D1602521

KHAKI SHADOWS
Pakistan 1947–1997

KHAKI SHADOWS
Pakistan 1947–1997

General K.M. Arif

DS
283.5
.A2
A83
2001
West

OXFORD
UNIVERSITY PRESS

OXFORD

UNIVERSITY PRESS

Great Clarendon Street, Oxford OX2 6DP

Oxford University Press is a department of the University of Oxford.
It furthers the University's objective of excellence in research, scholarship,
and education by publishing worldwide in

Oxford New York

Athens Auckland Bangkok Bogotá Buenos Aires Cape Town
Chennai Dar es Salaam Delhi Florence Hong Kong Istanbul Karachi
Kolkata Kuala Lumpur Madrid Melbourne Mexico City Mumbai Nairobi
Paris São Paulo Shanghai Singapore Taipei Tokyo Toronto Warsaw

with associated companies in Berlin Ibadan

Oxford is a registered trade mark of Oxford University Press
in the UK and in certain other countries

© Oxford University Press 2001

The moral rights of the author have been asserted

First published 2001

All rights reserved. No part of this publication may be reproduced,
translated, stored in a retrieval system, or transmitted, in any form or by any
means, without the prior permission in writing of Oxford University Press.
Enquiries concerning reproduction should be sent to
Oxford University Press at the address below.

This book is sold subject to the condition that it shall not, by way
of trade or otherwise, be lent, re-sold, hired out or otherwise circulated
without the publisher's prior consent in any form of binding or cover
other than that in which it is published and without a similar condition
including this condition being imposed on the subsequent purchaser.

ISBN 0 19 579396 X

Typeset in Times
Printed in Pakistan by
Mehran Printers, Karachi.
Published by
Ameena Saiyid, Oxford University Press
5-Bangalore Town, Sharae Faisal
PO Box 13033, Karachi-75350, Pakistan.

CONTENTS

List of Plates (between pp. 30–31)

Annexures (between pp. 62–63)

FOREWORD

Pakistan has been in existence as a sovereign country for 53 years. At the time of Independence, there was no doubt in any one's mind that Pakistan would be a democratic state where authority would be exercised through the chosen representatives of the people. Yet the history of this nation has witnessed several martial laws—both partial and total—interspersed by short periods of civil rule. The civilian governments, even those with strong majorities in Parliament, have lacked confidence and lived under constant fear of the 'Khaki Shadows'.

What are the circumstances which have led to frequent military interventions? Why do the armed forces continue to exercise such power and influence over civilian governments? What are the sensitivities and priorities of military governments? What are their strengths and weaknesses? What can be done to bring stability to the political process? Will there ever be a time when Pakistan will have an un-interrupted democratic dispensation? What measures can be taken to bring this about?

These are some of the issues, amongst many others, which have been dealt with by General K.M. Arif in this highly interesting and readable account which spans half a century of politics and power in Pakistan.

The book is a mixture of biography and current history. It is history through the eyes of a person who has experienced it with great intensity at close quarters. During the period 1977 to 1988, when the late General Ziaul Haq was president, General Arif held sensitive and important assignments; firstly, as Chief of Staff to the President, and later, as the Vice Chief of the Army Staff. He was thus privy to many matters of state and can speak with direct knowledge of those events. He was a close confidant of the late president. Accordingly, his account of this important period has special significance. He gives us deep insight into the personality of the late president, his likes and dislikes, his habits and proclivities, which help us in understanding his actions. I cannot think of any other person who could have given a more authentic and perceptive analysis of the events of these years.

Sometimes minor incidents in one's life have a major bearing on shaping one's character and personality, and influencing decisions taken at a later stage. Many such incidents in the life of the late General Ziaul Haq are recounted in this book. We are told, for example, that on Eid day the young Zia visited the Junior Commissioned Officers mess of his Unit wearing *shalwar kameez* (native dress). This annoyed the British Commanding Officer who would not tolerate such nonsense in the heydays of the British *Raj*. He was given another posting as a punishment. It was perhaps this insult which led him to actively promote the national dress when he became president.

Any government which comes into existence through military intervention almost immediately faces the question of legitimacy—moral, legal and political. Every martial law imposed so far has been challenged before the courts. The dissolutions by the president under discretionary powers conferred by the 8th Amendment were also similarly questioned. I am discussing military interventions and presidential dissolutions in the same context because the latter could not have been accomplished without active military support. However, taking such matters before the courts has raised essentially political questions with the result that the courts have shown unease, hesitancy, and inconsistency in their handling of such matters. Both the martial laws of 1958 and 1977 were validated by the Supreme Court. The earlier on the grounds that every successful revolution is a legal revolution, and the latter on the grounds of necessity. On the other hand, the martial law imposed by the late General Yahya Khan was held to be invalid. He was declared a usurper in very strong and uncompromising terms. The decision, however, came when he had been ousted from power and a civilian government had taken charge. General Arif also points out how in 1977, the then Chief Justice of the

Supreme Court was prevailed upon to modify his judgment and give powers of constitutional amendment to the Chief Martial Law Administrator when he was informed that otherwise, he would have to be replaced by the previous incumbent.

The judiciary has not been alone among institutions that came under strain. Over the years, the fate of parliaments has been the same; parliament has been used less as a body involved in making laws and more as a respectable cover for laws already prepared by the executive. The committee system has been ineffective and the role of parliament as a check on the executive has been illusory.

General Arif has rightly observed that the executive branch of government has been the most dominant and the most powerful organ of the state. This has been so, whether the form of government has been parliamentary or presidential, as it was during the Ayub era. The executive government has vast powers to benefit as well as to cause harm, with no checks either way. Bureaucracy has acted as an untamed horse allowing itself to be manipulated by a strong rider but throwing him off the saddle if he is unable to control it. All this has led to the creation of a powerful, monolithic, executive structure. The fate of the other two institutions has always been one of subordination.

One may legitimately ask if the lack of balance between the three organs of the state has been the reason for instability and disruption of the democratic process. Can some measures be taken to bring about such a balance, so that we can have normality in the political process as well as in the relationship between the civilian and the military forces?

General Arif has also dealt with purely military matters in a style and manner intelligible to a person with no military background. The wars of 1965 and 1971, conflict in the Rann of Kutch and operation Gibralter, and later, Grand Slam in Kashmir have been analysed with depth and expertise. Exercise Brass Tacks held in 1987, during which Pakistan and India came close to open war, has been discussed in great detail and with authority naturally because at that time General Arif was the effective head of the Pakistan Army. Moves and counter moves by both sides make interesting reading. The exercise shows that India is always ready to take advantage of any real or perceived weakness in Pakistan's defence and, therefore, there is need for constant vigilance. During this crisis, the political and military leadership acted in harmony. Vision and mature handling avoided a disastrous war. These qualities are required in even greater strength today, as both India and Pakistan are nuclear powers and a conflict between them would have unimaginable consequences.

General Arif has a military background but he has also had the advantage of close association and interaction with civilian governments. His experience is, therefore, vast and his canvas large. He has analysed the emergence of the Muhajir Quami Movement, a phenomenon of the 1980's, and its implications and impact on the politics of Pakistan. Many new facts come to light here. He has also discussed major foreign policy issues including Kashmir, relations with the United States, the nuclear issue and the conflict in Afghanistan. He speaks with direct knowledge on all these subjects and brings a new approach and freshness in discussing these important matters.

Khaki Shadows is a comprehensive book. It deals with a variety of subjects. One observation made by General Arif needs to be particularly noted in the context of the politics of Pakistan. He remarks that a democratic order needs patience and perseverance, two qualities that are generally in short supply in Pakistan. Can the politicians and the military develop the much required patience and perseverance for the democratic process to succeed? Can the military also learn lessons from history and realize that military solutions may not be the best? Can both civilian and military forces develop a healthy balance of co-existence? Any one who reads General K.M. Arif's book will be better placed to answer these questions.

WASIM SAJJAD
Former Chairman,
Senate of Pakistan.

PREFACE

In 1996, I received an invitation from Villanova University, PA, USA, to participate in a seminar to be held in October 1997 to commemorate the golden jubilee of the birth of Pakistan. The panellists from Pakistan in the seminar included Mr Justice Javed Iqbal, a retired judge of the Supreme Court of Pakistan, Mr S. M. Zafar, an eminent international jurist, Mr Munir Ahmad Khan, former Chairman, Pakistan Atomic Energy Commission, Mr Abdul Sattar, former Secretary and Minister of Foreign Affairs of Pakistan, and myself. All the participants were given one separate theme each. The organizers had shown foresight in inviting a judge, a jurist, a diplomat, a general and the chairman PAEC for an analytical study of Pakistan's performance in its first fifty years as an independent state. The timeframe of the seminar and the themes chosen for it are a tribute to the vision and skill of the coordinator, Dr Hafeez Malik.

The theme of my presentation—the role of the military in politics, 1947-1997—was topical, intellectually stimulating and provocative. The thinking, study and research that went into my presentation was the beginning of a thought process that moved to new horizons and ultimately to this book, *Khaki Shadows*.

On entering the Villonova Room of the Connelly Center, Villanova University for the inaugural session of the seminar on 24 October 1997, I glanced at the seating arrangement and was pleasantly surprised to notice that the seat to my immediate right was that of General Anthony Zinni, Commander-in-Chief of the US Central Command (CENTCOM). This reflected the thoughtfulness of the organizers. Zinni told me that since he was scheduled to undertake an official visit to Pakistan within the next couple of days, the seminar offered him a useful opportunity to update himself on Pakistan on the eve of his tour.

I doubted if any Pakistani service chief would have attended a day-long session in any university-sponsored seminar in his own country, as Zinni did, to acquire further knowledge about a target state? The quest for knowledge in developed countries has taken them to dizzy temporal heights with the attendant prestige, confidence and power. Those who have distanced themselves from the fountains of knowledge, as many in Pakistan have done, are dwarfed to insignificance in the international power game, despite their considerable inherent power potential. Pakistan's democratic journey might have been less thorny had its pen and sword been harmonized for the good of the country.

The insatiable curiosity of inquisitive minds has taken man to the moon and beyond. The people of Pakistan, however, have generally lagged behind in this race for knowledge. Commensurate with the size and potential of the country, very few books are published here. Many of our schools and universities churn out semi-literate *baboos* (clerks) as they used to do during the colonial era to serve the imperial *Raj*. Bright, intelligent and curious young minds are not encouraged, and there is an enormous brain-drain, as many brilliant people leave the country to live in a free society, filled with opportunities that Pakistan does not offer.

University professors, scholars and academics hesitate to write on many crucial and sensitive issues, including defence and security, due to state pressure or fear of the unknown. Our national reservoir of scientists, scholars and journalists who are capable of speaking coherently and writing logically on nuclear-related and strategic issues is, therefore, limited.

Settlement of major inter-state disputes may promote durable peace but conflict resolution cannot be achieved by adopting an ostrich like approach. Remedial measures are imperative.

My book, *Working With Zia*, published by Oxford University Press, Karachi, in 1995 had its supporters and critics. I respected their comments and benefitted from their observations. I believe, therefore, that the impact of the various military rules—the Zia rule (1977-1988) in particular—on the country, and on the military itself deserves a fuller analysis. I hope the effort made in this narrative prompts others to write on this controversial era. No human effort can ever boast of finality. I shall be willing to update my own observations and conclusions in the light of fresh evidence that may surface in the future.

The presence of 'khaki shadows' in Pakistan and their influence on the national life of the country for most of its 53 years cannot be denied or wished away. They deserve an impartial and impassioned analysis to enable us to identify the errors made in the past by the military in national politics, both for the sake of recording history and benefiting future generations. Eyewitnesses to the events of the past shall do a service to the country by making public their own experiences and observations.

Some do not wish to share their experience with others for personal or other reasons. Others are hesitant because of the low tolerance limit of government and state officials. The Official Secrets Act, a fossil of the past, needs to be updated to meet the requirements of the present age. The government, police force, and intelligence agencies have always considered themselves eminently qualified to issue certificates of patriotism and disloyalty to the public at large. They have arrogated to themselves the right to be the sole custodians of the country's security, and those who expose the excesses and blunders of the administration and policy makers run the risk of getting midnight knocks at their doors. Notwithstanding such hurdles, the end goal must always be the truth.

Pakistan, a country weakened by prolonged crises in its top leadership, needs to put its house in order. An objective and indepth assessment of the past performance of governments and a review of the political-military acts of omission and commission would definitely benefit present and future generations. The country needs a culture of tolerance and the freedom of expression guaranteed in the Constitution.

Pakistan, unfortunately, lost its founder within a year of independence. Prime Minister Liaquat Ali Khan tried to fill the vacuum created by the loss of Muhammad Ali Jinnah, the

Quaid-i-Azam, but he was assassinated in 1951. The country started drifting from its political moorings. In 1953, General Mohammad Ayub Khan, the army chief, was authorized by the government to pave the way for a cooperative relationship with the United States. This eclipsed the Foreign Office and inducted the army into national politics. The 'khaki shadows' appeared in the country and, barring some intervals, have been present ever since in varying degrees and shades.

This book, spread over eleven chapters—each part complete in itself—is an attempt to focus discussion on the role of the military in national politics and the manner in which this influenced the country and the military itself. The purpose is not to eulogise or criticise but only to record history with accuracy to benefit posterity and the future historian in evaluating events in their true perspective.

The opening chapter briefly describes army life as it existed in the early years of Pakistan. It also provides a brief review on how martial law was first introduced in the country.

For reasons hard to justify, Pakistan brushed under the carpet the events of the Indo-Pakistan War of 1965, and not much was allowed to appear in the media in the country on what happened or failed to happen, and why, in this fateful era. The myopic vision of policy makers and the misplaced over-emphasis on the secrecy of information kept the people of the country in the dark. Pakistan's case remained unexplained to the world, which was fed a one-sided story of the war as narrated and fabricated by her adversary. Chapter 2 is a brief narration of this war in which I was a participant and an eyewitness in the now famous Chawinda Sector where the largest tank battle since the end of the Second World War took place. This may provide a lesson to our political leaders and military planners.

We mourned the death of East Pakistan but reconciled to the emergence of Bangladesh as inevitable under the circumstances that prevailed in 1971. But why Pakistan came to that pass is yet to be critically and analytically examined. A professional and academic analysis of the crisis in East Pakistan needs to be conducted in the National Defence College and in the Staff

Colleges. Our achievements and our failures are a part of our history, and deserve both analysis and debate at the professional levels in a fair and frank manner.

Along with the physical fall of Dhaka, Pakistan was also defeated in 1971 politically, diplomatically, and psychologically. For reasons of political expediency, the Hamoodur Rahman Commission was given a limited charter of duty and its report remains unpublished in Pakistan even today. A national commission should, therefore, be formed to ascertain the causes of our acts of omission and commission that converted East Pakistan into Bangladesh.

My association with Ziaul Haq may make my views and assessment of this era subjective. But I was privy to confidential information and this provides me with a unique opportunity to evaluate the influence of Ziaul Haq's policies on the country, and on the military establishment. The Zia era was a blend of success and failure in which 'khaki shadows' played a prominent part, but which eventually gave birth to a certain kind of democratic order. General Zia had claimed that he had imposed military rule to preserve the unity of the country and the solidarity of the army both of which, in his opinion, were threatened by the rule of an elected civilian autocrat hiding under the veneer of democracy.

To judge military rule by democratic standards is like equating night with day. General Zia did restore elected order, though late. I accept my share of the blame for this delay, for I had urged an early transfer of power to an elected government. Power has a toxic effect that is better understood by those who themselves have wielded authority.

The Mohajir Qaumi Movement (MQM) is now a part of our national milieu and its performance deserves an objective analysis. The history of the emergence of the MQM and its journey to becoming a political party are included in this narrative.

In 1987, Exercise Brass Tacks brought India and Pakistan to the precipice of war. This 'War That Never Was' as it was called by the Indian author, Ravi Rikhye, sharply illustrates the reality that Pakistan's internal weakness tempted India to adopt a coercive policy towards her. India's military brinkmanship was, however, blunted by Pakistan's timely countermeasures. The manner in which Pakistan's political and military leaders responded to the unprovoked threat of war would be of interest to the reader.

Democracy moves on the triad wheels of parliamentary, judicial and executive bodies. The charters of responsibility of each of these independent institutions of the state are clearly defined in the constitution and the three branches draw their authority from it. The elected governments in Pakistan have, however, adopted a two-track approach to the constitution; praising it in rhetoric, and often manipulating it for reasons of political expediency. The struggle for power between the presidents and the prime ministers often imposed a strain on the judiciary which frequently became an arbiter in the struggle for the distribution of political power. Political streaks were clearly visible in some judicial judgments, and the higher judiciary was criticized for this trend.

To add to the anxiety of the democratic polity, the constitution was stabbed, more than once, with the dagger of martial law. This had a negative, long-term effect on all aspects of national life. The impact on the judiciary was even more direct and damaging.

A weak judiciary co-existed with a strong civil and military executive, and this imbalance weakened the nation and the judiciary. In addition, the judiciary weakened itself through infighting which harmed its image and prestige.

The lure of power and its impact on the country are the burden of Chapter 8. The following chapter provides glimpses of foreign relations during the military rules of Presidents Ayub Khan, Yahya Khan and Ziaul Haq. The concluding part of the book describes my retirement from the army on the completion of my fixed three-year tenure as army commander.

Much more must be written on this subject. We have cause indeed to ponder over the ways of our political leaders and the legacy they have left behind. Pakistan has great potential and much of it remains unexplored. It is my conviction that a healthy review of our past errors will be good for the country. Out of the difficulties of the past shall emerge a vibrant, modern and moderate Pakistan in accordance with the vision of our forefathers.

I am indebted to Mr Wasim Sajjad for writing the foreword. And, I also offer my profound thanks to those who were helpful in reading parts of the manuscript and offering useful suggestions namely General Muhammad Shariff (late), Air Chief Marshal, Jamal A. Khan, Lieutenant-Generals Mohammad Aslam Shah, Syed Refaqat and Nishat Ahmed, Mr Justice S. A. Nusrat, and the former foreign Secretaries Mr Niaz A. Naik and Mr. Abdul Sattar. Major-General Malik Abdul Waheed read the manuscript and made valuable suggestions. I am grateful to my brother, Mr A. M. Tabassum for his help in making the Index. I hasten to confess that the conclusions drawn throughout the book are entirely my own and I accept full responsibility for them. Finally, I cannot help admiring the patience of my wife, Khalida, who suffered long hours alone to enable me to complete this work.

1

DOWN MEMORY LANE

These selected glimpses cover the route taken in early years, so that the pattern of life that existed soon after independence may be brought back to mind. These reminiscences may interest those military veterans who wish to look back into their youthful era, to remember those times and perhaps laugh at themselves. The narration may also provide a chance to the serving military generation to learn from and, indeed, reflect on the history of their chosen profession and the course it followed over the decades. There will be food for thought in this, some palatable and the rest, hard to swallow.

One not familiar with military life or the prevailing national and regional environment may learn from this book that, by accident or design or by both, the military in Pakistan got involved in the political quagmire of the country very early on, and stayed there for a long while. The politicians blame the army for entering the prohibited area of national affairs reserved for them. The military accuse the politicians for inviting and luring them into this domain by their acts, deeds and misdeeds, directly as well as indirectly. The debate is endless.

A well-knit and strong military establishment co-existing with a self-opinionated, inefficient and politically pliable bureaucracy has been the fate of Pakistan. In this scenario, the card of 'national security' has generally been overused by successive civil and military administrations to hide their own misdeeds on the pretext of keeping away public discussion and debate on military affairs. The establishment is so strong in Pakistan that any information of value is usually not accessible to the people at large.

Working under such conditions, the military, a dynamic entity, has generally maintained its conservative traditions, while moving with the march of time and has generally responded well to the call of duty.

Military service was remote from my mind as family tradition had psychologically groomed me for a civil career. Besides, the Gurdaspur District, to which I belonged, with its lush green fields and a large industrial base, had a seductive charm of its own so its youth had no compelling reasons for joining military service. To me, the term 'martial race' was a cleverly coined colonial ruse by the wily rulers to give us a sense of artificial pride and bravado. The colonial rulers wanted a human nursery for the defence forces of British India, to serve and preserve their Empire.

This imperial policy paid dividends. Poverty was writ large in the traditional Muslim recruitment areas—Balochistan, North-West Frontier Province and parts of the Punjab—at the time of independence. Barren and backward, this region could neither boast of industry nor of education facilities. As a consequence, Pakistan did not inherit any industrial complex worth its name in 1947. The border belt in India's North-West had been kept backward industrially and economically as a matter of imperial policy to recruit gun-fodder for the Empire. The primary British strategic anxiety in the area was to keep Russia, the 'Polar Bear', at bay and to deny her a route to the warm waters of the Arabian Sea.

A Pakistan Army advertisement appeared in the national newspapers in 1948. My college friends, euphoric about a military career, urged me to apply along with them. Their persuasion induced me to opt for a career of challenges, adventure and national service. My father readily permitted me to adopt a profession of my choice. However, a rush of motherly anxiety visibly gripped the face of my mother when she gave a nod of approval. The General Headquarters-sponsored academic tests for the course were held at the local brigade headquarters, Michni Road, Peshawar, on 20-21 December 1948. My roll number was 3987. This hurdle crossed, every successful candidate was interviewed by a selection team at the Garrison Theatre, Roberts Lines, Peshawar Cantonment on 11 February 1949. The interview letter intimated that dearness allowance at the rate of rupees five per day was admissible. The inflation rate was low then.

On entering an ill-furnished hall, I confronted three serious-looking army officers sitting straight behind a bare table. I had hardly sat down when the colonel fired the first salvo, 'Do you have a claim on the army?' I silently cursed myself for attempting to enter the off-limits club reserved for the scions of the martial races and quickly concluded that the military practised its own brand of apartheid. The brigadier in the centre seat interjected saying, 'He means do you have any relative serving in the army?' This rubbed salt on the wound of my injured pride and I decided to speak out. 'Sir, I understood the question the first time,' I said in a low deliberate voice, adding, 'But if this is the criterion for joining the Pakistan Army, I doubt if I shall ever wear a uniform.' My gut reaction was that my military dream had turned sour and I would be shown the door. To my surprise, the faces of the panel beamed and I realised that the men in khaki could smile. I felt petty for having such misplaced apprehensions about the defence services.

Basic Military Training

Weighing 112 pounds at the age of eighteen, I joined the First OTS course at Kohat on 17 March 1949, along with 508 other cadets. As Number 121 GC, K. M. Arif, I joined platoon number 5 in Alpha Company. My Platoon Commander was Captain M. G. Smith, while Major Richardson commanded A Company. The school, a make-shift institution, was located in the lines previously used by an infantry battalion that had been renovated to start the course. The instructors were a mix of Pakistani and British officers, with the latter outnumbering the former. The Commandant, Colonel Halsay, was a fatherly figure. The training area and the teaching environment was new to both the

instructors and the cadets, as was the syllabus. Training aids
were minimal. The first course cadets were used as the
proverbial guinea pigs for experimentation. Everything was new
except Kohat, an old and stable town, proud of its history and
reluctant to change with the march of time. It grew good quality
guavas and perhaps nothing else of substance.

After completion of the basic military training, the course
was split into two groups. The gentlemen cadets selected for
infantry remained at the OTS, Kohat, for advance training. Those
earmarked for other arms and services joined their respective
schools for special technical training. Under this arrangement,
thirty-four gentlemen cadets travelled from Kohat to Rawalpindi
by train on 30 June 1949, and after a night's stay at Transit
Camp, Rawalpindi, continued their train journey to Nowshera
to join the Armoured Corps School. Here the training emphasis
shifted from the physical conditioning of the body with subjects
like weapon training in the OTS to technical subjects in gunnery,
wireless and automotive fields.

The Armoured Corps School was established in Nowshera in
late 1947 with bits and pieces of outdated equipment and some
charts called 'training aids' inherited from Babina, India. Their
most striking feature was their antiquity. The school was a
modest entity, commanded by a Major with a Captain Adjutant
and a modest headquarters. Its three wings—Gunnery, Wireless
and the Driving and Maintenance—were each commanded by a
Captain. It had one Range and Model Officer. This small and
bare-bone establishment combined economy with efficiency.
This state did not last long. Soon, the school started
accumulating organizational fat—horizontally and vertically—
without correspondingly enhancing its professional efficiency
and output.

The teaching staff, composed of the junior commissioned
officers and the non-commissioned officers, possessed fair
experience in the art of instruction. Their lack of basic education
was partly compensated by learning through a process of trial
and error. The officer instructors occasionally visited the classes
for short periods of time but avoided sharing their professional

expertise with the students. They considered silence a virtue and exposure a risk not worth taking.

The Pakistan Armoured Corps inherited on Independence six regiments. The three tank regiments—13 Lancers, 19 Lancers and Probyn's Horse—were each equipped with Sherman tanks. The remaining three—Guides Cavalry, Prince Albert Victor's Own (PAVO) Cavalry, and 6 Lancers—were reconnaissance regiments all equipped with Humber and Daimler armoured cars and Stuart tanks. Every regiment was a well-knit family, 'ever right, never wrong and always the best'. Regimental affiliations were strong, visible and everlasting. The Armoured Corps *esprit de corps* was not as robust, though the officers took pride in calling the Armoured Corps the king of the battlefield. The black beret was a symbol of elation, a sign of excellence, and a mark of respect.

The non-armoured corps officers mocked their armoured corp colleagues for wearing un-military socks, carrying flashy handkerchiefs, sporting long hair, and having a self-assumed exaggerated sense of importance. In turn, they were teased as pongos. Both laughed at one another and at themselves. The inter-arm rivalry was mere fun, and bore no ill-will or jealousy.

The mess life was a parade. Table manners and mess etiquette were sacrosanct and inviolable. During meals, the fork and knife were used in an atmosphere of aristocratic silence. Chewing with the mouth open was undignified. Raising one's voice in the mess or at the table was considered uncivil. One invariably argued on all issues with the power of logic and never with the strength of vocal cords. A smile was preferred over loud laughter. It was a taboo to stretch one's arms across the table to pick up pepper or salt. Courtesy demanded that the neighbour be requested, 'May I have the pepper please,' and that he be thanked after he had obliged. The waiters were neither shouted at nor asked for a second helping. It was impolite to drag the dining chairs while sitting down or getting up. On all dinner nights one officer dined with the cadets. On these occasions the cadets sat straight, looked cheerful, spoke less and ate modestly.

On arrival at the OTS the young cadets were painstakingly groomed through a process of guidance, practice and supervision to chisel them into refined human beings. It was an essential pre-requisite for all cadets to acquire the military code of conduct before becoming officers. It was ingrained in the gentlemen cadets by acts and deeds that they were gentlemen first and cadets later. Professional excellence remained incomplete without practising worthy military conduct.

D-Day arrived. The graduation parade was held on 12 November 1949 in the polo ground, Nowshera. It was a small function as the number of participating cadets was small but the occasion was big in the lives of those who were entering the officer corps of the Pakistan Army. I was posted to the PAVO Cavalry (11th FF) along with four other colleagues, second-lieutenants Mohammad Anwar Khan, Mohammad Aslam Hayat Khan, Ghulam Mohammad Khan Durrani and Fida Mohammad Khan.

The *tonga* journey that took me from the Rawalpindi railway station to the Ojheri Camp, a thirty minute drive, cost one rupee. It was 22 November 1949. A waiting military truck took second-lieutenants Anwar, Aslam, Durrani, Fida and myself to a camp near Taxila where the regiment was engaged in winter training.

The adjutant, Captain Usman Shah, assigned the incoming subalterns to squadrons. After a pep talk, my squadron commander Major Rao Liaquat Ali, posted me to a troop. The regimental second-in-command, Major Syed Nayyer Raza, a quiet, unassuming person, advised us to read the history of the regiment and become its worthy members.

The Commanding Officer, Lieutenant-Colonel Abdul Rashid met the fresh arrivals after three days. The grim-faced Rashid nodded his head in a royal manner, when the five young officers were introduced to him by the adjutant. 'Your real training starts now,' said Rashid firmly in a voice devoid of warmth, and cautioned the officers that he would be initiating reports on them about their suitability for the army.

Rashid, a bachelor with nine years service then, was a pleasant personality who loved hard drinks and soft company.

He married while in command of the regiment but kept pushing his liver too hard to keep pace with his fast lifestyle. This brilliant officer lost his life at a relatively young age.

The senior subaltern, Sadiq Ali Khan, called one 'pippers' the lowest form of humanity, fit only to be seen, not heard. With a rich reservoir of juicy and unprintable jokes, Sadiq's indulgent lifestyle was in conflict with the demands of military service. His premature retirement from the army deprived his colleagues of his pleasant company and witty humour.

Collective training ended in 1949 with a regimental exercise. A spectator's stand was erected on the hill astride the Grand Trunk Road with Nicholson's Monument perched on it. I escorted the guests to their seats. These included female friends of the commanding officer. Sadiq Ali cautioned me to ensure that my own interest did not clash with that of my commanding officer. 'In the army', warned Sadiq, 'seniority takes precedence over youth.'

So perfectly did the regimental communication system work during the exercise that the Director of Signals at the GHQ attending the exercise, suspected that the unit had played a pre-recorded tape. He was all praise for the regiment after he satisfied himself that the performance was real and not fake. The PAVO's had always been proud of maintaining a high standard of communication network.

The PAVO Cavalry, a century old unit then, was an amalgamation of the 1st Punjab Cavalry and 3rd Punjab Cavalry, both raised on 18 May 1849. During the reorganization of the Indian Army in 1921, these two units were renamed as 21 Punjab Cavalry and 23 Punjab Cavalry respectively. Still later, in 1936, these two units were merged to form the PAVO Cavalry (11th FF). The regiment derived its name from Prince Albert Victor, the prince consort of Queen Victoria.

The words 'Frontier Force' indicated that a regiment was a part of the 'Piffers' group about whom Rudyard Kipling had written:

You must know that along the North-West Frontier of India is spread a force whose duty is quickly and ostentatiously to shepherd the tribesmen in front of them. They move up and down from one desolate post to another; they are ready to take the field at 10 minutes notice; they are always half-in and half-out of a difficulty somewhere along the monstrous line; their lives are as hard as their muscles and papers never say anything about them.[1]

Lord Ismay, the Secretary-General of the North Atlantic Treaty Organization, writes:

I went into battle young, joining Prince Albert Victor's Own Cavalry on the North-West Frontier of India when I was only 20. In those days cavalrymen did not enjoy the highest regard. A familiar story of the period began, 'There was once a cavalryman who was so stupid that even his fellow officers noticed it.' The colonel was more like the patriarch of a tribe than the iron disciplinarian of the story book. Punishments were very rare. 'You have let the regiment down,' was far worse than punishment.[2]

In World War Two, the PAVO Cavalry was the only regiment in the Indian Armoured Corps that participated in operations against the Germans and the Italians on the Western front, and the Japanese on the East. Since 1947, it has performed with distinction in the defence of Pakistan.

Mess Life

The senior regimental officers were amiable to the juniors in the mess, but on parade they stayed aloof and turned into snobs. It was customary for officers to assemble in the officers mess after the games period for a cup of tea or a cold drink. They left the mess before sunset as the sports gear violated the mess decorum in force then.

It was not considered officer-like to wear non-Western clothes outside one's home, including mess premises. Discussion among the officers in the mess centred on matters of professional and general interest that encouraged them to be acquainted with national and international affairs. Discussion on politics and women was taboo in the mess. The mess had a 'ladies room' reserved for women. Food was not served in the rooms except for those who were placed in sick quarters.

The junior officers clicked their heels on entering the mess and leaving it. They took permission from their seniors before reading a magazine or tuning in on a radio set. Urdu newspapers were not kept in the mess. Nor were the officers expected to listen to Pakistani music. The officers talked among themselves in the English language. The mess waiters were called in the imperial style, '*koi hai*', and spoken to in an anglicized Urdu accent. The British officers had been replaced by the brown *sahibs* who took visible pride in imitating them.

Four dinner nights and two supper nights were held per week. A dinner night with Blue Patrols was the Commandant's parade. The dinner was preceded by drinks and snacks. Smoking was allowed on the dining table after the toasts. The seniors entered the dining room first, and the senior dining member sat at the head of the table. After the meals, the seniors left first. The dress for the supper nights was dinner jacket and black bow.

The Director Armoured Corps, Brigadier H. M. el-Effendi, was once distressed at seeing some Armoured Corps officers wearing ready-made bows with dinner jackets. He issued a letter to the units saying, 'In the West, ready-made bows are worn by third-rate waiters in third-rate restaurants, and that too during their probation period....'

The Lahore Martial Law

The Qadianis (who call themselves Ahmadis) in Pakistan were a small but well-knit group. Most of them considered the head of their sect to be a prophet. This belief was in direct conflict with the cardinal point in Islam that the Holy Prophet (PBUH) was the last messenger of God and that there shall be no other prophet after him. This doctrinal difference was agitated by the (now defunct) Majlis-e-Ahrar (Ahrar party), a minor political group in the Punjab, that had opposed the creation of Pakistan and was a bitter opponent of the Qadiani sect. The issue had religious and sentimental appeal for all Muslims. The Punjab Chief Minister, Mian Mumtaz Mohammad Khan Daultana, soft-paddled the anti-Qadiani agitation when it first took a serious turn in 1952. So did the central government in the hope that the storm would blow over. Both were proved wrong.

The anti-Qadiani volcano erupted in Lahore on 27 February 1953. The Jamaat-i-Islami joined the Ahrars while the Muslim League sympathized with the core issue in dispute. A convention held in Lahore raised three demands. One, the Qadianis be declared a separate, non-Muslim minority; two, the Foreign Minister, Mr Mohammad Zafrullah Khan, a Qadiani, be removed from the Central Cabinet; and three, all Qadianis be relieved of key posts in the country. Caught between the conflicting demands of his religious belief and the political need to maintain public peace, Mumtaz Daultana played his political card.

With the agitation reaching its peak on 6 March 1953, he issued a statement appealing for peace and giving an assurance that his government was prepared to open negotiations with the leaders of the movement. The implied impression of conceding to the demands was bitterly resented by the public. Massive street violence engulfed the city of Lahore and people's emotions ran high. The law and order situation rapidly deteriorated. Sensing the public mood, Daultana reneged from his statement. But the damage had been done.

Political expediency caused the drift. At first, the Punjab Chief Minister, in contradiction with the policies of the Prime Minister Khawaja Nazimuddin, deliberately took a passive attitude for local political gains. He ignored the warnings given by the intelligence agencies about the developing political storm. Sensing the gravity of the situation, the civil administration gave up, and was eager to pass the buck on to another agency.

Daultana's offer of negotiations with the leaders of the movement greatly embarrassed Khawaja Nazimuddin who held the religious scholars in high esteem. With the situation getting out of control in Punjab, the central government imposed limited martial law in Lahore, and directed the Pakistan Army to restore order.

For an elected government to resort to the draconian act of imposing martial law to extricate itself from a self-created political quagmire was a major blow to democracy. The army acted with speed and promptly restored order in troubled Lahore. But the peace achieved was a Pyrrhic victory. The army brass was elated at succeeding in a task in which the civil administration had failed. The military action—firm and fair— was hailed by the public. This public response might have given ideas to the top military leaders that a repetition of martial law in the future would not provoke a negative reaction from the masses. The agitation also made clear the fact that religious sensitivity was easy to ignite but difficult to control.

The army responded quickly and effectively and proved that it could manage civil affairs with judicious application of force. Major-General Muhammad Azam Khan, the local martial law administrator, seized the opportunity to punish the miscreants, protect the citizens, expose the 'bloody *mullahs*', and prove his own worth. He cleverly launched a media campaign to publicize the *jawans* and to display his own authority. The military tasted the heady effects of publicity when its performance in civil affairs was reported widely in the print media in superlative adjectives. The Lahore martial law enhanced the image of the military and inflated the ego of its top brass.

The Lahore martial law was the turning point in Azam's military career. From the obscurity of his army appointment, the exuberant major-general suddenly rose to extreme prominence at the national centre stage, with his stars still on the rise. During his address to the Lahore garrison officers, General Ayub praised Azam for putting up a 'damn good show'. Azam was soon promoted to the rank of a lieutenant-general. A few years later he was included in Ayub's kitchen cabinet when martial law was clamped on the country in 1958. His hunger for publicity persisted, and he became a well projected minister in

Ayub's cabinet. He was later assigned Governor of East Pakistan where he earned respect and popularity with the people.

The slogans of 'Pakistan Army *Zindabad*' in the streets of Lahore, and the pro-army publicity in the state-controlled and state-influenced media was a high potency tonic to the military. To project the military as the (only) saviour of the country was a short-sighted and dangerous scheme. But those who mattered were more interested in quick and tactical gains. The long-term impact of such a proposition was either ignored or indeed deliberately suppressed. The emphasis was on projecting the image of the military's ability in countering political chaos, correcting administrative wrongs and excelling in conditions where the civil administration had failed or bungled. Such a myopic viewpoint led to the Lahore martial law—a forerunner of the military adventures or misadventures in the years that followed.

Horse and Cattle Show

The first Horse and Cattle Show was held at the Fortress Stadium, Lahore, in 1954 under the management of the Pakistan Army. This well conceived and brilliantly conducted spectacle drew large crowds and demonstrated the army's ability to provide a plethora of healthy festivities and recreation to the public. That considerable time and effort had been invested in planning this function was evident from the celebrities that graced the occasion. The foreign dignitaries attending the show included Prince Aly Khan, Prime Minister Louis Laurent of Canada, and a former *maharaja* with a polo team from India.

Why the army wished to organize a non-professional event of such high profile and grandeur was a moot point that was conveniently submerged in the blaze of publicity and glory that the show created in the media. The military possessed a few horses but this did not qualify it to organize an event of national importance. The people of Lahore were euphoric, and the image-building exercise for the army was an instant success. The director of the show, Major-General Azam Khan, had once again demonstrated his skill in the art of staging a high publicity drama. It goes without saying that he enjoyed the full backing of the Commander-in-Chief of the Pakistan Army.

The national Horse and Cattle Show became an annual feature, providing fun and festivity to the people, and a source of publicity and income to the organizers. The smart, polished and well-behaved military officers came into contact with the civil officials, and at times became well-acquainted with them. Such informality had its advantages and drawbacks. At the senior level, the military officers boasted of the national popularity that the annual festivity had earned them, and claimed that without the army's active participation, the civil administration would have found it difficult to organize the event. There was much truth in this claim. But it was not mentioned how much time, money and effort the army spent every year in running the show.

Army's Reorganization and Training

General Ayub Khan earned the distinction of being the first Pakistani Commander-in-Chief of the Pakistan Army. His assumption of office in January 1951 placed on him the onus of grooming the army into a well-oiled and cohesive fighting machine capable of meeting the defence needs of the country. This was a precarious time for the country and, in Pakistan's perception, India was looking for an opportunity to harm her. Ayub began enthusiastically, and devoted considerable time and energy in formulating the army's reorganization plan and implementing it with great speed. The reorganization included establishing and revamping training centres, the military schools of instruction, modification in the old military doctrines, improving the logistic infrastructure and injecting realism in the performance of the field formations. This was a tall order needing resources that the country could not indigenously generate.

In 1951, India concentrated her forces on the border of Pakistan as she had also done a year earlier. Prime Minister Liaquat Ali Khan clenched his fist while addressing a huge a public meeting at Lahore to symbolize Pakistan's determination to resist any aggression. This political rhetoric won the hearts of the people. The mailed fist was adopted as the emblem of the First Armoured Division when it was organized a couple of years later. Months later, Liaquat Ali Khan was assassinated in October 1951, and the country came to be ruled or misruled by political leaders—neither efficient nor popular— for whom the task on hand was beyond their ability to handle.

An aggressive neighbour and inept domestic leadership posed a security problem for Pakistan which had tragically lost two senior founding fathers in quick succession. Under these circumstances, Pakistan concluded the Mutual Defence Assistance Agreement with the United States in May 1954. The military hardware that came in its wake helped in replacing some of the old and obsolescent equipment in the Pakistan Army and in the Pakistan Air Force. The Pakistan Navy, the more orthodox of the three services, maintained its traditional links with the British Navy.

During the decade 1954-64, the Pakistan Army absorbed the new hardware in its units and formations at the technical and tactical levels. A number of medium to large scale exercises with troops were then held to amalgamate the men and equipment, and to test the changes made in tactical concepts and doctrines in simulated operational environments. These included Exercises Vulcan (1953), November Handicap (1954), Agility (1956) and *Tezgam* (Nimblefoot—1960).

Vulcan was a small armoured brigade-size exercise held in the Punjab terrain to test the mobility and deployment of armoured units and armoured brigade. At that time, the army did not have any armoured division.

November Handicap was a large, month long, two-sided exercise run in the plains of Punjab in the region Gujrat-Talagang. 1 Corps (Azam Khan) was exercised with 7 Division (Habib Ullah Khan) acting as the enemy. The exercise helped in training commanders from battalion upwards to the corps level under realistic, war-like conditions. In the process it exposed some weaknesses in command and in the obsolescence of Second World War vintage equipment still operational in the army. The latter helped in expediting the inflow of US military aid.

The largest peace time manoeuvre held in the country since 1947, Exercise November Handicap was a well publicized training effort that attracted high ranking observers from Australia, Britain, Ceylon, Iran, and the US. A VVIP camp for the foreign observers was established at the picturesque site, Kallar Kahar, where the guests were entertained with the warm hospitality traditionally offered by Pakistan.

Exercise Agility was the first two-sided, double division manoeuvre held after the receipt of US aid had enhanced the mobility of the army and improved the firepower of its units. The exercise involved crossing a major water-obstacle at night, and was witnessed by President Iskandar Mirza and Prime Minister H.S. Suhrawardy, some observers from SEATO and the Baghdad Pact countries and a number of correspondents. Coming in quick succession within two years, Exercise November Handicap and Agility gave confidence to military planners and perhaps a false sense of having attained perfection. Military exercises are excellent vehicles for learning but they are a weak substitute for actual combat with the enemy.

Exercise *Tezgam* held in the Sargodha region in central Punjab under very hot and oppressive summer weather conditions was to test the mobility and firepower of the recently acquired American Patton tanks. The exercise produced mixed results. M-47 Patton tanks were installed with a problematic and unreliable range finder, and were heavy for terrain with high, sub-surface water table. Notwithstanding these problems, the Pattons provided a psychological advantage, and the tank crews were elated to get machines that were far superior to the Sherman tanks previously held by them.

Exposure to GHQ

In 1954, I was posted to the Armoured Corps Directorate, General Headquarters. At the end of my first day in office the peon expertly collected the writing material from my table and quietly deposited it in the table drawer. As I looked at him in surprise he innocently remarked that the office hours were over. I learnt that the union hours were sacrosanct in the GHQ, nicknamed by some as a 'Mad House'.

The AC Directorate had five officers—one brigadier, one lieutenant-colonel, one major and two captains. The work load was divided between the major and the captains, each working directly under the lieutenant-colonel. The major spent a large part of his time with polo and hounds. A part of his official work was frequently assigned to the two captains to 'educate' them in staff duties.

Much time and effort in the GHQ was spent in convincing the omnipotent financial advisers that the expenditure proposed to be incurred on new proposals was justified and inescapable. These know-all financial watchdogs virtually held a veto power and could delay the finalization of proposals for prolonged periods. The system of financial controls prevented the defence services from keeping pace with the march of time. The army officers silently grumbled against the in-built tyranny of the system, but the financial shackles were too strong to be cut loose.

The GHQ was not only prone to accumulating organizational fat but was also frequently hit by the epidemic of vertical and horizontal rank proliferation. So also was the case of the static establishments in the army. The officers posted to GHQ, especially those already over the hump in their professional careers, relished its steady pace of work.

In 1954, Brigadier Sahibzada Yaqub Khan became the Director Armoured Corps. The calculating and aristocratic Yaqub maintained a healthy distance from his subordinates. One day he was extra affectionate to me. With a poker face he explained to me the virtues of regimental soldiering to earn a regular commission. Sensing his plan, I patiently listened to his sermon. The inevitable happened just two days later, when Captain Muzaffar Khan Malik, Yaqub's adjutant during his command assignment, was posted to replace me. Yaqub's liking for Muzaffar was a well known fact, and his posting to the AC Directorate made sense. Yaqub's tact in easing me out showed his diplomatic quality. After retiring from the army he served for a number of years as Pakistan's ambassador in France, the Soviet Union and the US. Later, he was the foreign minister in seven different administrations.

Training Cadets

In 1957, I was posted to the Officers Training School, Kohat, to teach at the institution that had once groomed me. Suspicious by nature, the Commandant, Brigadier Nasir Ahmad Khan, trusted others—including his own shadow—only to the extent that was necessary. He used his colourful Punjabi vocabulary to unburden himself whenever his partner blundered during the game of Bridge, his favourite relaxation after parade hours. Later, he was replaced by Brigadier Mohammad Muzaffar, a gunner who loved the artillery board and hated the pack of cards.

The Chief Instructor, Lieutenant-Colonel M. Rahim Khan, was an introverted workaholic with a subtle sense of humour. On the eve of his posting, he received a letter from the OTS postmaster, a civilian, eulogizing his services. Rahim wrote on the margin, 'My confidential report from the postmaster.' Rahim was replaced by an extrovert Hamid-ud-din Khan, sporting an impressive overgrown mustache. The shrewd, *pan* (betel leaf) chewing Major Mansoor Sheikh excelled in sugar-coating his double-talk with a fine icing of subtle humour. The sharp and smart Major Luqman Mahmood was too bold to escape trouble for long. The on-going low stake in the game of Bridge was 'chicken feed' for his high-style life. A brilliant conversationalist, he kept his audience amused with witty remarks. Captain Saadat Ali Sheikh, the

adjutant, was a terror for the cadets and a remarkable individual
for his friends. His full-throated laugh cheered up many somber
moments. Captain Rahat Ullah Khan Jarral excelled in the leg-
pulling technique to put others on the defensive. He had the
knack of appearing busy.

There was never a dull moment in the company of the ever
jovial Captain Fazal-Ur-Rahman. For him, life was a rainbow
on a dreary, cloudy sky. Gaiety spontaneously oozed out of his
vibrant and restless system. Then, suddenly one day it was all
gone. With grief writ large on the faces of his friends, Fazal lay
dead, tragically killed in a road accident. It was a moving scene
when Fazal's aging father, a veteran soldier, sought permission
from the commandant of the OTS to take away the body of his
son for burial. His composure at the time of extreme grief left a
deep and lingering impression on those present.

The Fire Eaters

Captain Kamal Said Mian, a tribal from Parachinar, often
fascinated his friends with absorbing stories of men from his
area who played with burning charcoal without sustaining injury
on their persons. It hurt the ego of the proud Pathan when his
listeners always dismissed his story as incredible fiction. He
decided to prove his point. A bus load of eager officers from the
OTS reached Kamal's *hujra* at Thall for a stag dinner. Living
up to his traditional warm hospitality, the beaming host served a
sumptuous meal to his guests. Nearby, some log-wood stacked
in the courtyard was set ablaze. A group of about fifteen adult
performers was introduced to the guests. They spoke perfect
Pushto and showed no abnormality in their behaviour. By the
time the dinner was over, the logs had turned into bright burning
charcoal.

They started a drum beat, initially at a leisurely pace but
gradually accelerating in tempo. The performers started moving
around the red hot charcoal in rhythmic, measured steps. Their
movements gained momentum as the drum beat became louder

and quicker. Suddenly, they started singing a chorus in some unfamiliar language, not understood by the audience, including those who spoke Pushto. Even the host could not decipher the words. The faster the drum beat, the greater was its impact on the dancing group. Soon they were visibly excited, greatly agitated and noticeably hysterical. As the drummer went crazy so did the performers. They removed their footwear and started walking with bare feet on the burning coal without showing any visible ill effects. It was an amazing performance.

While the spellbound audience watched aghast, the dancing hysterics picked up pieces of the burning charcoal. Some tossed them from one hand to the other. Others held them in their teeth. This was an unbelievably fantastic performance. The slowing down of the drum beat initiated the winding down process of the strange and spectacular show. Minutes later the performers, totally exhausted, were back to normal. They did not recollect what they had sung and in which language. There were no burn wounds. The act defied logical explanation. Were we all mesmerized? Perhaps not. Or, was it a mystical performance? This was certainly not a magic show. Whatever it was, those who did not believe in the claims earlier were noticeably perplexed and convincingly silenced. The Pathan honour stood vindicated as a smiling Kamal bid farewell to his amazed guests.

Staff College, Quetta

It was February 1960. The rail journey from Kohat to Quetta took forty-four hours. Air travel was not common then. Besides, my wife and I did not believe in travelling light for a year-long stay in Quetta.

Established in 1905, the Staff College, Quetta, enjoys international stature as a premier institution of learning. Here the students work against time to produce workable plans of action. The work tempo is fast, the competition is tough and the course performance determines the officers advancement in their future professional lives.

We had likeable neighbours. Major Nasir Ullah Khan Babar mercifully kept his ferocious alsation dog tied to allow his neighbours freedom of movement. He prematurely retired in 1975 as a major-general at the request of Prime Minister Z. A. Bhutto to enrich national politics. I telephoned him to inquire whether to congratulate him or sympathize with him on joining politics. Later, Babar served as a minister in the cabinet of Ms Benazir Bhutto. Soldiering remained an unmistakable style in his political life.

Major Faqir Mohammad Khan maintained a healthy balance between his studies and pleasure. His smile and humour kept his Capper Road neighbours in good cheer. He retired a Brigadier. Major Mazhar Ali Shah, a bookworm, took the course and life as seriously as a keen gunner conducts an artillery shoot. His advice on work and life was mature and correct. He retired a Lieutenant-Colonel.

The happy-go-lucky Major Fazil Shah had no pretensions of being an academic. He took the course in his stride and was ever ready to ditch his studies to accompany his friends on shopping trips to downtown Quetta. A lovable and jovial personality, Fazil's spontaneous wit and humour removed gloom from any dull day and added life to our company. Eat, drink and be merry was his philosophy on life and he considered laughter the best medicine. In 1964, Fazil Shah was struck by jaundice. As his illness gradually drained the life out of his body, he remained cheerful and courageous till the end. Every time his wife entered his room in the Combined Military Hospital, Peshawar, Fazil would sport a smile on his ashen face, pick up a book and pretend to read to re-assure his spouse. He died the way he wanted to, gallantly. May God bless his soul.

The 1960 staff course, Quetta, was attended by seventy-eight students including eighteen foreign officers from fourteen different countries. While every participant played his part, some were more conspicuous than others. The college magazine 'The Owl 1960' records their contributions under the heading, 'They will be Remembered,' thus:

Major Mohammad Ahmad, for introducing colour, variety and romantic delicacy in his uniform;

Captain Syed Anwar Hussain, for bringing drought in Quetta in general and staff college in particular;

Major Nasir Ullah Khan Babar, for denying everyone, including the directing staff, the right of free speech;

Major Fazil Shah, for disagreeing with all concepts;

Captain F. R. Fleming (UK), for using his sunny smile to remove classroom depressions;

Major Fateh Khan, for exploiting his personality to the maximum, by not exposing it;

Major Syed Fazal Hussain Gilani, for always taking the audience into confidence before giving his views;

Major D. O. A. Magee (Australia), for giving detailed explanations as to why his answer could not be brief;

Major E. J. Mills (UK), for luring some students to join him on his hikes and losing them as good friends;

Major Malik Mohammad Sharif, for allowing his voice to overshadow his arguments;

Major Riaz-ul-Haq Malik, for his generous advice on every professional problem to one and all, except his own sub-syndicate;

Major Mohammad Yusaff Bin Ibrahim (Malaysia), for giving his views so diplomatically as to commit himself to nothing;

Captain Syed Mohammad Muslim Zaidi, for remaining in a perpetual flap during the course.

The lack of space forced the editorial board of the Owl to focus attention only on a few lucky individuals. In its collective wisdom it denied the pleasure of being commented upon by a large number of remaining student officers that included this author.

The course over, I joined my regiment at Mansar Camp, a cluster of World War II vintage wooden huts that might have been liveable when constructed. The huts did not boast of ceiling fans because the wooden roofs were too delicate to bear the load. Instead, each hut was provided with only one, old table fan. This unreliable and solitary cooling machine in each house worked occasionally. Air conditioners were rare then. The GHQ was requested to authorize use of military transport to buy items of daily use from the nearby town of Campbellpur, now Attock, to which the response was that as Mansar Camp was located on the Grand Trunk road, it did not qualify to get other amenities.

Worldly Temptations

In February 1962, I became the president of the summary military court working at District Courts, Lahore. The army officers were nominated on this duty for a period of three to four months, and it was my turn to rough it out.

This duty enabled me to assess the performance of the corruption-riddled police department from close quarters. The First Information Reports (FIR) were not written without fear or favour. The investigative efforts were shoddy and the concept of speedy justice in a court of law was a far cry. It was sad to observe that the custodians of law and order became partisan in disputes and indulged in questionable practices.

The police officials deliberately selected weak and half-baked cases for trial in the military courts, as if to tarnish the image of military justice. In some instances, the FIRs were falsely recorded, with some vital details left out to favour or damage one or the other party. In one case two FIRs, both diametrically opposed, had been recorded to confuse the issue. The investigative process was painfully slow, the trials were held at a leisurely pace, and the prosecution witnesses included police touts.

The army authorities neither enhanced the military image nor provided fair justice to the people by accepting such suspicious and half-baked cases for trial in the summary military courts. Perhaps too much faith was placed in the police departments to select cases for trial only on merit. It was conjectured that the police officials bargained with and blackmailed the accused on the mode of trial in a civil or in a military court. The discretionary powers of the police officials to decide which cases went for trial to civil or military courts was *ipso facto*, a miscarriage of justice.

The army officers were not immune either from the lure of corruption. The president of a summary court (a major) was seemingly an insignificant appointment unworthy of serious attention. Despite that, I was suddenly made conscious of my importance. My privacy was invaded by friends, relatives and acquaintances. One case illustrates the point; from the time this case was received by me for trial I was inundated with requests for favours. At first I ignored the advances but eventually, the pressure became too long for me to ignore. I went to the deputy martial law administrator's headquarters, explained all the facts to the officer concerned and requested for the transfer of the case from my court. The DMLA, Brigadier Sadiq Ullah Khan, rejected my request and directed me to proceed with the trial. The trial was completed in a single day and judgment announced in an open court. The summary military court proceedings were then submitted to the DMLA Headquarters for confirmation, as was required under the law.

A couple of weeks later, I was summoned to Headquarters 10 Division, Lahore. Despite my request, the agenda of the meeting was not disclosed to me. The mystery deepened further on being told that the Colonel Staff, Colonel A. O. Mitha desired to meet me. There was no plausible reason for the interview because a major was too humble a rank to merit the attention of the Colonel Staff. The haze cleared when the divisional staff told me that the summary military court proceedings of the trial held by me had been submitted to Mitha and were still pending with him. It was the same case which Sadiq Ullah had declined to withdraw from my court.

Mitha inquired if the case had been tried by me. I affirmed that it was and sought permission to apprise him of the facts before he asked any questions. He conceded to my request with a smile. I told him the facts of the case and disclosed to him the names of all the persons who had contacted me directly and indirectly to influence my decision. Mitha listened patiently, thanked me for the briefing and said, 'Keep doing your work.' I asked the purpose of summoning me and invited questions to clarify any lingering doubts. He smiled even more broadly, stood up and warmly shook hands with me. This was a hint for me to leave. I did not hear about this case again.

There were other temptations. An army major requested an early meeting to discuss what he called an important issue. The gentleman, who was not known to me, was hesitant to divulge details on the telephone. I agreed to meet him in order not to appear discourteous to a fellow officer. As he entered my modest drawing room he introduced himself by mentioning somewhat pointedly that he was a member of the Border Land Committee posted at Lahore. This committee scrutinized the cases of the allotment of the border lands to military officers. Sensing a catch, I evaded the bait and inquired about his problem. It was his turn to ignore my question. 'You don't have any border land in your name', said my visitor. He had obviously done his homework before meeting me. 'The thought of becoming a landlord', I said humourously, 'never occurred to me.' This was the opening my clever visitor wanted. With a meaningful smile spread on his face he said, 'Give an application and leave the rest to me.' I thanked my guest and told him that I would contact him when I needed his help. The visitor was persistent. 'Be quick', he said, adding, 'The land is shrinking and the claimants list gets bulkier every day.' By then the visitor had gained enough confidence to come to the point. He talked of a case of illegal occupation of property that was pending trial in my court. He showed his discomfort when reminded of the impropriety of his request. The major lost his case. I lost the land.

Was the 1958 Martial Law Inevitable?

General Mohammad Ayub Khan became the first Pakistani Commander-in-Chief of the Pakistan Army on 17 January 1951. To rise to the pinnacle of the professional ladder at the age of forty-two with only twenty-two years of military service to his credit posed a challenge to him. Ayub was intelligent, compassionate and widely respected.

A mere eight months later, Prime Minister Liaquat Ali Khan was assassinated in Rawalpindi on 16 October. With the nation dipped in utter gloom, it was a time for the vested interests to take hold. For the ruling politicians, 'the termination of the Prime Minister's life had come as a beginning of a new career for them.'[3] Ayub benefitted indirectly. The more the political minions indulged in power intrigues to elbow out their competing rivals, the more they weakened the fragile political structure in the country. Correspondingly, the army's stature and authority kept growing.

By 1953-4, the scheming and feuding politicians had created political anarchy, and a free-for-all ensued. The country was still without a constitution. The Muslim League had split. East Pakistan nourished a grudge against West Pakistan. Gradually, the army became a factor in national politics. This role fascinated Ayub Khan, whose eyes were increasingly focused on the political arena.

In Ayub's own words:

> I was staying on 4 October 1954, at a hotel in London...I could not sleep (because) the news from home was disturbing, the portents ominous...I was feeling uneasy that Governor-General Ghulam Mohammad might do something reckless...He and the Prime Minister Mohammad Ali Bogra were feuding with each other. I had a premonition that Ghulam Mohammad might draw me into politics which I wanted, above all things, to avoid.[4]

While claiming to avoid indulging in politics, Ayub nevertheless wrote that night 'A short appreciation of present and future problems of Pakistan,'[5] a comprehensive and lengthy analysis totally political in content. A study of this paper leads one to the inevitable conclusion that the scheme had long been in the making in the mind of its author.

Ayub was well informed. The ailing and headstrong governor-general, Ghulam Mohammad, was the real fount of power. His arbitrary approach created an ugly situation with the prime minister. In September 1954, the federal government introduced a bill in the Constituent Assembly which provided that the

'Governor-General shall be bound by the advice of the Prime Minister.' This provision, hailed by the press,[6] infuriated the wily Governor-General who felt betrayed by his own appointee.

In retaliation, the governor-general dismissed the federal government and dissolved the Constituent Assembly on 24 October 1954 'with deep regret'. Strangely enough, the deposed prime minister, Mohammad Ali Bogra, was asked to reform the government, an offer he did not dare to refuse. Seemingly in an attempt to keep Bogra in check, the governor-general offered the post of the defence minister in the new cabinet to General Ayub Khan. Ayub accepted on the condition that he remain the army chief, because he wanted 'to act as a buffer between the politicians and the armed forces.'[7] This claim does not ring true. The real reason was that 'Ayub Khan was now recognized as the man behind the throne'[8] and was keen to stay in his power base. General Iskandar Mirza, the new, powerful Home Minister unabashedly advocated, 'controlled democracy'[9] for Pakistan. Democracy was being throttled by non-politicians.

Appointing the commander-in-chief as defence minister, in a cabinet of tottering politicians, was like putting a cat among the pigeons. It gave Ayub and Iskandar Mirza an opportunity to assess the calibre and the weaknesses of their political cabinet colleagues from close quarters. Ayub's assertion that he desired to act as a buffer between the politicians and the armed forces was a euphemism for indulging in politics and showed his lust for power.

Ayub Khan was due to retire from military service in January 1955 after completing his four year command assignment. Instead, he was granted an extension. This enabled the commander-in-chief to entrench himself further and meddle in politics.

'Iskandar Mirza was the only *de facto* authority after 1955.'[10] A constitution was enacted in 1956 but it was not given time to run. By mid 1958, the duo of Iskandar Mirza and Ayub dominated the national scene. The politicians had eroded themselves and their prestige had nose-dived. With the government struggling to survive, Ayub was in no mood to retire from service. Firoz Khan Noon, the weak prime minister, gave him a further two year extension on 9 June 1958. Noon did what Ayub had demanded.

The axe fell on 7 October 1958. The 1956 Constitution was scrapped by President Iskandar Mirza on the plea that it was 'unworkable' and that 'more sacred than the constitution (was) the country.'[11] Pakistan was placed under martial law. Iskandar Mirza failed to comprehend that the power in martial law was provided by the gun firmly held by the army chief. On 27 October, Ayub sent three generals—Burki, Azam, and Khalid Sheikh—to President Iskandar Mirza, who meekly signed on the dotted line of his own resignation. Ayub emerged as the absolute ruler.

The grant of extensions to the senior military commanders, a double-edged weapon, runs counter to the interests of military service. Extensions allowed to a few cause frustration to many others who are denied promotion in their due turn despite their experience and qualifications. Besides, the beneficiaries develop exaggerated opinions about themselves and personalities start dominating the institutions. Ayub's martial law was a premeditated affair. The country might have followed a different political course had Ayub Khan not been given an extension in service.

Serving in Azad Kashmir

In 1963, I was posted as Brigade Major, 102 Brigade, located at Kotli, Azad Kashmir. The Nikial sector was then semi-active and exchanges of fire across the cease-fire line were a common phenomenon. I decided to visit this sector to gain first-hand knowledge. This involved a long march over the hills. The Brigade Commander, Brigadier Khalil Ahmad cautioned me to go slow. Arrogating myself to be in a super-fit physical state, I took his advice lightly. Khalil quipped with a poker face, 'Hills are seldom good-going for tanks.'

The prestige of the armour and my ego were at stake.
I accepted the implied challenge and decided to prove the
brigade commander wrong. The three day trek over the hills
was more strenuous than playing the tough games of basketball
that I was used to. On my way from Nikial to the Kallargala
post, about two and a half hours walk, I was put to shame by
the porter carrying my luggage. He merrily kept trotting up the
hill while I kept gasping for breath every few minutes. The
journey back was worse because my body was stiff and in pain.
It was only my wounded pride that kept me going. My legs
ached, knees wobbled and spirit was bruised by the time the trip
was completed. I learnt the hard way that ascending hills sharply
drained out human vitality if the leg muscles were not
sufficiently tuned for such a trek.

GOC 12 Division, Major-General Shaukat Ali Shah, was
more interested in minor issues than in the higher aspects of
command. He showed a remarkable capacity for checking that
no person in the formation spent more than twenty days casual
leave during a year. At times he made interesting observations.
One Education Officer serving in 102 Brigade, father of a large
family, including a mentally retarded child needing regular
medical care, submitted a petition requesting that his next
posting be in a station that provided a suitable medical facility
for his ailing child. General Shaukat endorsed the application
thus, 'Why has this officer produced so many children and what
has the Brigade Commander done about it?'

Brigadier Khalil was replaced by Brigadier Mahmood Hussain
as Commander 102 Brigade; a fine gentleman who had a
successful encounter with a royal Bengal tiger while serving in
East Pakistan. Soon thereafter, Major-General Akhtar Hussain
Malik took over the command of 12 Division from Major-
General Shaukat Ali Shah. A clear headed professional, Akhtar
Malik injected dynamism into his command and took difficult
decisions easily and speedily. His remarkable stamina for hard
work was easily matched by his ability to hold his glass.

From Kotli to Fort Knox

In June 1963, I was selected to attend the Armor Officer's Career Course at the School of Armor, Fort Knox, Kentucky, USA. It was attended by 222 military officers, including seventeen from fourteen different allied countries. I found the American officers intelligent, inquisitive, professionally competent and patriotic. Most of them knew Europe and its problems, but to them Africa was a dark continent. Except for Japan, Korea, the Philippines and the Far-East, Asia was considered a distant land mass with ancient history, mystical culture and abject poverty.

For most Americans, China either did not exist or was not worth knowing about. Mao Zedong and Ho Chi Minh were presented as horrible monsters out to harm the free world, and devour Western culture. Everything they stood for in their own country or in world affairs was wrong. Everything the US said about them was correct and justified. The troops were frequently indoctrinated against these two 'devils' of the East. In contrast, despite the on-going cold war, the Soviet Union leadership was disliked, but not despised.

The Americans took pride in their technological superiority and boasted of clobbering Vietnam in the combat which had just then begun. The professionals relished the opportunity of testing their high-tech weapon-systems and operational doctrines in the Vietnam battlefields. When reminded of the fate of the French forces at Dien Bien Phu in May 1954, the US military officers, without being rude to the French, arrogated themselves to be in a more advantageous position, economically, militarily and diplomatically. The optimism of the US administration to emerge victorious in the Vietnam conflict was largely shared by American academics and the media. Their arrogance was widespread and all pervasive. Vietnam was apparently a gift from the heavens for the US to test its combat power.

Years later the tables turned. The Americans were shocked when Vietnam triumphed over the US in combat. The US learned the hard way that despite all the conventional high technology weapons used in the battlefield, and despite its visible supremacy in other fields, the arrogance of power could not conquer the spirit of the people. Military might proved inferior to the peoples rights. A stunned America suffered a Vietnam syndrome from which it took decades to recover. The intoxication of power had blinded the US policy makers and they made the fatal error of underestimating their adversary.

The Americans were sympathetic to the Jews and felt they deserved special consideration because of the grave injustices done to them by the Germans in the Second World War. Why the Palestinian Muslims were suffering for the atrocities committed by the German Christians on the Jews was a question left unanswered. Some Americans confessed that, while both the Jews and the Palestinians had claims on the disputed territory, Israel enjoyed a special status for them. The Jewish lobby in America was strong, in the media and in the financial institutions.

Oil from the Gulf was important because it was the lifeline of the European and the US economy. The US did not show concern about the presence or absence of democratic governments in the Gulf region. For it, oil was more important. The major US concern was to deny the Soviet Union diplomatic inroads into this strategically vital region. The bulk of the military exercises conducted during this period were planned in the setting of Central Europe.

Most Americans were not well versed with Pakistan. They were astonished when told that Pakistan possessed the relics of stone age man in the Soan Valley near Islamabad, claiming a possible antiquity of about half a million years. They could not believe that Kot Diji, in Upper Sindh, dated back to 2800-2500 BC, and that two great civilizations had flourished in the cities of Harappa and Moenjodaro around 2350 BC. Ignorance about Pakistan—her history, geography natural resources, varied culture etc.—was pathetic. However, being a new country on the map of the world, Pakistan should have made efforts to educate other nations about her cultural and strategic importance. The Foreign Office failed to play its due role in this respect.

For example, while speaking to a Church group in Fort Knox, I was asked if Pakistan had roads. There was a loud burst of

1. Field-Marshal Ayub Khan.

2. General Muhammad Yahya Khan.

3. Zulfikar Ali Bhutto.

4. General M. Ziaul Haq.

5. General Pervez Musharraf.

6. Generals Zia and Arif, Field Area, Kohat, November 1986.

7. Generals **Sawar** Khan, Arif and Zia. Installation Ceremony: Arif as Colonel Commandant, Regiment of Artillery, Attock, April 1986.

8. Lt-General Mirza Aslam Beg and General Arif—Successor and Predecessor—Sindh Regiment Reunion, Hyderabad, February 1986.

9. Generals Zia and Arif, Mess Function, Rawalpindi, 1985.

10. Justice Sajjad Ali Shah, former
Chief Justice of Pakistan.

11. Justice Ghulam Safdar Shah, Judge,
Supreme Court of Pakistan.

12. General Arif and General John A. Wickham Jr., Chief of Staff US Army, July 1985.

13. (From left to right) Lt-General Fazle Haq, Chief Minister NWFP, General Ziaul Haq, General Arif, and Col. Abdul Ghafoor Hoti, Governor NWFP, Peshawar, 1986.

14. General Arif calling on the President of Turkey with the Pakistani ambassador, Ankara, 14 October 1985.

15. Z. A. Bhutto and Nusrat Bhutto, 30 September 1974.

16. Zia and Arif, visiting troops in Azad Kashmir, 1986.

17. Services Chiefs with Former Prime Minister Nawaz Sharif, Horse and Cattle Show, Lahore, 2 March 1986.

18. Pakistan–China friendship—Pakistan delegation with the Chinese hosts, Great Hall of China, 1984.

19. General Arif with wife, Khalida and son, Amer Arif, Rawalpindi, 1984.

20. General Arif with wife Khalida. The Great Wall of China, 1978.

laughter when I replied, 'No. We live on trees.' Some of the audience thought that girls were not permitted to attend schools, and every man in Pakistan had four wives. A girl asked, 'How do you compare the standard of morality in the US with that in your country?' When I pointed out that in my part of the globe men did not kiss their wives in public, there was a unanimous noisy chorus, 'But, why not?' The diversity in the two cultures stood exposed.

The regular non-commissioned officers—the backbone of the US army—were efficient and well trained. On the other hand the US conscripts were a mixed bag. I once asked a young soldier how much service he had to his credit, to which the prompt retort was, 'One month and eleven days to go.' Military duty, he complained, stood between him and his love.

President J. F. Kennedy was assassinated on 23 November 1963. We heard the news during the tank gun shooting on the Fort Knox field ranges. A pall of gloom spread among us, but the firing continued. Each student had fired two rounds of the main gun on a moving target which appeared to travel at a healthy Olympic speed. By lunch time, 100 students had fired 200 rounds. While the students had their field lunch, the instructor went to the moving trolley to record the number of hits scored. To our embarrassment, only four rounds had hit the target. While announcing our poor performance, the instructor looked at me and said, 'Major Arif, how will you grade the quality of firing?' The class burst into laughter when I said, 'I wonder who got the other two hits.'

During the course we benefitted professionally, and made good friends. One day, a senior student announced that, 'the longest pregnancy in history has come to a successful end. Captain (name deleted) of the Indonesian army, who has been in the United States for the last one year, has been blessed with a son back home. We all congratulated him. Some cigars were placed on the dais to celebrate this happy occasion.'

The students enriched the military lexicon by adding new definitions to the glossary of terms. Some examples. Infantry: Hundreds of years of tradition unhampered by progress.

A tanker: A member of a uniformed force; may be a soldier. Decisive engagement: When all freedom is lost and one has no option but to marry.

At the end of the course, I went to Canada, West Germany, France and Spain on a sight-seeing tour. Captain Lobo, a fellow student from Spain, and I travelled together in his car from Fort Knox to Canada and back to New York to take the flights for our respective homeward journeys.

En route to Canada, we stopped in Chicago to see the M-48 tank assembly plant. Weeks earlier, Lobo and I had sought permission from our respective national embassies in Washington DC to see this factory. We had also sent our request to the tank factory through the School of Armor. The Pakistani Mission in Washington did not care to reply, despite the fact that the trip was to cost nothing to the State exchequer. By the time the course ended my request had neither been sanctioned nor rejected. I convinced myself that the silence implied acceptance and embarked on the journey.

From our hotel in Chicago we called the factory and found them cooperative enough to show us the armoured car plant. We were interested, we insisted, in seeing the tank plant. The gentleman on the line apologized for the communication error because they had received a security clearance from their head office to show us the armoured cars production plant. He requested for a few minutes to settle the confusion. Twenty minutes later, a guide was on the way to the hotel to escort us to the tank factory.

We were told that after our telephone conversation the management contacted their head office located in a different city which in turn checked our *bonafides* from the School of Armor before granting security clearance. This process took only twenty minutes, demonstrating the efficiency of communication channels in the US, and the efficacy of their decision makers. I admired their system of work.

Lobo and I were escorted by a senior official and given VIP treatment during a guided tour of the tank plant. We felt embarrassed. The hospitality included a lavish meal by those who consider free lunch a taboo. The hosts gave us exaggerated importance on a mistaken notion that we were evaluating the tank on behalf of our countries. Mercifully, our governments remained unaware of our visit.

A week later, while travelling in Frankfurt, I started talking to a cab driver who spoke intelligible English. 'Were the Allied troops liked in their respective occupation zones in Berlin?' I inquired. The driver replied firmly, 'No.' I asked if they differed in their behaviour? With contempt writ large on his face, the driver replied that they were all chips of the same block, adding, 'the Americans are more broad-minded than others.' Finding him responsive, I fired another salvo, 'Do you think Hitler made errors in war?' His brutally frank reply showed the German pride, 'Hitler made only one mistake. He lost the war.'

A waitress in a restaurant in Paris looked at me in amazement when I asked for a glass of water with lunch. 'The French wine tastes well,' she insisted with a captivating smile on her face. She could not comprehend a person preferring water over wine.

My duty impelled me to observe protocol and call on Pakistan's Ambassador in Paris. At first a clerk and then a junior officer in the Pakistan Embassy grilled me to extract the real purpose of my audience with the ambassador. My insistence that it was only a courtesy call compounded their doubts. They inquired if I had a visa or a financial problem or had run into a difficulty with a local? Did I wish to ring up someone or send a message to Pakistan? Did I wish to locate some person or needed transport? I was treated like a hardened criminal evading searching questions. Then, the junior officer disappeared into a room, ostensibly to announce me to the unapproachable representative of Pakistan in France. He failed to return. I left the Mission in disgust without calling on His Excellency, the ambassador.

My return to Karachi in July 1964 might have been erased from my memory but for a ridiculous incident. The prevailing rule required all returning Pakistani citizens to declare the foreign currency in their possession at the port of entry, and later get the amount exchanged for local currency from a bank.

The foreign currency amount in my pocket showed my poverty. Nevertheless, I made it public by declaring it. The gentleman at the counter returned the declaration form with an earthly advice, 'This is too small an amount to declare. Keep it with yourself.' As five dollars and six DM could not make me rich, I decided to be honest, followed the law and declared the amount. A week later, I carried the coins to a bank for exchange which declined to accept them on the plea that the banks did not deal in coins. I wrote to the State Bank of Pakistan, explaining the situation and requesting permission to retain the coins as souvenirs. It took three months for the 'competent authority' to approve my request with the vital proviso that, 'prior permission of the State Bank will be required if ever the coins were used for commercial purposes.' Someone had a sense of humour.

NOTES

1. Rudyard Kipling, *The Lost Legion*, quoted by Major-General M. Hayauddin in *One Hundred Years-History of the Punjab Frontier Force*, Civil and Military Gazette Press, Lahore, 1950.
2. Lord Ismay, 'The Best Advice I Ever Had', *Readers Digest*, October, 1953.
3. Mohammad Ayub Khan, *Friends Not Masters,* Oxford University Press, Karachi, 1967, p. 41.
4. Ibid., p. 186.
5. Ibid., pp. 186-91.
6. *Dawn,* 22 September 1954.
7. Ayub Khan, *Friends Not Masters,* p. 53.
8. Altaf Gauhar, *Ayub Khan,* Sang-e-Meel Publications, Lahore, 1993, p. 96.
9. Ibid., p. 97.
10. K. K. Aziz, *Party Politics in Pakistan 1947-1958*, National Commission on Historical and Cultural Research, Islamabad, 1976, p. 226.
11. Ayub Khan, *Friends Not Masters,* p. 246.

2

FOLLIES IN WAR

Introduction

This is not the history of the India-Pakistan War of September 1965. Nor is it a detailed battle account of the military formations engaged in combat during that period. Many books written on the subject by Indian writers have appeared in print. They give a fairly comprehensive account of the war, but largely with a one-sided, pro-India bias, and a strong injection of Indian nationalism in the narrative. Such attempts are more political than academic in content. Pakistani writers have generally shied away from the war account, partly because official sources of information are denied to them, and also because the sword of the Official Secrets Act hangs over their heads. Such restrictions should be removed, specially at this belated stage, so that freedom of expression enables history to get recorded in a fair, balanced and correct perspective.

Keeping in view the broad-based scope of this book, this chapter is a postmortem of some major acts of omission and commission of Pakistan's political and military policy makers in 1965. The aim is to learn from their experience. The appraisal is attempted in the hope that it may benefit our political leaders and military commanders in the future. Additionally, this effort would eminently serve its purpose if it provokes other writers to conduct a full, comprehensive and dispassionate analysis of this war.

The 1965 war is one of the classic examples of an unintended war. Pakistan did not bargain for general hostilities. Perhaps, neither did India. Limited and local events and episodes followed one after another, increasing tension and triggering jingoism.

Each side reacted disproportionately to the perceived provocation by the other and in the end lost control. India and Pakistan reacted, on occasions excessively, to each other and plunged into a war that neither had planned.

The origin of the 1965 war is traceable directly to the Kashmir question. This dispute had continued to fester as Indian intransigence obstructed and blocked the implementation of the United Nations Security Council resolutions, according to which the people of the state were to decide the question of the state's accession to India or Pakistan. They agitated against Indian colonial rule, which India ruthlessly put down. The people of Kashmir displayed their determination to be masters of their own destiny. Pakistan felt increasingly frustrated as Kashmir became a pawn in the Cold War. The Soviet Union used its veto power shamelessly to shield India in the Security Council. The United States, too was increasingly reluctant to maintain a principled position, especially after India's border clash with China in 1962. As has happened frequently in history, fatigue and frustration eroded the will to maintain peace.

Historical Background

With an area of 84,471 square miles and a population of 13.30 million in 1999 (estimated), the strategically important State of Jammu and Kashmir borders Afghanistan, China and Tibet. The rivers flowing out of it—Indus, Chenab and Jhelum—provide the only source of water to Pakistan and constitute its lifeline. History and geography link Kashmir with Pakistan. So do the customs and traditions of their people, their cultural ties, language affiliations, trade routes, religion and contiguous location. Pakistan and Kashmir constitute one single geographic unit that is politically and economically inseparable and strategically vital to each other.

Under the 1846 Treaty of Amritsar, the State of Kashmir (77 per cent Muslims, 22.2 per cent Hindus and 0.8 per cent Buddhists) was sold by the British rulers to the Hindu Dogra chieftain, Gulab Singh, for a sum of Rs 7.5 million. Gulab Singh and his successors imposed tyrannical rule in the state that denied human rights, clamped arbitrary and harsh taxation measures and imposed despotic and repressive measures in which the slaughter of a cow carried the penalty of death, later reduced to ten years imprisonment.

Hari Singh, the ruler of Kashmir in 1947, had ascended to the Dogra throne in 1925. While a vast majority of its people wanted Kashmir to accede to Pakistan, the Hindu lineage of Hari Singh pulled him towards India. The people rose in revolt and took control of a part of the state. Sensing power slipping out of his control, Hari Singh proposed, on 12 August, a Standstill Agreement with India and Pakistan 'on all matters.' Pakistan agreed but India procrastinated and sought discussion.

India and Hari Singh then indulged in an intrigue that would have put Machiavelli to shame. A drama was staged for the military occupation of Kashmir by India. On 7 October 1947, Sardar Patel wrote to his cabinet colleague, the defence minister of India, 'I hope arrangements are in hand to send immediately supplies of arms and ammunition to Kashmir state. If necessary we must arrange to send them by air.'[1] On his part, Hari Singh secretly secured the services of a contingent of gunners from Patiala State to guard the Srinagar Airfield and the Patiala infantry to reinforce defences in Jammu.[2] These contingents 'were moved as part of the supply convoys despatched to Jammu and Kashmir by the Government of India.'[3]

At the other end of the spectrum, Kashmiri freedom fighters endeavoured to gain control of the state. They captured Domel on 22 October 1947. The route to Srinagar was just 100 miles away with no major obstacle on the way. About 3000 tribesmen entered Kashmir. On 24 October, the Poonch revolutionaries declared independence and Hari Singh lost the writ to rule. The dethroned ruler rushed Deputy Prime Minister R. L. Batra to New Delhi to seek military assistance from India.

Mountbatten and Nehru kept Pakistan in the dark and hatched a plan to annex Kashmir. The Maharaja was made to sign on the dotted line and Indian troops were air dashed to Kashmir.

At the time of 'accession' India declared that, '…as soon as law and order have been restored in Kashmir and her soil cleared of the invader, the State's accession should be settled by a reference to the people.'[4] Belatedly, Nehru informed Liaquat Ali Khan on 31 October in a telegram thus, 'Our assurance that we shall withdraw our troops from Kashmir as soon as law and order are restored and leave the decision regarding the future of this state to the people of this state is not merely a promise to your government but also to the people of Kashmir and to the world.'[5]

Alastair Lamb lists four reasons that makes the instrument of accession legally invalid. First, the Maharaja had already been toppled by his people two days before he signed the accession document. Secondly, it was in violation of the Standstill Agreement that the state of Kashmir had made with Pakistan. Thirdly, the accession was conditional 'on the will of the people'. And finally, Mountbatten's Viceroyalty was dominated by acts of fraud.[6]

India took the Kashmir dispute to the UN Security Council on 1 January 1948, under Article 35 of the UN Charter. The UN Security Council adopted two resolutions, one on 13 August 1948 and the second on 5 January 1949. India and Pakistan accepted these resolutions which declared that the question of accession of Kashmir to either India or Pakistan would be decided through a fair and impartial plebiscite. This dispute remains unresolved.

Himalayan Skirmish

India's war with China in 1962 had an indirect but important bearing on the Kashmir dispute. This border conflict exposed India's miscalculation and military inadequacy. The utter confusion in which her troops reeled back helter-skelter under modest Chinese pressure in the Himalayan mountains, without a serious fight, destroyed Nehru who could not recover from the shock of national humiliation for the rest of his life. Nehru's forward military policy in the disputed areas had misfired.

India, using the China Card, quickly sought and received military aid from the US-led Western countries that pursued a policy of containing China. India went to the extent of asking the US to bomb strategic sites on the Chinese mainland, and requested that the US Air Force provide air cover to India to release the Indian Air Force for combat duty. Such unprecedented requests exposed the frailty of India's claim on non-alignment. On its part, the US showed excessive eagerness in wooing India and in this process violated the 'assurance of prior consultation' personally given by President Kennedy to President Ayub in July 1961.[7]

The Sino-Indian border conflict offered a tempting chance to Pakistan to benefit from India's preoccupation in combat. On face value, Pakistan could up the military ante in Kashmir. The US advised Pakistan to show restraint against such an attempt. Ayub did not take advantage of India's weakness. Nor did Pakistan stab India in the back. Whether Ayub succumbed to US pressure or he was too honourable a person to hit his adversary below the belt, is open for discussion. Or, did he foresee something which others failed to observe? Whatever the case, the fleeting opportunity quickly consumed itself when China, displaying maturity and statesmanship, unilaterally ceased fire and withdrew her forces from the disputed territory. This gesture conveyed to the bewildered Indians that the Chinese intention was, in fact, to register a protest and not to rub salt on their wounded pride.

With the advantage of hindsight it became obvious that the duration of the Sino-Indian hostilities was too short to provide a meaningful opportunity to Pakistan to initiate any worthwhile activity in Kashmir. A major change in policy takes time to implement. Besides, it might have created a false impression internationally that China and Pakistan had acted in unison in the Himalayas and in Kashmir. Such an accusation would have embarrassed both China and Pakistan.

The US expected Pakistan to help India and oppose China during the Himalayan skirmish. She found it inconceivable that Pakistan, an ally, would adopt an independent course that was

different from US policy in the area. America was hurt when
Ayub did not accept the unsolicited US advice to distance Pakistan
from China. The prospects of a China-Pakistan understanding
alarmed the US, and America exerted pressure on Nehru to start
negotiations with Pakistan to settle the Kashmir dispute.

Bilateral negotiations on the Kashmir dispute started at the
ministerial level. The talks were aborted in May 1963 after six
rounds. The crisis in the Himalayas over and the external
pressure removed, India was no longer interested in peacefully
settling the Kashmir dispute. Nor did she show interest in settling
her dispute with China. India reverted to the policy of Nehru
during the heydays of *Hindi-Chini bhai-bhai*. He had told an
Indian cultural delegation before their visit to China in 1952,
'Never forget that the basic challenge in South-Asia is between
India and China...Never let the Chinese patronize you.'[8]

Brigadier J.P. Dalvi had aptly titled his book on the Sino-
Indian border conflict of 1962 as the 'Himalayan Blunder', and
as Brigadier Dalvi called it, it was Nehru's folly and India's
misadventure that brought them shame. India used the China
Card to camouflage her defeat and to earn Western sympathy
and support. This conflict prompted India to expand and
modernize her armed forces and rehabilitate their self-respect.
India's mix of poverty and power was ominous for South Asia
and dangerous for Pakistan, her declared Enemy Number One.
New Delhi looked for an excuse to re-establish her military
image, preferably in a conflict with the weaker Pakistan.

The Rann of Kutch Operation

The 8,400 square mile Rann of Kutch, a wasteland of low sand
dunes, is situated between the province of Sindh, Pakistan and
the Indian State of Gujrat. Its undemarcated border made it
disputed territory between India and Pakistan. This area, mostly
unfit for human habitation, gets flooded with sea water between
the months of June and September each year. Small clusters of
mud huts, scattered here and there, show sparse signs of life.

The cattle population in the Rann of Kutch belonging to the local Indian and Pakistani villagers move unhindered in the disputed area and graze there at will. In 1956, India's border forces impounded the intruding cattle and drove out the Pakistani villagers from their ancestral homes. A small military contingent from Pakistan returned the Indian compliment and evicted the Indian force from the area. An uneasy calm returned to the region.

In early 1965, Indian military patrols adopted a provocative, aggressive posture in the disputed area and fired at a Pakistani border patrol in the vicinity of the half-ruined fort of Kanjarkot. The Indian patrols also shadowed the Pakistani posts at Mara, Rahim-ki-Bazar, Ding and Surai. On 19 February 1965, Indian fighter planes violated Pakistan's air space in the region. In March, India held a brigade group exercise code-named Arrow Head inside the disputed area. On 7 April, India's Home Minister declared in the *Lok Sabha* (lower house) that steps would be taken to end Pakistan's intrusion in the area. Such unprovoked, intimidatory acts led to a chain reaction in which both the countries reinforced the disputed area. The Pakistani military assessed that India aimed at capturing Kanjarkot.

On 10 April 1965, small-scale skirmishes took place in which the Indian forces abandoned the Sardar Post. This caused a red alert in both the countries and Pakistan inducted elements of 8 Division in the area. She decided to improve her defensive posture by capturing two posts—Karim Shahi and Chhand Bet. This mini-operation began on 26 April. Biar Bet was captured after a brief encounter, and this cleared the way for the Pakistani forces to block the enemy's retreat line. The Pakistani troops were ordered to consolidate their gains and let the enemy retreat, which it did in visible panic. This minor military setback to India from a country smaller in size and power potential, infuriated the policy planners in New Delhi. If India had planned to wash off the stigma of her 1962 defeat by achieving a military success in the Rann of Kutch, her plans misfired.

A political storm gripped India. Mr U. M. Trivadi, the Jan Sangh leader in the *Lok Sabha*, wanted the Indian military forces to go, 'right up to Lahore to bring Pakistan to its senses.'[9] The socialist leader, Dr R. M. Lohia, wanted India to overrun Pakistan. Mr P. V. Shastri, independent, wanted his country to march on to Karachi.[10]

Pakistan proposed a cease-fire and withdrawal of forces from the disputed area. Field Marshall Ayub Khan said, 'If Pakistan wanted to commit aggression it would have chosen a better area than the mud flats and also a better time when the Indian forces were on the run after their defeat at the hands of China (in 1962).'[11] India rejected Pakistan's proposal. On 28 April, Prime Minister Lal Bahadur Shashtri thundered, 'If Pakistan does not listen to reason, Indian army will decide its own strategy and employment of its own manpower and equipment in the manner which it deems best.'[12] This was a threat of war, and Shastri lived to carry out his commitment.

On the initiative of the British Prime Minister, Harold Wilson, India and Pakistan signed an agreement on 29 June 1965, which called for a cease-fire in the Rann of Kutch from 1 July 1965, the disengagement of forces within seven days, the restoration of the status quo as of 1 January, and ministerial discussions on the demarcation of the border. The dispute was agreed to be referred to an impartial tribunal in case the ministerial discussions were unsuccessful. The award of the tribunal would be final.

Pakistan was satisfied. However, the reaction from India was mixed. India's Defence Minister, Mr Y. B. Chavan called it 'an honourable agreement.' India's Foreign Minister, Krishna Menon, felt differently, 'It is not at all what I would have wished.' The ultra right Jan Sangh leader, Atal Bihari Vajpayee (now Prime Minister of India) called the agreement, 'thoroughly dishonourable.'

On 18 August, India proposed that the Rann of Kutch dispute be directly referred to a tribunal without first holding bilateral ministerial discussions on the subject. Pakistan agreed. The Rann of Kutch Tribunal settled this dispute by awarding nearly three-fourth of the Rann to India and the remaining one-fourth to Pakistan. This was the second time that an Indo-Pakistan dispute was settled with the intervention of a third party. The Indus Basin Water Treaty between India and Pakistan had earlier been negotiated in 1960 under the World Bank.

The mood in Pakistan was buoyant. Lieutenant-General Gul Hassan Khan, then Director of Military Operations, writes that 'military morale could not have been higher.' Another writer maintains that Ayub Khan allowed an escape route to the trapped Indian troops because he 'was reasonably confident that the Rann of Kutch accord (if reached) might serve as a model for the settlement of the Kashmir dispute.'[13] This was wishful thinking, based on a misreading of the Indian psyche. The word 'goodwill' does not exist in India's diplomatic diction when it comes to dealing with her neighbours, particularly Pakistan.

Even Pakistan's Foreign Minister and Foreign Secretary Aziz Ahmed, 'had convinced himself that Pakistan was in a position to dislodge the Indians from Kashmir.'[14]

'The perceived reverse in the Rann of Kutch gave India a grudge to nourish and a score to settle.'[15] India strongly protested to the US over the use of American-supplied weapons by Pakistan in the Kutch. Washington promptly announced an embargo on the further supply of weapons or spare parts to both the countries, knowing well that such a ban would hit only Pakistan. The Indian military was equipped with Soviet-supplied weapon-systems. America's 'equal treatment' drew a sharp response from President Ayub Khan that 'Pakistan sought friends not masters.' The Indian perception of defeat and the Pakistani perception of victory fired emotions of vengeance on one side, and euphoria on the other.

Developments in Kashmir

In October 1963, New Delhi embarked on legal manoeuvres to integrate the disputed territory of Jammu and Kashmir into the Indian Union, a position illegal and unacceptable to the people of the State as well as Pakistan. Nehru wanted to gradually erode the special status of Kashmir, to renege out of the personal commitments given by him to the people of the disputed area to decide their own future through a UN-sponsored referendum. The people of Kashmir opposed these legal measures.

The peoples agitation took a serious turn when, on 26 December 1963, the *Moo-e-Muqaddis*—a hair of the Holy Prophet (PBUH)—was stolen from the Hazratbal shrine, near Srinagar. The people were outraged and a spontaneous insurgency erupted in all the cities and towns of the Valley. Great tension prevailed in the State, even after the recovery of the holy relic. The crisis further deepened due to India's repression against unarmed people whose only fault was to demand the right of self-determination, a right that is timeless and sacrosanct.

On Pakistan's appeal, the UN Security Council held lengthy debates on the Kashmir dispute, first in February 1964, and then in May that year. The efforts in the apex organ of the United Nations were frustrated by the Soviet veto. This was a serious blow to the prospects of peace between India and Pakistan. The perception that the Security Council decisions were influenced more by *realpolitik* than by justice, fair play and the merits of a dispute, eroded public confidence in the organization.

Among other reasons, the Hazratbal agitation forced Nehru to release Sheikh Abdullah on 8 April 1964 from prison, where he had been incarcerated since April 1954. A clever politician and an admirer of Nehru, Abdullah felt that Nehru wanted a resolution of the Kashmir dispute, a belief shared by Jayaprakash Narayan, who showed courage by criticising Indian policies in Kashmir, and arguing that elections held by India in Kashmir did not constitute a vote of integration with this country. In this positive scenario, Ayub invited Abdullah to visit Pakistan, and Nehru did not try to frustrate the trip.

Sheikh Abdullah came to Pakistan in May 1964, and was awarded red carpet treatment by Ayub Khan. He maintained an ambivalent position on bilateral contentious issues by criticizing India's policies in Kashmir but remaining loyal to his country. In his assessment, a settlement of the Kashmir dispute without

Pakistan was not possible. At his suggestion Ayub Khan agreed to visit New Delhi for a meeting with Nehru. Providence willed otherwise. The next day, 27 May, Nehru died. With the death of Nehru, the hope for a summit meeting between India and Pakistan receded into the background. Nehru's successor, Lal Bahadur Shastri, did not follow up on Abdullah's suggestion for a meeting with President Ayub Khan.

Shastri revived the policy of constitutional measures to integrate Kashmir with India, and adopted India's double-track policy of speaking of negotiations but acting unilaterally. With the chance for peace gradually decreasing, a drift ensued and the two countries were put on a collision course.

Tension between India and Pakistan grew as the former resumed repressive measures in Kashmir. In May 1965, Sheikh Abdullah and Mirza Afzal Beg, leader of the Plebiscite Front, were arrested on their return from Hajj. This caused another popular upsurge in Kashmir. India used force to crush the struggle.

Such developments led to the inevitable conclusion in Pakistan that internationally, the United Nations had put the Kashmir dispute in a deep freeze, and the use of the veto by any of the five permanent members could keep it there for a long time. Both the superpowers, the US and the erstwhile Soviet Union, did not display any urgency in getting this dispute amicably settled. At the bilateral level, India did not show any desire to meet the firm and unequivocal commitments made by her in the United Nations, and to the people of Kashmir and Pakistan to decide about the final accession of Kashmir through a UN-sponsored plebiscite. Instead, India increasingly felt that given her favourable balance of power in South Asia, there was no urgency for her to honour her commitments on the issue. Sooner or later, India would be in a position to force a decision about Kashmir based on her own terms. Pakistan would, therefore, have to do something herself to pull the Kashmir dispute out of the deep freeze before the power ratio got decisively tilted against her in the future.

The more proximate cause of the war was the chain of actions and disproportionate reactions with regard to Kashmir. In order to focus world attention on Kashmir, Pakistan took the fateful initiative, code-named Operation Gibraltar, to send volunteers for sabotage in the Indian occupied part of Kashmir in August 1965. India responded by large-scale military action, its armed forces crossing the cease-fire line, occupying Azad Kashmir territory, and threatening the capital Muzaffarabad. India also brought its air force into action and bombed a village in Pakistan. Finding loss of the mountainous areas unacceptable, the Pakistan army mounted an assault in the Chhamb sector in the southern part of Kashmir. This confronted India with a threat to its line of communications in the state. India now decided to launch an attack on Lahore across the international boundary. Thus, the limited war in Kashmir expanded into a general war.

Operation Gibraltar

Conceptual Input

General Headquarters (GHQ) is mandated to conceive, plan and implement all land battles involving Pakistan. For some reason, Ayub Khan allowed Foreign Minister Bhutto and his confidant, Foreign Secretary Aziz Ahmed to remain in the vanguard of the planning stage of the Kashmir operations. Their action violated the institutions and put the country on a war path. Former Foreign Secretary Abdul Sattar, who worked as Director in Foreign Secretary Aziz Ahmed's office in 1965 maintains that while, 'Foreign Minister Bhutto and Foreign Secretary Aziz Ahmed were involved in the process, the "Foreign Office" was ignorant about Operation Gibraltar. The Foreign Ministry did not get an opportunity to conceive, examine, analyse or plan this operation.'[16] This might be so, but Bhutto and Aziz Ahmed could only interfere in the highly sensitive matter in their official capacity as Foreign Minister and Foreign Secretary respectively. That they kept their own ministry officials in the dark on the vital issue of national security causes their motives to become suspect. Besides, the domineering role of personalities showed the failure of institutions. Another writer says, 'Operation Gibraltar came into existence at Bhutto's behest and with Ayub Khan's approval.'[17]

In 1964, General Ayub Khan created a Kashmir Public Committee with Foreign Secretary Aziz Ahmed as its Chairman to keep the Kashmir situation under review. The members of the Committee were Secretary Defence, Director Intelligence Bureau, Chief of the General Staff and the Director Military Operations. Aziz Ahmad told the Committee that the 'President had ordered GHQ' to prepare two plans, one to encourage sabotage activities across the cease-fire line and the other to provide 'all out support for guerrillas to be inducted into Kashmir.'[18] GHQ assigned both the tasks to HQ 12 Division located at Murree.

In mid February 1965, another plan prepared by Aziz Ahmed and the ISI Directorate was placed before the intelligence committee of the cabinet. General Musa attended this meeting but conspicuously absent were the Commanders-in-Chief of the Navy and the Air Force. They had not been invited and surprisingly General Musa did not show any concern about their absence.

General Musa says, 'Bhutto and Aziz Ahmed, spurred on by Major-General Akhtar Hussain Malik, who was commander of our troops in Azad Kashmir, pressed the government to take advantage of the troubled situation in the valley and directed the army to send raiders into Indian-held Kashmir for conducting guerrilla activities there.'[19] Musa's lament is supported somewhat by another observer who says that the Kashmir Cell was 'greatly influenced by the views of Aziz Ahmed and his minister, Zulfikar Ali Bhutto. Bhutto had also taken to lobbying senior officers at their residences, and seeking to impress them with the indispensability of launching raids across the Cease Fire Line. These visits led Musa to complain to Ayub Khan that Bhutto was brainwashing his officers.[20]

Altaf Gauhar, Ayub's highly active and influential Secretary
of Information, maintains that Aziz Ahmed, in concert with the
ISI, took excessive interest in operational matters. When the
plan jointly prepared by them was presented before the
intelligence committee of the cabinet, Ayub inquired, 'Who
authorized the Foreign Office and the ISI to draw up such a
plan? All I asked them to do was to keep the situation in Kashmir
under review.'[21] Ayub's remark showed that initially he was not
inclined towards this operation. Notwithstanding his displeasure,
Bhutto and Aziz Ahmed kept working on the theme that India
was in a weak position in Kashmir and Pakistan should take
advantage of the favourable situation. The military success in
the Rann of Kutch had reinforced the conviction of this lobby.

The persuasive Bhutto had greater access to Ayub's receptive
ears than the Army Chief General Musa. Slowly, Bhutto
convinced Ayub of the logic of his strategy. He maintained
contacts with Major-General Akhtar Malik who was respected
in the army on professional matters. Ayub went to Murree on
13 May to attend a sand model presentation made by Akhtar
Malik on Operation Gibraltar. General Musa and the military
brass from the GHQ attended the presentation. The Naval and
Air Chiefs were not invited. Ayub approved the plan. This was
a victory of individuals over the institutions. The fate of the
country was decided by the judgement of a nominated few.

Playing his cards with finesse, Bhutto had brought Ayub
around to his own reasoning with a written assurance given to
him that India was, 'at present in no position to risk a general
war of unlimited duration for the annihilation of Pakistan.'
Cleverly, this assurance was conveyed on the eve of Ayub's
visit to Murree. Bhutto's psychological gamesmanship with his
president worked.

General Musa writes that, 'Those who controlled the Ministry
of Foreign Affairs...did not appear to believe that India would
use deep raids, in a disputed territory, as a reason for escalating
a wider war, for the sake of Kashmir.'[22] Musa adds, 'I went on
opposing the whole proposal, both verbally and in writing, till
I was ordered to implement it, despite my opposition.'[23] This

explanation is flawed. Surely Musa knew the last honourable option open to him if his professional advice on the vital issue of peace and war was rejected.

Plan in Outline

Small groups were planned to be inducted in the Indian-held Kashmir (IHK) on a broad front to destroy or damage military targets—bridges, ammunition and supply dumps, formation headquarters, lines of communications, military convoys—to create panic, arouse hatred against the occupation power and encourage the oppressed people to rise in revolt. The aim was to take advantage of the anti-India feelings nursed by Kashmiris. The infiltrators carried arms and explosives and a limited quantity of rations with them. Thereafter, they planned to live off the land and rely on local hospitality.

The operation comprising six groups—Babur, Ghaznavi, Khalid, Qasim, Salahuddin and Tariq—began on 7 August 1965. It had a primitive communication network and an *ad hoc* logistic support system. The infiltrating teams achieved minor gains but because of conceptual flaws and inadequate planning, Operation Gibraltar fizzled out without achieving the aims set by its planners. Indeed the unachievable goals had little chance of success. India reacted strongly, and despite the valiant resistance offered by the small bunch of infiltrators, the operation failed. The flaw in strategy gave India a pretext to impose a war on Pakistan.

Operational Analysis

A freedom movement may succeed if it is indigenous in nature. Outside support and assistance can play a part provided it is substantial in material as well as personnel resources. Its success or failure depends on the capacity and the sustained ability of the oppressed people to resist the tyranny imposed on it by an occupation power. The seeds of the movement germinate within the area when the people are ready to sacrifice their lives. The Polish rebellion during World War II, and the Algerian and the Vietnamese revolutions in the post-war era are some examples. Outside help is a bonus and an advantage if it is provided by a contiguous neighbour.

A freedom movement begins slowly and takes time to gain momentum. Its leadership tiers—visible and underground—are established, and an infrastructure is created to implement planned political, psychological and military acts. The momentum, if lost, takes considerable time and effort to re-establish. An underground movement is not an affair to be employed arbitrarily for producing instant results.

Assessed in this context, Operation Gibraltar failed for a variety of reasons:

- The operation was conceived on faulty political assessment and flawed assumptions.
- The people of Kashmir had not been consulted or taken into prior confidence. They did not rise in a war of liberation fearing brutal reprisals by the Indian military forces.
- The planning time was excessively telescoped and the plan was implemented prematurely.
- Excessive secrecy prevented the flow of essential information to all concerned on a need to know basis.
- Intelligence failure.
- Inadequate communication, logistical and administrative arrangements.
- Lack of inter-service and inter-arm coordination.
- Inadequate training for the specialized operation.
- Inadequate attention to the diplomatic and psychological fields.
- The Pakistan Army possessed limited and mostly theoretical expertise in launching a guerrilla operation or combating it. The prescribed institutions were bypassed and operational planning violated the prescribed channels. Some of the planning errors might have been corrected had the relevant institutions been consulted.

Bhutto Dominates

Operation Gibraltar was conceived or misconceived with serious limitations. After giving the green signal to launch Gibraltar, Ayub retired to the cool valley of Swat, ostensibly for rest and relaxation. This was an intriguing development. It was expected of a soldier-President to personally guide and direct the situation. Or, was rest a pretext to show confidence over developments in Kashmir? The ground realities in the Valley should have caused anxiety because the plan had run into serious snags. Ayub's journey to Swat distanced him from the minute-to-minute front-line news emanating from Kashmir which ought to have been his primary concern. Instead, he was fed with information that was stale, second-hand and perhaps tailored by others to suit their own convenience. 'His absence from the capital gave Bhutto and Aziz Ahmed the freedom to take control of Gibraltar, not only in the context of Foreign Affairs, but also in the field of military planning and manoeuvres.'[24] An additional handicap was that, at this critical juncture, the country did not have a full-time Minister of Defence. With Ayub, who was in charge of the Ministry of Defence, temporarily away, Bhutto assumed authority far in excess to what his appointment otherwise indicated.

Ayub's well-informed media chief Altaf Gauhar, writes that the president left for Swat for 'inexplicable reasons'. This adds to the confusion and creates a mystery. The serenity of Swat could not have given Ayub peace of mind when Pakistani troops were fighting against heavy odds in the Valley.

With Operation Gibraltar failing, Bhutto dashed to Swat and got a directive signed by Ayub on 29 August 1965. Addressed to the Foreign Minister and the Commander-in-Chief, the directive stated that Pakistan's political aim was to bring India to the 'conference table without provoking a general war ... whilst confining our action to the Kashmir area we must not be unmindful that India may in desperation involve us in a general war...we must, therefore be prepared for such a contingency.'[25] After initially putting the country on the war path, Bhutto inserted a safety valve to escape personal responsibility. The directive placed him in a pre-eminent position to interpret it to his convenience.

Higher Direction of War

War is a political decision which the military transforms into an operational strategy. Defence planning, a professional, serious and sacred responsibility, demands cool nerves, vision and logic by the planners. The territorial integrity of the country is an important but only one aspect of national security. Others include the political, diplomatic, domestic, economic and psychological fields.

The Kashmir operations were planned in 1965 in the firm belief that India would not cross the international border and widen the conflict. To their everlasting discredit the military yielded to Mr Bhutto's persuasive logic without seriously questioning the validity of the argument advanced by the articulate foreign minister, who had no military experience to his credit. In so doing, it violated the cardinal military principle that one should assess one's adversary on the basis of his capability and not on his stated or perceived intentions. Pakistan paid a heavy price for this error in judgement.

Pakistan's Higher Defence Organization (HDO) consists of three tiers, the Defence Committee of the Cabinet (DCC), the Defence Council (DC) and the Defence Services Chiefs Committee (DSCC).

The DCC, presided over by the Head of the Government, includes the ministers for defence, foreign affairs, finance, interior and information. They are assisted by the secretaries of defence, foreign affairs and interior as well as the director-general of inter-services intelligence. The Cabinet secretary keeps the records. The three services chiefs invariably attend the DCC as military advisers without the right of vote. This decision-making authority evolves national defence policy and gives political guidance to the national defence effort. Its meetings are held when required at the convenience of its chairman. Strangely, the DCC did not meet during the immediate pre-crisis period and during the war. Instead, all decisions were taken on an *ad hoc* basis which negated the purpose of the DCC. If Ayub did not take the initiative for holding the meeting of the DCC, none of the others down the ladder complained about the dormant nature of this vital, policy-making organ of the state.

This lamentable attitude of bypassing a vital decision-making body violated the norms of good governance and harmed the country. To reduce the HDO to the status of a dormant body, in peace and in war, was to play with the destiny of Pakistan. The army in general, and its chief in particular, bear a heavy burden of responsibility for this lapse. If General Musa was driven by a sense of blind obedience to his superior, Ayub Khan, and he dutifully obeyed the dictates given to him, he showed a weakness in the performance of his responsibilities.

The DCC, working under the chairmanship of the minister of defence with all the services chiefs as members, is responsible for transforming the defence policy into a military action plan. In the absence of a full time minister of defence, the defence effort suffered because of political expediency. The president devoted attention to matters of defence from whatever time he could spare from his multifarious responsibilities of the state. The routine work of the ministry was done by the defence secretary, Nazir Ahmed, who had his limitations in a rank and status conscious society. The dynamic Bhutto virtually controlled military operations, outdistanced Musa and told others only what he desired to convey. The institutions weakened under the strong personalities of Ayub, Bhutto and Akhtar Malik, and the docility of Musa.

The DSCC is the highest military body that examines all military problems affecting national defence and renders professional advice to the government. In 1965, the commander-in-chief of the Pakistan army was its head. Operation Gibraltar was neither discussed nor approved by this body. To deny the top military brass of the country an opportunity to conduct the professional scrutiny of an operation was to deny the defence services of Pakistan the benefit of advice from their own commanders. Musa's failure to consult the navy and the air force chiefs was deeply resented by them.

The air chief and the navy chief were as security conscious as the army chief was. They should have been active participants in planning the operation. It is indefensible to argue, as was done, that the navy and the air force chiefs were excluded because the operations in Kashmir were only land-based. The PAF dropped supplies in the combat zone and the extension of the raids concerned all the three services. An uncharitable view is that some 'hidden hands' might have wanted to create a rift between the three military services chiefs by rushing through the adventure in Kashmir without subjecting it to an in-depth inter-services scrutiny. Even if it is true, this does not absolve the military from its failure.

India reacted swiftly and ruthlessly. The Kashmiri political leaders were harassed, arrested, tortured and the population was subjected to severe reprisals for helping the 'infiltrators'. The people were terrorized and frightened. The raids made some local gains, but on the strategic level they failed to create the desired impact.

Concurrent with Operation Gibraltar, HQ 12 Division had thinned out some posts in the upper regions of Azad Kashmir to muster additional troops for Operation Grand Slam. It was in the knowledge of GHQ that such partial withdrawals would create pockets of weakness. And yet, nothing was done to prevent it. Taking advantage of this local imbalance, India launched a series of attacks to capture territory and pose a threat. Pir Sahaba and Budil fell to India on 26 August. The following day, the Indian forces captured Bharat Gali and Sarpir. Hajipir Pass fell on 29 August. The loss of these posts endangered the security of Azad Kashmir and necessitated the launching of a counter-offensive by Pakistan to re-establish military balance.

These instances show that our 'higher direction of war' failed to put its act together in its ability to conduct war. Our strategic offensive in Kashmir failed because of faulty planning, *ad-hoc* conduct and inability to maintain the momentum of the operation after its launching.

Operation Grand Slam

Background

12 Division, commanded by Akhtar Malik, had its area of
responsibility stretching from the Leh-Kargil zone in the north,
with the heights of the lofty peaks varying between 12,000 and
18,000 feet, to the low foot-hills of the Chhamb-Akhnur zone in
the south. Except for Akhnur, the ground was suitable for limited
armour operations. The terrain was suitable for defence and an
offensive would be time consuming and costly.

Major-General Akhtar Malik, an exuberant, articulate and
ambitious commander, had his limited military resources
overextended for a defensive battle. He had no reserves. The
deployed troops of 12 Division were fully engaged in providing
passage to the infiltrating columns into Indian-held Kashmir
and in facilitating their return to Azad Kashmir. The resources
of the Division were over-stretched on these tasks.

Aim and Objective

Operation Grand Slam was not a pre-planned finale of a grand
design. It was necessitated by the failure of Operation Gibraltar.
The primary aim of this manoeuvre was to release the pressure
of enemy action in upper Kashmir. The re-establishment of the
tactical military balance in Kashmir under operational
environments created a strategic imbalance at the national level.
This was a serious development that should have been foreseen,
and guarded against. A war plan should be conceived, planned
and implemented as a single operational entity to maintain the
momentum of the effort and to achieve the desired goal. As
against this, the Pakistani military planners indulged in an
unsteady, patch-work effort with disastrous consequences.

In the context of an Indo-Pakistan conflict, the numbers game
shall always favour the former. India shall invariably have
numerical superiority in the armed forces, and in the materials

and hardware, a dimension that is likely to remain constant in the foreseeable future. This poses a challenge to the leadership in Pakistan to produce strategic and tactical efficiency, at least at critical times and in critical areas, that can achieve more with less. It demands very well educated and superbly motivated leaders whose superior quality of character and professionalism can override quantity. Given this efficiency, dedication and sense of purpose, a smaller force can prevail over a larger adversary. This has happened before in the history of warfare.

But the insurmountable can become otherwise only when the top leaders personally set an example and are emulated, in letter and spirit, by the leaders at the middle and at the lower levels. By and large, Pakistan's higher military command did not rise to the occasion and this weakness permeated down the ladder. Many junior leaders achieved spectacular results in the battlefield, but their gallant acts of heroism and sacrifice were submerged in a sea of mediocrity in the higher echelons of command.

The terrain-oriented Operation Grand Slam was launched with the limited aim of capturing Akhnur. The success of this operation would have isolated the Indian forces in Indian-held Kashmir from their base, besides providing Pakistan further openings towards Jammu and Rajauri. Pakistan adopted a strategy of indirect approach, both physically and psychologically, and the operation launched in a vacuum achieved the element of surprise. The semi-mountainous terrain facilitated the use of armour on a small scale, with the River Chenab providing flank protection in the south.

Contingency planning for Grand Slam, a manoeuvre in desperation, was completed by 30 August. The attack was along the axis, Bhimber-Chhamb-Akhnur. Its success hinged on the speedy capture of Akhnur to choke the lifeline of the enemy forces in the Naushehra-Poonch sector.

The operation started under Akhtar Malik on 1 September 1965. The troops assembled via a circuitous route that kept them within the disputed territory in Kashmir. The direction of attack too was chosen to prevent undue provocation to the enemy. Such measures paid dividends and the attack 'came as a complete surprise'[26] to the enemy who had anticipated a Pakistani 'venture into the Jhangar area.'[27]

An Indian writers says that 'Pakistan sliced through the Chhamb Sector in a blitzkrieg offensive,'[28] an operation in which the regiment of the author—11th Cavalry (FF)—participated along with other units. 'At 2030 hours,' the narration continues, '191 Infantry Brigade (India) was ordered to withdraw to Akhnur because it would not be able to hold out for long against the strong onslaught of the enemy (Pakistan).'[29] The enemy's apprehension proved correct, and Chhamb was captured by Pakistan early on 2 September. With the tactical battle going as planned, the River Tawi was secured. At this point, Jaurian stood between the attackers and Akhnur, the jugular vein of the enemy. Originally, Jaurian was planned to be bypassed and a quick manoeuvre launched against Akhnur. Instead, a fatal twist turned the tables. Just one hour before the prescribed time of contacting Jaurian, a change in command inducted HQ 7 Division in battle and relieved HQ 12 Division who were reverted to Murree.

Modifying the original plan, GOC 7 Division decided to capture Jaurian first before advancing further. The inherent delay, unavoidable in a change of command, lost thirty-six valuable hours—time Pakistan could not afford to lose. The Indian author writes that, 'Our forces, reeling under the impact of relentless onslaught so far, regained a measure of balance. It was a providential reprieve.'[30] The providential relief to India gave a fatal blow to Grand Slam.

Jaurian fell to Pakistan on 4 September. So fierce was the Pakistani attack that 161 Field Regiment (India) 'abandoned its guns and fled the field. It was a most disgraceful action that no unit could ever live down.'[31] The eighteen 25 pounder guns captured by Pakistan were later inducted in its army as 40 Field Regiment Artillery. The enemy withdrew 41 Mountain Brigade from Jaurian area to Akhnur on the night of 4 September. The capture of Jaurian brought the Pakistani troops in contact with the line—Nanga Chak and Harpal. The delay provided time to the enemy to reinforce Akhnur, just six miles away. Operation Grand Slam ran out of steam.

General Musa says that while visiting the battle front on 2 September he was amazed to note that, 'Akhtar could not brief me on the latest situation.'[32] Besides, he found Akhtar's tactical headquarters understaffed and relying excessively, 'on the means of communication of the corps artillery headquarters[33] for conducting the battle', and, 'there was no proper articulation of command and grouping of forces.'[34] Hence the induction of General Yahya Khan in battle.

General Musa calls the midstream change of command as 'pre-arranged' and not an 'after thought', a view also supported by the Pakistan Army's official historian who writes, 'While Grand Slam was being planned it was realized that it would be difficult for the GOC 12 Division to control operations on the entire front from the Northern Areas to Akhnur...It was, therefore, decided that the GOC 12 Division would control the operation till the capture of Tawi; thereafter GOC 7 Division would take over.'[35]

These assertions do not ring entirely true for several reasons. First, 7 Division and 1 Armoured Division had an offensive task assigned to them. In terms of time and space, 7 Division was located away from Kashmir. It's sudden induction in lower Kashmir for operations beyond Tawi created a strategic weakness in operational plans at the national level and deprived Pakistan's main punch i.e., 1 Armoured Division, of it's only infantry support (7 Division). The negative implications of this change are discussed later.

Secondly, had the change of command been pre-planned, Akhtar Malik would not have unilaterally planned operations beyond the Tawi River, which he had done. He was too honourable a person to impose himself on others or create difficulties for them. Thirdly, General Yahya would not have taken thirty-six extra hours in planning to capture Jaurian if he had been forewarned about the change in command. And finally, the GHQ was fully aware that the presence of HQ 12 Division at its permanent location, Murree, was an operational necessity, and that Akhtar had planned to use Tactical HQ 12 Division for

Operation Grand Slam. The static location of HQ 12 Division at Murree mostly had fixed communications to meet its needs. It was imprudent for Akhtar Malik to shift them for Grand Slam. If the communication facilities at Chhamb were inadequate, GHQ might have had them reinforced before the battle was joined.

One workable option might have been not to burden Akhtar Malik with Grand Slam, to enable him to concentrate exclusively on the defensive battle on his vast divisional front. This choice was not adopted. Speed, which was of the essence for the success of Grand Slam, dictated that the entire operation be conceived and implemented under one commander to maintain the momentum of the offensive.

An alternative choice might have been to task GOC 7 Division or another division to plan and implement Grand Slam in its entirety. This did not happen because initially 7 Division had a different task. The mid-stream change of command, the worst option, guaranteed the surrender of initiative to the enemy.

A great opportunity was lost. India's GOC-in Chief, Western Command writes, '... for had it (Grand Slam) succeeded, a trail of dazzling results would have followed in it's wake,'[36] and 'with the capture of Akhnur bridge by the enemy a point of no return would soon be reached.'[37]

General Musa laments that, 'General Yahya should have pursued the enemy faster after the fall of Jaurian. Despite that, however, it would not have been easy to capture Akhnur quickly because the enemy had reinforced it substantially by then.'[38] Musa contradicts himself. The capture of Akhnur demanded quick, surgical action with a premium on speed and ferocity. Such an approach received a setback with the change of operational command in battle. The chances of success receded with every hour. By the time Jaurian fell, the opportunity of capturing Akhnur had been lost.

History might have been kinder to General Musa if he had accepted the blame. Perhaps General Yahya had his own reasons for going slow with the on-going operation. Sharp as he was, he must have assessed that the chance of capturing Akhnur had receded with the passage of every hour and did not relish the thought of being accused for a failed operation. Much was at stake for him then.

Recoiling, India did the obvious—reinforced the Munawwar Gap and inducted additional forces to strengthen Akhnur defences. The fate of the plan was sealed. Akhnur, the elusive town, remained so near and yet so far away. It did not fall. It was not even attacked. Grand Slam was guillotined, not by the enemy but by Pakistan itself. India pre-empted its burial by attacking the heart of Pakistan, the historic city of Lahore on 6 September 1965. Soon after the war, General Yahya Khan told a visitor at Jaurian, *'Panga liya hai. Ab hamaisha aik division is area mein rakhna pare ga.'*[39] (We touched India's raw nerve and now we will always have to maintain one division in this area in the future)

Operations in Kashmir reflected the psyche of both the nations rather prominently. Pakistan entered the war in an overconfident mood. The Indian attitude, cautious and calculating, was to wait for an opportunity to launch its military operations.

Indo-Pakistan War–1965

India attacked Pakistan in the early hours of 6 September. The advantage of surprise and the superiority in numbers and weapon systems made the Indian military high command euphoric. Confident of achieving a military blitzkrieg, General J. N. Chowdhri, Chief of Staff of the Indian army, told his officers that he would march through the city of Lahore and have a drink at the Lahore Gymkhana that evening to celebrate an Indian victory.[40] The boastful general misread Pakistan's defiant mood. President Ayub Khan echoed the determination of his people with the words, 'The Indians don't know what people they have taken on.'[41] Subsequent events proved him right. The enemy offensive was blunted. Lahore became Pakistan's Stalingrad. Those desiring a victory drink in Lahore were made to swallow their insult.

India's Military Plan

Some Indian writers argue that the vulnerability of Akhnur forced a war on their country to relieve pressure from this town. This claim is belied. The strategic objectives chosen by India and the quantum of forces used to achieve them led to the inevitable conclusion that the minimum objective of India was to destroy Pakistan's offensive capability. India's offensive plan had the following main elements (Annexure 1):

1. A Main Effort in the corridor formed between the rivers Ravi and Chenab with four divisions supported by six artillery brigades, along with a Diversionary Effort in the Jassar Sector.
2. The Fixation Efforts in the disputed State of Kashmir and in the Sialkot Sector.
3. An Auxiliary Effort in the Ravi-Beas corridor with three divisions with the aim of capturing Lahore, the second largest city in Pakistan.
4. A second Auxiliary Effort in the Rajasthan sector.
5. India did not attack East Pakistan for military, political and psychological reasons. Militarily, she avoided a war on two fronts, as Pakistan did, but the advantage enjoyed by the aggressor was greater. Politically, she tried to drive a wedge between the two wings of Pakistan to disrupt their unity. And psychologically, she attempted to create a feeling in East Pakistan that her defence needs were neglected.

Pakistan's Response

Pakistan's response to the contingency was to:

1. Hold the enemy in the Lahore, Sialkot and Kashmir sectors.
2. Initiate local efforts in the Sulaimanki sector and in Rajasthan.
3. Launch a riposte on the axis Khem Karan-Amritsar.
4. Blunt enemy's Main Effort.

The Holding Efforts

India's Auxiliary Effort opposite Lahore in the Ravi-Beas sector failed. After some initial confusion, the first line of the Pakistani defences, based on Bambanwala-Ravi-Bedian Link Canal, successfully brought the Indian attack to a grinding halt. The tenacity of the defenders dominated the timidity of the attackers and the war was reduced to exchanging minor punches between the opposing forces. The courage and tenacity of the defenders of the city of Data Darbar so demoralized Major-General Niranjan Prasad, GOC 15 Division, (India) that he earned the dubious distinction of being relieved of command on the first day of war.[42] His removal was a tribute to Pakistan's defence effort in the Lahore sector.

India's division-size fixation effort in the Sialkot sector had the twin objective of checking a threat to Jammu and protecting the flank of her Main Effort. The military tug-of-war remained confined to the border belt.

India's diversionary effort in the Jassar Sector eliminated the small Pakistani enclave east of the River Ravi. Besides, it aimed at imposing dispersion by drawing on local reserves. This diversionary effort coincided with the Main Effort on the night of 6/7 September. 115 Brigade was deployed in this sector with 3 Punjab guarding the Jassar Bridge. The churning of the tanks across the river led the defenders to the faulty conclusion that the enemy was in the process of crossing the bridge. Confusion prevailed. To the added misery of the defenders, HQ 115 Brigade was incommunicado with HQ 15 Division headquarters for a short but vital period when uninterrupted contact was urgently needed. Both the headquarters were to be blamed for this blackout. During the interregnum, the bridge was prematurely blown up by the defenders without first cross-checking the authenticity of the initial false alarm. By the time it was subsequently learnt that the enemy had only closed up to the river-line as a defensive necessity, the damage had been done.

The error in judgment unnerved HQ 15 Division. The confusion caused during the night was discussed in the field HQ

INDIAN MILITARY PLAN

PAKISTAN

Boundary: International, Province ....
Division, Tribal ....
Capital of Country ....
Head-quarters: Province, Division ....
River ....

FIXATION EFFORTS

MAIN EFFORT

DIVERSIONARY EFFORT

AUXILIARY EFFORT

AUXILIARY EFFORT

FRONTIER UNDEFINED

DISPUTED TERRITORY

CHINA

JAMMU & KASHMIR

ISLAMABAD

I N D I A (B H A R A T)

Gilgit Agency

Gilgit

Malakand

Peshawar

Abbottabad

Rawalpindi

Kohat

N.W.F.P.

TRIBAL

D.I. Khan

Sargodha

Gujranwala

Lahore

Faisalabad

Multan

D.G. Khan

Bahawalpur

P U N J A B

A F G H A N I S T A N

I R A N

B A L U C H I S T A N

Quetta

Sibi

Kalat

Larkana

Sukkur

Mirpur Khas

Hyderabad

Karachi

S I N D

Turbat (Makran)

A R A B I A N   S E A

Scale 1:7,500,000

0   50   100   200   300 km
0   100   200   300 miles
Lambert Conical Orthomorphic Projection

OPERATION NEPAL

Annexure 2

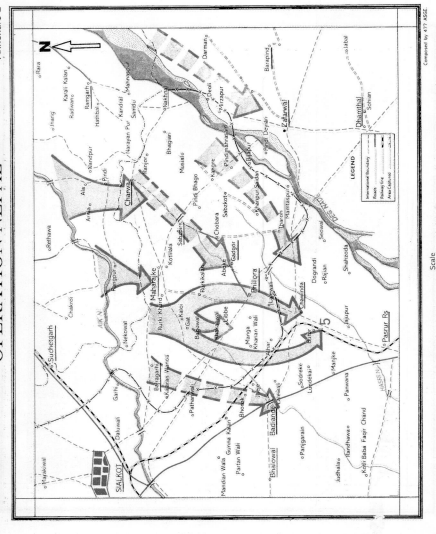

Composed by 477 ASGE.

Sketch drawn by Maj-Gen Sahibzada Yaqub Khan, illustrating the deployment of an armoured division in a defensive battle, 10 September 1965.

Annexure 3

ANNEXURE 4

MESSAGE FORM

OP IMMEDIATE

FROM : 6 ARMD DIV   DTG: 102030

TOP SECRET

TO :

LIST E		
4 CORPS	ARTY	G-0925
14 (P) BDE	24 BDE	
11 CAV	25 CAV	4 BALUCH
AQ BRANCH		

INFO : 1 CORPS

---

fol regrouping/moves will take place on ni 10/11 Sep 65 (.) ONE (.)
14 (P) BDE (.) moves from present loc to area ZAFARWAL (.) route
(.) PASRUR - QILA SOBHA SINGH 9588 - along the tr DEPOKE
0293 - DHAMTHAL 0895 - ZAFARWAL (.) TWO (.) 9 FF closes
around Phillaurah 9007 (.) relieves 24 BDE (.) THREE (.) 11 CAV
moves from present loc to relieve 25 CAV (.) on arrival new loc will
come under comd CO 9 FF (.) route (.) PASRUR - CHAWINDA 8902
- PHILLAURAH 9007 (.) FOUR (.) 24 BDE incl 25 CAV less arty
units sqn 33 (33) TDU R&S COY AP and Sup P moves on relief to
PASRUR (.) route (.) PHILLAURAH - CHAWINDA - PASRUR (.)
GUIDES CAV remain present loc temporarily (.) FIVE (.) Sqn 33
TDU moves to ZAFARWAL and comes under comd 14 (P) BDE on
arrival (.) Coy R&S ex 24 BDE moves to ZAFARWAL and comes
under comd 14 (P) BDE on arrival (.) SIX (.) DIV HQ will move area
PASRUR on 11 Sep (.) loc later (.) SEVEN (.) tfc con arrangements

(.) sec cons at PASRUR and CHAWINDA under arrangements OC MP Unit (.) tfc con arrangements enroute explained to OC MP Unit verbally (.) EIGHT (.) AQ Branch issuing order regarding estb of rec posts (.) NINE (.) conc areas at new locs already explained to all concerned verbally (.) TEN (.) fwd loc state on arrival new loc.

18/10/GS(0)   Sd/ Lt Col

10 Sep 65

                                                (NAZIR AHMED KHAN)

BATTLE OF CHAWINDA (SEPTEMBER 1965)

Annexure 5

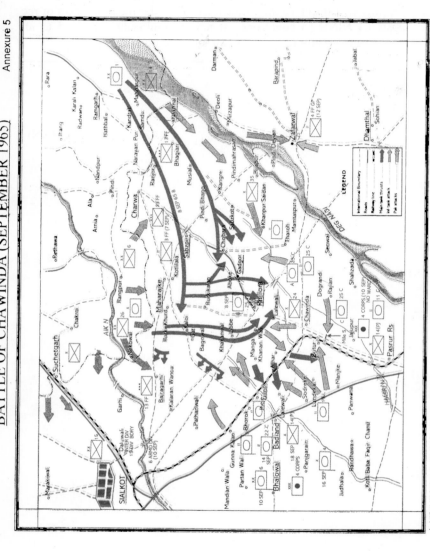

15 Division at 1100 hours on 7 September. Those who attended, besides the formation commander and his staff, included Lieutenant-General Bakhtiar Rana, Commander 1 Corps, Major-General Abrar Hussain, General Officer Commanding 6 Armoured Division, Brigadier A.A.K. Chowdhry, Commander 4 Corps Artillery and myself. The tiny enclave across the River Ravi in the Jassar area was indefensible and its loss was not unexpected. This did not cause any surprise. However, the alarm bells raised during the night, the blowing up of the Jassar bridge, the communication blackout and the movement of 24 Brigade group exposed command and staff limitations. These got further highlighted when a shaky presentation was made by the colonel staff 15 Division. The acting GOC 15 Division briefly intervened but without inspiring confidence. Throughout the meeting, a grim and glum Bakhtiar Rana kept his poise but mostly kept silent. That he felt grievously hurt was writ large on his solemn face.

At about 1800 hours on 7 September, 24 Brigade was ordered by 15 Division to move to Jassar to stabilize the situation in this sector. In view of the enemy concentration opposite his own area, the Brigade Commander suggested that his units might not be uplifted. His advice was turned down. This created an imbalance in the divisional defence effort.

24 Brigade moved with 2 Punjab and 25 Cavalry less one squadron. The Brigade Commander along with his 'O Group' reached HQ 115 Brigade at Narowal and found GOC 15 Division already present there. The battle situation was confused but it was clear that the enemy had not crossed the Ravi.

GOC 15 Division soon left for Sialkot on getting the report that the enemy had attacked. At 2300 hours, 24 Brigade was ordered to concentrate at Pasrur, halfway between Narowal and Chawinda. At this time the Brigade-less 25 Cavalry was at Narowal. 25 Cavalry was on the move near Qila Sobha Singh. The move to Pasrur was completed before last light on 8 September.

Commander 1 Corps acted fast to restore order. GOC 15 Division and Colonel Staff 15 Division were relieved of their

respective assignments. General Tikka Khan took over
15 Division.

The Fixation Effort in the disputed State of Jammu and
Kashmir kept the cease-fire line active at most places, but no
major engagement took place. The opposing troops maintained
eye to eye contact and fired at each other but generally the
status quo prevailed. The areas lost by both sides in the
skirmishes held in August remained in adverse possession. This
had caused a setback to Pakistan, particularly in the Badori
bulge and in the Uri-Poonch Sector.

The Sulaimanki Sector

105 Brigade defended the Sulaimanki Headworks. This brigade
captured a sizable area across the Headworks on 6 September,
to improve its defensive posture. The enemy counter-attacks to
regain lost territory were beaten. Thereafter, *status quo* prevailed
during the war.

The Desert Sector

India had 11 Infantry Division deployed in the desert sector, as
against Pakistan's 51 Brigade supported by a small desert force
comprising of Rangers and some Hurs (civilian volunteers).
Captured documents reveal that India had aimed at capturing
Khokhrapar, line Umarkot-Chhor, Mirpur and Hyderabad. The
plan targets were rather ambitious for the limited resources
deployed by the enemy.

India opened a 'second front' on 8 September by launching
operations in the desert belt. The Gadra salient fell and the
enemy's eyes were now focused on Khokhrapar. Three days
later, 51 Brigade captured Munabao Railway Station and a
couple of other posts. This imposed caution on the enemy and a
slogging match ensued. The enemy captured Shakarbu which
was subsequently regained by Pakistan on 16 September.

Another post, Dali, was captured by India on 19 September and recaptured by Pakistan the next day. By this time India's offensive capability had been effectively thwarted.

Up north, in the Reti-Rahimyar Khan Sector, a force of Rangers and Hurs captured a large chunk of enemy territory in the Jaisalmer area that included the Kishangarh salient. These territorial gains surprised the enemy and improved Pakistan's bargaining position during the post-war, inter-state negotiations on the exchange of each other's territories captured during the war.

Pakistan's Riposte

The Pakistan Army faced a problem in the articulation of command as it had only one corps headquarters. General Headquarters (GHQ) sought the government's sanction for the raising of one additional corps headquarters. The proposal moved at a snail's pace because of the resource constraints faced by the country. Eventually, GHQ's perseverance paid dividends and the sanction was belatedly granted by the government. It was now the turn of the GHQ itself to hibernate on the issue. General Musa defends the delay by claiming that by the time the government sanction arrived, 'a number of dramatic developments took place in quick succession...Rann of Kutch...concentration of forces ...Operation Gibraltar...Operation Grand Slam...and finally, an all-out war.'[43] Besides, he did not wish to make major changes in the higher command and staff appointments in a hurry. Such inverted logic had seldom been seen in a military establishment. It leaves one aghast that despite the 'dramatic developments' listed by General Musa, GHQ kept doing business as usual and did not act urgently to improve the army's command structure in a quicker time-frame.

Brigadier M. Attiqur Rahman, Vice Chief of the General Staff, says, 'Musa sent for me. He was feeling awkward as his shoulders were twitching. "What is all this about a new corps headquarters being raised?" "Sir, you know that we want it for an operation plan", I replied. "Yes, yes, but what are we going to do with it in peace time", Musa querried, "we do not want another lieutenant-general wandering about in GHQ?"[44] The GHQ was spared the inconvenience. Months later, the agony was felt by the whole nation when Pakistan's riposte failed. Among other reasons, the articulation of command of the counter-offensive force was faulty.

Pakistan's riposte, code-named Mailed Fist, comprising 1 Armoured Division and 11 Division, was launched on 7 September in area Khem Karan with the aim of capturing bridges over the River Beas at Harike. The success of this plan might have unhinged enemy defences in the Lahore sector.

The riposte launched in a fair, tank-going area was directed at the enemy's imbalance. With the River Beas providing flank protection in the South, the remaining water obstacles in the area ran parallel to the line of advance and did not cut across it. Raya Bridge was a sensitive objective. The Rohi Nullah and Khem Karan were the impediments enroute. The well-conceived plan had a strategic orientation.

The funneling effect restricted the manoeuvre of the tank formations and their optimum combat power was hard to generate in the area. Carefully laid minefields further restricted the freedom of movement of the advancing elements. Besides, the water obstacles enabled the enemy to inundate a part of the area.

11 Division, working with six infantry battalions instead of the standard nine, and holding an important sector, was not enough to provide infantry support to 1 Armoured Division on whose success depended the outcome of the war. Consequently, the bridgehead made by it on the night of 7/8 September was weak. This was against tactical doctrine according to which the bridgehead should have been large and spacious enough to provide space and security to an armoured division to fan out. The shortage of infantry was apparent from the time Mailed Fist was launched. The withdrawal of 7 Division from this sector, for induction in the Tawi operations only a few days before this operation, created a serious imbalance in the grouping from which the force did not recover. As the induction of 1 Armoured Division in the bridgehead commenced, a misfortune struck.

A bridge over Rohi Nullah collapsed and another bridge had to be constructed at the cost of considerable time. This upset the planned time schedule and the resultant confusion caused an early setback to the operation.

Khem Karan was captured on 8 September. 5 Armoured Brigade advanced up to Valtoha and Chima but, because of the shortage of infantry, pulled back at night for replenishment to a leaguer at Khem Karan. 4 Armoured Brigade, led by 4 Cavalry, was given the task of cutting off the road Khem Karan-Bhikiwind at mile 32. A loss of direction derailed this advance. This was caused by the high sugarcane and cotton crops that restricted visibility and allowed cover to the anti-tank teams to operate. India also breached the Madhupur canal to inundate the terrain to impede the advance of tanks. Mailed Fist came to a standstill, and was called off on 11 September. 1 Armoured Division less, 5 Armoured Brigade, was moved to the Sialkot Sector.

A good opportunity was lost. The enemy escaped the trap after it had been cornered and outwitted. The riposte failed largely because of Pakistan's own command and logistic weaknesses at the field level. These included:

1. The absence of a corps HQ in conducting the offensive effort. GOC 11 Division exercised the dual responsibility of commanding his division as well as the remaining riposte force. This *ad hoc* arrangement lacked the command, control and communications infrastructure for handling the additional workload. Additionally, HQ 11 Division was itself a recently raised formation.
2. Unbalanced grouping of the force. One additional infantry division would have created a balanced effort.
3. The GOC 1 Armoured Division, an infantryman, lacked experience in armour operations even though he had earlier raised and commanded in peace time an armoured brigade. Oversensitive by nature, he trusted his subordinates with reservations and commanded a loosely knit team.

4. Lack of coordination between the fighting and the administrative echelons of 1 Armoured Division created logistic problems at critical moments.
5. Lieutenant-Colonel Sahibzad Gul, Commanding Officer 6 Lancers, an excellent unit, was killed in battle while leading his regiment from the front. Earlier, this unit had also lost Major Dost Mohammad Utra while entering the bridgehead. These deaths at critical moments had adverse effects.
6. Loss of direction by one tank regiment and lack of logistic support to it at a crucial time affected operations.
7. For inexplicable reasons the Rohi Nullah, an obstacle, was not marked on the Pakistani maps. This was a serious failure at the planning level.

A conceptually sound plan suffered because of Pakistan's own tragedy of errors. The enemy played a small and secondary role in the failure of the Mailed Fist. The operation failed because of policy mistakes and faulty planning, inadequate grouping of forces, lack of a dedicated controlling headquarters, shortage of infantry support, and competent leadership with some exceptions at the lower levels.

Operation Nepal

India's Main Effort, code named Operation Nepal, was launched with 1 Armoured Division, 6 Mountain Division, 14 Infantry Division, 26 Infantry Division and six artillery brigades on the night of 7/8 September. Three sensitive documents captured from the enemy during the war provide details of the attack plan (Annexure 2). This was:

1. 6 Mountain Division and 14 Infantry Division to make a bridgehead in the area Bajra Garhi—Maharajke—Charwa on night 7/8 September.
2. 1 Armoured Division to pass through the bridgehead and capture Chawinda.

3. 14 Infantry Division to take over from 1 Armoured Division, on orders.[45]

India's Strategic Orientation

India's strategic orientation was geographically appropriate. It aimed at threatening the sensitive objective—Grand Trunk road (Lahore-Gujranwala)—a vital communication centre located in the heart of the country. The ground permitted armour manoeuvre and the two water obstacles, Eik Nadi and Deg Nadi, provided a degree of natural flank protection. Besides, no other man-made, anti-tank dry barriers existed in the area. These advantages notwithstanding, the strategic direction had some drawbacks. The restricted space, particularly at the start of the manoeuvre, hindered the generation of the optimum combat power inherent in the force. The Marala Ravi Link/Upper Chenab Canal, lying across the line of advance, was a major obstacle. Besides, the enemy had to cover over fifty miles to reach strategic depth.

The Battle of Frontiers

Operation Nepal was launched on the night of 7/8 September 1965 against the sparsely held border posts and the covering troops of 15 Division operating between Eik Nadi and Deg Nadi, a frontage of about 20 miles. The enemy advanced slowly and cautiously. In this phase, 3 FF suffered casualties which adversely affected the unit's subsequent performance.

15 Division had 24 Brigade, commanded by Brigadier Abdul Ali Malik in this sector. This Brigade, deployed at Gadgore-Phillaurah, had two battalions (2 Punjab and 3 FF) plus 25 Cavalry, and 31 Field Regiment. 3 FF had been deployed by the Brigade in an observation role on the border to facilitate its projected mission.

14 Para Brigade, commanded by Brigadier A.A.K. Niazi joined this sector on 10 September and was initially located at

Pasrur. It was 'para' in name only—the symbol was a relic of its past parachuting capability.

Concurrent with her Main Effort, the enemy launched a diversionary effort in Jassar Sector which resulted in the premature blowing up of the Jassar Bridge. In a hurry, 24 Brigade was directed to reinforce the Jassar sector. This created a vacuum in the defence effort at a critical time when the enemy's Main Effort was imminent. The crisis was mercifully averted because of the slow pace of the Indian offensive and an element of luck for Pakistan.

24 Brigade, back in Pasrur, was out of touch with 15 Division and was keen to reoccupy its defensive positions to restore balance in the defence effort. To gain time, 24 Brigade ordered 25 Cavalry to counterattack the enemy whose precise location and strength were still uncertain. Acting boldly, Commander 25 Cavalry took the unconventional step of attacking on a broad front with everything placed in the show window. The enemy was contacted between Chawinda and Phillaurah, and was pushed back to Gadgor. They were so surprised that eight Centurion tanks were captured at Gadgor with their engines running, and the tank crews busy brewing tea. The booty included one copy of Operation Nepal, 16 Cavalry OO No 1, dated 7 September. The show of force, combining boldness with mobility and optimum use of space, paid dividends and misled the enemy. Her first contact with the Patton tanks made the Indians erroneously believe that Pakistan's 6 Armoured Division had counterattacked. India had incorrectly placed 25 Cavalry on the Order of Battle of 6 Armoured Division. The enemy 'fell into the trap,'[46] and recoiled to consolidate its limited gains. The defenders seized the initiative, albeit temporarily, and this respite was used to improve the Phillaurah defences.

The 6 Armoured Division, not yet fully raised, was also moved that night to its forward concentration area. It was under reorganization from 100 Independent Armoured Brigade Group to an armoured division. A division in name only, it merely had the units of the brigade group it was replacing. Devoid of its integral brigade headquarters, and having only the skeleton of its authorized command, support and logistic elements, it might have given a false sense of security to some chronic optimists, but in the professional sense it was an unbalanced formation with a limited combat potential.

The Division's persistent attempts to get the process of its raising expedited had been scuttled by a combination of financial constraints, bureaucratic hurdles, procedural rigmarole and in-service inertia. Structurally defective, ill-equipped and incomplete, 6 Armoured Division became GHQ's strategic reserve located in the Sialkot Sector under 1 Corps. It had operational tasks in 1 Corps area.

The General Officer Commanding 6 Armoured Division was Major-General Abrar Husain, a soft-spoken and quiet infantry officer without armour experience. His selection had raised many eyebrows. His long spell of staff assignments was a disqualification to his critics. A well groomed scion of a respected ancestry—Abrar—gifted with polished poise, conducted himself with dignity and grace. He entered the war as a dark horse on whom even his friends were reluctant to bet. His courteous nature disguised his strong nerves. He had splendidly moulded his team into a cohesive fraternity with his leadership qualities.

6 Armoured Division was in location by the first light of 8 September. The scattered trees in a graveyard at Bhallowali provided some cover from view to the Division Headquarters. A small dilapidated Rest House served as a field kitchen. As General Abrar stepped out of his caravan on the morning of 8 September, he curiously glanced at the sprawling cemetery, slowly paced up to the command vehicle and softly addressed me, 'Arif, don't you think we have come to this abode rather prematurely?'

Prelude to the Tank Battle

When 25 Cavalry was engaged in a fierce battle at Phillaurah, the Director Military Operations at the GHQ, Brigadier Gul

Hassan Khan, urgently inquired from me about the type of enemy tanks confronting this unit. Lt. Col. Nisar Ahmad Khan (Kaka Nisar), Commanding Officer 25 Cavalry, was more interested in knocking out the enemy tanks opposite him than diverting his attention in answering seemingly innocuous questions. Gul Hassan's purpose was eminently served when 'Kaka' indicated that his unit faced Centurion tanks. This convinced GHQ about the presence of the enemy's 1 Armoured Division in the area as only this formation of the Indian Army was then equipped with these type of tanks.

The presence of 1 Armoured Division in the Samba area had previously been reported to GHQ by 15 Division on 3 September, when one motor cycle despatch rider (MCDR) of this formation was ambushed. His captured satchel contained the mail of the divisional units. Despite this hard evidence, the military intelligence directorate at the GHQ did not rule out the possibility of a plant by the enemy to confuse the location of India's main strike formation. Hence Gul Hassan's anxiety.

24 Brigade Group, deployed at Phillaurah-Gadgore, had prepared Chawinda as its alternative position. Knowing that this sector was poised for a major engagement, HQ 1 Corps ordered a regrouping on 9 September in which 6 Armoured Division assumed responsibility for the defence in this sector with effect from 0001 hours on 10 September.

This proved right the lurking fear of the 6 Armoured Division that the war might overtake its projected reorganization. A formation yet to participate in a single exercise in peace time assumed a dominating role in war, a task usually performed by an infantry formation. An armoured division, an offensive formation, is best employed to strike deep into the heart of the enemy to create an impact of strategic dimensions. It is a trump card sparingly used for achieving decisive results. India had employed her 1 Armoured Division in this role.

An armoured division is short of infantry to fight a defensive battle for prolonged periods of time. It is under-utilized if deployed in mobile defence. In advance and in attack, the territory captured by an armoured division is usually handed over to an infantry formation to enable the armoured division to be employed again in an offensive role or kept in reserve.

14 Para Brigade and 24 Brigade Group were placed under the command of 6 Armoured Division. The grouping of the Division underwent frequent changes in the next two weeks to meet the requirements of the changing operational environment. This exposed the pitfalls of its initial *ad hoc* structure. Lying in the pathway of the enemy's Main Effort, the Division became the focus of attention of the enemy as well as its own country. Its success would put a feather in Pakistan's cap. Its failure was riddled with catastrophic consequences. Hence its importance.

Doubts emerged about the ability of Abrar to handle the forces placed under his command. Unsolicited postings of senior armour officers to the division became a routine. These gentlemen created more problems than they were supposed to solve. Individually, they were fine people, well-meaning, competent and cooperative. Notwithstanding their professional expertise and eagerness to contribute in the defence effort, their collective nuisance value outstripped their positive contribution. This is discussed in greater detail later. For the present the following is just one example to illustrate my point.

The war found Lt. Col. Farzand Ali, General Staff Officer 1, 6 Armoured Division at the wrong place—on a long vacation in Europe. Commander 1 Corps could not hide his surprise on learning in late August 1965, during a visit to the HQ 6 Armoured Division, that Farzand was away from the place he was needed most. On 8 September, he attached one armoured corps lieutenant-colonel serving in HQ 1 Corps to temporarily act as GSO 1 in HQ 6 Armoured Division. The vacuum persisted despite this timely decision. The officer tended to become a transient Corps HQ representative rather than merging himself with the divisional environment.

Within hours of assuming the defence responsibility of the sector, the enemy attacked Gadgore-Phillaurah. The attack was successfully countered but not without creating a realization that 24 Brigade Unit, which had fought well, deserved a well-earned respite. Besides, Chawinda provided a stronger defensive locality than Gadgore-Phillaurah. This was a sure recipe for catastrophe.

Lull Before the Storm

On 10 September, Major-General Sahibzada Yaqub Khan, the new GOC 1 Armoured Division in place of Nasir, visited HQ 6 Armoured Division. While discussing the battle situation with Abrar, he drew a sketch to explain the mechanics of deploying an armoured division in a defensive battle. In a philosophical discourse he explained that an armoured division with its inherent shortage in infantry was better suited for mobile defence on the basis of anvil and hammer. The anvil (base) comprises a small but a mobile force. Should the base be attacked, the division launches a violent counterattack (hammer) on one of the flanks of the attacking force. The sketch drawn by him is given in Annexure 3.[47]

Based on this concept, one tank regiment/battalion group was selected to form an anvil at Chawinda to lure in the attacker. Both the flanks of the anvil were secured by deploying one tank regiment/battalion group at Badiana and a brigade at Zafarwal. The balance of the division was to be located at Pasrur. The plan, later discussed at HQ 1 Corps, was approved but without subjecting it to a staff discussion at HQ 6 Armoured Division. During the day, the acting GSO 1 Nazir passed verbal orders to all concerned individually to implement the plan. All the staff officers of the Division, except Nazir, remained unaware of the projected change over.

At 1800 hours on 10 September, Nazir collectively briefed GSO 2 (Ops) and GSO 2 (Int) and asked the former to issue confirmatory notes for the implementation of the orders during that night. This hit the juniors like a bolt from the blue resulting in unpleasant scenes. Nazir was annoyed at hearing from GSO 2 (Ops) that there was inadequate time to implement the relief operation that night. His face turned red with rage when advised that it would be more appropriate if verbal orders were issued by the GOC collectively to the 'O Group'. Such sudden impertinence from a junior officer was not acceptable and, with anger writ large on his face, Nazir firmly admonished him, 'Don't forget that you are only a staff officer. Just do your work.' The adamant junior retorted that it was his official and moral responsibility to apprise the GOC of the shortage of available time to implement the task given to the units, and loyalty demanded that he highlighted the risk involved. An angry Nazir warned his junior to mind his own business and disclosed that he had already passed the orders to all the unit commanders and none had raised any objection.

My heart was not in the confirmatory note that I drafted, on orders, and my conscience told me that standard teaching practice was being violated. While checking the typed note, I could not convince myself to sign the stencil. A feeling of unease and a sense of guilt gripped me. Caught between the conflicting pulls of military duty in combat and the dictates of my conscience, I asked the clerk to get the document signed by Nazir, which he did. This was the only time in war when I burdened someone else to sign an order which would have normally borne my signatures. The confirmatory note is attached as Annexure 4.[48] Salient points contained therein were:

1. 14 (Para) Brigade moves to area Zafarwal.
2. 9 FF Group closes around Phillaurah and relieves 24 Brigade.
3. 11 Cavalry moves to relieve 25 Cavalry and comes under command 9 FF.
4. 24 Brigade, on relief, moves to area Parur.

24 Brigade received the orders for the relief operation in two parts. Brigadier Ali Malik was conveyed the gist of the plan on the telephone and his Brigade Major (BM) was summoned to HQ 6 Armoured Division to get the details. The BM reached the Division HQ just before dusk, met the GSO 1 Nazir, who urged upon him to rush back to his HQ as the orders for relief had already been passed to Commander 24 Brigade. Aware of how Brigadier Ali functioned, the BM suggested to Nazir that

instead of the relief operation, the combat group of 9 FF-11
Cavalry be placed for operations under 24 Brigade for a limited
offensive action, adding that the troops had high morale and
were not exhausted. Ignoring the unsolicited advice, Nazir asked
the BM to rush back to his HQ.

BM 24 Brigade (Major, later Lieutenant-General Mohammad
Aslam Shah) reached his HQ at about 20:00 hours and in his
words:

> I noticed the packing up activity. I also saw Commander 24 Brigade
> briefing CO/2IC of 11 Cavalry, CO 9 FF and CO 1 SP Field Regiment
> who were already present there. Brigadier Ali then talked to Brigadier
> Riazul Karim at HQ 6 Armoured Division and while opposing the
> relief operation desired that the 9 FF-11 Cavalry combat Group be
> placed under his command for an offensive operation, already planned
> by him earlier. His request was not accepted. The conversation ended
> with Ali's remarks that the new defensive arrangements will be weak,
> particularly in the absence of a minefield.[49]

The doctrine of mobile defence by an armoured division and
the strategic philosophy behind it, so lucidly explained by
Yaqub, was neither new nor unique. It was hurriedly adopted
without analyzing the implications of the realities of equipment,
mobility and spaces. This doctrine had not been adopted in the
Pakistan army due to lack of resources. In the present case, the
following factors inhibited its adoption:

1. The structural weakness of the unbalanced 6 Armoured Division.
2. The inferior mobility of our own force as compared to that
   enjoyed by the attacker.
3. The enemy flanks were naturally protected by the Eik Nadi
   and the Deg Nadi within the restricted space available for
   manoeuvre.
4. Weak armour-heavy reserves held by 6 Armoured Division
   to produce the hammer effect when launched.
5. The doctrine of mobile defence had not been adopted by the
   Pakistan Army.
6. The risk in experimentation.

At 2030 hours on 10 September, Lieutenant-Colonel Abdul Aziz Khan, Commanding Officer 11th Cavalry telephoned from HQ 24 Brigade and spoke first to the GSO1 and then to Brigadier Riazul Karim Khan at HQ 6 Armoured Division. He expressed apprehension that the 9FF/11 Cavalry combat group might be too weak for the task given to it. Till then, neither of these units had arrived at their projected destination. The Brigadier assured Aziz that the Division had sufficient reserves to meet any unexpected development. He then spoke to Commander 24 Brigade, asking him to help the 9 FF-11 Cavalry group in implementing their assigned task. Ali confirmed that the relief operation would be implemented during the night.

Ali's optimism was in contrast to the pessimism expressed by Aziz. The ground realities were cause for concern for the unit commander and he had good reason to be unhappy. The lack of time had perforce telescoped the relief operation and the change-over process was neither smooth nor as prescribed in the training manuals of the Pakistan Army.

9 FF reached Phillaurah just before midnight. An element of haze covers the details thereafter. On arrival, this unit found that except for the guides detailed for it, the battalions of 24 Brigade had already vacated their positions. The incoming company commanders had not seen the defensive positions earlier, and the lack of inter-battalion coordination and liaison placed 9FF in a difficult situation. BM 24 Brigade maintains that while the unit layout parties had gone to the new locations, the Main Body was still present. However, proper relief could not be carried out because of darkness.

Time was running out for CO 9 FF as he could not collect his 'O group' in one place. Instead, Lieutenant-Colonel Abdul Majid individually briefed his company commanders who only had a rough idea of the location of their adjoining companies. Majid had himself not been personally briefed about his operational task because his commitments during the day had prevented him from leaving his unit. Instead, he had sent his second-in-command to HQ 6 Armoured Division to attend a 'coordination conference', which in fact turned out to be a briefing from GSO 1. 9 FF and

11 Cavalry had yet neither established a communication link nor
had liaison officers been exchanged between them.

11 Cavalry went into a leaguer at Kalewali, and held its 'O
Group' at 0045 hours. By 0500 hours, 11 September, its
squadrons were located in their hastily occupied battle positions.
It was unaware of the layout of 9 FF.

The 9 FF Group struggled through the whole night, and
hastily occupied battle positions unseen by them earlier during
daylight hours. It did not get the chance of gaining from the
ground experience of the previous units. The priority for
24 Brigade was to achieve an orderly exit to occupy its new
positions during the hours of darkness.

The Day of Distress

The dawn of 11 September was the beginning of the day of
distress. With 9 FF and 11 Cavalry still adjusting their defensive
positions during the pre-dawn hours, the enemy attacked
Phillaurah. The folly of short-circuiting the battle procedure for
a relief operation, and denying daylight reconnaissance to the
troops resulted in heavy losses. 9 FF and 11 Cavalry bore the
brunt of the massive attack with determination and courage but
the dice was heavily loaded against them. To their added agony,
the commanding officer (Aziz) and the second-in-command of
11 Cavalry (Major Muzaffar Malik) were seriously wounded
and Lieutenant-Colonel Abdul Rehman, Commanding Officer 1
(SP) Field Regiment Artillery was killed in battle—all by enemy
artillery fire. This unit had already earned the unique honour
of firing the first shots from the Division in war. Days later, it
also fired the last shot in the artillery duel just preceding the
cease-fire.

Phillaurah was lost but not before the tenacity of the defenders
had blunted the attack with their blood and spirit. An impromptu
counter-attack launched by the division stabilized the situation.
The casualties for the day were heavy on both sides.

General Abrar visited the front-line, ordered readjustments in the defensive layout, inducted 24 Brigade back in the Chawinda position and recalled 14 FF from its location at Raya. He accepted the responsibility and did not blame anyone else. He was too dignified a commander to pass the buck to others.

Action at Zafarwal

In the afternoon of 12 September, an air observation post spotted enemy concentration at Sabzpir moving towards Zafarwal. 14 (Para) Brigade was directed to task one battalion with a squadron of tanks from 22 Cavalry to hold Zafarwal. 4 FF moved up to Dhamtal in transport and the Brigade Commander (Brigadier A. A. K. Niazi) accompanied this force. Niazi sent a message that Zafarwal was held by the enemy and sought permission to recapture it. 4 FF occupied Zafarwal by 0100 hours on 13 September against minor resistance. This operation imposed caution on the enemy and he made no effort subsequently to operate east of Deg Nadi.

The Battle of Chawinda

The enemy used the next three days to consolidate its gains and its plan of action was now an open secret. Its cautious approach helped the defenders to get ready for a decisive engagement at Badiana and Chawinda.

The Enemy Plan

India employed (Annexure 5) 6 Mountain Division with 62 Cavalry under command and 99 Infantry Brigade with 2 Lancers less one squadron under command to hold firm bases at Bhagowal and Phillaurah respectively. 1 Armoured Division advanced on two axes, with (a) 43 Lorried Infantry Brigade moving towards

Bhagowal, and (b) 1 Armoured Brigade on axis Chobara-Phillaurah with the 'intention' to 'capture area Chawinda and in the process destroy the remainder of enemy's 6 Armoured Division.'[50] The destruction-oriented mission began on 14 September.

Dispositions—Own Troops

24 Brigade Group had a compact (6000 yards) defensive position between Jassoran in the West and Dogranwali in the East with Chawinda a central strong position. It had three battalions. 14 Baluch (Lt. Col. Z. K. Shinwari) in the centre and front with 3 FF (Lt. Col. Sadiq Akbar) and 2 Punjab (Lt. Col. Mohammad Jamshed, MC) on the two flanks with 25 Cavalry in the middle to manoeuvre interior lines within the brigade area.

14 Para Brigade (Brigadier A.A.K. Niazi) was initially located at Pasrur but was later moved to Badiana. Guides Cavalry (Lt. Col. Amir Gulistan Janjua) was deployed on the West of 24 Brigade along the railway line and linked up with 22 Cavalry. 22 Cavalry (Lt. Col. M. Yasin Khan) covered the extreme left of the division between Gunna Kalan and railway/track junction 8108.

4 Corps Artillery (54 guns), which functioned as HQ 6 Armoured Division Artillery, was boldly deployed well forward between Chawinda and Pasrur. Later, 36 more field guns became available from 15 September onwards, and were deployed on the Badiana axis. Lieutenant-Colonel Naseer ud Din Ahmed, GSO 1 HQ 4 Corps Artillery, remained at the Division HQ to maintain a communication link with the Artillery HQ.

The Tank Battles—14–19 September

The stage was set for the decisive phase of war in 1965. The challenger had exercised the advantage of selecting the time and place of attack to exploit the numerical superiority of its balanced force. Its twin objective, in its own words, was 'to capture Chawinda and destroy 6 Armoured Division.'

For ten vital days the strip of land between the Eik Nadi and the Deg Nadi was the scene of attacks and counter-attacks by the opposing sides in the biggest tank battles since World War II. In these fierce engagements, the enemy's armoured division was systematically degraded in successive operations. It made repeated efforts to capture Chawinda and Badiana during the day, and took advantage of its infantry resources to consolidate positions at night. In the process, the enemy kept reinforcing failure and suffering heavy losses in men and materials.

The shortage of infantry in 6 Armoured Division imposed a great strain on men and machinery as the firm bases—Chawinda, Badiana and Zafarwal—faced sustained pressure. The tank regiments covered wide frontages and the tanks deployed in the crop-covered area were exposed to tank hunting parties at night. Besides, the wide dispersal of units created problems of logistics—maintenance, repairs and replenishment—during night hours.

At 1630 hours on 15 September, with a furious tank battle raging opposite Badiana, HQ Task Force (Lt. Col. S. Wajahat Hussain) reported that two enemy tanks had broken out and were heading towards the Division HQ located in Bhallowali. The Deputy GOC, Brigadier H. M. el Effendi, ordered the evacuation of all vehicles not in use to a safe location in the rear and asked the staff to select a new location for the Division HQ. Noticing some camouflage nets being rolled down, General Abrar promptly rescinded the order with the firm direction, 'There shall be no rearward movement. Everyone stays and fights from here.' Even a token movement to the rear might have created an alarm. The GOC's firmness and foresight earned him the admiration of all those present.

In response to the call of duty, the defence troop in the divisional HQ waited to deal with the unwanted guests, with their personal weapons and high spirits supported by two light tanks—the heaviest hardware available. The alleged intruders failed to show up. It was later discovered that two tanks from

B Squadron 19 Lancers got detached from their Squadron and
moved towards their previous location (near Badiana) with their
guns pointing in the wrong direction. Both the tanks were
knocked out by 22 Cavalry. Errors in war, even minor ones, can
cause major damage. A failure to abide by the basic drills seldom
goes unpunished.

The repeated frontal attacks on Chawinda having failed, on
16 September the enemy launched a two regiment strong tank
attack to envelope its defences with concentric hooks from the
west and rear. The well conceived cartwheel movement
employed 17 Horse in the inner circle and 4 Horse in the outer
circle. The success of this bold effort would have also exposed
our gun areas where the bulk of the artillery had been deployed
centrally and well forward for ease of command and control.

16 September was a day of heavy fighting and fluctuating
fortunes. Village Jassoran fell to the enemy. So did Village Sodreke.
The Western flank of Chawinda got partially denuded when 3 FF
could not hold the part of its remaining Battalion. After a fierce
fight, Village Butter Dograndi was lost to the enemy. At this tense
moment, the enemy commander was heard on the intercept urging
Commanding Officer Poona (17) Horse to, 'Cut the road at Mile 5
and Param Vir Chakra will be lying at your feet.' If the
enemy was desperate to envelope Chawinda, the troops defending
this town were no less determined to prevent this breakthrough.
Lt. Col. A.B. Tarapore made a brave effort and came within one
mile of his objective when his tank was hit and destroyed. India
honoured him posthumously with the promised award. The
following day 25 Cavalry captured 1 Armoured Brigade OO No 3
of 13 September from Tarapore's tank.

The pressure showed on both sides. At 1630 hours Commander
24 Brigade spoke to General Abrar over the telephone and
expressed his concern about the Chawinda defences. He stated
that if the situation worsened, he might be compelled to readjust
his defensive position at an appropriate location. Abrar said, 'Ali,
you know what there is in the kitty. We shall fight to the bitter
end from where we are.' Reassured, Ali accepted the challenge
with the discipline expected of the army. Ali was decorated in the

war with the *Hilal-i-Jurat*, which he richly deserved for his qualities of leadership and competence.

The danger was averted. Chawinda—a small, obscure and dusty town located in a remote border belt—suddenly came under international focus as a symbol of Pakistani determination, pride, and soldering. The enemy offensive was brought to a grinding halt. The failed Main Effort saw Chawinda being turned into a graveyard of Indian armour. The gun area kept functioning without interruption. The tenacity of the Pakistani military withstood the test of war. Bruised and shaky, the enemy retreated with the uneasy realization that it had failed to subdue its smaller adversary.

Turn of the Tide

The opposing forces put salve on their battle wounds on 17 September and planned for the next step to be taken. The previous day had left a large area in possession of the enemy and the possibility that it might be used as a springboard for further aggression could not be ruled out. A limited counter-offensive was launched on 17-18 September to eliminate the penetration. This task was largely performed by HQ 4 Armoured Brigade which had joined the Division on 16 September. 19 Lancers, 22 Cavalry and 14 FF were placed under command 4 Armoured Brigade for this task.

Pakistan recaptured villages Buttar Dograndi, Mundeke Berian, Khupra, Sordeke and Jassoran. These successes reduced the enemy salient between Badiana and Chawinda but the speed of operation was slow. The GOC visited the forward areas twice on 18 September to speed up the pace of attack. The shortage of infantry had prevented a faster combing of the recaptured areas which were littered with dead bodies, disabled tanks and damaged equipment.

The enemy made one last effort to capture Chawinda on the night of 18/19 September. This was effectively checkmated. The time had finally arrived to regain lost territory.

A major regrouping took place on 20 September. 8 Division took over operational responsibility for the Chawinda area and its east from 6 Armoured Division. The defensive responsibility was thus finally transferred to an infantry division, thereby releasing 6 Armoured Division for its counter-offensive mission. A plan was quickly formulated. For this task, HQ 6 Armoured Division had two armoured brigades and two infantry brigades under its command. The GOC 6 Armoured Division held his O Group at 1830 hours on 21 September for a counter-offensive to be launched at 0430 hours, 22 September. The stage was set for Operation Wind Up, as it was named. It was called off minutes before the H Hour because of the impending cease-fire.

A message received on 20 September summed up the mood in the country. It read:

For Imam (commander) 6 Armoured Division,

The President of Pakistan has commanded that his personal congratulations be conveyed to all ranks under your command for the exemplary, courageous and successful battles they have fought. The President and the whole nation are proud of these untarnishable deeds of valour.

Hazards of Command

Senior commanders should either be fully trusted or instantly sacked. They must be given complete freedom of action within the limits of their allotted operational tasks to produce results. It is unfair and often counter-productive to hamstring them whether in peace or in war.

Major-General Abrar Hussain earned the high gallantry award, the *Hilal-e-Jurrat*. This silenced critics who were sceptical of his command ability and knowledge of armour tactics. Some brass in GHQ did not trust his judgement completely. For, how else can one explain the constant flow of 'specialists and advisers' to HQ 6 Armoured Division to enlighten its GOC with the pearls of their wisdom on tank warfare. Their presence created embarrassment for all, including the unwanted visitors. It is easy to offer advice when the burden of responsibility lies on the shoulders of others. What ought to be done is aptly stated thus, 'After the battle the King may dispose of my head as he will, but during the battle he will kindly allow me to make use of it.'[51]

The structural flaws of 6 Armoured Division caused frequent regroupings to meet the needs of changing situations. The following major formations and units were placed under the command of 6 Armoured Division:

7 September—11th Cavalry (FF)
9 September—24 Brigade—4 Baluch
10 September—14 Para Brigade—4 Baluch (detached)
11 September—10 Brigade
12 September—3 Armoured Brigade
13 September—Ad hoc Task Force created
16 September—HQ 4 Armoured Brigade
17 September—Ad hoc Task Force broken up
21 September—54 Brigade

Success in battle builds up the morale of a unit just as failure dips it to a low. Good performance by a unit in its first engagement with the enemy is important because a second chance may not present itself in a war of short duration. The reverse creates a psychological weakness that tends to linger on. This is what happened to one battalion which suffered some casualties in its first contact with the enemy. The shock adversely affected its subsequent performance. On two occasions, its stragglers were picked up from the artillery gun area and sent forward to rejoin their unit. GOC 6 Armoured Division was surprised when some persons from this unit were subsequently decorated without his recommendation. The brigade commander of the unit was no less affronted on being bypassed in the process. It transpired that Commander 1 Corps desired to raise the morale of the dazed unit. He asked Major-General Nasir Ahmad, who was attached with HQ 1 Corps after losing the command of 1 Armoured Division, to visit the battalion and suggest corrective measures. Nasir rose to the occasion and the efficient Corps staff did the rest. The violation of the chain of command and bypassing the military institution bestowed an undeserved bonanza.

Personal Reminiscences

Brigadier Abdul Ali Malik, Commander 24 Brigade, showed his leadership traits by his calm demeanor and confidence. His brigade major, Aslam Shah, was meticulous, efficient and pleasant, knew his job and remained calm under pressure. Brigadier A. A. K. Chaudhry, Commander 4 Corps Artillery, deployed his guns boldly and used them effectively in the high tradition of the Regiment of Artillery, Pakistan Army. Brigadier A. A. K. Niazi, Commander 14 (Para) Brigade, had a soft sector to command but earned his decoration with a *finesse* that left others bewildered. His brigade major, Major Imtiaz Ali, a fine professional officer, learnt after retirement that politics was a messy business. Colonel Jahanzeb, Colonel GS 1 Corps, was always alert and receptive to demands and his helpful attitude were valuable assets.

Lieutenant-Colonel M. Gustasab Beg, GSO 1, 6 Armoured Division, excelled in native humour, narrating anecdotes and getting work out of his subordinates. A lovable and down-to-earth person, Lieutenant-Colonel Ghouse Mohiuddin (Assistant Adjutant and Quarter Master General, 6 Armoured Division) was always busy with the work created for him by his sharp subordinate. The bright, witty and affable, Major Mir Abad Hussain, GSO-2 (Intelligence) 6 Armoured Division, was a devoted professional and good friend. He became a successful diplomat after moulting his uniform. Major Syed M. Hatim Zaidi (DQ, 6 Armoured Division)—lively, smiling and humorous—never tired of arguing that logistics was a far more difficult nut to crack than making an operational plan with the red and blue arrows drawn on the map. Major Aman Ullah, (DAAG, 6 Armoured Division), wielded his pen as effectively in his office as he used his gun during partridge shoots in the field. Captain Jahangir Karamat, aide-de-camp to General Abrar, endeared all. He loved to read books, would monitor enemy intercepts, listen to home and foreign news, and always sport a charming smile. Captains Aftab Ahmad Jan Qazi, (GSO 3 (ops)) and Qadir Saeed, (GSO3 I), were workaholics *par excellence*, always busy and ever cheerful. Captain Sanjaf Khan, the staff captain, fed us well with the traditional hospitality of an honourable Pathan. Major Farid Malik, Field Interrogation Unit, and Captain R. N. Joshua, Military Police, interrogated the prisoners of war.

Majors Abdul Rehman and Mohammad Jamal, both of HQ 1 Corps, were always available on the telephone with a quick and positive response. Lieutenant-Colonel Mohammad Jamshed CO 2 Punjab, greatly influenced the operational planning in 24 Brigade. A taciturn man with nerves of steel, Jamshed was not a flamboyant personality in peacetime, but he radiated confidence and courage in war.

The Other Fronts

The immense contributions made by the Pakistan Navy and the Pakistan Air Force in the national war effort, deserve a comprehensive analysis and a full record without which Pakistan's war history will remain incomplete and wanting. Suffice it to say that Pakistan's navy conducted naval operations against a bigger adversary with tremendous courage, and put it on the defensive. Pakistan's Air Force so excelled in counter-air operations against its numerically superior counterpart that it earned the appreciation of knowledgeable neutral observers. Without the timely and effective support provided by it, the task of the Pakistan Army would have been much more difficult. The excellent performance of the Pakistan Air Force in the Chawinda sector was a feat to remember.

'War is a continuation of diplomacy by other means.' A discussion on war cannot be complete without taking into consideration the prevailing international scene, and the diplomatic and regional realities of the time.

The effect this war had on East Pakistan was serious. It left a psychological impact on the people of the eastern wing, who felt isolated and ignored during the crisis. To them, the concept of the defence of East Pakistan lying in West Pakistan, as advocated at the time, appeared meaningless and selectively self-serving.

The operational employment of the Special Services Group (SSG) was less than praiseworthy. Despite the planning flaws, the troops cheerfully implemented the difficult tasks assigned to them with courage and determination. Their devotion to duty and sense of responsibility reflected the traditions of the Pakistan Army.

Gains and Losses

'An official spokesman disclosed that in the operations which ended yesterday, the Pakistan armed forces have seized 1600 square miles of Indian or Indian-held territory. As against this, India holds 450 square miles of Pakistani territory.'[52] This statement, factually correct, shows the obvious but hides the vital. Pakistan's territorial gains were mostly either in the desert belt opposite Sindh or in the Chhamb area in Kashmir. On the other hand, India had seized territory mostly in the fertile Sialkot sector in Punjab and Kashmir.

The relative battle losses suffered by the two opposing sides, as officially claimed by Pakistan, were as under:[53]

	Pakistan	India
Killed	1,033	9,500
Wounded	2,171	11,000
Missing	630	1,700*
Tanks lost and damaged	165	475
Aircraft	14	110

* According to Indian estimates

Additionally, Pakistan suffered a loss of a different kind that, for reasons unknown, has remained hidden. Soon after the war,

GHQ ordered all the formations and units of the Pakistan Army to destroy their respective war diaries and submit completion reports to this effect by a given date. This was done. The war diaries constituted first-hand source material in recording history and in helping the historian in sifting fact from fiction. Their destruction, a self-inflicted injury and an irreparable national loss, was intellectual suicide. A cloak of official secrecy protected the perpetrators of this crime. The hidden hands remain undiscovered because those issuing the orders made sure they destroyed all the evidence at source. The official records have not yet been released by the government for public examination.

One half-hearted attempt was made but it did not yield any positive result. Soon after assuming power in 1977, the Zia administration directed the Ministry of Foreign Affairs to reconstruct the events of the 1965 war period from its archives. The intention was to examine the role played by Pakistan's major policy makers of the time.

The diplomatic records maintained in the Foreign Office, the cypher telegrams exchanged during the relevant period and other vital communications received from foreign capitals constituted a wealth of information. Their collection, collation and synthesis would have been of great help in recording events. Surprisingly, all the relevant records of the time pertaining to the crisis in East Pakistan were found missing. The Ministry of Foreign Affairs reported that these papers had (perhaps) been destroyed as a matter of routine, although no note to this effect was available on record. Most probably, the destruction was the result of a planned effort to distort history, and to cover up the actions of those who had something to hide. This abominable job was expertly done by those who were privy to the records. The Foreign Office cannot escape responsibility for this misconduct.

The destruction of the war diaries in the Pakistan Army and the disappearance of the war-time records in the Foreign Office could not be simple coincidences. It is logical to suspect ulterior motives behind these misdeeds. These were premeditated acts of a sinister master plan prepared by those who wielded authority.

The End Result

This ill-conceived and ill-planned war gave a new dimension to relations between India and Pakistan and left an indelible mark on the psyche of both the nations. It is a rebuke to their collective political wisdom that these two close neighbours have spent most of their post-independence years as adversaries. Their bilateral enmity persists and enhancing their combat power takes precedence over peaceful options and philosophies.

The war ended in a stalemate and caused frustration to both adversaries. India failed to defeat Pakistan, a country weaker than her, or destroy Pakistan's armed forces, despite her numerical superiority over them. One Indian writer says, 'At strategic levels, our war aims were not achieved.'[54]

Pakistan felt satisfied that she had frustrated Indian designs by effectively checkmating her in combat. But the more substantive issue—the Kashmir dispute—remained unresolved though it briefly came under sharp global focus.

International opinion began to grow weary of the Kashmir dispute. It desired peace in South Asia but did not have a formula for achieving this goal.

The frailty of foreign aid and the unreliability of external crutches showed rather prominently. The weakness and untrustworthiness of US friendship with Pakistan stood exposed.

Pakistan's major failings included:

1. Faulty assessment of the Indian reaction.
2. Failure to put political, diplomatic and military acts together.
3. Weak 'higher direction of war'.
4. Failure of institutions and their domination by individuals.
5. The Gibraltar blunder, a gamble that was doomed to fail.
6. Absence of a full-time minister for defence.
7. Weak articulation of command in the Pakistan Army.
8. Mishandling of Grand Slam.
9. Command and logistics failures.
10. Outdated concepts and techniques of fighting.

The 1965 war was a military blunder in which both India and Pakistan failed to achieve their respective national aims and military objectives. Despite many errors, Pakistan managed a stalemate in the battlefield, largely because India made bigger blunders and quickly lost the advantage traditionally enjoyed by the aggressor.

The Pakistani military left behind for posterity numerous tales of blazing glory and grit of *Shaheeds* and *Ghazis* who excelled in combat under adverse conditions to keep the flag of their country flying high. Words fail to describe their acts of valour and the intensity of their zeal and determination in performing their assigned tasks, often well beyond the call of duty. Their acts of heroism and bravery are beacons of light for the people of Pakistan.

NOTES

1. White Paper on Jammu and Kashmir Dispute, Government of Pakistan, January 1977, p. 12.
2. Lt-Gen L. P. Sen, *Slender was the Thread: Kashmir Confrontation, 1947-48*, New Delhi, India, 1969, p. 64.
3. Alastair Lamb, *Kashmir—A Disputed Legacy*, p. 131.
4. Chaudhri Muhammad Ali, *The Emergence of Pakistan*, p. 295.
5. Ibid., p. 296.
6. Alastair Lamb, *Kashmir—A Disputed Legacy*, p. 155.
7. Altaf Gauhar, *Ayub Khan*, Sang-e-Meel Publications, Lahore, Pakistan, 1993, p. 205.
8. Frank Moraes, *Witness to an Era*, London, 1973, pp. 220-21.
9. Altaf Gauhar, *Ayub Khan*, p. 310.
10. Ibid., p. 310.
11. Major-General Shaukat Riza, *The Pakistan Army War 1965*, printed for Services Book Club by Wajidalis, Lahore, 1984, p. 99.
12. Ibid., p. 99.
13. Altaf Gauhar, *Ayub Khan*, p. 312.
14. Ibid., p. 319.
15. Rafi Raza, *Pakistan in Perspective 1947-1997*, Oxford University Press, Karachi, 1997, p. 91.
16. Interview, Abdul Sattar, 21 January 1999.
17. Sherbaz Khan Mazari, *A Journey to Disillusionment*, Oxford University Press, Karachi, Pakistan, 1999, p. 646.
18. Lt-General Gul Hassan, *Memoirs*.

19. General Mohammad Musa, *My Version: India-Pakistan War 1965*, Wajidalis, Lahore, Pakistan, 1983, p. 43.

20. Sherbaz Khan Mazari, *A Journey to Disillusionment*, p. 646.

21. Altaf Gauhar, Ayub Khan, pp. 320-1.

22. White Paper on Jammu and Kashmir, quoted by General Musa, *My Version: India-Pakistan War 1965*, Wajidalis, Lahore, Pakistan, 1983, pp. 2 and 4.

23. Ibid., p. 43.

24. Altaf Gauhar, *Ayub Khan*, p. 329.

25. Ibid., p. 328.

26. Major-General Jogindar Singh, *Behind the Scene*, Lancer International, New Delhi, 1993, p. 118.

27. Ibid., p. 118.

28. Ibid., p. 118.

29. Ibid., p. 118.

30. Ibid., p. 118.

31. Ibid., p. 119.

32. General Mohammad Musa, *My Version*, p. 41.

33. Ibid., p. 41.

34. Ibid., p. 25.

35. Major-General Shaukat Riza, *The Pakistan Army War 1965*, printed for Services Book Club, GHQ, by Wajidalis, Lahore, 1984, p. 121.

36. Lieutenent-General Harbakhsk Singh, *War Despatches Indo-Pak Conflict 1965*, Lancer International, New Delhi, India, 1991, p. 57.

37. Ibid., p. 129.

38. General Musa, *My Version*, p. 42.

39. General Yahya Khan to Lietenant-Colonel M. Gustasab Beg in September 1965.

40. General Musa, *My Version*, p. 49. Also Brigadier Gulzar Ahmed, *Pakistan Meets Indian Challenge*, Islamic Book Foundation, Lahore, Pakistan, 1967, p. 111.

41. Altaf Gauhar, *Ayub Khan*, p. 337.

42. Lieutenant-General Harbakhsh Singh, *War Despatches*, p. 94.

43. General Musa, *My Version*, p. 50.

44. M. Attiqur Rehman, *Back to the Pavilion*, published by Ardeshir Cowasjee, Karachi, 1989, p. 137.

45. 1. 16 CAV OO No 1, No. 7501/GS(ON), 7 September 1965.
    2. IMPORTANT INFORMATION, No. 2207/1/S, HODSON'S Horse, 7 September 1965.
    3. 1 Armoured Brigade OO No. 3, 13 September 1965.

46. Major-General Jogindar Singh, *Behind the Scene*, p. 210.

47. Annexure 1.

48. Annexure 2.
49. Interview Lieutenant-General Mohammad Aslam Shah.
50. 1 Armoured Brigade OO No. 3, (captured in war).
51. Seydlitz at the Battle of Zorndorf, quoted by Field Marshal Erich Von Manstein, *Lost Victories*, Methuen and Co. Ltd., London, 1958, p. 361.
52. *The Pakistan Times*, Lahore, 25 September 1965.
53. Pakistan Inter Services Public Relations Directorate, *Pakistan Repels Aggression*, 7 January 1966.
54. Major-General Jogindar Singh, *Behind the Scene*, p. 8.

3

DEBACLE AT DHAKA

The Indo-Pakistan war of 1965 eclipsed President Ayub Khan's political image. His popularity graph dipped low and his grip on the administration loosened. The Tashkent Declaration, perceived by the people of Pakistan as pro-India, further dwarfed Ayub's status. Initially, Foreign Minister Bhutto vehemently defended the Tashkent Declaration, but, sensing the defiant and peevish public mood, he not only distanced himself from it but also chided Ayub Khan for a sell-out. Ayub relieved Bhutto from his cabinet post, and Bhutto became a bitter foe.

Ayub's cardiac disorder in 1968 left him a lame-duck president, unable to rule firmly but reluctant to quit. Intrigues surfaced against him. Mr Bhutto used these circumstances to secure a place for himself and for the Pakistan Peoples Party, newly formed by him. Ayub's political cronies and media experts put him on a collision course with his critics and the agitating public. With the streets filled with anti-Ayub agitators, his hand-picked sycophant associates misused the state-controlled electronic media and made a futile attempt to celebrate the 'decade of reforms' of the Ayub era. As usually happens, the over-projection of the president assisted in ousting the tottering government of the once strong Ayub Khan.

By March 1969, the persistent anti-Ayub Khan public agitation and street violence left the president with no option but to relinquish authority. His resignation made him vulnerable to a process of accountability being initiated against him. To escape from this danger, he asked the Army Chief, General Yahya Khan, to 'carry out his legal obligations', a euphemism for preventing civil rule and for imposing martial law. The twin objectives of the wicked strategy—personal safety for Ayub and transfer of power to Yahya—fulfilled the mutual interests of both the general officers. It was irrelevant to both that their bilateral deal was unconstitutional and undemocratic. Yahya's martial law lasted till December 1971, when East Pakistan became Bangladesh.

The Yahya interregnum, traumatic and turbulent, witnessed Pakistan's defeat in war and the amputation of its Eastern wing. This monumental tragedy has remained an unexplained affair and the truth has still not emerged regarding Pakistan's disintegration and military surrender. This would expose the political and military blunders made since 1947, a risk not acceptable to the policy makers. The details of the 1971 war have been written by the winning side in which facts have been falsified, with bias injected in the narration rather generously.

'The history of failure in war can be summed up in two words: Too late.'[1] Pakistan lagged behind events in East Pakistan, lost the initiative, chased shadows and met her doom. Under the inspiring leadership of Sir Winston Churchill, Great Britain had converted the defeat at Dunkirk into victory. Conversely, Pakistan, reeling under the impact of defeat and the stigma of surrender in 1971, naively consigned its political, diplomatic and military skeletons to the safety closets and marked them TOP SECRET.

Public Alienation

The war of 1971 did not erupt in a vacuum. Pakistan's internal failures started the fire and the smouldering ashes were fanned and fuelled by a hostile India. Pakistan had joined the community of independent states in 1947. Just twenty-four years later, she faced shame when the same generation that had created a new homeland earned the dubious distinction of destroying half of its cherished motherland.

The East Pakistan catastrophe demands identification of the individuals who failed and betrayed the country during that tumultuous period. No less vital is it to determine the causes—

real and percieved—that created a sense of deprivation in the
people of East Pakistan. The alienation that affected the Bengali
mind soon after 1947 was caused by many factors including the
backwardness of the area; gross shortage of trained manpower;
and the cultural domination of society by the Hindu population.
The post-independence era witnessed administrative follies
committed by the centre, creating the impression that the Eastern
wing was being denied even-handed treatment. The devious role
played by India in Pakistan's internal affairs contributed in
fomenting trouble in the province.

Initially, some seemingly minor grievances were voiced. For
example, there was a muted claim that the capital of the country
should have been located in the majority province, ie, East
Pakistan. The Quaid-i-Azam's decision on the issue closed the
matter. The politically conscious people of East Pakistan visibly
resented the stiff-necked behaviour of the non-Bengali speaking
bureaucrats from West Pakistan who occupied key posts in East
Pakistan. The popular feeling was that such job opportunities
rightfully belonged to the 'sons of the soil'.

The Bengalis agitated when Urdu was declared the national
language of Pakistan. Three students of Dhaka University were
killed by police firing on 21 February 1952 during the pro-Bengali
agitation. A *Shaheed Minar* (martyrs monument) was constructed
on the site, and 21 February came to be observed annually as the
Language Martyrs Day in East Pakistan.

The post-1954 provincial elections Jugtu (united) Front
government formed in East Pakistan with Maulvi Fazlul Haq as
the Chief Minister was dismissed within two months of its
formation, and the province was placed under Governor's rule.
This undemocratic step sowed the seeds of discontent in the
province.

The Hindu minority exercised control on the economic,
cultural, educational, and social life of the province far in excess
of its population ratio. The Bengali bond was so strong that
East Pakistan had greater cultural affinity with West Bengal in
India than with its provinces in the Western Wing. Tagore was
preferred over Iqbal. The Bengalis learnt Urdu to communicate

with the people of West Pakistan, but they were incensed that the people in West Pakistan were reluctant to reciprocate and learn Bengali.

East Pakistan lacked the trained manpower to fill in its allotted quota of seats in the federal ministries. And yet it complained that its representation at the centre was not in accordance with the population ratio of the provinces. The shortage of Bengali officers was particularly visible in the senior posts. The fresh induction of civil servants from East Pakistan was a time-consuming process. Besides, the new entrants needed time and experience for holding senior appointments. This delay was exploited by vested interests.

The Bengalis complained about unequal economic growth and development between East and West Pakistan, and the criticism was mostly directed towards Punjab and Sindh. East Pakistan had started from a weak economic base in 1947, and its per capita income was lower than in the economically better developed West Pakistan.

History played an important part in the issues that confronted East Pakistan. During and after India's failed war of independence in 1857—titled the great Indian mutiny by the imperial power—as a matter of imperial policy, the British patronized the Hindus as a counterpoise to Muslim power. Prolonged official support enabled the Hindus to gain influence and dominance over the Bengali Muslims who constituted 57% of the population of undivided Bengal.

The pro-Hindu tilt was so pronounced that Sir W. W. Hunter, a British civil servant, recorded that the Bengali Muslim was frustrated as 'every honourable walk of life was closed to him and he was excluded from the share of power and the emoluments of government which he hitherto almost monopolised and saw them passed into the hands of the hated Hindus.[2] The British had, therefore, deliberately kept the Bengali's away from the Indian armed forces, and this factor eventually created an anomaly in 1947 when the largest province of Pakistan, in terms of population, found itself lacking in appropriate representation in the defence forces of the new

nation. Efforts were made to correct this imbalance. The youth
from East Pakistan started joining the military services in
reasonable numbers. But the deficiencies, large as they were,
could not be compensated in a short time. The selection of
candidates for regular commission in the army, navy and air
force—all on the basis of national merit—attracted some
candidates from East Pakistan, but their numbers were small
compared to their compatriots from West Pakistan.

The people were unhappy when three prime ministers hailing
from East Pakistan—Khawaja Nazimuddin, Mohammad Ali
Bogra and H. S. Suhrawardy—were unceremoniously dismissed
because of intrigues hatched by the West Pakistani coterie
wielding power at the centre. The martial laws of Ayub Khan
(1958) and Yahya Khan (1969) reflected the domination of West
Pakistan, as both the generals hailed from the Western wing.

It was commonly argued that East Pakistan was under-
defended by the military. This feeling gained momentum during
the Indo-Pakistan War of 1965, when the people felt isolated
and threatened by India. A higher military presence in East
Pakistan might have provided psychological security to the
people. The notion that the defence of East Pakistan lay in West
Pakistan did not make sense.

Feelings of isolation and unease prompted Sheikh Mujibur
Rahman to announce the Six Points formula. In 1968, he faced
trial on the charge of sedition in the Agartala Conspiracy Case.
At about this time, Ayub was facing public agitation in West
Pakistan against his rule. The political parties pressurized Ayub,
and secured the release of Mujib, and the withdrawal of the
Agartala Conspiracy case against him.

General Yahya inherited this political scenario. The
controversy between the two wings of Pakistan was not his
creation, but as the military supremo it was expected of him to
restore order, and to achieve national unity out of the prevailing
chaos. Public expectations were high. So were their emotions.
All eyes were focused on him. Whether or not he was able and
prepared to clean up the political mess firmly and effectively
was a question seriously debated.

Yahya's Career Profile

General Agha Muhammad Yahya Khan, HPK, HJ, SPK, PSc, (1917-1981) an impressive, Persian speaking Pathan, was commissioned in the Indian Army in 1938 from the Indian Military Academy. He served in the Worcestershire Regiment, British Army, for one year before joining 3/10 Baloch. He later served in 4/10 Baloch in Italy during the Second World War, and was taken a prisoner of war by the Germans. As a major, Yahya Khan served as general staff officer 2 (operations) in General Headquarters, India, between 1945-1946. In July 1947, he was posted as an instructor to the prestigious Command and Staff College, Quetta.

When he was lieutenant-colonel, Yahya Khan commanded two infantry battalions and had two stints in staff appointments, one in the Military Training Directorate in GHQ and the other as general staff officer 1 in an infantry division. Yahya had the distinction of becoming a brigadier at the young age of thirty-four. He commanded an infantry brigade, served as brigadier general staff in a corps HQ and as the deputy chief of the general staff at the GHQ.

As major-general, Yahya Khan commanded three separate infantry divisions, two in West Pakistan and one in the Eastern Wing. Such a varied and wholesome experience made him well aware of the defence problems of both wings of the country and the peculiar sentiments and sensitivities of the people of East Pakistan. His appointments as the vice chief of the general staff and the chief of the general staff at the GHQ groomed him in higher defence responsibilities in the Pakistan Army. Lieutenant-General Yahya Khan was made Deputy Commander-in-Chief in March 1966 before he took over as the Commander-in-Chief in September 1966.

In the annual confidential reports of his early years, Yahya was described as an intelligent and hardworking officer with a logical mind and a sharp brain—a valuable, all-round officer, who was an asset to the army. As a senior commander and staff officer he was good in his professional work and took clear and concise decisions promptly and fairly. He was also a pleasant conversationalist brimming with confidence and possessing a subtle sense of humour.

Yahya made no secret of his preference for hard drinks and female company. In his own words, 'I do not present myself as a model of rectitude or piety. As a sinful man there exist many flaws in my personal character for which I seek forgiveness from Almighty Allah.'[3] Yahya continues, 'I claim to be a professional army officer who is nothing if not a soldier. I did not force Ayub to relinquish power in my favour... but welcomed the chance to take power away from him.'[4]

Yahya on Bhutto

'Zulfikar Ali Bhutto was power-crazy and would mortgage even his soul to acquire any office....'[5] 'He was a complexed person who could not help doing mean things....'[6] He is a scorpion who cannot help but sting even the hand which feeds him....'[7] 'It has been my misfortune to be the target of a campaign of slander on the part of Bhutto even when he was a minister in my cabinet'[8] '...I was projected as a licentious person. I have been portrayed as an alcoholic sex-maniac. It is not for me to throw stones at others. Bhutto himself had a serious drug problem. He was almost an addict. Although quite capable of telling a story or two which would make even a shameless person such as Bhutto blush, I shall never do so till the end of my life...'[9] 'Bhutto was an unprincipled egocentric who could go to any length to acquire and use power. He wanted East Pakistan to secede....' 'Of course, Pakistan broke when I was at the helm of affairs. Of course, the Pakistan Army was defeated when I was its Commander-in-Chief. However, much more than myself, it is Zulfikar Bhutto who is responsible for the defeat and disintegration (of Pakistan)'.[10]

Yahya on Mujib

'Mujib is an extremely unreliable and immature person who thrives on publicity and mass hysteria...he is an agitator—pure and simple—who can gesticulate and shout (but) has no capacity to analyze or think...he is a born liar...he thinks he is clever but essentially he is a simpleton who was exploited by the Indian secret service agencies as well as by Zulfikar Ali Bhutto...Mujib has described in detail the arrangements arrived at between him and the representatives of some Indian political parties in the Agartala meetings. Substantial amounts were received by him from the Indians, most of whom have been identified as government functionaries working directly under instructions from the Indian Prime Minister. The idea of Bangladesh was carefully planted in his mind.'[11] '...Curiously, both Bhutto and Mujib were pressuring me for the same objective. Each wanted to take one wing of Pakistan away and set it up as his own private realm. Bhutto wanted to separate the western wing so that he could rule it without the "Bengali brother", as he used to term it.'[12]

Yahya takes Charge

I [K.M. Arif, the author] was commandant 11th Cavalry (FF) at Kharian. At 2 p.m. on 22 March 1969, I received a telephone call from the Military Secretary's Branch at the GHQ, Rawalpindi, directing me to report to the Military Secretary at his residence at 0900 next morning. I was not apprised about the nature of duty despite my inquiry.

As I entered his house, I found the Military Secretary, Major-General Mohammad Nawaz, lounging in a chair under a tree, with a white sheet wrapped around him. This was perhaps the only time in the history of the Pakistan Army when its Military Secretary had interviewed an officer while having a hair cut. Nawaz directed me to report to Brigadier Mohammad Rahim Khan in the conference room of the Adjutant General's Branch.

He was not forthcoming about the nature and duration of my duty.

Rahim, a secretive introvert, was not communicative either. He told me that we had been assembled to make a 'contingency plan' for the military to act in case the anti-Ayub disturbances went out of control. During the day, Brigadier Mohammad Iskander-ul-Karim (Bachu Karim) and Lieutenant-Colonel Abdul Rashid joined us. We worked unobtrusively for the next forty-eight hours as 24 March was also a closed holiday and the GHQ was empty. The Adjutant General, Major-General S. G. M. M. Peerzada, visited us frequently to give instructions and supervise the plan.

President Ayub Khan's hold on the national administration had loosened, and his control on the affairs of the state was wavering. He had become indecisive, and authority was exercised mostly in his name by a small group of his trusted bureaucrats like Altaf Gauhar, whom General Yahya called the Rasputin of Ayub Khan. On 23 March, Ayub confirmed to Yahya Khan his decision to quit power and it was so agreed between them that his address to the nation, due on 25 March, would be pre-recorded. On the advice of his close associates, Ayub changed his mind. He hinted about postponing the date, but Yahya told him firmly that the army had been alerted for the take-over. Ayub now also wanted his address to be broadcast and telecast live—a request turned down by Yahya Khan.

At 7 p.m. on 25 March 1969, President Ayub Khan announced his own retirement and asked General Yahya Khan to 'fulfil his responsibilities.' Yahya put the country under martial law and himself became the Chief Martial Law Administrator. The 'khaki shadows' loomed large once again on the quasi-military rule.

Field Marshal Ayub Khan wanted to stay on in Rawalpindi. His presence in the capital was irksome to the new supremo who had conveyed explicitly that the former president might like to shift to another city. Ayub had no option but to take the hint and go to Swat.

The President's Secretariat was converted into the Chief Martial Law Administrator's Headquarters (CMLA HQ) with

Major-General Peerzada becoming the Principal Staff Officer (PSO) to the CMLA. Brigadiers Rahim and Karim became Brigadier Martial Law and Brigadier Civil Affairs respectively. Both the brigadiers were assisted by two officers each in the rank of lieutenant-colonel. I worked under Rahim. Colonel A. R. Siddiqui became the Press Secretary to the CMLA. Major M. A. Hassan was posted as the legal expert.

Peerzada's contacts with his staff officers were impersonal and infrequent. Meticulous in his work and suspicious by nature, he maintained his distance and permitted no one to enter his office without prior appointment. Only Rahim and Karim were permitted to speak to him on the internal communication system. Peerzada (Peeru to Yahya Khan) had a lucid expression, spoke fluently and wrote with a running hand that on occasions he found hard to decipher himself. Peerzada soon found out that Major Abdul Qayyum, his personal staff officer, wrote with circumspection and envious clarity. One day, he asked Qayyum how did he learn to write so well? As Qayyum told me later, this was how he explained it:

'Sir', replied Qayyum, 'I learnt it the hard way.'
'I have tried no less hard', said Peerzada, 'but perfection has eluded me.'
'My father helped me in smoothening the rough edges,' said Qayyum, with a faint, mischievous smile on his poker straight face.
'How?' asked an insistent Peerzada.
'Sir, every time my written effort was not neat, my father placed pencils between my fingers and pressed my hand hard. I had the option of either having crooked fingers or straightening my hand writing.'

The Inherited Scenario

Unlike most countries, Pakistan was split in two parts and separated by a hostile power. East Pakistan was a single, cohesive administrative entity with a single provincial assembly, a rich Bengali language and a distinct cultural identity. On the other hand, West Pakistan consisted of four different sized provinces each having their own provincial legislature. The smaller provinces were uneasy about the largest province, Punjab.

A feeling of neglect prevailed among the people of East Pakistan, who felt they were dominated by the Western wing in general and Punjab in particular. The Yahya government inherited a parity formula by which East and West Pakistan had an equal number of seats in the National Assembly, despite the numerical superiority of East Pakistan. As a balancing act, the four provinces of West Pakistan were merged into a single province named One Unit.

The formation of the One Unit generated mixed feelings. The merger of four provinces was conceived in haste and implemented with inadequate preparation. The financial and administrative powers were over-centralized at the provincial headquarters—Lahore—which created practical difficulties for people living away from the seat of provincial headquarters, and psychological problems for the inhabitants of the smaller provinces.

The senior bureaucrats were opposed to the de-centralization of authority for reasons of self-interest, and desired to retain real power with themselves. This caused frustration among the people. Also, the calculating bureaucrats felt that their avenues of promotion might be adversely affected by de-centralization.

The domination of the Punjab aroused misgivings in other provinces. Some politicians felt uneasy at the possibility of a reduction in the provincial assembly seats. Others felt that reductions in the provincial cabinets might deprive them of the chance of becoming ministers.

General Yahya quickly shed the controversial political load accumulated by the Ayub administration. To the satisfaction of the smaller provinces, One Unit was dissolved. The parity formula was discarded and the system of 'one-man one-vote' restored. This step was acclaimed, particularly in East Pakistan. National elections were promised in which the provinces were to get representation in the National Assembly on the basis of their population ratio. The status of Balochistan was raised to that of a province, to bring it at par with other provinces. The former princely states of Dir, Chitral and Swat were merged to form the Malakand Agency—a step towards greater national integration.

These sound and far-reaching decisions enjoyed political consensus in the country, and showed that General Yahya, despite being an unelected ruler, had his fingers on the national pulse. He did not get sufficient credit for these important acts because they became clouded under the shadow of defeat that the country subsequently faced.

Military Team

Lieutenant-General M. Attiqur Rahman was the Governor of Punjab. His fertile mind generated innovative ideas at a rapid pace. A great story-teller and a strict disciplinarian, Attiq expertly intermingled wit and sarcasm in his flowing oration that left his audience perplexed. A dedicated professional striving for perfection, he took pleasure in pointing out any flaw in a soldiers salute or dress. My first impression of him stays fresh in my memory.

In May 1954, while attending the Piffer reunion at Abbottabad, I was sitting in the Piffer Mess reading a magazine. A gentleman occupied the seat next to me and said, 'Young man you seem to be from Cavalry.' Looking at the stranger, I replied, 'Sure, I am.' Back came the censure, 'You won't keep long hair when you come to attend the staff course.' I quickly learnt that Brigadier Attiq was then Deputy Commandant Staff College, Quetta.

Lieutenant-General Rakhman Gul, the Governor of Sindh, was flexible in his approach to administration. He earned Bhutto's goodwill by consulting him frequently on important issues, and was compensated when Bhutto came to power. Later, Rakhman Gul represented Pakistan well as an ambassador.

Air Marshal Nur Khan took his assignment to prepare a new
labour policy and a new education policy for the country very
seriously. He hired talented young people—whiz kids—and with
their help created a mini government within the government. A
dynamic personality, he hated interference in his work but did
not mind offering advice to others or questioning their authority.
The labour and the education policies prepared by him contained
some good features, but, on the whole, they created more
problems than they tried to solve. His quick exit from the
government did not surprise those who knew his temperament
and style of work.

Fateful Elections

The elections promised by Yahya Khan were held in 1970 under
a Legal Framework Order. This was the first phase of the
government's political plan. The next was to frame a constitution.
The final phase involved the transfer of power to the elected
representatives of the people. The first phase was completed
despite a massive natural calamity that hit East Pakistan
(a cyclone). Some politicians recommended a postponement, a
proposal to which Yahya Khan did not agree. The elections were
assessed to be fair and impartial, not a minor achievement in a
country in which general elections had not been held since it
became independent in 1947. That a military dictator gave an
electoral culture to the country which his civilian predecessors
had failed to offer, was a feather in the cap of Yahya Khan.

Phase two of the political plan—framing a constitution—
proved a tough nut to crack. Luck deserted General Yahya Khan.
His asset turned into a terrible liability for him. The National
Assembly did not meet. The government was not formed. The
transfer of power remained a far cry.

Sheikh Mujibur Rahman's Awami League swept the polls in
East Pakistan, winning 160 out of 162 seats reserved for this
province. Despite its enormous success, it remained a regional
party because it did not win a single seat in West Pakistan.

Mr Bhutto's Pakistan Peoples Party, won 81 seats from West Pakistan out of 138 reserved for it, and emerged as the largest party in the Western wing. It did not contest a single seat in East Pakistan.

Opposing Views

Had Pakistan been a single, compact, territorial entity, the electoral outcome—emergence of regional groups—might not have created a serious difficulty. However, the physical separation of its two wings polarized the country. The regional split was accentuated by the egocentric attitude of the two charismatic and populist leaders—Mujib and Bhutto—whose irrational behaviour and uncompromising attitudes put the country on an irreversible collision course.

Mujib exploited his electoral success in East Pakistan to the hilt. His views on Awami League's 6 Points Programme, an issue on which he had earlier maintained an ambiguous and flexible approach during the pre-election period, now hardened. He claimed that the people in East Pakistan had spoken on the issue and that he could not change public opinion. His stern and uncompromising attitude aroused public emotion and created anti-army and anti-Punjab feelings.

Bhutto argued that no single political party could frame a constitution without safeguarding the legitimate interests of all the federating units. He alleged that 'Mujib wanted to establish an independent, fascist and racist regime in East Pakistan as he did not believe in the integrity of the country.'[13] He claimed that there were two majority parties in the National Assembly, the Awami League for East Pakistan and the PPP for West Pakistan. He threatened to 'break the legs of the elected members of the Parliament who dared to attend the session of the National Assembly at Dhaka'[14] and warned them to travel on a one-way ticket. Bhutto even talked about two prime ministers in one country.

Both the intransigent leaders created a political dead-lock
that put General Yahya Khan in a quandary. His effort to frame
a constitution through consensus failed because both Mujib and
Bhutto operated on different wavelengths. Mujib insisted that
the constitution-making process could only be initiated inside
the National Assembly. Wishing to avoid a constitutional
deadlock inside the National Assembly, Yahya urged Mujib to
arrive at a compromise with the PPP and other parties through
mutual negotiations. The electoral victory had made Mujib
headstrong and uncompromising. His priority did not include
listening to the advice given by his president. Yahya declared
publicly that Mujib would be the next Prime Minister of
Pakistan. This annoyed Bhutto, who did not support the
government's policy of appeasement towards his political
opponent. Despite this, Mujib apprehended that the army might
not permit Yahya Khan to transfer real authority to the elected
representatives of the people, even if the president wanted to do
so. A crisis of confidence gripped the country.

The Legal Framework Order required the National Assembly
to frame a constitution within 120 days, and thereafter convert
itself into a legislative body. The political parties having
contested the elections under the LFO were perceived to have
accepted this condition.

Post-Election Strategy

A split verdict in the election created a hung parliament and
prompted the political parties to manoeuvre for their role in the
crucial parlays that lay ahead. Their first priority was to
demonstrate their own importance in the planned constitution-
making process. Immediately after the declaration of election
results, the Awami League became impatient that the date for
the inaugural session of the National Assembly be announced
by the President. At a massive public meeting held at Dhaka on
3 January 1971, the MNAs and the MPAs elected from the
Awami League took a pledge of loyalty. The undeclared purpose

of this unusual display of public solidarity was to send a signal to the government and to the political parties in West Pakistan that the Six Point Programme was not negotiable.

The Awami League fired a political salvo with the declaration that, 'Punjab and Sindh are no longer the bastions of power. The Awami League was quite capable of framing a constitution and (in so doing) the cooperation of parties other than the PPP will be sought.'[15] The Awami League's general secretary, Mr Tajuddin, declared that, 'The Awami League is quite competent to frame a constitution and form the central government without PPP's support.'[16] The Hindu students in Dhaka University chanted slogans of 'Quit Bengal' and 'Jai Hind' (Victory to India).[17] Emotions ran high in the charged political atmosphere and it was threatened that 'the traitors would be hacked to pieces,'[18] if the constitution was not based on the Six Points Programme.

Bhutto was no less adamant. His hyper-sensitivity and shrewdness did not permit him to leave the political arena free for his opponents. He proposed that President Yahya, along with the AL and PPP should jointly evolve a constitution based on a bipartisan consensus between both the major parties. Alternatively, both the major parties might make separate constitutions for their respective wings.[19] He emphatically stated that 'No constitution could be framed nor any government at the centre be run without PPP's cooperation.'[20] The diametrically opposed views of Mujib and Bhutto on substantive issues caused great concern.

General Yahya tried to play a mediating role in pacifying the political storm brewing between the hardline views of the AL and the PPP. He met Sheikh Mujib and his close associates at the President's House, Dhaka, on 13 January 1971 for a personal assessment of the prevailing situation. While conceding the right and the technical ability of the AL to form a central government by its own party strength, he advised Mujib to include some persons from West Pakistan in his cabinet for smoother conduct of the business of the state. Yahya carefully avoided naming any parties.

Mujib agreed to meet the West Pakistani politicians, including Bhutto, but maintained that his personal status vastly differed from that of the PPP leader. 'While I am the sole and unrivalled elected representative of East Pakistan enjoying total support', said Mujib, 'Mr Bhutto's position is different in West Pakistan. Other parties have won a considerable number of seats in the Western wing and we can associate them with us.'[21] Mujib favoured a unicameral legislature for the country. He hoped that other parties would not have mental reservations against the Six Point Programme. Yahya impressed on Mujib the need to show flexibility in framing a constitution, as the process demanded more than a simple majority in the legislature.

Yahya Khan's advice fell on deaf ears, and Mujib remained firm on the basic issues. He did not show flexibility on the Six Point Programme, nor did he compromise on the constitution making process. His views on the PPP were also as resolute as before.

On his return journey from Dhaka to Islamabad, General Yahya Khan stopped at Larkana to meet Bhutto, to publicly demonstrate his even-handed treatment to the two leaders. The Yahya-Bhutto meeting was less than cordial. Bhutto vehemently argued that a constitution framed by the majority party without achieving a prior, national consensus would be a 'barren exercise.'[22] In his view, the election results had created three options. One, the AL and PPP could jointly form a government and frame a constitution. Two, the AL could muster the support of some smaller parties in West Pakistan to the exclusion of PPP and form the government. And lastly, all the three power centres—the AL, PPP and the army—could form 'a three-legged stool to govern the country.'[23]

Reacting strongly to the third option, General Yahya told Bhutto that the army would not indulge in any political wheeling-dealing. It will be subservient to civil control and perform its task of maintaining law and order.[24] The sharp-witted Bhutto finally proposed something that was even more bizarre than his third option. He requested General Yahya Khan to advise Mujib to include Bhutto in the government, in the national interest, failing which the army might use force. A stunned Yahya explained the ground realities to Bhutto. Mujib could not ignore him and both might work in unison to frame a constitution. If a coalition was not possible, Bhutto could be the leader of the opposition, a choice distasteful to him.

That a self-appointed *Quaid-e-Awam* (leader of the masses) could influence a military dictator to take anti-democratic steps to place him in the power saddle, highlighted the tragedy of Pakistan. History was repeating itself. Bhutto was not the first culprit in this infamous game. Some of his predecessors in politics had also sought the military ladder to climb to political heights. Politicians had covertly hobnobbed with the men in khaki to topple democracy. Politicians sought power and the means to acquire it was a matter of secondary importance to them.

On 27 January, Bhutto went to Dhaka. Mujib and Bhutto discussed the Six Point Programme, with the latter conceding all but half a point. The Awami League, to everyone's surprise, with Bhutto present in East Pakistan, unilaterally announced a draft constitution which, among other issues, stated that East Pakistan would be named Bangladesh; the naval or the air headquarters would be shifted to Bangladesh; the centre would be invested only with foreign affairs, defence and currency and would be stripped of all taxation powers except to levy tax on provinces within the sliding scales prescribed in the constitution. Mujib ignored Bhutto's proposal for sharing power and giving him a key appointment in the government. A dejected Bhutto returned empty-handed to West Pakistan despite conceding to most of the Six Points. Mujib knew Bhutto well and was as wily and possessive of power as Bhutto was.

Deepening Crisis

Mujib's hardened attitude and the failure of the Mujib-Bhutto parleys was an eye-opener for President Yahya Khan. Yet he took almost two weeks to react. On 9 February 1971, he invited

Mujib for a meeting to Islamabad. Notwithstanding his differences, decency and protocol demanded that Mujib respond positively to the invitation sent by the head of the state. With most of the political cards held by him, Mujib arrogantly declined a journey to the national capital. His preference was confrontation not conciliation. His base of power, Dhaka, was a more useful place for him to stay to achieve his goal.

Mujib—euphoric with his electoral success—wanted the inaugural session of the National Assembly to be held at Dhaka on 15 February 1971. An early session did not suit Bhutto, who wanted sufficient time to evolve a consensus on all the contentious issues before the inaugural session was held. 23 March was his choice. A cornered General Yahya met Bhutto on 11 February, and two days later chose the middle path. On 13 February 1971, the National Assembly was summoned to meet at Dhaka for its inaugural session on 3 March. This was perhaps done without prior consultation of the political parties with the notion that a couple of weeks either way was inconsequential. Subsequent developments proved Yahya wrong, and he learnt it at a bitter personal and national cost.

Both Mujib and Bhutto were up in arms, insistent on acceptance of their own demands. Yahya was caught on unfamiliar ground and he evinced his inability to take political decisions. He was now dealing with elected politicians who, unlike him, enjoyed a freshly obtained public mandate. The whip of the Legal Framework Order was still held by Yahya, but the fear of its use was eroding every day. Yahya could not reject the reasonable demands of both the majority party leaders for fear of facing a sharp internal reaction and criticism from foreign agencies. Mujib and Bhutto were acknowledged agitators and demagogues of a high calibre. Both were experts in playing with the sentiments of the people and exploiting them to their own advantage.

General Yahya did not make a public issue of Mujib's rebuff and kept hoping that, with the summoning of the National Assembly session, political passions would reduce and sanity return to the elected leaders. On 15 February 1971, Bhutto telephoned Yahya's Principal Staff Officer, Peerzada, from Peshawar and complained that he had not been consulted before the date of the summoning of the National Assembly was announced. Peerzada gave him a bureaucratic reply that under the constitution he was not required to be consulted. A peeved Bhutto retorted, 'You will face the music when my party does not attend nor permit others from West Pakistan to do so.'[25] That day Bhutto announced that, 'PPP will not attend the National Assembly session,' and 'we cannot go there (to Dhaka) to endorse the constitution already prepared by a party and to return humiliated.'[26] Bhutto threatened a 'revolution from Karachi to Khyber' and predicted that the National Assembly would be a 'slaughter house.'[27]

General Yahya made another attempt to break the deadlock. On 17 February 1971, he once again invited Mujib to meet him at Islamabad. Mujib expressed his inability to travel to the capital to meet the President. His consistent refusal for a dialogue made his intentions suspicious. His goal was to create an *impasse* and take his life-long ambition to its conclusion for which he had been promised active support by India.

General Yahya was not an ignorant head of state. The national intelligence agencies had kept the government fully informed about India's deep involvement in Sheikh Mujibur Rahman's plans. With Mujib acting quietly, and Bhutto posturing publicly, General Yahya and his close associates viewed the shrinking political choices with concern, and prepared alternatives.

Bhutto met the president on 19 February 1971. The wily politician sensed Yahya's unease about Mujib, reinforced his doubts about the AL leader and urged him to act firmly against the forces of national integration. In Bhutto's assessment, the weak-kneed Governor of East Pakistan, Vice Admiral S. M. Ahsan, was a 'pliable tool in the hands of Awami League.'[28] The following day, while addressing the PPP's elected members of the National and Provincial Assemblies he proposed that, 'The government should either postpone the National Assembly session or waive the 120 days time limit' for framing the constitution.[29]

With tension rapidly increasing, Governor Ahsan and the MLA Sahibzada Yaqub Khan impressed on the president the need to visit Dhaka for an on the spot assessment of the prevailing situation. General Yahya and his advisers in West Pakistan felt differently. The Agartala Conspiracy case had made Mujib suspicious in the eyes of many in West Pakistan. To the military brass, his links with India's 'underground' were well established and deep rooted. His Six Points Programme was considered a subterfuge to harm Pakistan in the garb of protecting the interests of East Pakistan. This had reinforced the doubts of Mujib's opponents about his allegiance to the country which the constitution demanded he defend and protect.

General Yahya held a two-day meeting of the Governors and MLAs at the President's House in Rawalpindi on 22-23 February 1971, primarily to review the situation in East Pakistan. Those attending included selected government functionaries, the GHQ's top brass, heads of the intelligence agencies and police, Chairman of the National Security Council and Major-General Rao Farman Ali Khan. Yahya took exception to Mujib's refusal to visit the capital, and admonished those present for being unassertive in handling the agitation. He wanted firm action against Mujib and Bhutto who shared responsibility for vitiating the political climate and creating an *impasse*.

Yaqub and Ahsan explained the mood of the people of East Pakistan who felt betrayed and had risen in revolt to 'protect' their rights. Both opposed the use of force against the people who had supported the Awami League during the elections. In their assessment, the use of force would bring the situation to an undesired climax and might lead to the disintegration of the country. They recommended a political solution for which pressure would be exerted on the leadership of both wings of the country, particularly on Bhutto.

To many in the government Mujib, the villain, deserved to be disciplined for not keeping the extremists in the Awami League under control. While they criticized Bhutto's rhetoric, they opposed taking firm action against him to prevent agitation in West Pakistan. Bhutto sensed the predicament of the administration and exploited it to his advantage. The official attitude towards the two principal actors was uneven, firm against Mujib and lenient towards Bhutto.

General Yahya stated that in the polarized political climate it was inappropriate to hold the National Assembly session on 3 March 1971. This view shocked Ahsan and Yaqub, who strongly advocated against such a step. They argued that local sentiments were highly charged and bruised Bengali nationalism might lead to the erosion of national unity, with the gravest consequences. Sensing strong opposition, Yahya asked General Hameed, Ahsan and Yaqub to meet him separately in an adjoining room.

This was not one of the most genial meetings presided over by Yahya Khan during his turbulent tenure as the President of Pakistan. He told his exclusive audience that he had decided to personally control the law and order situation in East Pakistan. The presence of General Hameed in the meeting indicated that the military supported the decision. Yaqub painted a grim scenario. According to him, East Pakistan was 'slipping out of the federation.'[30] The civil administration and the intelligence agencies were no longer trustworthy, and the military and para-military forces of East Pakistani origin were under strong, local political pressure. Any military action could ignite a spark resulting in bloodshed, and India's covert support might initiate a local uprising with serious consequences. Yaqub recommended a political solution and a serious effort to put the onus of responsibility on the political leaders, especially in West Pakistan, if the National Assembly session was not held. Politicians, not the army, Yaqub argued, would be responsible for the failure. Ahsan agreed with Yaqub's sombre diagnosis.

Yahya did not share Yaqub's 'pessimism' and adjourned the meeting to reassemble at 10 a.m. the next day, with the remarks that he had decided to act firmly in East Pakistan. This decision made the military, the visible arbiter of national destiny, subservient to Mujib and Bhutto. Little did the assembled dignitaries know then that the decision meant a gory end to Quaid-i-Azam's Pakistan.

Admiral Ahsan and General Yaqub returned to Dhaka with their martial law swords reluctantly drawn out of the scabbards. On instructions from the president, they informed a shocked Mujib on 1 March that the assembly session due two days later was postponed. Mujib suggested that a revised date be simultaneously announced failing which it might be impossible for him to control the situation. His advice was not accepted. At midnight on 1 March, the postponement of the National Assembly session was announced without indicating a revised date. The situation took a serious turn.

The political reaction to the postponement was mixed. At one end of the opinion scale, the PPP announced that the president's decision was based on good intentions.[31] With his immediate purpose served, a calm Bhutto opined that, 'surely nothing is lost.' At the other end, the Awami League concluded that West Pakistan would not transfer power.[32] An enraged Mujib vowed that 'the postponement would not go unchallenged.' He called for a strike on 7 March. In between the two extreme views, while some small parties in West Pakistan blamed Bhutto for stalling the democratic process, others were against postponement. But all wanted an early restoration of democracy. The Yahya government later declared that the National Assembly session was postponed because one major party (PPP) had refused to attend the session on 3 March, and more time was needed to reach an understanding on the constitution making process. This belated explanation did not alleviate tensions.

Ahsan was relieved of his duties and Yaqub took over the dual charge. Yahya had not forgiven Ahsan for not persuading Mujib to travel to Islamabad to meet the president.

Reaction in East Pakistan

Public reaction in East Pakistan was spontaneous and hostile and the postponement was seen by the people as a conspiracy against the Bengalis. Dhaka came to a standstill with government offices closed, shops shuttered down, and the roads and streets overtaken by slogan chanting activists. 3 March, the date on which the National Assembly was to convene, was declared a day of mourning with a province-wide strike. Emotions ran high. The Quaid-i-Azam's portrait was burnt. The national flag was desecrated. The West Pakistanis were taunted, the army was abused and essential supplies to the cantonment were stopped. The Bangladesh national anthem was played on the state-controlled Dhaka TV that had been taken over by the AL political activists. The Dhaka cantonment was besieged, the mobs clashed with the police, and the army, and people were killed. This added fuel to the fire.

Yaqub, the new governor, asked President Yahya Khan to visit Dhaka. Yaqub renewed his invitation on 3 March. On the night of 4/5 March, Yahya conveyed to Yaqub his inability to visit Dhaka for the present. The refusal was a rebuff that Yaqub could not accept. He immediately requested, first verbally and then in writing, to be relieved of his responsibilities.

General Yahya Khan invited Shaikh Mujib to meet him at Dhaka on 10 March 1971. Mujib declined the invitation saying, 'unarmed civilians are being killed and I will be asked to sit with certain elements [Bhutto] whose devious machinations were responsible for the death of innocent peasants, workers and students.'[33]

Lieutenant-General Tikka Khan, the new Commander, Eastern Command, reached Dhaka on 7 March. He wanted to meet Mujib who was agreeable provided the venue was his (Mujib's) house. Tikka suggested a neutral place—the Government House. Mujib declined, and the two did not meet.

In West Pakistan, Bhutto pursued his one-point agenda, acquisition of power. On 10 March 1971, he sent a telegram to Mujib suggesting that, 'The two wings of Pakistan must immediately reach a common understanding if the unity is to be saved.'[34] Days later he was more explicit when he said, 'Because of the geographical separation (of East and West Pakistan) the majority rule does not apply,'[35] and 'power should be transferred to both the majority parties.'[36] The gulf of opinion between the PPP and the Awami League remained wide and un-bridged.

Negotiations Aborted

President Yahya Khan belatedly arrived at Dhaka on 15 March 1971. By that time the people of East Pakistan were in a defiant mood. Significantly, his reception line at the Tejgoan airport did not include any Bengali politician or bureaucrat. The fear of retribution for attending the reception ceremony weighed heavy on the people of East Pakistan. The following day, Mujib arrived at the president's house, flying a Bangladesh flag on his car, to meet the President, Yahya Khan. He proposed a confederation between East and West Pakistan, and demanded that the talks could not be tripartite, meaning he would not like Bhutto to join their bilateral parleys.

The government-Awami League negotiations were held between 16-24 March 1971. On the invitation of the president, the West Pakistani political leaders arrived at Dhaka on 19 March to participate in the talks. They included Mumtaz Daultana, Sardar Shaukat Hayat Khan, Mufti Mahmood, Khan Abdul Wali Khan, Sahibzada Abdul Qayuum, Ghouse Bakhsh Bizenjo, and Maulana Shah Ahmad Noorani. Mr Bhutto joined them at Dhaka on 22 March, after Mujib agreed to meet him. On the suggestion of Yayha, Bhutto and Mujib had an exclusive conversation in which they agreed to disagree with each other on substantive political issues. They could not achieve convergence of views because their thinking was regional-based. While they vehemently hated each other, their suspicion about Yahya's motives was the same.

Two negotiating teams, each individually representing the government and the Awami League, prepared two separate draft constitutions. A ray of hope was created that a solution was possible. It fizzled out rapidly. The Awami League negotiators were in an uncompromising and strident mood. They outwardly wanted confederation, but actually wanted separation. Yahya had been warned by the intelligence agencies that the Awami League had alternative secret plans ready. The details of this were explained to him. He made a final effort to maintain the unity of the country. He also advised the West Pakistani political leaders to urge Mujib to be reasonable and realistic. Mujib insisted on a settlement on his own terms.

Sensing the failure of the talks, on the afternoon of 24 March, General Yahya ordered General Tikka Khan to launch the already conceived Operation Searchlight, a military contingency plan, for restoring normalcy. Hours later, he flew back to Karachi with Tikka Khan ready to exhibit the military muscle.

Sheikh Mujibur Rahman had aroused strong Bengali emotions in East Pakistan by consistently spreading venom against the Western wing in general, and the Punjabi 'Shala' in particular. All the ills of the province were dumped in the lap of West Pakistan. Initially, India played a subtle role in instigating such hatred. So did the Hindu minority in East Pakistan. In the final stages of the crisis, the Mukti Bahini was influenced strongly by India.

Between 2-26 March, the people of Bihar and West Pakistan living in East Pakistan became hostages in their own country. Mujib's party activists went berserk at Santahar, Chittagong, Mymensingh, Dhaka and elsewhere and indulged in acts of loot, violence, rape and murder. The people were ambushed, molested, and killed, and their houses were torched and property destroyed. According to one estimate, about 100,000 non-Bengali and West Pakistani persons were killed by the Awami League political activists during March 1971.[37]

One gory incident was perhaps the nadir of human behaviour. 'On the night of 25/26 March, Major Ziaur Rehman, later President of Bangladesh, woke up his (West Pakistani) commanding officer Lieutenant Colonel Janjua, took him to the offices of 8 East Bengal in his night clothes, made him sit in the commanding officer's chair and made the colonel's batman shoot him dead.'[38] The premeditated, cold-blooded murder was a deceitful and cowardly act.

The news of this episode spread fast and was widely known in the Pakistan Army. Years later, Ziaur Rehman, now the President of Bangladesh, visited Pakistan. In addition to the official functions held in his honour, President Ziaul Haq held a luncheon for the visiting dignitary to which I was also invited.

I requested that I be excused from this function. Assuming that my request was based on national sensitivity General Zia counseled, 'Bangladesh is now a reality and we should accept it without reservation.' I told President Ziaul Haq that my personal instinct prevented me from lunching with a murderer who had stooped so low as to have his own commanding officer gunned down.

Military Action

The intelligence agencies had warned the government that the Awami League, with the support of the Bengali elements of the East Bengal Regiment and the East Pakistan Rifles, had planned to seize the Dhaka airfield and the Chittagong sea port in the early hours of 26 March 1971, and Dhaka cantonment was to be stormed.

Operation Searchlight was launched at 1 a.m. on the night of 25-26 March 1971. Its immediate military objective was to arrest the prominent Awami League leaders; disarm all Bengali troops; control all the naval bases and airfields; ensure the security of all the towns; and re-establish the writ of the government by firmly enforcing law and order in the province. Sheikh Mujibur Rahman was arrested from his house in Dhaka in a swift commando action. By this time, all the other AL leaders had fled to neighbouring India where they were received with open arms. Dr Kamal Hussain, legal adviser of the Awami League, surrendered in Dhaka on 4 April.

The Dhaka University hostels, which had become the militant student wing headquarters of the Awami League, were cleared of all students during the night. The radical groups among them had been 'training students in the use of fire arms' reported one foreign observer.[39] The troops exchanged fire with the weapon-wielding students residing in the hostels, and sixty-six Bengali students and four soldiers lost their lives. Another estimate put the figures as 167 dead. The soldiers were said to have 'over reacted' because they had been 'taunted, insulted and spat at during the last one month.'[40]

Twilight Zone

Bhutto flew back to Karachi on 26 March, and declared, 'By the grace of Almighty God, Pakistan has at last been saved.'[41] The same day, General Yahya Khan addressed the nation on the electronic media. He banned the Awami League and bitterly accused Mujib of being an 'enemy of Pakistan.' Sheikh Mujib was sent to West Pakistan where he was tried for treason by a special tribunal headed by Brigadier Rahimuddin Khan that sentenced him to death. General Yahya Khan put the verdict in abeyance.

On 30 March 1971, both the houses of the Indian Parliament passed a resolution assuring the people of East Pakistan that, 'their struggle will receive the wholehearted sympathies and support from the people of India.'[42] This was an understatement. In reality, Mrs Indira Gandhi had already ordered the Indian military to attack East Pakistan. India's cautious Chief of the Army Staff, General Manekshaw, wanted six months to launch the operation as he did not want his army to get stuck in the 'quagmire of monsoon.'[43] November 1971 was selected as the month of invasion to destroy Pakistan.

Within six to seven weeks of the launching of Operation Searchlight, General Tikka Khan had restored a reasonable modicum of normalcy in East Pakistan. While not all the immediate military objectives were fully achieved, the writ of government stood restored, and the cities and towns started pulsating with civil life. Economic activity picked up, and trade gained momentum, bazaars buzzed with people. Schools and colleges reopened and attendance in offices became normal.

An accurate assessment of the human casualties is not possible because of the absence of reliable statistics. They vastly vary between one million civilians quoted by India to 34,000 stated by General Tikka Khan[44] and 30,000 assessed by the

Western missionaries working in East Pakistan.[45] The military had 237 officers, 136 JCOs and 3,559 other ranks killed and wounded[46] up to November 1971.

Errors were made. The escape of the Awami League leaders to India was a failure of intelligence. This kept the party alive and functioning in East Pakistan, albeit underground, with its leaders remaining under the effective influence and firm control of India. From March through November, the Awami League activists received directions and guidance from their party leaders living in safe havens just across the border.

The members of the East Bengal Regiments were disarmed as planned. They trekked across to India which was only too eager to provide them weapons and reorganize them into the Mukti Bahini. Later, these elements formed the vanguard and led the Indian army to the Pakistani defences so familiar to them.

East Pakistan needed a political recipe to assuage the hurt feelings of the people in order to bring them back into the national mainstream. The policies of the Yahya government fell far short of public expectations, and the prospects of a peaceful and political breakthrough dimmed rapidly. The elections polarized the country and started a political tug of war between the main contenders of power, Mujib and Bhutto. Yahya tried to bridge the gulf between their vastly conflicting views, but he failed in his attempt. The country needed a renewed political plan of action to break the *impasse*. Yahya's strategy was different. Instead of achieving a national consensus by taking the political parties and the nation into confidence, he put a military plan into gear after consulting his close advisers.

The national institutions were dormant because the country was under one-man rule. But even those still existing were bypassed. There is no evidence to show if the military brass was collectively consulted as a body. Nor indeed was the federal cabinet taken into confidence about the failure of the Yahya-Mujib-Bhutto political negotiations at Dhaka. It remained a hush-hush affair and details surfaced rather late after the military action had already been launched. The rulers arrogated to know all, and the security of information prevailed over the security of the state.

General Yahya Khan had confidentially directed Commander Eastern Command, Dhaka, to be ready to launch Operation Searchlight in the event of the failure of the ongoing political negotiations. On 24 March 1971, he took the fateful decision to launch military action to discipline the Awami League, and to re-establish the failing writ of his government. Little did he know then that this was the beginning of the end of Quaid-i-Azam's Pakistan.

Operation Searchlight had multiple objectives, long-term and short-term. Its immediate objectives included the disarming of Bengali troops in East Pakistan; arresting prominent Awami League leaders and stiffening martial law in the Eastern Wing.

The imposition of Yahya's martial law was hard to sell abroad, particularly in the Western countries, as it was an anti-thesis of democratic dispensation. They praised the holding of fresh and fair general elections in the country. Their eyes were then focused on the next logical step, the restoration of democracy and return to the rule of law. This did not happen. Instead, the failure of political parleys at Dhaka caused not only an internal setback to Pakistan but its ramifications in the free world were also serious and pronounced. The military action added fuel to the fire. The Western countries, which had hoped that Pakistan would move forward towards democratic rule, were taken aback when it suddenly got derailed from the democratic track. This caused resentment in the West, and Pakistan was politically and diplomatically isolated in the comity of nations. This seclusion put Pakistan on the defensive to such an extent that her initiatives in maintaining her own territorial integrity were criticized by outside powers.

Pakistan's press relations effort was also weak. To ask the foreign journalists to quit Dhaka, as was done, was a media blunder of serious proportions. This ostrich-like approach was indefensible and counterproductive. Similarly, the white paper issued by the government on the East Pakistan crisis failed to create the desired impact on the targeted audience.

The military force needed to restore normalcy was used excessively. The gulf of mistrust kept widening to the advantage of a hostile India that exploited the situation to its own benefit.

India's Machiavellian Role

The military action in East Pakistan caused some trans-border migration. They were mostly Awami League activists escaping from the grip of the law, and the Hindu population, some moving across as a precautionary measure and others encouraged by India to do so for reasons of tactical necessity. Their exact number was kept secret by India, which did not permit international agencies to visit the so-called refugee camps. India put their number as ten million. Later, India used the pretext of the influx of Bengali refugees to launch an attack on East Pakistan.

Had refugees been a genuine issue, India would have welcomed foreign assistance in returning them to their homes. Instead, she prevented the refugees from leaving her territory[47] or permitting the UN personnel to handle them.[48] India did not even accept any proposal to curb guerrilla activity from her own territory.[49] An Indian writer maintains that, 'Eighty five percent of the Bengalis who left East Pakistan were Hindus who would have gone away to West Bengal in any case.'[50] 'Utter rubbish,' says another analyst who insists that India attacked Pakistan to settle the refugee problem, adding, 'India went to war to satisfy the nationalist and popular view that the dismemberment of Pakistan was in the long (term) interest of India.'[51]

As discussed earlier, Prime Minister Indira Gandhi had ordered an attack on East Pakistan in March 1971, and she spent the next six months fabricating a plausible justification for her military adventure.

The Military Factor

Background

Geography was against Pakistan[52] from the day of her independence, and the two parts (wings) separated by 1,600 kilometers of hostile Indian territory posed daunting problems to national defence planners. This peculiarity justified the raising of two independent sets of armed forces, one for each wing, to meet the minimum essential security needs commensurate with the magnitude of the threat posed to them respectively. Such an option was foreclosed by the weak national economy.

The alternative was to maintain a smaller force in the less threatened zone, while keeping the main defensive military strength in the other wing, a choice that was adopted. This bulk of the defence services was consequently located in West Pakistan—the larger geographic entity, the heartland of the country and the hub of its industrial and military power. Judged by strategic, economic and military yardsticks, this decision was inherently sound and made sense. However, East Pakistan looked at it largely from a provincial rather than a national viewpoint and protested against 'depriving' the Eastern wing of adequate sinews of military power for defence.

Initially, after independence, only one infantry brigade was located in East Pakistan. Subsequently, the strength was raised to one infantry division out of the total army component of nearly four and a half infantry divisions.

East Pakistan did not face the vagaries of war during India's aggression on Pakistan in 1965. But the Bengali politicians were quick in playing up the theme that the security of the Eastern wing had been neglected, and the centre had not done enough in this regard. This influenced the minds of the Bengali people who were increasingly disillusioned by the theory that the defence of East Pakistan lay in the Western wing. However, this remained the official policy and the military strategists subscribed to its viability and reliability in letter and spirit.

In 1969, one corps headquarters, 3 Corps, later called Eastern Command, was raised in Dhaka and Lieutenant-General Sahibzada Yaqub Khan took charge. Some additional troops were also inducted in East Pakistan. 3 Corps was tasked by GHQ 'to defend East Pakistan.'

The 1970 general elections, held after a year long electoral campaign, polarized the country. Sheikh Mujibur Rahman wanted nothing short of the Awami League's Six Point Programme. Mr Bhutto was too impetuous to become the Leader of the Opposition in the House. The country was politically split from within, and the Yahya administration did not have a solution to offer.

On 17 September 1970, HQ 14 Division issued its operational instruction in which its mission was specified 'to defend East Pakistan' and to 'ensure the defence of Dhaka at all costs.' This was based on the directive received earlier from GHQ and clearly shows the extreme significance attached to the defence of the capital city, Dhaka.

The situation in East Pakistan underwent a dramatic change after the elections. With the stamp of public approval affixed on the Six Points Programme, the Awami League became increasingly arrogant and uncompromising in its negotiating strategy with the government. Army troops were deployed on internal security duties.

The Turning Point

As the threat from India became overt, the population became hostile, the Bengali troops deserted, and promptly slipped across the border to receive arms, training and moral and logistic backup from India. In this deteriorating law and order situation, the government airlifted two infantry divisions, 9 and 16, into East Pakistan via Sri Lanka because India had banned Pakistan International Airlines from flying over Indian territory. These two infantry divisions lacked guns, armour and engineering support. Besides, most of the troops had not previously served in East Pakistan, and were unaware of its terrain and political environment.

With the situation in East Pakistan rapidly deteriorating, Commander Eastern Command Lieutenant-General Sahibzada Yaqub Khan developed differences on policy matters with the government and resigned on 5 March 1971. He was replaced by Lieutenant-General Tikka Khan. Military action ordered by Tikka Khan in March 1971, was the beginning of the end. From then onwards, it was West Pakistanis against Bengalis; the Pakistan Army against the Mukti Bahini. By antumn, General Tikka Khan had established the writ of the government, and an uneasy calm prevailed in the province. This created a misplaced euphoria, but the stage had been set for the division of the country. General Tikka Khan's military crackdown achieved some success but at a heavy political price. General Tikka Khan was a ruthless commander and a strict disciplinarian. The people of East Pakistan suffered terribly. A modification in strategy and a change of face was needed. Tikka Khan was replaced by Lieutenant-General A. A. K. Niazi as Commander Eastern Command on 3 September 1971. The choice was unfortunate and exposed his professional limitations. He was to learn later, the hard way, that the apparent calm prevailing in Dhaka was, in fact, the lull before the storm.

Operational Plan

In August 1971, Eastern Command had sent a new plan to GHQ for the defence of the province. This envisaged the defence of the major towns as fortresses and strong points, and a plan to defend the provincial capital, Dhaka, at all costs. Additionally, some offensive action was planned across the border including the capture of Farrakha Barrage and a threat to be posed to Calcutta.

Such offensive tasks, in reality 'missions impossible', reflected the fact that GHQ was out of tune with the realities in East Pakistan. The induction of two additional but truncated infantry divisions in East Pakistan were not sufficient to enable the force commander to carry out the necessary tasks. Soon, military prudence prevailed, the offensive missions were deleted and GHQ directed the Eastern Command to concentrate on its defensive battle.

Relative Strength

India waited for the end of the monsoon season to start the war of attrition. For operations against East Pakistan she had up to eight infantry divisions, nearly three dozen Border Security Force Battalions, and about 100,000 Mukti Bahinis, besides her second line forces. This gave India an overwhelming superiority in numbers over the weak ground force held by Eastern Command. Additionally, India had total control over the sea in the Bay of Bengal, enabling it to impose a naval blockade of East Pakistan. India's superiority in the air was no less telling. She had deployed 11-12 fighter squadrons, and one bomber squadron against one single squadron of twelve inferior fighter aircrafts of the Pakistan Air Force based on Dhaka airport. It was obvious to all that Dhaka airport would easily be rendered inoperable by the enemy within one or two days of the start of hostilities, and the PAF would be grounded in East Pakistan.

Threat Assessment

India's impending offensive was known to Pakistan. The ISI Directorate had done its job. It had placed India's offensive strategy plan on the table. The information had been provided well in time. However, Yahya and GHQ failed to take advantage of the forewarning given to them.

In October-November 1971, the GHQ and Eastern Command had assessed that the Mukti Bahini, supported by the Indian Army, might try to capture some territory in East Pakistan to provide India an excuse to recognise 'Bangladesh'. Such a development being unacceptable to Pakistan, military steps were taken to frustrate this possibility. Niazi did expect an Indian attack, but he was inclined to preclude an all out military operation by the enemy. This was a faulty assessment. It appears that even GHQ did not foresee a sudden and serious operational development in East Pakistan. For how else can one justify GHQ directing Eastern Command on 15 November 1971, to submit a revised operational plan for approval. At this time the enemy was already knocking at the doors of the country and its intentions should have been obvious to all.

Niazi deployed his forces for defence, but did not earmark a dedicated reserve for the defence of the vital nucleus, the Dhaka bowl, strategically located at the confluence of three mighty rivers. It was believed that after fighting their delaying battles, the troops would fall back to occupy the defensive perimeter at Dhaka. This was an unwise decision because uncertainties dominate in combat and to leave one's vital base unattended amounts to surrendering the initiative to the enemy.

Army's Role

East Pakistan faced a great human tragedy. The Dhaka University hostels, converted into fortresses by emotionally charged students and professors, were raided by the military on the night of 25-26 March 1971. The troops were fired at by the entrenched students who had barricaded themselves in well-prepared positions. A mini-military action was launched to get the hostels vacated by students who should have been holding books not weapons in their hands. The blood that was shed in the process weakened Pakistan still further.

The rebellious Bengalis from the East Bengal Regiments were disarmed, and this action increased East-West hatred. General Tikka Khan soon felt the shortage of troops that had been thinned out throughout the province for internal security duties— clearing road blocks, securing communication centres and occupying important junctions. He requested reinforcements from West Pakistan, which began to arrive by air from 1 April. The fresh arrivals were without tanks, heavy equipment and direct support artillery. This deficiency adversely affected their performance in the war that followed. However, by the end of May, the insurrection in East Pakistan had been suppressed and the writ of the government restored.

In March 1971, thirty-five foreign journalists operated from East Pakistan. For reasons betraying professionalism, Pakistan expelled all of them from her Eastern Wing before the military action started. The military government also tried to revamp commercial activity in East Pakistan at this time. This attempt met with stiff resistance, and it was largely unsuccessful as the Awami League, that unofficially ruled East Pakistan, was in confrontation with the government. The government had secured all major towns, but the vast countryside remained under the control of the dissidents.

The government re-established its control on radio and television stations, but a clandestine radio station operating from Indian territory spread venom against Pakistan. Attempts to pacify East Pakistan obviously did not suit the policy objectives of India which had laboured hard for nine months in preparing its political-military-economic strategy to convert East Pakistan into Bangladesh.

Furthermore, the political and military action plans concerning East Pakistan were conceived and implemented in isolation of each other. An integrated approach was not used in adopting these plans, and relevant institutions were bypassed in adopting policy options. Such patch-work planning did not speak well either of the CMLA Headquarters or of GHQ, or indeed of the federal government.

Military Surrender

India attacked East Pakistan with eight divisions in November 1971, as accurately forewarned by Pakistan's intelligence agency. At 4.31 p.m. on 16 December 1971, Lieutenant-General Amir Abdullah Khan Niazi, Commander Eastern Command, signed the instrument of surrender at the Ramna race course ground, Dhaka. He surrendered his revolver and his badges of rank to Lieutenant-General Jagjit Singh Aurora, GOC-in-C Eastern Command, Indian Army, in a ceremony held on the occasion. The surrender ceremony humiliated the military and shall haunt Niazi for the rest of his life.

Bangladesh was born out of the ashes of East Pakistan. Pakistan lost the war without seriously defending her Eastern Wing or opening a second front in West Pakistan. Minor skirmishes and low level engagement took place at various places, but the battle of strategic dimensions was not fought by either side. India won without a single, serious military encounter above minor levels.

For the people of Pakistan this time was traumatic. General Yahya Khan led the Pakistan Army to defeat and presided over the destruction of the country. For these acts, he was neither tried in a civilian or military court of law, nor convicted. Belatedly, the Supreme Court declared Yahya a usurper and condemned him unheard.

Pakistan was beaten politically, morally, diplomatically and, above all, militarily, more so because of the follies committed by her own leadership than by the skill of her adversary. Her dismemberment was the result of many self-sustained injuries inflicted over a prolonged period of time. India simply took advantage of the situation and played her cards right. The Hamoodur Rahman Commission covered only the tip of the iceberg—the military surrender. Other vital factors, political and othewise, were deliberately swept under the carpet, and the true facts were hidden from the people of Pakistan.

Lessons Learnt

This narrative will remain incomplete without analyzing the mistakes made. Self-criticism may help in recording history and benefiting our future generations.

Political Neglect

East Pakistan nurtured political grievances since 1947 which needed sympathetic consideration and political accommodation by the federal government. Instead, successive governments avoided taking difficult decisions and hoped that time would somehow mellow down regional sensitivities. The opposite happened. Growing regional restlessness gave India an opportunity to meddle in the affairs of East Pakistan by covert and overt means. The seeds of separation were sown.

India embarked on a long-term strategy to dismember Pakistan and prepared for this development politically, diplomatically and militarily. On the other hand, Pakistan wasted energy and resources on internal dissension that eroded her national unity from within and isolated her internationally.

India invested in the creation of Bangladesh to promote her own national interest. The amputation of East Pakistan, a blow to the unity of Pakistan, was, however, in the shape of Bangladesh, a re-confirmation of the Muslim League's Two-Nation theory. This theory might have been negated had Bangladesh opted to merge with India and lose its separate identity. Independent Bangladesh confirms the validity of the Two-Nation theory.

Trial of Politicians

The Agartala Conspiracy Trial made Sheikh Mujibur Rahman a hero and champion of the downtrodden people of East Pakistan. Thereafter, his political stars remained on the rise, and he became bolder and more determined to divide Pakistan.

Operational Policy

Military policy is influenced by the political objectives of a country. Defence and counter-insurgency are two different operations, each requiring a distinctly separate professional approach. While a defensive effort against aggression demands the concentration of forces and retention of reserves to regain vital or important areas if lost, counter-insurgency operations justify dispersion of effort to deal with minor incidents. Niazi's operational policy remained unclear, with minimum guidance given to the fighting units. The end result was that, to quote one example, Dhaka was denuded of troops when it needed them most. That the vital area remained un-defended, as was the case in Dhaka, boggles the military mind.

Fortress Defence

This demands a strong positional defence reinforced with bunkers, trenches, barbed wire, minefields, booby traps and other such defensive arrangements. The 'fortresses' and the 'strong points' ought to be mutually supporting, and the gaps between them fully covered, with patrolling at regular intervals. Given the operational environment in East Pakistan, and the paucity of military resources, the 'fortress' defence, except at a few critical points, was not a viable option. Military resources were frequently frittered away, and the best result was not extracted from the quantum of troops available in Eastern Command.

Operational Flexibility

War is a game of fleeting opportunities and fluctuating fortunes. Many a time, even a brilliantly conceived and carefully prepared plan of action requires modification at short notice to meet unforeseen developments. During combat, an inflexible senior military commander may surrender the initiative to the adversary at critical times. Likewise, a military leader who cannot read the mind of his adversary with a reasonable degree of accuracy, usually comes out second best. Inadequate flexibility of conduct and mind brought General Niazi to where he found himself in December 1971.

Niazi took charge of Eastern Command under extraordinary conditions and during the short tenure proved to be inadequate to the task.

Concept of Operations

The Indian high command had neither foreseen the capture of Dhaka nor tasked GOC-in-C Eastern Command as its mission. The Indian success covered many glaring flaws in their military plan. So quick was the collapse of the top brass defending East Pakistan that even the Indian army was amazed at the success achieved by the Mukti Bahini-led forces. The Bengalis, familiar with the defensive layout in various sectors, guided the aggressors to their targets via the safest available routes. East Pakistan was surrendered without a fight. Despite the odds against him, General Niazi cannot escape the responsibility of a surrender. Obviously, there were others, in the GHQ and in HQ CMLA, who shared the blame in varying proportion.

It was naive to believe that India would, at best, provide maximum support to the Mukti Bahini without its army physically crossing the international border. The sanctity of the border was argued to be the reason for this misconceived optimism. Such wishful assessment ignored India's hegemonic performance in the past. Since 1947 it had merged Sikkim, colonized Bhutan, blackmailed Nepal, destabilized Sri Lanka, engineered a coup in Maldives, provoked China in the Himalayas, and grabbed Kashmir. The sanctity of the borders of its neighbours had been frequently violated by New Delhi for self-serving reasons.

The faulty assessment of the enemy's intentions gave birth to defective plans that created a strategic imbalance of forces in terms of time and space. Weak leadership expedited the military fiasco.

Troop Fatigue

Prolonged deployment of soldiers on internal security duties, an unpleasant and unwelcome task for the military even at the best of times, causes attrition and fatigue in the troops. The military anguish in East Pakistan was tragic because the unfortunate conflict was fratricidal in nature, and local public sympathy was largely with the agitators. Working under such conditions for months at a stretch, the troops faced considerable psychological and emotional stress.

Higher Direction of War

East Pakistan, surrounded by hostile India and cut off from its power base in West Pakistan, faced an unenviable situation. It could neither be reinforced from the Western wing at short notice nor could its battle casualties be evacuated for rest and recovery. This difficulty, inherent in its geography, was a known phenomenon. While it could not be completely eradicated, its intensity could have been minimized. An effective system should have issued appropriate and timely directives to assist Commander Eastern Command in the planning of his defence effort, and in the implementation of the GHQ approved plans without interfering in the conduct of actual operations.

However, the reverse happened. The principle of the unity of command was violated. The battle raging a thousand miles away deserved full time supervision and constant guidance to retain control. This did not happen. The President did spend time in the GHQ operations room, but at times he was not instantly available to give orders on rapidly changing developments in the battlefield. There were communication gaps between the Eastern Command and the HQ CMLA and GHQ. HQ CMLA and GHQ functioned at separate places, and frequently one was unaware of what the other did or failed to do. The army's chain of command did not function smoothly. To make matters worse the Chief of Staff, General Hameed, the Principal Staff Officer to the President Lieutenant-General Peerzada, and the Chief of General Staff, Lieutenant-General Gul Hassan Khan were neither constantly available nor were they mentally tuned to a single frequency. The functioning of different power centres in combat was an invitation to disaster. After the war, each tried to escape responsibility by shifting blame onto the other.

Physical inter-wing contact between the commanders was not possible. In the Eastern wing, Niazi remained in his office during critical periods. This was against military training which required officers to lead from the front. Even an occasional visit by the senior commanders to the forward areas could have done wonders.

In short, the organization of the higher direction of war failed to function as an efficient, well-oiled machine during the war. The geographic separation of the two wings demanded extra effort to achieve overall coordination of developments in the battlefield. Instead, the controlling HQs worked in isolation. The inevitable happened. When catastrophe hit the country like a thunderbolt, each power centre blamed the other, and claimed to be an innocent spectator. In fact, they were all guilty of neglecting duties. If Niazi lost his will to fight at Dhaka, those directing the war from Islamabad did no better.

The military surrender at Dhaka was the culmination of the political, diplomatic, administrative and military failures of Pakistan spread over a prolonged period of time. At the final critical stage, the loss of political will in Islamabad and military skill in Dhaka combined to turn the tables on them. While many others share the blame for this monumental tragedy, neither President Yahya Khan nor the military can escape responsibility.

The East Pakistan catastrophe resulted from the cumulative failure of the country in political, diplomatic and military fields. While Pakistan was bifurcated in December 1971, the seeds of separation, eventually leading to her political and military defeat, were planted soon after the dawn of independence in 1947. They kept gaining strength with the errors of judgement made by all the political and military governments that ruled the country. They all share censure in varying degrees. Pakistan's blurred vision and national disunity encouraged hostile India to interfere in her internal affairs, first covertly and then with no holds barred.

Pakistan's failure to strengthen her political institutions and her political frailty were an invitation to disaster. If the politicians blunderd, weakening the national political system, the military harmed the country no less with its repeated intervention in civil affairs. Both are at fault, and both accuse each other for causing greater disservice to the state.

The fall of Dhaka resulted from a faulty political vision and weakness in generalship. While impetuous Bhutto and unfaithful Mujb share considerable blame for the national tragedy in 1971, General Yahya Khan bears the stigma for presiding over the destruction of the country. Pakistan's gallant soldiers, sailors and airmen did not get a fair chance to defend their country and demonstrate their skill while facing the orchestrated challenge of internal subversion and external aggression.

NOTES

1. General Douglas MacArthur, quoted by Richard Nixon, *The Real War*, Warner Books Inc., 1980, p. 1.
2. Sir W.W. Hunter, *The Indian Musalman,* London, 1871, reprinted in Lahore, Pakistan, 1961, p. 127.
3. Dr A. Basit, *The Breaking of Pakistan,* Liberty Publishers, Lahore, Pakistan, p. 112.
4. Ibid., pp. 25-26.
5. Ibid., p. 116.
6. Ibid., p. 114.
7. Ibid., p. 98.
8. Ibid., p. 111
9. Ibid., p. 113.
10. Ibid., p. 127.
11. Ibid., p. 129.
12. Ibid., p. 133.
13. *Dawn,* Karachi, 28 March 1971.
14. General K.M. Arif, *Working with Zia,* Oxford University Press, Karachi, 1995, p. 21.
15. *Pakistan Observer,* 22 December 1971.

16. Siddiq Salik, *Witness to Surrender,* Oxford University Press, Karachi, 1978, p. 31.
17. Lt-General Kamal Matinuddin, *Tragedy of Errors,* Wajidalis, Lahore, 1994, p. 158.
18. Ibid., p. 159.
19. Safdar Mahmood, *Pakistan Divided*, Ferozsons Ltd., Lahore, 1984, p. 92.
20. Salik, p. 31.
21. Kamal Matinuddin, *Tragedy of Errors*, p. 161.
22. Maudood Ahmad, *Bangladesh—Constitutional Quest for Autonomy,* University Press, Dhaka, 1976, p. 211.
23. Kamal Matinuddin, *Tragedy of Errors*, p. 163.
24. Kamal Matinuddin, *Tragedy of Errors*, p. 163.
25. Ibid., p. 166.
26. *Dawn,* 16 February 1971.
27. Ibid., 17 February 1971.
28. Z.A. Bhutto, *The Myth of Independence,* Oxford University Press, Lahore, 1969, p. 30.
29. Ibid., p. 28.
30. General K.M. Arif, *Working With Zia,* p. 22.
31. Maulana Kausar Niazi, *Pakistan Times,* 3 March 1971.
32. Kamal Matinuddin, *Tragedy of Errors,* p. 177.
33. *Dawn,* 1 March 1971.
34. Z.A. Bhutto, *The Myth of Independence,* p. 33.
35. *Dawn,* 16 March 1971.
36. Z.A. Bhutto, *The Myth of Independence,* p. 36.
37. Major-General Fazal Muqeem Khan, *Pakistan's Crisis in Leadership,* National Book Foundation, Islamabad, 1973, p. 57.
38. Brigadier Z.A. Khan, *The Way it Was*, DYNAVIS (Private) Ltd., Clifton, Karachi, 1998, p. 284.
39. Paul Martin, *London Times,* 25 March 1971.
40. Kamal Matinuddin, *Tragedy of Errors,* p. 250.
41. *The Pakistan Times*, Rawalpindi, 27 March 1971.
42. General K.M. Arif, *Working with Zia,* p. 30.
43. Sukhwant Singh, *Liberation,* p. 19.
44. Kamal Matinuddin, *Tragedy of Errors,* p. 260.
45. Qutubuddin Aziz, *Blood and Tears,* Din Muhammad Press, Karachi, 1974.
46. G.W. Choudhry, *Last Days of United Pakistan,* C. Hurst and Company, London, 1974, p. 85.
47. R. Sisson and Leo E. Rose, *War and Secession: Pakistan, India and the Creation of Bangladesh,* University of California Press, Berkeley, LA, p. 190.
48. Dr Henry Kissinger, *White House Years,* Little Brown and Company, Boston, MA, 1979, p. 863.
49. Ibid.

50. Kuldip Nayar, *Distant Neighbours,* Vikas Publishing House, New Delhi, p. 155.
51. K. Subramanyam, interview with Kamal Matinuddin, *Tragedy of Errors,* p. 282.
52. A.K. Azad, *India Wins Freedom,* Bombay, India, 1959, p. 227.

4

THE MILITARY UNDER ZIA

Zia in Various Roles

I first met Captain M. Ziaul Haq in 1952 when he arrived from his unit to become adjutant, Armoured Corps Centre and School, Nowshera, where I was serving as Wireless Instructor in the Technical Training Wing. Our respective duties—administration for Zia and training for me—kept us separate during parade hours and our infrequent contact was mostly in the officers mess. This was not a daily routine because Zia, married, lived with his family while I, a bachelor, lived in the mess. Zia had a dual personality, pleasant and jovial during off duty hours but formal and disciplined while on parade. During our nearly eighteen months stay at Nowshera, we developed a healthy respect for each other and maintained relations which were correct, official and reasonably affable.

During the next twelve years, I met Zia only on brief and rare occasions as we never served together in the same station or in the same formation. I met him while attending the Officers Career Course at the US Armor School, Fort Knox, Kentucky. Lieutenant-Colonel Zia, then on Associate Command and General Staff Officer's Course at Fort Leavenworth, attended a week long course at the Armor School, Kentucky, and we both frequently met during this week.

Promoted to brigadier in May 1969, Zia took command of 9 Armoured Brigade at Kharian where I was commanding a tank regiment. However, both of us were soon posted out, Zia went to Jordan on deputation, and I joined General Yahya Khan's HQ CMLA Secretariat at Rawalpindi. In mid 1971, I was

Colonel Staff (Colonel) 1 Armoured Division when Brigadier Zia, returning from Jordan, was attached with HQ 1 Armoured Division, pending his posting to command this division.

This was the beginning of our long association. During the command of 1 Armoured Division by Major-General Zia, I worked as Colonel Staff and later commanded 5 Armoured Brigade in the same division for two years. In March 1976, Zia became the army chief. I was then serving as Director Military Operations at GHQ. On my promotion to the rank of Major-General in 1976, Zia asked me to serve as Military Secretary in GHQ for a year before taking command of 1 Armoured Division. Fate intervened. Martial law was imposed in July 1977. Instead of commanding a field formation, I became Chief of Staff to the CMLA, and Zia kept me on this assignment till March 1984 when, on promotion to the rank of four-star general, I became Vice Chief of the Army Staff, a post from which I retired in March 1987. My prolonged association with Zia enabled me to observe national developments from close quarters, and actively participate in policy planning and statecraft.

Zia—the Person

A conservative human being, General Zia (1924-1988), was neither a saint, as eulogized by his admirers, nor a fiend, as condemned by his critics. A practising Muslim, he was a model of humility. Groomed under the influence of eastern culture in his boyhood, this value system had moulded his outlook on life. He neither advocated Pakistan adopting the mores of western permissive society nor did he impose his own beliefs on others. He desired his fellow citizens to follow their own faith and practice their own convictions and avoid criticizing the religious beliefs of other faiths and the cultural sensitivities of other doctrines. A perfectionist with a pronounced ego, Zia took pride in being a Pakistani and was a staunch nationalist.

A gracious and generous host, Zia had the knack of putting his visitors at ease with his modest nature and courteous manners. He received his guests and bid farewell to them with a disarming broad smile, a double-handshake and a courtesy unspoiled by the arrogance of officialdom expected of his elevated position. His unaccustomed visitors usually first entered his house with the apprehension of facing a stern, solemn, and serious-looking military ruler indulging in a monologue to justify his undemocratic rule. To many of them Zia was unduly fascinated with the Islamic way of life, and was a spoiler in the adoption of western democracy by Pakistan. The civil nature and the soft demeanour of the general-politician swiftly disarmed his guests, including such critics. While not all of them agreed with Zia's convictions expressed on national, international and other affairs, they were invariably impressed by his forthright views and firm approach, and the ease with which he calmly replied to provocatively needling and loaded questions. Zia did considerable homework with a select group of specialists before meeting the more important guests. Such meetings helped in evolving a strategy for presenting his point of view.

A workaholic by nature, Zia demanded well-drafted, neatly produced, and error-free written effort from his staff for his signatures. Typing mistakes irritated him. He would admonish his lower staff with remarks like, 'Isn't there a dictionary in your office?', or, 'It helps to be awake while typing', or, 'Perhaps you need a proofreader?' He dictated fluently and copiously to his steno-typist and left it to his personal staff to polish the draft to perfection.

He expected his Chief of Staff and his Military Secretary to be the encyclopedia of their respective spheres of work with their fingers always firmly placed on the pulse of all developments concerning their responsibilities. He demanded instant and accurate replies to his queries about events that had happened or had failed to occur. He wanted to keep abreast of all major developments and expected his senior staff officers to be instant human computers. A reply such as, 'I will check the details and let you know', was unacceptable to him, and such a person usually had a short tenure with him.

His non-military background and a humble lineage had injected a religious streak in young Zia that developed with age and experience, and became visibly pronounced as he rose in status. During the early years of his military life he was as attentive to his religious obligations as he was to music, films and sports. As he started climbing the professional ladder, he became a devout practising Muslim but he was not a bigot. He was moderate and modern in his religious thought-process and he invariably adopted a strategy of indirect approach to influence others. For example, he would keep a slot for prayers in the programme of work but would not ask others to join in if they desired to stay away from *salat*. He never imposed his personal religious beliefs on others, directly or indirectly. It was a matter of faith with him to combine politics with religion and govern an Islamic country in accordance with the dictates of the Quran and *Sunnah*. Zia's Military Secretary, when asked to comment on his religious beliefs and sensitivities described him as a 'very humble person, tolerant in religious issues and having a genuine love for Islam.'[1]

A staunch nationalist, Zia institutionalised wearing of the national dress in all official functions and promoted the use of Urdu, Pakistan's national language. These measures enjoyed popular support and became symbols of national identity. Such changes were grudgingly accepted by many of Pakistan's Western educated intellectuals and the stiff-necked bureaucrats who were used to wearing Western dress and conversing in English, at times with a heavy native accent. This was their way of asserting authority and supremacy in public dealing. While most of them could converse in not too elegant Urdu, their ability to write in the Urdu script was limited. The bureaucrats had always created hurdles in the promotion of the national language in the country.

Zia's humility was proverbial, almost captivating. One former air chief recalls that, 'Much after my retirement from service, I was once playing golf at Rawalpindi. Having noticed that President Zia was following behind I stopped at a tee point and waited for the general to catch up. After an exchange of greetings, I requested the president to overtake me as I had the time to play at a leisurely pace. Zia politely declined, despite my insistence, because it was "against the golf ethics." The President kept waiting till I teed off.'[2]

Zia—the Man and the Soldier

Zia showed a sustained stamina for work and commitment for soldiering that was noted by his seniors and colleagues even in his early military life. He attended the basic professional courses without any distinction and quickly adjusted himself to the military environment. One setback jolted Zia and left a lingering impression on him. After successfully completing his basic military training in the Officer's Training School, Mhow, India, Zia was commissioned in the Indian Army on 12 May 1945, and posted to 13 Lancers, then serving in Burma during the Second World War.

On Eid day, a holiday, the young Zia visited the mess of the Junior Commissioned Officers of his unit wearing *shalwar-kameez*. This surge of nationalism, an unacceptable 'unofficer like misconduct' in the heyday of the British *Raj*, earned Zia the ire of his British commanding officer who would not tolerate such 'nonsense' from a youngster. As a punishment he was posted to 6 Lancers, which took him for a short stint of service to Java and Malaya. This humiliation perhaps influenced his decision, later in life, to promote the wearing of the national dress in governmnet circles in Pakistan. Barring this incident, Zia's early soldiering was uneventful. He had a habit of losing his temper and occasionally using unprintable military language. His close friends called Zia a '*Maulvi*'—because of his visible religious proclivity.

A late sleeper and a late riser, Zia struggled hard throughout his military life to start his day at the appointed early hour. He never boasted of punctuality as a striking quality throughout his professional career—a trait that kept aggravating as he rose in life. But once he started his day, he worked without a break till late and remained remarkably fresh during his busy, often hectic, work schedule.

A patient listener, Zia held marathon meetings and encouraged all participants to present their views candidly and frankly, for or against the issues under discussion. He took copious notes and summed up the discussions at a leisurely pace, then issued clear and firm orders. Thereafter, he expected the participants to support the decisions wholeheartedly, irrespective of their own views on the subject.

Zia wore a denture after he lost two front teeth as captain in a cycle-polo match. The ball hit him so hard on his upper lip that his teeth were knocked off. He developed the habit of removing his false denture and adjusting it again with his tongue during the meetings. This looked odd, if not ugly, to his audience. He stopped fiddling with his false teeth in the later stage of his life.

Zia—the Commander

Zia, a graduate of the Command and Staff College, Quetta (1955) and Fort Leavenworth (1964), USA, became the Brigade Major in 3 Armoured Brigade. This appointment groomed him to shoulder higher responsibilities in his professional career. He took over command of his unit (1967-68) when its previous commanding officer was sacked after a lacklustre performance. Through painstaking effort he transformed the unit into such an effective fighting machine that it became the envy of the armoured division.

Zia's command of an armoured brigade (1969) was intercepted by his posting to Jordan. At that time, Jordan was engaged in combat with Syria and the Palestine Liberation Organisation. Zia's professional ability brought him into contact with the royal family and he developed a personal rapport with King Hussain and Crown Prince Hassan that lasted till his death. Zia's successful military performance was disliked by the authorities in Syria and by the PLO, and was a subject that he avoided discussing.

General Zia commanded an armoured division (1972-75) with enthusiasm and dedication. His style of command was direct, personal and unconventional. He deeply involved himself in training activities, and in the process kept himself and his subordinates engaged in hectic professional pursuit. This made him well acquainted with the performance of his units, and officers in the division. He left the armoured division a well-oiled striking formation—trained, motivated and ready to take the field at a short notice.

Zia was a quick, almost hasty, decision-maker who usually trusted a story on face-value and frequently issued orders without first ensuring the accuracy of the facts involved. On occasion the petitioners presented half-truths or a tainted version of a situation to elicit a decision favourable to them. This tendency often created difficulties for Zia when it was detected that the decision made had been based on faulty premise. Zia did not hesitate to modify his orders if convinced that they were based on inadequate data. When advised that a prior staff check might have saved him the embarrassment, Zia invariably had a simplistic reply, 'I trust all till they are proved wrong.'

The city of Multan, the home of an armoured division, was a professional cantonment that Pakistani and foreign visitors kept away from, particularly during its prolonged and inhospitable summer months. It provided adequate training opportunities unhampered by the burden of protocol and diversion to other, non-professional engagements. The close proximity of the training and firing areas permitted Zia to train the armoured division in its primary task. A typical training year included at least one division-scale signal exercise and three or four such exercises for every armoured brigade. In addition, every armoured brigade conducted one brigade-size exercise with troops. The units had one exercise per year with troops. These events were invariably attended by General Zia. In addition, he was often present during the squadron and company level exercises planned and conducted by the units.

Such events provided frequent opportunities to Zia to address the troops during the postmortem of the exercises held. On such occasions he spoke at length, was generous in praising good performance, and sternly but fairly criticized faults. The troops appreciated his personal involvement in training activities and his forthright analysis of their performance.

While comfortable with a command assignment, Zia hated staff work. He avoided leafing through the pages of files and endorsing orders on the cases submitted to him. Consequently, the reports and returns required to be sent to the higher headquarters under his personal signatures were usually delayed, at times beyond reasonable limits. He needed constant prodding to attend to his filework and the in-trays in his office were seldom empty. He was lethargic, almost phlegmatic, about writing the annual confidential reports on officers and was invariably in arrears. When his own formation staff or those from the Military Secretary's Branch in the GHQ pointed out to him that the absence of the ACRs might adversely affect the promotion and career planning of the officers, Zia usually put his right hand on his chest and remarked, 'I will personally protect their interests in the Army Selection Boards.' General Zia left behind dozens of incomplete ACRs requiring his remarks at the time of his death in an air crash. Some had not been endorsed for years. The affected officers suffered because he was no longer alive to protect their legitimate interests in the Army Selection Boards.

Zia—the Friend

Zia had a large group of acquaintances but his intimate friendship was restricted to a selected few. A pleasant go-getter, he was affectionate to his friends and helpful to them in their hour of need. He interacted well socially despite being an introvert. He spoke easily, laughed heartily, cracked jokes, was a chain smoker and never took hard drinks. He occasionally met his select group of old friends to relax from the demanding official routine. In such meetings they were nostalgic and laughed at themselves, recalling their own follies and achievements.

Zia knew whom to meet and when. Some of his immediate retired military associates suggested meeting him periodically to keep him abreast with certain ground realities which the official agencies might not be reporting to him. Zia would always welcome such suggestions but he never availed their unsolicited offers. On such matters he followed the Arab tradition of taking refuge behind religion to cover up his reluctance by saying 'inshallah'. The old guard had limited utility for Zia. It was his tactical compulsion to keep them amused and away from his official work. A ruler likes to hear what he wants to hear. Sincere advice does not fall in this category. He periodically rotated his close team to emphasize that he was the boss.

Zia was a helpful superior, quick to promise help to the needy. He seldom said 'no' to a request but his 'yes' did not mean that the request had been immediately granted. He honoured his commitments in his own timeframe and usually after being reminded a few times. He had developed the art of an imperial attitude to create personal loyalties in others.

Zia received his guests, friends and visitors—formal and informal—with courtesies far beyond the dictates of official protocol. Civil and obliging, President Zia treated them with a high degree of respect. The guests usually admired his humility and his disarming courtesy became proverbial during his lifetime. Even his critics acknowledged this quality but they called him a hypocrite, aiming to divert public attention by such gimmicks, from the stigma of being a dictator. To be fair to him, Zia never pretended to be a democrat. He was a dictator and he confessed with pride that the military was his constituency. To argue that Zia outwitted the people for eleven long years, is to insult the intelligence of so many placed so high. Zia had his failings, some too glaring and obvious to miss. But in hospitality and humility, as in politics, he outplayed many democrats in Pakistan who occupied dizzy heights.

One personal example illustrates Zia's helpful attitude. In the spring of 1981, I asked him for a week's leave, indicating my intention to visit a foreign country. 'What for?' inquired Zia. I told him that I had to attend a family wedding. He fired a second question, 'So, you will be accompanied?' Feeling uneasy about my financial position, I confessed that I could afford the expenditure for one person only, adding that I had given the option to my wife to represent our family at the marriage but she did not relish the thought of travelling alone. 'Family obligations have their importance', quipped Zia, adding 'Both of you should attend.' My wife and I were included in a delegation which happened to be visiting that country during the same time as the wedding. At times, I still feel uneasy that I yielded to the temptation and availed the offer that combined duty with pleasure.

Zia—the Family Man

Zia and Shafiqa, married on 10 August 1950, had five children, two sons and three daughters. The youngest daughter, Zain Zia, was a 'special' child and as moody and demanding as she was adorable. Her demands were biblical commands for Zia who did not, or could not, say no to the mentally challenged girl. On one occasion, she insisted on visiting Abbotabbad by helicopter and a dignitary had to be detained at short notice to accompany the child. On another occasion, she demanded that she be decorated in an investiture ceremony on 23 March at a function held at *Aiwan-e-Sadr*. Immediately after the formal closure of the official investiture ceremony, President Zia stood up to announce an unofficial private function. To the amusement of the assembled dignitaries, Zain Zia smartly walked up to the dais and received a fake decoration from her father.

When away from his home, General Zia spoke to his wife daily and frequently wrote to her. He was a devoted husband and a loving father. The family usually had dinner together when the evening was free from any official function. Their post-dinner conversation at the dining table was normally a prolonged affair.

Zia's military secretary describes Mrs Zia as 'a very noble lady' and all the members of his family as being 'very cooperative and helpful' in official dealings. Begum Zia normally did not interfere in the official business of the state, except on occasions when someone close to her demanded a personal favour. The military secretary found Zia very helpful to the lower personal staff working in his house and averse to changing them. On the contrary, he was harsh with the military secretary and at times showed his annoyance.[3]

Zia—the Senior Commander

Unlike official mail, General Zia was prompt in handling his personal correspondence and demi-official letters. The mail bag of his demi-official letters was usually heavy as he maintained personal and regular correspondence with his subordinates and contemporaries. As the division commander, it was normal for him to address letters directly to the unit commanders and at times to individual officers, copies of which were sent to the relevant brigade commanders under separate covers.

Major-General Zia was respectful to Commander 2 Corps, Lieutenent-General Muhammad Shariff under whom he worked, but their mutual relations were more formal and official than cordial or intimate. Both were respected, professional commanders but their personalities, working habits, lifestyles and social attitudes were very different. Shariff maintained a distance but Zia freely mixed with those serving under his command. His relations with the principal staff officers at General Headquarters were normal, but it was a difficult for them to extract reports from Zia on any special task given to him by the GHQ. In his own younger days Zia, the staff officer, did his paperwork with meticulous care and painstaking accuracy. While so doing, he invariably placed a premium on the quality of effort rather than on the timely submission of a report.

By the time he commanded a division, Zia had considerably mellowed down temperamentally. But occasionally he would use four-letter words to unburden himself. On one occasion he demoted a major on the spot for committing an error in training.

While the officer was at fault, prudence demanded that Zia show greater tolerance.

Zia took over command of 1 Armoured Division in early 1972. At that time, national morale was low and its impact was clearly visible in the army. However, the military speedily absorbed the shock of defeat in East Pakistan, and rehabilitated its bruised professional image.

Acting swiftly, the dynamic Z. A. Bhutto worked rapidly to restore the confidence of the people. The Pakistan Army was shaken once more when the Army Chief, Lieutenant-General Gul Hassan Khan, appointed on 20 December 1971, was unceremoniously retired on 3 March 1972.[4] Bhutto found Gul Hasan reluctant to accept political interference in the internal functioning of the army. He was given an ambassadorial assignment in Portugal to keep him at a safe distance from Pakistan.

General Tikka Khan, who had been bypassed for promotion only months earlier, replaced General Gul Hassan Khan as Chief of the Army Staff. A down to earth soldier, Tikka Khan was gifted with a phenomenal memory, a dogged resistance, native wisdom and nerves of steel. As Director Military Operations, if my telephone buzzed after midnight or just before dawn, the person on the other end was often the Army Chief seeking information about some event on some hot spot on the border. Tikka Khan kept his fingers on the pulse of events and he knew every thing that happened in the Pakistan Army. Tikka had no inhibition in reaching down to any junior to collect the information required by him. In March 1976, he became due for retirement from the Army and his successor was to be appointed.

Zia—the Army Chief

Bhutto, riding the crest of his political popularity, was firmly entrenched in the seat of power, or so it appeared to his supporters and critics alike. Weak and fragmented, the opposition parties did not have in their ranks any person of the stature and calibre of Bhutto. He was firm and decisive in exercising his authority. The 1973 constitution had authorized Prime Minister Bhutto to select a new army chief to replace General Tikka Khan. No one had the authority or the courage to question his nomination.

The seniority order of the then lieutenant-generals was Muhammad Shariff, Muhammad Akbar Khan, Aftab Ahmad Khan, Azmat Bakhsh Awan, Agha Ali Ibrahim Akram, Malik Abdul Majid, Ghulam Jilani Khan, and Muhammad Ziaul Haq. Prime Minister Bhutto had a personal rapport with all these eight general officers. The intelligence agencies and other instruments of the state had painstakingly checked their credentials, suitability and competence for further promotion. Besides, Bhutto's kitchen cabinet had evaluated every individual and rendered its advice. The assessment and the selection process took months to complete and nothing was left to chance.

The prime minister, known for his 'no-forgive, no-forget' temperament, had personally observed the performance of the panel of candidates, and had reservations mostly on non-professional issues. In Bhutto's own judgement some were too independent-minded to rise higher, others were unacceptable for being 'Ayub Khan's protégés, and yet others had qualities not to the liking of the prime minister.

Bhutto dug deep and appointed the junior most—Muhammad Ziaul Haq—to command the Pakistan Army. To his mind, Zia was the best choice for the country and for the army, and the safest for him personally.

The law required the prime minister to appoint the chairman of the Joint Chiefs of Staff Committee (JCSC), and the services chiefs of the army, navy and air force at his discretion which was absolute, unqualified and unquestionable. By convention, such appointments usually involved a few supercessions. However, the supercession of as many as seven general officers senior to Zia raised some eyebrows although this was not such an unusual phenomenon.

The Chairman JCSC and the services chiefs earn their posts because they are judged to be the most suitable commanders by the prime minister for their respective appointments. This selection is a legal responsibility that is supposed to be exercised with great care, after indepth reflection. All decisions that affect national security are taken after due deliberation. By appointing Zia to command the Pakistan Army, therefore, Mr Bhutto performed his legal duty to the best of his ability and in the national interest. This was not a favour to Zia. It is uncharitable to Bhutto to suggest that he wilfully appointed an undeserving Zia to lead the Pakistan Army. Bhutto knew what he did and why. He was too sharp a person and too experienced an administrator to indulge in experimentation in the game of power.

It is hypothetical to speculate if a person other than General Zia would have imposed martial law in 1977, or taken a lenient view of Bhutto's crime and conviction in 1979. Under those circumstances, any other person might not have acted differently from Zia. The ground realities provide the indicators. Zia's military commanders had unanimously approved the imposition of martial law; the people supported the act by their conduct and behaviour; and the Supreme Court upheld the decision as lawful. Similarly, a unity of military command existed during the trial and execution of Bhutto. The latter was a complex and painful decision involving numerous factors, constitutional, legal, political, psychological, moral and diplomatic. Bhutto was convicted by the civil courts after a full, open and transparent trial spread over months.

Zia—the Politician

General Zia had a political instinct that was seemingly dormant but surfaced occasionally from the time he became a major-general. The country faced a difficult period when he was promoted to command 1 Armoured Division soon after the fall of Dhaka. The field formations were then deployed, and Zia employed his division personnel on anti-malaria mosquito duties and on area cleaning and hygiene work in the nearby villages without any request made by the civil administration for military assistance. The news carried to the top that the military was voluntarily participating in projects of public welfare.

Back in Multan, General Zia maintained contact with senior civil officials of the division who were invited to his house in military functions. A distinguished visitor to his residence was Bhutto himself during his tour of Multan, when the military wives and children respectfully lined up along the Fort Colony road *en route* to Zia's house showering flower petals on his motorcade. The merging of politics with military duty raised many eyebrows. A little later, General Zia addressed the garrison officers. One junior officer mustered the courage to ask Zia during the question hour the necessity of route lining by the military families during Bhutto's visit. The impertinence of the inexperienced youngster became the beginning of his long and arduous tribulation in service. His military career was cut short and he was soon hounded out of the army.

Major-General Zia presided over the military court that tried the persons accused in the 1973 conspiracy case. The then ISI chief, Lieutenant-General Ghulam Jilani Khan, states that Bhutto was personally obliged to Zia for convicting the persons, and for keeping him informed about the progress of the trial. Bhutto had also appreciated the gesture of appointing him as Colonel-in-Chief of the Armoured Corps, an appointment permitted under the rules. General Zia was then the senior most Armoured Corps officer, but the proposal for Bhutto's appointment had been initiated by Major-General S. Wajahat Hussain GOC 6 Armoured Division who held the installation ceremony at Kharian. Zia had agreed with Wajahat's plan.

'General Zia was one of the most extraordinary men I have met. Power makes men arrogant, proud, short-tempered and corrupt, and absolute power corrupts absolutely,'so writes Mr M.P. Bhandara, adding, 'In Zia's case it seemed to have the opposite effect. The more firmly he was in the saddle, the more benign be became. People would say that his extreme courtesy to all and sundry was a put-on job. I think not'...'Unlike most rulers he would never dominate a conversation; an attentive listener who would put any interlocutor at total ease. His courtesy was legendary.'

'Zia's years were a waste. His Afghan policy was courageous. He should be immortalized by the Americans for playing such a large part in the unraveling of the Soviet Union. But, his regime was a paradigm of virtue, compared to the corruption of his successors.'[5]

Bhandara told me that he had once asked Zia why Bhutto's government was toppled. Zia gave an evasive reply saying, 'some day I will give you information about Bhutto that will make your hair stand on end.' Zia told Bhandara that the disintegration of the Pakistan Army was unacceptable to him.

Those who rule have to judge the public mood to stay in power, know the tolerance limit of the people on taxation and other harsh policy measures, and steer a safe course to escape public wrath and trouble. They must outwit their political opponents and deny them a chance to remove the political rug from under their feet. General Zia had the political acumen to do all this, and more. Starting as a political novice, he soon made his presence felt and gained stature and authority internally and internationally. One may differ with his policies, views and preferences, and there were good reasons for such criticism, but his prolonged rule for eleven years was a testimony to his political skill. He might have remained at the helm of affairs in the country for some more time but for his mysterious death at the prime of power.

Zia had developed a knack of judging people and commenting on them in his lighter moments. He promoted a general officer to a safe and secluded appointment to ease him out of a public dealing assignment because he was averse to meeting people. Senator Maulana Kausar Niazi became a bitter critic of Zia in the parliament. At the time of re-election to the Senate he did not enjoy sufficient electoral support for success. He approached Zia for a meeting to explain matters. Zia did not respond. Niazi requested me to intervene and arrange his audience with Zia. I mentioned to the president that his 'friend' wanted his help to get a Senate ticket. Immediately sensing the person, a smiling Zia told me, ' If Niazi is a "Bas...d" I am a bigger one.'

Bhutto Outsmarts Zia

General Zia took charge of the Pakistan Army with the proverbial zeal of a new incumbent. His elevation coincided with several retirements in the senior echelons of the army, and Zia desired to fill in these vacancies with fresh promotions on a priority basis. Quick promotions, Zia felt, would create a healthy first impact on his command. The promotion of the general officers involved the government's approval which caused some delay because of bureaucratic routine. Zia desired a quick decision.

The army chief met Prime Minister Z. A. Bhutto, informed him about the vacancies pending in the general officers ranks and requested that his recommendations for fresh promotions and retirements may be processed with speed. 'An early announcement will be well received in the army', argued General Zia.

Supporting the request, the prime minister gave his approval. He went on to advise Zia that since all military promotion cases were routinely processed through the Inter-Services Intelligence Directorate, he might discuss his recommendations with Lieutenant-General Ghulam Jilani Khan first before submitting the proposals to the Ministry of Defence. This would save time argued Bhutto, adding, 'I will ask Jilani to contact you.'

Jilani met Zia the following day, who apprised the ISI Chief about the proposed immediate promotion and retirement plan. The retired list contained the name of Major-General Abdullah Malik. Jilani conveyed to the prime minister the gist of his conversation with Zia, pointing out that from the scrutiny point of view he had no comments to offer on the changes being proposed by the new army chief.[6] Bhutto's purpose was served. He was forewarned about Zia's name list.

The spadework completed, the Bhutto-Zia meeting was held to consider the retirement of major-generals and promotion of major-generals and brigadiers. Taking the promotion cases first, General Zia named the major-generals recommended for further promotion in the order of their seniority, starting with the senior most Mohammad Iqbal Khan. 'Oh', interrupted the forewarned

Bhutto, 'This will mean appointing a new Chief of the General Staff'. Unaware of Bhutto's scheme, Zia replied in the affirmative. Beaming with confidence, Bhutto said, with a smiling face, 'You must have a team of your own choice', adding, 'Go ahead, I approve your promotion plan in toto.' A relaxed and happy Zia thanked Bhutto who assessed that the time was ripe for him to strike.

Before Zia could name a person from the list of the proposed retirement plan, Bhutto bowled a political googly and said, 'I think Abdullah Malik will make a good Chief of the General Staff.' A cornered Zia, who had this general officer on his retirement list, was caught on the wrong foot. Discretion guided him to accept the inevitable without reservation. Bhutto promptly ordered a fresh cup of coffee, and directed his staff to put him through to Abdullah Malik. In the presence of Zia, he congratulated Abdullah Malik on his new and prestigious assignment. The Bhutto guile humbled Zia. This was Bhutto's first political recipe for the new army chief. I may state that the above said conversation was narrated to the author by General Jilani.

Zia Heads the Army

With his unorthodox work habits and personalized command style, Zia started as the army chief on a high note. His armour background was an asset as well as a liability for him. Asset, because he was free from the professional rivalries in the infantry-dominated Pakistan Army built in the British tradition, and a liability because his direct contact with infantry had been infrequent as he had mostly served in the armoured formations. The non-armoured troops had seldom heard him on professional issues. While he was respected in the armoured corps, the bulk of his contemporaries in other arms and services did not know him too well.

Innovative and dynamic, Zia was receptive to new ideas and encouraged his subordinates to experiment. He allowed freedom of expression, even dissent, knowing that once a final decision was taken, his military team would implement it in letter and spirit without any reservation in the proverbial tradition of the Pakistan Army. He had tuned his command to his frequency and knitted a well-oiled team. Generous in praise, he gave credit where due without reservation and often followed his verbal approbation with a written communication personally signed by him. He was equally frank in criticism. He was generous in providing a helping hand to the needy, but only at public expense!

General Zia commanded the Pakistan Army from 1 March 1976, till his death in the aircraft crash on 17 August 1988. This made his command the longest and the most controversial in Pakistan's turbulent history. His prolonged tenure as the head of state cum the head of government made him the absolute ruler and his 'own constituency'—the military— came to occupy the centre-stage in national politics.

General Tikka Khan, Zia's predecessor, had introduced a New Military System (NMS) that had reduced the army's manpower ceiling to 85 per cent of its sanctioned authorization. Under this system, some units and formation headquarters were converted into 'caderized form' with their manpower reduced between fifty to seventy-five per cent of their authorized Tables of Organization and Equipment. The intention was to curtail military expenditure in peace time, and to bring up the caderized units to their full manpower complement at the time of national emergency. The reduction in manpower was made at a time when the the threat posed to national security had not diminished. This created an operational imbalance in the army, and the NMS was resented by all formations.

The NMS was introduced on an assurance that the government would provide additional funds to buy hardware and military equipment to compensate for the loss of the army's manpower. In practice, while the army's manpower ceiling was reduced, the promised additional equity remained elusive. Zia sought the government's permission to dismantle the NMS. As Director of Military Operations, I made a presentation to the federal cabinet for reversing its previous decision. After a lively discussion, the NMS was discarded but the army ceiling remained at 85 per cent for reasons of economy. It took the Pakistan Army two decades to get its manpower ceiling restored.

The Zia command period witnessed a number of positive developments that improved the army's operational plans and its logistic capability. While its professional review is outside the scope of this narration, a few indicators are listed to illustrate the point. For example, the Army Aviation was upgraded into a separate corps, the Army Medical College was established, an Officers Training School was created, and a Junior Academy formed to act as a feeder for the Pakistan Military Academy, Kakul. Besides, the Financial Regulations were revised that improved the handling of the annual budgets of the three services, and rationalized the financial powers of the services chiefs. Okara and Gujranwala cantonments were established, and a plan was made for a housing scheme for army officers.

One general-officer, Lieutenant-General Saeed Qader, closely associated with General Zia for over a decade, has listed his three good qualities as, 'humbleness, strong determination and ability in selecting his team members.' In his opinion, Zia's weak traits were, 'hypocrisy, reluctance to punish defaulters and financial laxity at public expense. His lavish style set a bad precedence.'[7]

The Tajammal Episode

Major-General Tajammal Hussain Malik, a courageous general officer with infantry background, enjoyed a healthy professional reputation. His valour and courage in combat had earned him the respect of his colleagues and contemporaries. He was serving in East Pakistan in the rank of brigadier when Dhaka fell in December 1971, and he became a prisoner of war. Interned in a camp at Bareilly, India, he was repatriated to Pakistan in April 1974. Promoted to the rank of major-general in November 1974, Tajammal commanded an infantry division located at Jhelum.

The stigma of defeat in East Pakistan left a deep scar on Tajammal's mind. The humiliation of captivity was distressful but his personal robustness sustained him in facing the twin ordeals of surrender and captivity. Tajammal's wounded pride turned him into a practising religious devotee. His views on life hardened, and he became self-opinionated and over-sensitive.

Frustration took the better of Major-General Tajammal when he was superceded for promotion to the rank of a lieutenant-general in 1976. He silently sulked and criticized the promotion system that had earlier elevated him to the rank of major-general. He reflects his own state of mind by claiming to have asked Major-General Akhtar Abdur Rahman, also superceded in 1976, on 30 March *'coup kar dayo'* (carry out a *coup d'etat*).[8] Akhtar spurned the offer, 'just smiled' and walked away. A little later Akhtar went back to Tajammal and said, 'We haven't talked.' Tajammal replied, 'Don't worry, we haven't talked.' The incident was hushed up and the sensitive conversation remained unreported to the higher authorities.

The bug planted in Tajammal's mind kept nourishing in secrecy and the time came when he could suppress his frustration no longer. He conceived a scheme to topple the Bhutto government and discussed his plan with his Colonel Staff, Colonel (later Major-General), Mohammad Aslam Zuberi, asking him to join in. Zuberi was loyal to his immediate commander but he was more loyal to the institution he served. He spilled the beans to his corps commander, Lieutenant-General Faiz Ali Chishti. The game was over for Tajammal. His military career abruptly ended when, in his own words, the Army Chief, General Zia, told him on 3 April 1976, 'You are a fanatic, I have decided to retire you.'[9]

After his forced retirement from military service Tajammal took refuge in politics. He joined Tehrik-i-Istaqlal, only to leave it, and formed his own political party. He realized soon enough that the responsibility was difficult to handle. Disillusioned, he turned against Zia and became his bitter foe. As confessed by him, 'I thought I must play my part in getting the nation rid of the curse of military rule. I, therefore, started working for a military/politico revolution to overthrow General Zia's illegal and un-Islamic military leadership.'[10] How his own failed effort would have been 'legal' and 'Islamic' was left unexplained by Tajammal.

Four years later, it was past midnight when the telephone on my bedside table rang. The caller requested an urgent meeting, insisting that he could not wait till dawn to unburden himself. Minutes later he arrived, along with an army major, who narrated a conspiracy which on face value appeared credible and too sensitive to ignore. I telephoned the DGI Major-General Akhtar Abdur Rahman and asked him if he had any house guests. Surprised, he inquired if all was well with the president. 'He is resting,' I replied, adding, 'but I need a hot cup of coffee at your house in the next few minutes along with two accompanying guests.'

A visibly worried Akhtar was waiting in his drawing room when I pulled up my car in front of his house, in the very early hours of the day. Both of us met alone for a few minutes before my two guests were requested to join us. The major repeated his story and mentioned that he was attending a course of instruction at the College of Military Intelligence, Murree, and had only four more hours available after which he would have to rush back to the hill station to join his class. He confessed that he had travelled to Rawalpindi during the night without seeking permission from the College and was keen to keep his journey a secret. He was allowed to leave after Akhtar fixed with him the time and place in Murree where his designated nominee would meet the major after office hours that day.

I asked Akhtar to take charge of the case and launch a surveillance effort to identify the scheming individuals. 'Should we not inform the old man first,' inquired Akhtar? 'This is an odd time to disturb his rest', I replied, adding, 'I will brief him in the morning.'

The major attending the course at Murree had good reason for his midnight escapade to the federal capital. Based on the information provided by him, it was easy to launch a surveillance effort. The bits and pieces of the *coup* plan when collected, collated and synthesized with speed made sense. The plan envisaged the arrest of all the corps commanders assembled at

Rawalpindi for a preplanned formation commanders conference. Also to be arrested were Akhtar Abdur Rahman and myself. Simultaneously, General Zia was to be captured alive from his residence at the appointed time on the designated night and forced to record a message transferring power to a Revolutionary Command headed by Tajammal. This done, all the general officers commanding divisions were to be retired.

General Zia was to be taken into custody after duping the military sentries performing guard duties at the President's House. It so happened that Tajammal had once commanded the battalion that was presently performing guard duties at the President's House. His own son, Lieutenant Naveed Tajammal Hussain, and his nephew Major Riaz Hussain, were then serving in this battalion. These two officers, as co-conspirators, were to arrange entry into Zia's residence on the pretext of checking the guard. The misconceived adventure backfired because it was simplistic and naive. Tajammal was arrested in the early hours of 6 March 1980, from Lahore. He and his son and nephew were tried by a field general court martial in May 1980, and were found guilty. Tajammal was sentenced to fourteen years rigorous imprisonment. His son and nephew were sentenced to ten year's rigorous imprisonment each.

Officers Promotion System

The Pakistan Army officers promotion system is competitive, institutionalized and increasingly demanding at each successive level of command. The rank structure of the officers is like a pyramid with a large base that sharply tapers upwards to form the apex which has just enough space for one person—the Chief of the Army Staff. An officer ascends the promotion ladder after passing through a tough selection process developed over a prolonged period of time.

Promotions up to the rank of major are made on the basis of seniority from amongst those who qualify in the prescribed promotion examinations. Beyond the rank of a major, all promotions are made by the Selection Boards on the basis of seniority-cum-efficiency. The criteria for efficiency has been quantified into mathematical figures.

Regional selection boards comprising nominated general-officers recommend promotion cases from major to lieutenant-colonel. The board proceedings are placed before a ratification board presided over by the army chief. This board may approve, reject or modify the recommendations made by the regional selection boards. The decision taken by the ratification board is final.

Promotion to the ranks of colonel and brigadier are made by another broad-based selection board with all the formation commanders and the principal staff officers at the General Headquarters as its members. This board, presided over by the chief of army staff, makes recommendations with respect to each officer. The board proceedings are submitted to the government for approval.

Brigadiers are considered for promotion to the rank of major-general in a board comprising all the corps commanders that is presided over by the chief of the army staff. The board recommendations are subject to approval by the government.

The selection boards consider the demonstrated performance of the affected officers. The dossiers are forwarded to the Ministry of Defence along with the board's recommendations for obtaining government approval. This permits an independent assessment.

An officer superceded by the board has the right to appeal to the government and such an appeal, if and when made, cannot be withheld by General Headquarters. Experience shows that the right to appeal is exercised only by a small minority. This implies that the promotion system enjoys the confidence of a vast majority of the officers.

Such in-built checks and balances make the selection process fair, competitive and transparent. The high suppression rates are reflected by the fact that only about three per cent of the total officers reach the ranks of lieutenant-colonel/colonel and a mere one-third of one per cent rise to the rank of a major-general.

For a system to work perfectly, those who implement it must be perfect too. Even a fair system gets eroded if institutions are weakened by strong personalities for extraneous reasons. Some examples of army promotions illustrate the point. Brigadier Luqman Mahmood was approved for further promotion by the selection board. Prime Minister Bhutto vetoed his promotion because he considered this officer too 'sharp.' His professional career was abruptly cut short. The omnipotent Bhutto's intervention also resulted in the premature retirement of Brigadiers Bashir Ahmad, Mohammad Asghar Khan and Rashid H. Lodhi on the basis of unsubstantiated intelligence reports.

The 1975 Army Selection Board approved Brigadier Saeed Qadir for promotion to the rank of major-general. Bhutto withheld his promotion without corroborating it by any reason to GHQ. The Army Selection Board reconsidered the case of this officer the following year and again approved him for promotion. Mr Bhutto again stood in his way, and in April 1976 commented in a Pay Committeee meeting that 'this officer (Saeed Qadir) disagrees with our policies'. The Army Selection Board 1977 approved this officer's promotion for the third consecutive year. On this occasion, General Zia told Saeed Qadir that Bhutto wanted him to be retired but he had resisted the demand. Fate intervened. General Zia's martial law in July 1977, removed Bhutto. Saeed rose to become a lieutenant-general. After retirement from military service in 1985, he was elected a senator. But his woes followed him. It was the turn of Benazir to pick up the thread of vengeance against Saeed Qadir from where her father had left off. The Benazir government had him arrested, denied him freedom for two years and framed charges against him based on biased 'evidence'. After the fall of her government, the Nawaz Sharif administration withdrew the case and Saeed Qadir was exonerated.

During the command of General Tikka Khan, Brigadier Arbab Niaz was approved for further promotion by the Army Selection Board. In anticipation of his promotion, the army chief placed him in 18 Division to command this formation. An awkward situation was created when Bhutto withheld the promotion of this officer. Tikka Khan felt, and rightly so, that whereas the promotion was the prerogative of the government, the posting of the officer was his discretion. Arbab acted as the General Officer Commanding of the division for a whole year without wearing the major-general's rank. The Army Selection Board again approved Arbab for promotion the next year but the Bhutto government once again denied him the promotion. General Zia's martial law brought justice to Arbab, who later retired as a lieutenant-general.

Such was the officers promotion system inherited by General Zia in 1976. This institution worked smoothly during the early years of his command. However, the long military rule and the lack of political accountability of military acts eroded the system. Despite its firm roots and established traditions, the selection process was on occasions misused, violated or manipulated in a subtle way to benefit some officers and damage others.

By tradition, a brigadier who failed to get promoted to the rank of a major-general in his first attempt in an Army Selection Board was rarely elevated subsequently. The logic was simple. A potential major-general is usually a galloper who makes his ability to command a division felt before he gets promoted. The rank of a general officer must carry dignity and respect, and an unblemished record of service. During the Zia era, this distinction got diluted. His political compulsions to stay in power required him to selectively compromise on principles. He used a political approach in retaining the support of 'his own constituency' and in this process, the promotion policy came in handy.

'The key members in his military team were used and discarded by Zia. He encouraged personal loyalty by promoting some officers with inadequate qualifications or by ignoring the character failings of a few others. Such one-man acts weakened the institution.'[11] To quote one case, Zia appreciated the flying skill of the PAF's Falcon pilot who frequently flew him. In a surge of generosity, he told the pilot that he was promoted to his next rank. The air chief explained to the president that this promotion would supercede some officers senior to this pilot who were equally competent in their profession. Besides, it would violate the promotion system. Zia reneged.[12] This was neither the first incident of Zia's selective benevolence nor the last.

Zia institutionalized the system of inducting military officers into civil departments. This system had been followed in the past by different governments but on a case to case and *ad hoc* basis. This was a good utilization of experienced manpower provided the selection process remained even-handed. Normally, it was customary to retire major-generals and brigadiers on completion of their respective service limits. This tradition was relaxed with respect to some officers who got extensions up to their age limits and beyond to compensate for their personal loyalty. The more lucky and persevering officers were promoted despite repeated previous suppressions. Such acts, though small in number, eroded a fine system.

General Zia had a soft corner for a brigadier whose promotion, he knew, would be opposed in the Army Selection Board. He had his name deleted from the promotion list on the pretext that a 'clear vacancy' did not exist in the officer's corps. Months later, a vacancy was created and a nominated selection board was held on an *ad hoc* basis to consider the promotion of this solitary individual. The board rose to the occasion.

In the mid-eighties, one major-general approaching his retirement age felt that the army had not yet fully benefitted from his wisdom. A junior officer serving under him was known to have the ears of the 'old man'. He pressurized this junior to propose to General Zia that he be promoted to lieutenant-general. The bewildered junior resisted the demand of his insistent senior but not for long. Buckling under sustained pressure he mustered courage and explained his predicament to General Zia who pretended not to hear the request. The general officer kept goading his junior to repeat his request to the president whenever he found him in a receptive mood. The harrassed junior obliged. Perseverance paid. 'Go and tell him,' said Zia one day 'that he would be promoted.' He didn't have to wait for long to wear his new rank.

Normally a patient listener, General Zia could take criticism in a seemingly sporting style without showing annoyance. His senior military colleagues differed with him on numerous issues and presented their points of view at times with a touch of humour, on occasions forcefully and sometimes in a brutally frank manner. Rarely, if ever, did Zia show resentment against such verbal assaults. He knew that his colleagues were sincere and did not have any selfish motives. His military colleagues knew the limits of their criticism, and notwithstanding their in-house censure of policies, they invariably defended his decisions in public unanimously.

On the other hand, General Zia's poise concealed a complex personality. The person hidden deep inside him was different from the one normally seen. This inner personality tolerated criticism within certain limits only, and could be excitable and touchy. Zia easily forgave minor lapses of personal discipline but was less generous in forgetting or forgiving premeditated emotional outbursts made in public. During his military rule he addressed the defence services officers on many occasions. On a few occasions, some junior and middle-rank officers asked searching qestions concerning the more sensitive issues like the execution of Bhutto, the prolonged martial law and the postponement of the election schedule announced by him. Not taking such questions kindly, Zia showed his anger and vindictiveness. Those asking such questions came to grief and were invariably hounded in a manner that showed bias. The army lost a handful of upright and intelligent officers who had the courage to ask discerning questions.

Extensions to Services Chiefs

Pakistan's political performance might have been less arduous had the services chiefs regularly retired after completing their fixed four year tenure. In 1975, the Bhutto government reduced this time period to three years, but allowed the then army chief General Tikka Khan to complete his four year term.

General Zia retained this policy in letter but violated it in practice. He favoured a four year term for every service chief and liberally gave extensions to them on a case to case basis. Some served for more than four years. I once suggested to him to revert to a fixed four year tenure for all the services chiefs as the grant of extension on a discretionary basis went against the institution. With a cynical smile spread on his face he said casually, 'why amend the policy letter when the desired purpose was being served.' This meant that every retiring service chief might request for an extension, which Zia, in his benevolence might grant.

Bhutto's Political Eclipse

When General Zia became the army chief, Prime Minister Bhutto was deeply entrenched in power, and his popularity graph was on the rise, despite his harsh rule. The opposition, weak and fragmented, did not pose a serious electoral challenge to Bhutto's attempt for a second term in office for which elections were to be held in March 1977. The Gallup Polls predicted a comfortable majority for the ruling PPP in any fair electoral contest.

Bhutto planned an overkill of the opposition to muster a two-third majority in the new House to enable him to amend the constitution. The elections were blatantly rigged to satisfy Bhutto's lust for unbridled authority. The PPP's landslide victory (155 seats) with the opposition's Pakistan National Alliance, (PNA) getting only thirty-six seats, was the beginning of the end for Bhutto. The election 'farce' was rejected by the PNA and the people, and a popular, country-wide agitation destabilized the Bhutto government.

The public tide turned against Bhutto, who was called a wrongdoer and unworthy of further trust. His fate might have followed a different course if he had accepted his errors, apologized to the people and agreed to hold the elections again. But he was too egotistic to go down in history as the 'election-rigger'. By opting to defend his indefensible action he put himself on a downhill slope from which it was impossible for him to rise to power again.

Initially, General Zia stoutly defended the Bhutto Government and from March through July used military force to suppress the political agitation raging against it. The use of the military to support the once-populist leader put the army under great strain. The troops neither saw the logic nor relished the thought of using military force against their own agitating countrymen. They showed their sentiments when they fired their weapons in the air instead of directing them against the anti-Bhutto, slogan-chanting agitators. Three brigadiers in the city of Lahore declined to open fire on the protesters.

Such incidents ran the risk of eroding military discipline and caused great anxiety in the top echelons of the army's command structure. Zia was simultaneously pulled in two opposite directions. On the one hand, a split in the army was totally unacceptable to him. On the other hand, Bhutto wanted the military to bail him out from his self-created political quagmire. On Bhutto's prompting, the Chairman of the Joint Chiefs of Staff Committee and the three services chiefs issued an unprecedented press note on 27 April reiterating their loyalty to the government and pledging 'their constitutional obligations in support of the present legally constituted government.' This statement was legally flawed, morally unjustified and politically unwise for the services chiefs to make.

The ruling PPP and the agitating PNA held month long negotiations between them to evolve a mutually acceptable political settlement. An agreement was almost reached but the crisis in confidence failed to clinch the issue. The PNA wanted additional legally binding guarantees because it distrusted Bhutto's government in honouring the negotiated deal. General Zia decided to take over the country's administration on 4 July 1977. He backtracked at the last moment when it seemed that the elusive agreement was on the verge of being signed. On 5 July 1977, the military intervened and General Zia appointed himself as the Chief Martial Law Administrator. On face value, the country heaved a sigh of relief. The agitation ended and calmness returned. But the nation suffered a deep invisible cut of a different kind from which it bled for a long while.

Dual Duties

General Zia gave a ninety day agenda for his extra-constitutional rule of the country, and publicly pledged to hold elections on 18 October 1977. Little did he realize then that it was easier said than done. After two postponements, party-less elections were eventually held in February 1985.

The promulgation of martial law necessitated the appointment of a martial law administrator in all the provinces. Initially, the corps commanders at Peshawar, Lahore, Karachi and Multan, along with a small staff, were given the dual task of martial law duties. The system of dual duties worked to the army's disadvantage, and it led to the segregation of military duties and the full time appointment of serving lieutenant-generals as martial law administrators in the provinces. None of the general officers so appointed held the charge of the military formations as well except for Lieutenant-General Rahimuddin Khan, who continued to command 2 Corps at Multan. This exception, an odd arrangement, was not well received and was criticised. To be fair to Rahim, he had told Zia that he would accept the governorship only if he continued to command 2 Corps.

Each province also had some deputy martial law administrators and sub martial law administrators. They all held dual charges. In addition, some officers performed military court duties. As a matter of policy, they were frequently rotated every few months to keep them up-to-date with their profession and away from the temptations offered by the civil environment.

The early inductions at the federal level were Lieutenant-General Ghulam Hassan Khan as CMLA's Adviser on National Security and Lieutenant-General Faiz Ali Chishti, first informally, then as Chairman of the Election Cell, and still later as a minister in the federal cabinet. The members of the Election

Cell were Major-General Jamal Said Mian (MGO), and Major-Generals (Retired) Rao Farman Ali Khan (Chairman Fauji Foundation) and Ihsan-ul-Haq. I was the Chief of Staff of the CMLA.

The prolonged martial law necessitated changes in the military team, and at various times some serving general-officers were inducted as ministers in the federal cabinet. They were Lieutenant-Generals Chishti, Ghulam Hassan Khan, Saeed Qadir, J.S. Mian and Major-General Rao Farman Ali Khan (retired). All of them held dual charges.

At the time of the postponement of elections in October 1977, I told General Zia that it was not possible for me to do full justice to two full-time jobs concurrently; military secretary at the GHQ and COS to the CMLA. I desired to be relieved of any one assignment to fully concentrate on the other. Zia wanted to keep me as his COS. I, therefore, quit as military secretary.

The remaining general-officers—Chishti, Hassan, J.S. Mian and Saeed Qadir—strongly desired to retain their respective army assignments in addition to becoming ministers in the federal cabinet. Their logic was that the formations would not take them seriously if they were stripped of their army appointments. If Zia could wear two hats, his military colleagues could not be denied this advantage. Their preference was accepted by General Zia. Likewise, Farman was keen to retain the Chairmanship of the 'golden goose', the Fauji Foundation. Zia yielded to his request as well. Air Marshal Inamul Haq became an odd man out, and he held only his ministerial appointment.

With a large hostile India on Pakistan's eastern border, and a not so friendly Afghanistan on its west, the Army Chief, General Zia, had full-time involvement in matters of national security. His added worries included the no-peace no-war situation in Kashmir and the then on-going insurgency situation in Balochistan. The imposition of martial law on 5 July 1977, added a new and unfamiliar burden on the shoulders of Zia. His responsibilities increased and his priorities underwent a change.

In addition to dealing with issues of national security and internal security duties, Zia had to administer the country and bring it back onto the political track. In the process, perforce, military duties were relegated to a back burner. Zia's time was increasingly spent on matters of state. Consequently, he got distanced from the daily functioning of General Headquarters and his personal contacts with the field formations decreased. He maintained links with his military command, but the Pakistan Army was too large an organization, and it required a full-time incumbent. But for his considerable stamina and sustained effort, his grip on the military formations might have been less strong.

The inevitable happened. On many professional matters General Zia came to rely on his PSO's advice in formulating policy options. These sincere and mature general-officers worked to their optimum ability, but were denied on the spot guidance and the supervision that their chief would have normally given if he was readily available in the General Headquarters. The price paid for the dual charge might be hard to quantify but its impact was equally hard to deny. Besides, some PSOs developed streaks of arrogance in their behaviour. They started thinking that GHQ knew best and its wisdom was superior and unquestionable.

As per the system in vogue, the army chief used to hold a PSOs conference once a week. This enabled him to take decisions, enforce his policies and supervise their implementation. After the induction of martial law, the frequency of this conference decreased and later it gradually became a rare phenomenon. Resultantly, the weekly conference held by the chief of the general staff assumed more importance, and the CGS assumed responsibilities that did not rightfully belong to him. These included the purchase functions traditionally exercised by the master general of ordnance. The change in the system negated the principle of check and balance.

Also, the Military Secretary's Branch came to exercise greater influence and authority on matters of posting, transfers and retirement of officers. Much of the overseeing check routinely exercised by the army chief on the performance of this branch was diluted because of Zia's national commitments. As a result, the military secretary assumed unchecked control in the composition of the regional selection boards, in the posting and retirement of officers, and in their selection for lucrative assignments.

Some formation commanders complained to General Zia that the PSOs had become more assertive and less responsive to the needs of the formations. Zia was concerned at such reports. In mid 1978, Lieutenant-General Muhammad Iqbal, the senior-most corps commander was appointed as a full time deputy chief of the army staff to institutionalize the functioning of the Pakistan Army.

Iqbal's induction in GHQ was a partial success because he was delegated only restricted authority, which made him only half functional. For example, the military secretary took orders directly from the army chief, and the posting and transfer of officers was outside the purview of the deputy chief. The concept of authority lying with one person and responsibility with the other ran counter to the norms of military discipline and efficient administration.

With his wings clipped, the lame duck deputy chief lacked the tools to address the problems he was appointed to solve. Also, some protocol matters created hurdles in Pakistan's rank and status-conscious society. The corps commanders-cum-governors cold-shouldered Iqbal during his visits to their areas on the plea of being busy with 'pre-arranged' gubernatorial duties. On some occasions, the order of precedence for seating arrangements between the deputy chief and the Governors became a contentious issue. Strange as it may seem, some general-officers dipped low on matters of symbolic significance despite their own high status.

Iqbal was a man of principle, known for his professional qualities and a subtle sense of humour. Soldiering was deeply ingrained in his blood and he was incapable of willingly violating the norms of military discipline. He never complained in the presence of his subordinates but brought the institutional anomalies to the notice of General Zia. He was given marginal relief which indicated that the curbs imposed on him were premeditated. They helped Zia in getting briefed by two persons on every subject of military importance—by the deputy chief and the PSO concerned.

Zia learnt the art of governance fast. The lack of political legitimacy of his government haunted him. Legally, his military take-over had been justified by the Supreme Court under the 'law of necessity'. Politically, he was taunted by his critics that he was a dictator. His government worked under the 'khaki shadows', no matter what he did to justify his rule.

Bhutto's Trial and Execution

The military was not involved in the trial of Mr Z.A. Bhutto in the Lahore High Court and in the Supreme Court of Pakistan (11 October 1977-2 February 1979). The prosecution story was pieced together by the Federal Investigation Agency from the case that had previously been 'filed as untraceable' by the police authorities in October 1975, after getting orders from the PPP government in Punjab. The trial was held in the Lahore High Court. The federal govenment implemented the judgment of the Supreme Court and Bhutto's execution took place on 4 April 1979.

The shrewd Zia consulted the military brass in deciding the destiny of Bhutto. He alone had the constitutional authority to either implement the sentence or commute it to a lesser punishment. Exercising abundant caution, he discussed all the options concerning Bhutto's fate with his civil and military colleagues in the government. He held separate discussions with the services chiefs and the provincial governors, and jointly met the army formation commanders and the principal staff officers in GHQ before arriving at a decision on the mercy petitions. The in-depth discussions took long hours and those present fully participated in the deliberations. This was Zia's technique of involving 'his own constituency' in the decision making process. His entire military team, except for one single voice, supported his decision. This lone general-officer supported the punishment awarded but suggested that the final decision be put off for the next government to take.

The Martial Law Administrators Conference was another forum to keep the army brass associated with the functioning of the government, even when it did not have a direct responsibility in this field. Till the end of 1979, these meetings were invariably held in GHQ and, among others, the PSOs participated in them. Thereafter, the venue was changed to the CMLA Secretariat and the PSOs were no longer invited to attend. Some special occasions were an exception to this rule when the president desired to brief the PSOs or consult them on specified issues.

Soviet Forces Enter Afghanistan

The Soviet invasion of Afghanistan was aimed towards the fulfilment of Moscow's historic desire to reach the warm waters of the Arabian Sea. The rise in Soviet influence was in contrast to declining US interest in this region. Afghanistan's status was so low with Washington that the overthrow of President Daoud's government in April 1978 was almost a non-event for the Carter administration. Foreseeing expansionism, President Zia wrote to President Carter suggesting that the US might take a serious note of the strategic imbalance created in the region. Carter ignored the warning as an overreaction from a weak country.

America's shrinking global vision was an invitation to the Soviet Union, who with an expansionist past, moved in to fill the power vacuum. The Carter administration was caught off-guard when a 100,000 strong Soviet military force entered Afghanistan in December 1979. A stunned President Carter called it 'the greatest threat to peace since World War Two,'[13] and advised Brezhnev to 'either withdraw the Soviet military or face serious consequences'.[14]

The induction of Soviet military forces in Afghanistan disturbed the geostrategic equilibrium, destabilized the region and added to Pakistan's security concerns. With India as usual breathing fire on Pakistan's eastern border, a destabilized Afghanistan on her west created a two-dimensional threat to her national security. The Pakistan Army and the Pakistan Air Force readjusted their operational and deployment plans, and took the new ground realities into military consideration. This was a difficult task.

Soon, Afghan refugees started pouring into Pakistan seeking shelter and security. Provision of humanitarian assistance to over three million Afghan refugees placed a heavy burden on Pakistan's weak economy. While the bulk of expenditure was incurred by Pakistan, some foreign countries and agencies partially shared the cost. Without their help, Islamabad might have been in deeper economic and political straits.

The assistance was not without strings. The major powers wished to collect intelligence in the garb of providing relief to the uprooted and needy Afghans. Pakistan knew that the undercover world was having a field day. It was a case of evaluating the cost-benefit ratio of the incoming aid.

The twin threat posed to Pakistan's national security encouraged her prophets of doom to spread gloom in the country. They forcefully argued that Islamabad's weak power potential prohibited her from incurring the wrath of the Soviet Union, and self-interest dictated that Pakistan should not burn her fingers in Afghanistan's insurgency. They advised the acceptance of the *fait accompli,* particularly since the US had proved to be an unreliable ally in the past. When the Soviet forces occupy a territory, it was claimed, they do not vacate the area. The logic, not without substance, was hard to ignore by the policy makers.

India remained ambivalent on the induction of the Soviet military forces in Afghanistan. She owed gratitude to the Soviet Union for providing her military assistance and diplomatic support in bifurcating Pakistan in 1971. An obliged India did not condemn the Soviet invasion in the UN General Assembly or elsewhere. Also, Prime Minister Indira Gandhi frequently hurled threats and created an imaginary war hysteria to keep Pakistan under pressure, and to help its strategic partner in Moscow.

Zia showed skill and patience in guiding Pakistan's destiny in such precarious circumstances. His government took difficult decisions that withstood the test of time. One, Pakistan was in the vanguard for opposing the Soviet occupation of Afghanistan. This policy accepted the risk and the punishment that went with it. Two, Pakistan had assessed that despite its seriousness, the Afghan crisis would be diplomatically settled earlier than the Kashmir dispute with India. Three, to avoid facing a two-front scenario, Islamabad initiated a peace offensive with India to isolate this country in the comity of nations and to put it on the defensive. 'Zia's visit to Jaipur without a formal invitation, ostensibly for watching a cricket test, was an eloquent proof of the General's innate caution.'[15] It put Indira Gandhi on diplomatic tenterhooks. Four, Pakistan began providing covert military assistance to the Afghan freedom fighters in late 1978, four years before the first US aid package to Pakistan became effective in 1982.

Zia's political foresight and brinkmanship in Afghanistan annoyed the Soviet Union. At the diplomatic level, Moscow repeatedly warned Pakistan of dire consequences for waging a 'proxy war' against its forces in Afghanistan. So intense was the Soviet sensitivity and concern that at one time Prime Minister Desai of India was approached for jointly exerting Soviet-Indian military pressure on Pakistan. Desai declined. The Soviet diplomatic *demarches* were intermingled with the advice that Pakistan accept the regional realities and not trust her 'distant friend', meaning the US. Inducements were offered. Moscow also expressed its willingness to mediate the 'bilateral border issue' between Afghanistan and Pakistan.

Between the years 1980-1989, Pakistan's air space was violated 2,730 times from her Western border, causing 1,355 casualties. Additionally, during this period Pakistan suffered 1,007 casualties by ground violations committed by artillery fire. Such intrusions caused concern within the country in general and in the border belt in particular. The people felt unsafe and blamed the government for not retaliating against such premeditated acts of aggression. Pakistan's retaliatory policy against such provocative acts was carefully conceived.

Hostile aircraft could be engaged with anti-aircraft fire. 'The PAF fighters were only authorized to shoot down Soviet or Afghan combat aircraft that would appear regularly to bomb the *Mujahideen* encampments located alongside the border. However, the pilots were under strict orders never to violate Afghan air space and further to ensure—even in the heat of battle—that all enemy aircraft they shot fell inside Pakistan's own territory. Operating under such frustrating and unique 'political' rules of war, the PAF evolved workable and operationally viable tactics and downed eight Soviet and Afghan aircraft without a single loss to itself.'[16] This was a praiseworthy performance.

The Pakistan artillery was permitted to engage only the enemy gun areas and that too after prior clearance. To hit the population centres would have hurt the Afghan civilian population—a choice unacceptable to Pakistan. Working under such severe, self-imposed restrictions, Zia kept his people and the defence services united and responsive to his leadership.

The Soviet military forces established their writ on Kabul. The local puppet regime working under the shadow of its masters dutifully obeyed the dictates of its foreign advisers who wielded real power and exercised firm control on the Afghan decision-making process. Kabul did what Moscow wanted it to do. Such was the 'freedom' exercised by the government in Afghanistan.

The Soviet Union quickly learnt that Kabul was not the whole of Afghanistan. While the Kabul coterie controlled the capital city, the vast countryside largely remained under the writ of the Afghan freedom fighters. The Soviet forces were soon consumed in protecting a few communication centres and airfields besides providing security to Kabul and a couple of other cities and towns. In the assessment of Pakistan, the combined Soviet-Afghan military effort inside Afghanistan was inadequate to commit a major trans-border offensive operation against Pakistan. Besides, such an attempt ran the risk of international consequences of a grave nature for Moscow.

The Soviet forces revealed their weaknesses. Many troops in the 'Soviet military contingent' were raw, inexperienced and ill-motivated. Defections were not uncommon, and those doing so usually claimed that they became aware of their presence in Afghanistan only after reaching their destination. These soldiers exposed the simmering discord inside the Soviet Union.

Some Afghan pilots, defecting to Pakistan along with their Russian-made helicopters and aircraft, disclosed that the Soviet officers trusted Afghans only to the extent necessary and exercised firm vigilance on the Afghan soldiers. The machines flown by the defecting pilots to Pakistan provided research and evaluation opportunities to Pakistan and the US. Washington showed great interest in military technology of Soviet origin. This was an important by-product of the Afghan war for the US defence industry.

Afghan Fall-out on Pakistan

Did General Zia mastermind the Afghan crisis and prolong it to extend his military rule in Pakistan? This criticism is made by those cynics and analysts who excel in finding fault with any system. It is naive to allege that Zia had manipulated the entry of the Soviet military forces across the Amu River. The Soviet Union invaded Afghanistan to promote its own national interests and vacated this region, a decade later, badly burnt and with aims unachieved.

Besides, it is an insult to the Afghan people to allege that they were tools in the hands of Zia, who exploited them to fight against a superpower for a full decade to enable the dictator to occupy his power saddle in Pakistan. This is a preposterous allegation against the fiercely independent Afghans who fought very bravely for so long and against heavy odds to protect their national sovereignty and independence. History shall remember their epic struggle.

The Soviet misadventure in Afghanistan provided an opportunity to the Zia administration which took advantage of it in the national interest of Pakistan. This was a golden chance to put the bilateral Pakistan-Afghan acrimony on the Durand Line issue on the back burner, and to start a new chapter of friendship between Kabul and Islamabad. Zia seized this occasion and used it profitably. Pakistan supported the Afghan struggle willingly and unconditionally to achieve the withdrawal of the Soviet forces and also to avoid being destabilized herself.

Pakistan abhorred the military occupation of a weak country by its strong neighbour as such an act violated justice, law and the provisions of the United Nations Charter. The Zia government worked in concert with the Afghan *Mujahideen* who appreciated Pakistan's sincerity and support in those difficult days. Zia felt that Pakistan's investment in Afghanistan would yield long-term advantages to both these countries.

General Zia was not alone in this assessment. In the wake of the Soviet military intervention in Afghanistan in 1979, Pakistan's Afghan policy painstakingly evolved after a comprehensive analysis of the situation prevailing in and around this country. Those who participated in the policy planning process included the foreign office, federal cabinet, ISI directorate, the provincial MLA's, services chiefs, the army brass in GHQ and in the field formations, and all the concerned ministries in the federal government. All possible options were considered, and after indepth discussion and debate it was decided to fully support the Afghan freedom struggle.

Discussions were invariably held in a free and frank manner and participants expressed their points of view without reservation. Not everyone agreed with the views expressed by others. There were always differences of opinion and approach. Such rough edges were smoothened by counter arguments. In the final analysis, a consensus was reached. General Zia, a highly patient listener, took copious notes and usually summed up the discussion and announced decisions on the subjects under debate.

The decision to provide military support to the Afghan freedom fighters was never announced in the meetings nor made public. It was confidentially conveyed to all concerned and was kept a hush-hush affair. The military brass thus always a part of the decision.

The general assessment in the foreign office and in the ISI directorate was that the Soviet military forces were unlikely to vacate Afghanistan in the foreseeable future. So also thought the Western democracies led by the US. History proved them wrong. Those holding this view had underestimated the inherent strength of the freedom struggle, the resilience of the people of Afghanistan, and the internal turmoil that was eroding the Soviet Union from within.

Some regional developments influenced events that helped Pakistan. One, the departure of the pro-west Shah of Iran from his country in January 1979, and the hostages crisis in November that year had turned post-revolution Iran into a pariah for the US and the West. With the Iran-Afghanistan border denied, the only access to Afghanistan open to the US-led west was through Pakistan. This made Islamabad an important element in the western attempt to defeat the Soviet presence in Afghanistan.

Bhutto's execution in April 1979 upset many world leaders who nevertheless maintained that it was an internal affair of Pakistan. Some abroad expressed regret that Zia had not exercised his constitutional authority in commuting the sentence to a lesser punishment. Such concerns were mostly *pro forma* acts and Pakistan kept up its business as usual with the world. Developments in Afghanistan pushed the Bhutto tragedy into the background. The western media suddenly 'discovered' that Zia, the dictator, was in fact a 'good guy'. His opposition to the communist invasion in Afghanistan evoked sympathy and support. The western media projected him in favourable colours and his personal image improved globally. His views on the Afghan crisis were heard with attention, and Pakistan's decision to act as a conduit for western weapons to Kabul was eulogized. This enabled Zia to consolidate his grip on the country.

The Negative Impact

The Afghanistan crisis provided fertile ground to the intelligence agencies of foreign donor countries to establish their 'moles' in the area. At the official level, the ISI Directorate established mutually beneficial contacts with its counterparts in other states. The exchange of intelligence became a regular feature with many western countries, particularly the US. Some countries increased their intelligence presence in Pakistan with the approval of the government. Others did so unobtrusively on the pretext of running schools and hospitals for the Afghan refugee camps in Pakistan. Additionally, foreign-funded Non-Government Organizations mushroomed in Pakistan. While some did useful work, others were not as innocent as they claimed to be.

The traditionally porous Pakistan-Afghan border facilitated the transborder movement of men and material across the Durand Line. The principle of supply and demand came into play, and Pakistan became an international weapons-bazar where small arms, machine guns and explosives were freely traded. The weapons sale, starting at a trickle, gradually assumed serious proportions. A Kalashnikov culture took birth.

The narcotics trade developed between Afghanistan and the western countries via Pakistan. The demand for this commodity in the west, the lax laws in the western countries, and the lure of easy money in the sale transactions encouraged this trade. The cultivation of opium and an incredible increase in the number of drug addicts in Pakistan caused major problems. The image of the country also got bruised.

Zia, a fresh entrant in national politics and in international diplomacy, rapidly learnt the art of statecraft and played his political cards with skill and finesse. His military background had groomed him in the virtues of a proactive policy and the pitfalls of a reactive approach. Nominated teams of governors, ministers, secretaries and military officers invariably produced option papers that enabled the government to weather many a storm. The Afghanistan crisis catapulted General Zia from the status of a military ruler to that of an internationally recognised statesman.

Many democratic and autocratic rulers in Pakistan learnt the hard way that governance is a thorny business and political power is too mercurial a commodity to remain stable for long. The detractors of Zia's Afghan policy have too lightly brushed aside the fact that in the realities of those Cold War days, any placation of Moscow by Pakistan would have invited, ultimately, just its contempt. They fail to recognize that in 1979-80, Pakistan did not have any other options.

The wielding of power by General Zia for over a decade showed his tenacity. Success came to him because he kept the domestic front under control. Pakistan's monsoon economy behaved and the harvest of major crops was steady. The law and order situation remained reasonable despite the Bhutto factor and 'as the chief executive Zia was conscious of the pains of taxation and the tolerance limit of the people while approving new budget proposals.'[17] Pakistan's political parties were weak and unsure of public support. But for his sudden death in mysterious circumstances, General Zia might have dominated Pakistan's political scene for a few more years.

I was deeply distressed at the apparently engineered demise of General Zia. Over a million people attending his last rites at the foot of the Margalla hills in Islamabad showed that I was not the lone mourner.

US Aid Package

Given the flank protection of the Atlantic and the Pacific oceans and with weak neighbours located in its north and south, the US had difficulty in understanding the security predicament of Pakistan which faced a hegemonic India and its strategic ally, the Soviet Union. Most Pakistanis perceive the US as a fair-weather friend rather than a friend in need. India's size and power potential has usually worked to the disadvantage of Pakistan. President Carter displayed his bias when he visited Tehran and New Delhi during his presidential trip to the region but meaningfully skipped Islamabad. He lacked credibility in Pakistan when his administration offered a four hundred million dollar aid package to Islamabad in 1980, in the face of the Soviet occupation of Afghanistan. Zia rejected the offer. A foreign correspondent in Islamabad asked him the reason for rebuffing the proposal. 'When the Soviet weapons are breathing fire on Pakistan's border', replied Zia calmly, 'what can she buy with that measly amount to enhance her national security?' He then himself posed a counter-question: 'Peanuts?' Zia's 'peanuts' remark rejecting the aid offer reflected the public mood in Pakistan. President Carter turned into a successful troubleshooter for his country much after he left the White House.

The exuberant President Reagan, a master in dramatics, called the Soviet Union an 'evil empire.' In contrast to Carter, his election as the US President generated hope that he would pull his country out from the Vietnam syndrome and oppose Soviet expansionism in a firm and forthright manner.

In October 1980, former President Nixon called on General Zia at his hotel, Waldorf Towers in New York before the latter visited Washington D.C. to meet President Reagan. In this meeting where I was present, Nixon pointedly advised Zia to avoid discussing details of the issues he intended to raise with President Reagan. 'Speak to President Reagan in generalities and in broad outlines,' said Nixon, adding, 'let the details be handled by his staff and colleagues'. Nixon knew that Reagan was not a person of details and Zia gratefully took the hint.

Pakistan-US bilateral ties improved during the Reagan administration. Their cooperation on Afghanistan became intensive and extensive. Pakistan was offered assistance and a 3.2 billion dollar aid package for the period 1982-87 was negotiated in September 1981. The amount was equally divided between economic assistance and military sales. The US negotiators proposed soft terms for the military sales. To their amazement, Pakistan opted to pay more. The Agha Shahi-led foreign office was of the opinion that the acquisition of military hardware on concessional rates would compromise Pakistan's newly acquired status in the Non-Aligned Movement. Shahi's logic and apprehensions prevailed with General Zia and the Finance Minister Ghulam Ishaq Khan.

The proverbial zeal of the new convert ironically made the purchaser (Pakistan) pay more than was demanded by the seller (US). While this might have amused or surprised the US negotiators, Pakistan incurred some avoidable expenditure. In due course of time the NAM itself lost much of its utility and bargaining ability. But, to be fair to Shahi and his foreign office colleagues it may be conceded that the advantage of hindsight was not available then. It was also unpredictable then that the Soviet Union would implode and the bipolar system would collapse.

The diplomatic romance between Washington and Islamabad brought Pakistan under sharp and positive international focus, and Pakistan was lavished with praises like 'a pivotal state,' a 'wedge' and a 'front line country' worth eulogizing and supporting. Zia, the legendary dictator censured by the West, was now lauded as a statesman of calibre and an undaunting freedom lover helping the hapless people of Afghanistan in their sacred liberation struggle.

The enhanced importance of Pakistan was a temporary phenomenon created by force of circumstance. The US had a strategic interest in destabilizing the Soviet Union and making her military intervention in Afghanistan cost-heavy in order to promote her own national interests. The future of Afghanistan was of secondary concern to the US, her immediate objective being to fully cash in on the prevailing Afghan hostility against Soviet aggression. And, for this the US could enter Afghanistan only through Pakistan because the other option, the Iranian route, was closed to her as Iran-US relations were in a state of limbo.

The revived US interest was conceived in Pakistan as a tactical move. Nevertheless, it provided an opportunity to Islamabad to take advantage of it without compromising her principles. Consequently, an aid relationship was negotiated between both the countries. In the process, Pakistan's defence effort improved, and, to some extent, that gave confidence to her people. The US opposition to Pakistan's nuclear programme underwent a subtle change. However, Pakistan made it known to the US that her nuclear programme was not negotiable. And, Islamabad vigorously pursued it despite protests and veiled threats from Washington.

The Zia government evolved its major policy options with care and forethought, discussion and debate; a process in which all concerned, including the military, were always associated. Strange as it may appear to Zia's critics, the government made good use of the available institutions despite the fact that the country was under one-person rule. This was one reason for the longevity of the Zia rule.

The foreign military assistance was funneled to the Afghan *Mujahedeen* through Pakistan, and an elaborate network was established to collect military and economic intelligence from the Soviet Union and its troops in Afghanistan. The CIA and the Inter-Services Intelligence Directorate worked in concert with each other in providing tools and know-how to the different Afghan groups fighting in their respective operational areas within Afghanistan. What initially started as a covert operation maintained its secrecy during the Zia era. After Zia, it gradually became an open secret primarily because of the leaks appearing in the US media. Such leaks were less attributable to aggressive investigative journalism and more to deliberate plans of the US agencies to promote their own national interests. That, in the process they compromised Pakistan's position and endangered its security were matters of concern to Islamabad but of rudimentary interest to Washington.

The withdrawal of the Soviet forces from Afghanistan was a matter of strategic importance for the US. Thereafter, Kabul was not high on the US agenda. For Pakistan, the Soviet withdrawal was only the first essential step. The other objectives included an end to the fratricidal war in Afghanistan, return of normalcy in the country, achieving regional stability and preservation of the unity and territorial integrity of Afghanistan. While the immediate Pakistan-US aims were achieved, their long-term goals differed. For the US, Pakistan could now be sidelined and India wooed, as it promised to be a far bigger market for American investment and trade.

The initial joint strategy in Afghanistan was to obstruct the Soviet Union and make its occupation cost-heavy. Subsequently, the CIA planned to launch covert operations inside the Central Asian Republics through Afghanistan to erode the Soviet Union from within. Pakistan had neither the desire to indulge in such an activity nor the capability for such clandestine operations. It had no bilateral dispute with the Soviet Union either. It opposed it on principle and demanded vacation of its military forces from Afghanistan.

The aid package was negotiated on the Pak-US mutual understanding conveyed directly to the US Secretary of State, General Haig, that Pakistan would not compromise on its nuclear programme. Haig had replied that the nuclear issue would not become the 'centrepiece' of Pakistan-US relations. However, soon after the conclusion of the first aid package, Washington conveyed to Islamabad that the aid package and also the entire spectrum of bilateral ties would be seriously endangered if Pakistan pursued a weapon-oriented nuclear programme. With the changing US stance, Zia suspected that Washington could abandon Pakistan when its aims in Afghanistan had been achieved. The ISI was instructed that all meetings in Pakistan between the US officials and the Afghan leaders would take place in the presence of its representatives. This policy was implemented during Zia's life-time. The situation changed in the immediate post Zia era. The Benazir Government had an irresolute Afghan policy. Besides she wooed the US to stay in power. Inexperienced Benazir had yet to understand the fragility of external support and the changing moods of the foreign powers. The US fully exploited her domestic compulsions. Consequently, American interference in Pakistan considerably increased.

The military component of the US aid package was largely shared between the Pakistan Air Force and the Pakistan Army with a major share going to the former. The Pakistan Navy preferred getting equipment of British and French origin.

During the period 1978-88, Pakistan played a role in the Afghan conflict that was larger than its size and power potential.

The US-led west wanted a Muslim country to remain in the forefront of the Afghan struggle, and Pakistan was willing to play such a role for her own domestic and security reasons. The Western countries and the UN General Assembly fully supported Pakistan in her effort to oppose Soviet military aggression against Afghanistan. The opposition came largely from the Soviet Union and its major strategic ally—India. On occasions, Iran's position was ambivalent but Islamabad travelled an extra mile in keeping Tehran informed about the progress of *jihad* inside Afghanistan and in later years, about the on-going Afghan peace negotiations at Geneva.

General Zia frequently consulted the services chiefs and the army formation commanders on major developments on Afghanistan. Government actions were supported by the military and the major options often emerged out of consensus. This included acceptance of US aid and its distribution between the three services on the basis of a mutually agreed acquisition of military hardware.

In the final analysis, the Soviet military forces vacated Afghanistan, and Pakistan did not have to fire a single bullet to achieve this aim. This was a notable accomplishment whose significance deserves to be highlighted a great deal more than done hitherto. Despite facing Soviet and Indian pressures, Pakistan remained steadfast in her resolve and proved the virtue of her determination.

The price paid for the political advantage was considerable. Millions of Afghan refugees migrated to Pakistan putting pressure on her economy, social services, ecology, pasture land and water resources. A large number settled in Pakistan on a permanent basis. Pakistan faced the menace of the Afghan narcotic trade via her territory and the weapon culture created serious problems of law and order in the country. Many foreign countries established intelligence outposts in Pakistan, in the garb of providing humanitarian assistance to the Afghan refugees by their government and non-government agencies. The CIA-ISI intelligence link became strong and inter-dependent, with advantages and drawbacks to Pakistan. Above all, Pakistan's increasing dependence on the US ran the risk of losing most of the American gains if, at some point in the future, Washington pulled the political rug from under the feet of Islamabad once her own purpose had been served in Afghanistan. This last aspect did not get the priority it deserved and Pakistan, rather naively, trusted the US pledges in good faith, with the hope that the commitments made would be honoured in letter and spirit by the US. The fallacy of this assumption stood exposed in the post Geneva Accord period when America closed the aid tap, withdrew political support, and left Pakistan to fend for herself.

Zia—The Supreme Commander

General Zia belonged to the pre-independence category of Pakistan Army officers who rose to command the army without receiving formal high-level training. Despite the lack of academic and professional grooming he made good use of his considerable experience in the command and staff assignments held by him and his teaching stint at the Command and Staff College, Quetta. Zia's Military Secretary, Major-General Arshad Malik (1981-83), who heard him comment on issues of national strategy and operational strategy on numerous occasions says that 'Zia's understanding and grasp of such matters was deep and sound, and he possessed a striking ability to pick up the missing links from the operational presentations made to him by the commanders and the operational staff.'[18]

As supreme commander, defence minister and chairman of the defence committee of the cabinet, Zia's authority over Pakistan's national security policy and the management of its armed forces was absolute. This would ordinarily suggest a structure of autocratic dictation to the ministry of defence and the three services, but this was not Zia's way of exercising power.

Air Chief Marshall Jamal A. Khan says, 'Zia preferred to visualize the roles, tasks and missions of the three services in the context of an integrated military strategy that could provide the best security for Pakistan. He was successful in fostering this unified concept through the Joint Staff Headquarters. When presiding over many (often long and exhausting) meetings of the DCC, and presentations in other institutions on high-level defence issues, Zia almost never interrupted any minister, secretary or service chief and nearly always withheld his remarks till the end.'[19] His patience was inexhaustable, a rare quality for a person who wielded unquestioned and total power.

To a question whether Zia was fair or biased on inter-service matters particularly on the sensitive issue of the allocation of resources to the three services, the air chief said, 'Zia exhibited particular sensitivity to the concerns of the two smaller services. If he was partial to the army he never showed it. He encouraged discussion even when the views of others were clearly contrary to his own. This created an atmosphere of relatively subdued tensions when the services chiefs argued passionately their competing demands for budgetary support, particularly when the plans for the modernization and new weapon acquisitions by the three services were discussed. The affable chemistry generated by Zia in these meetings enlisted cooperation and, at times of sharp disagreement, caused minimum heartburn. Even when a proposed weapon system was not considered by Zia to be cost-effective or suitable, he would not condemn it publicly, preferring to express his reservations to the concerned service chief in private.'[20]

Questioned further about Zia's understanding of the air force, the air chief replied that, 'President Zia was quite knowledgeable about the significance of air power in the emerging era of high-technology warfare.'[21] On the state of the operational capability of the Pakistan Air Force during the Zia era, Air Chief Marshall Zulfiqar Ali Khan said, 'It remained static upto July 1978 when I relinquished command of the PAF. But after my retirement it got enhanced with the acquisition of F-16s.'[22] Air Chief Marshall Jamal A. Khan felt that the 'many serious challenges to Pakistan's security that Zia negotiated successfully have received insufficient examination, perhaps under the shadow of criticism heaped on his martial law rule over Pakistan. For instance, by insisting on and co-timing the accelerated induction of F-16s with the development of Pakistan's nuclear capability, the country's deterrent was given a credibility that was visibly noted in New Delhi.'[23]

Former Naval Chief, Admiral Iftikhar A. Sirohey, summed up General Zia's role in these words, 'General Zia understood the maritime compulsion of the country and tried his best to enable the Pakistan Navy to provide a credible maritime defence. He approved every request I made in the professional field. Had he lived, a lot could have been achieved in the maritime field.'[24]

The combat readiness of all the three military services was better when General Zia left the national horizon in 1988 as compared to what he had inherited in 1977 when he took charge of the country. The modernization and upgrading of the three services during the Zia era followed a carefully conceived and well-debated pattern to develop their combat effectiveness in an integrated manner. Zia had no hesitation in allocating the bulk of the resources received from the first US aid package to the Pakistan Air Force to create a visible deterrent capability. This priority was supported by the Chairman JCSC and all the three service chiefs. Pakistan was also keen to buy one Air Warning Aircraft (AWAC) E3A version mounted on 707 aircraft. India raised a hue and cry. Buckling under Indian pressure, the US reneged and offered to Pakistan the naval version E2A, Hawk Eye. The proposal was dropped.

Zia's omnipotence in national affairs weakened the institutions of the state and these included the ministry of defence. The services chiefs usually discussed their major problems directly with Zia and in some cases accepted his decisions. These cases were then processed through the ministry of defence to complete the formalities. In other words, the ministry controlling the services headquarters was used as a post office to issue formal approvals on the cases on which decisions had previously been taken by the president. This undermined the system because the ministry of defence was denied the opportunity of evaluating each proposal independently. Besides, its legitimate writ was compromised.

The weakening of the ministry of defence created an arrogance in the services headquarters which came to feel that every proposal submitted by them to the ministry must be quickly approved without raising any queries or objections. The objections and elucidation, when raised, were resented by the services headquarters and construed as hurdles for them.

The absence of parliament and an elected government, and the docility of the ministry of defence resulted in a lack of accountability of the military acts by the representative political leadership. The military developed a tendency that it knew best about defence issues. Such arrogance was misplaced and counterproductive. In the immediate post-Zia era, some army chiefs behaved like super prime ministers and indulged in acts that lowered the prestige of the defence services.

Patronizing Welfare Measures

Medical care of the sick and wounded was a passion with Zia. The Army Medical Corps received his personal attention and considerable boost. In 1976, the army was short of medical doctors. This shortage was largely overcome, the training of specialists received a high priority, and a structural review of the military hospitals improved their working condition. The parents of the defence services personnel were made eligible for treatment in military hospitals—a step widely hailed by all ranks.

Zia was liberal in sending abroad patients for medical and surgical treatment in those disciplines where advanced facilities were inadequate within the country. This imposed a considerable financial burden on the national exchequer. To Zia, the psychological satisfaction of the patients in distress outweighed the financial expenditure. This facility gradually came to be abused particularly by the influence wielding segments of society—ministers, judges, parliamentarians, senior bureaucrats and others occupying offices in the successive governments. It became a symbol of prestige and a source of combining duty with pleasure. Some members of this elite group had minor ailments treated abroad at the expense of the state.

The care and education of retarded children received considerable attention. Special education improved the quality of life of handicapped children. Zia's interest in this field was perhaps enhanced because he had a congenitally handicapped daughter.

Dr Mahbub ul Haq

Dynamic, extrovert and exuberant, Dr Mahbub ul Haq's (1934-98) innovative proposals on economic reforms and human resource development were frequently ingenious and controversial. A skilful debater and a chronic optimist who loved to generate public discussion on contentious issues to smoothen the rough edges of an economic tangle, Mahbub was a patient listener, a skilful synthesizer and a vibrant economist not hesitant to differ with the economic pundits and the policy makers of the time. The economic phrases coined by him were often provocative and controversial but his motives were sincere. To him the development of Pakistan took priority over other considerations.

A bureaucrat by profession, Dr Mahbub ul Haq was equally proficient in political double-talk. At times he supported proposals for reasons of political expediency knowing that he would not implement them. Two instances highlight this point. In 1986, Dr Mahbub ul Haq was the Minister for Finance. In accordance with established procedure he discussed the defence budget proposals with the ministry of defence during the pre-budget sessions and reached a consensus on the defence allocation. Hours before announcing the budget, the federal cabinet met to approve the budget proposals. To the surprise of his cabinet colleagues, Mahbub proposed that the defence allocation already agreed between him and the ministry of defence may arbitrarily be reduced by ten per cent. A discussion ensued. The reopening of an agreed case was unfair to the defence services chiefs who were not present in the cabinet meeting. The Prime Minister, Muhammad Khan Junejo inquired if the reduction proposal had been discussed with the ministry of defence and if so what was its reaction. He was visibly surprised to learn that this was a new scheme to ovecome 'financial constraints.' 'I am already fighting on many fronts', said Muhammad Khan Junejo, adding, 'I don't wish to add one more.' This closed the case.

In the eighties, Pakistan sent one armoured brigade to Saudi Arabia. The Saudi government paid the mutually agreed Service Charge to the Pakistan Army to train replacements for the loss of qualified personnel sent to their country. On receipt, this amount was merged by the ministry of finance into the Federal Consolidated Fund and was not released to GHQ. When several reminders failed to get a response for the release of this amount I, as Vice-Chief, requested the Finance Minister, Dr Mahbub ul Haq, for a joint meeting along with the Finance Secretary, Mr H. U. Beg and the Defence Secretary, Ijlal Haider Zaidi, to settle this case.

A meeting was held, and the finance minister agreed that the Service Charge would be kept under a separate head by the ministry of finance and the total amount would be released to the army. It was also agreed that GHQ would record the minutes of the meeting, and the ministry of finance would issue a policy directive after the minutes were approved by the finance minister. The GHQ sent the minutes to the ministry but the mutually agreed directive was not issued. Mahbub had a ready answer when, weeks later I complained to him about the delay. 'Arif *Bhai* I sympathize with your frustration. I assure you that the bureaucratic hurdles bewilder me no less. Beg is worried lest a precedence be set for the future. But I am determined to cross the fence. Give me a little time to get the rough edges smoothened.' Again, days passed without a reply. The silence led me to talk to the finance secretary. Beg confessed to me later that immediately after the GHQ meeting Mahbub had told him, 'I had to agree with GHQ because the army's demand was justified. But I have no intention of implementing the agreement negotiated with General Arif. Any reminder received from GHQ may be filed. Just sit over the case.'[25] The minister's directive was dutifully obeyed by his staff.

Zia—Handling State Affairs

In 1977, Mr H. U. Beg was Secretary Railways when the civilian government fell with the imposition of martial law. Just before this event Prime Minister Bhutto's wish had been conveyed to the ministry that the Divisional Superintendent's official residence in Karachi be sold to a person at the rate of Rs 200 per square foot. At that time, the market value of this property was Rs 1,300 per square foot. Besides, the ministry was, in principle, opposed to the sale of an official residence. Bhutto had overruled the objections raised by the ministry and a sale agreement was made. The declaration of martial law prevented the transfer of this property to a favoured buyer. The matter was reported to General Zia, who cancelled the agreement.[26]

Mr H. U. Beg worked as secretary finance under General Zia between 1979 and 1987. He worked in the Zia government 'without any fear and with total peace of mind.' To him 'Zia was a contrast to Bhutto' and the president 'never hurt his self-respect.' He 'was benevolent to individuals who sought help in the national development effort but he never asked the banks to help persons with bad bank loan records. Zia did not force decisions that hurt the banking sector.'[27]

Beg recalls that a British company, with a local partner, proposed to establish a Morris car plant in Pakistan to manufacture mainly taxis. The British government sent its Under-Secretary to Islamabad to facilitate the negotiation of this deal. The ministry of finance opposed the proposal on the grounds that the plant being supplied was old and outdated and the current trend favoured cars of Japanese origin. Zia agreed with this view and the Morris car plant was not imported.

Saeed Qadir called Zia a brave person who did not hesitate to take personal risks. He recalls that President Zia visited Pakistan Steel at Karachi despite an apprehension conveyed to him that its pro-PPP and highly active trade union might create a disturbance during his visit.[28]

Initially a fervent Bhutto admirer, Zia's views on the deposed prime minister underwent a dramatic change as the misdeeds of the Bhutto administration were exposed.

General Zia considered Nusrat Bhutto a political washout, devoid of leadership traits and unable to pose a political danger to him. She was permitted to go abroad for 'treatment' on the recommendations of a medical board and against the advice of the intelligence agencies. He never personally met the young and inexperienced Benazir Bhutto, but this lady was not without contacts within the government. She had an unpublicized meeting with a governor at a neutral place before she was allowed to go abroad in the mid-eighties. An unwritten understanding was reached between herself and Zia about her foreign visit.

The speed and manner in which the highly incendiary internal security situation inherited by Zia in Balochistan was appeased signified Zia's political understanding and statesmanship. Even some of Zia's close associates apprehended at the time that he was going too far too quickly, but time proved President Zia right.

Zia trusted the leaders of the Pakistan National Alliance in general, and those of the Muslim League (Pagara Group) and Mian Tufail's Jamaat-e-Islami in particular. He did not trust Mr Ghulam Mustafa Khar, had serious doubts about Mr Ghulam Mustafa Jatoi and visibly distanced himself from Maulana Kausar Niazi. He once called Mr Hamid Nasir Chatha 'a boy who refuses to grow.' Maulana Shah Ahmad Noorani had a meeting with General Zia in Karachi. Thereafter, Zia kept him in his place.

Khan Abdul Ghafar Khan, the Red Shirt leader and a disciple of Mahatma Gandhi, started his political journey in Pakistan on the wrong foot. He opposed the creation of Pakistan and remained steadfast in his belief till the end of his life. Perennially out of step with national politics, the Frontier Gandhi—Bacha Khan to his admirers—kept himself engaged in the narrow belt of his Pathan constituency in NWFP. A pleasant and frank personality, Ghafar Khan had a long spell of self-imposed exile in Jalalabad, Afghanistan, but carefully played his political game in Pakistan. He occasionally wrote to President Zia seeking assistance in his personal and property-related matters or raising some local issues. He died in Pakistan and as per his wish his mortal remains were taken to Jalalabad for burial.

Soon after Zia took charge of national affairs, Khan Abdul Wali Khan and some Balochi leaders arrested by the Bhutto government were set free. The Hyderabad Tribunal that was holding their trial on anti-state charges was dissolved. Zia frequently met Wali Khan in an effort to bring him and his Awami National Party into the mainstream of Pakistan's national politics. Wali Khan who had once declared that 'Bhutto and Pakistan cannot co-exist', supported the Zia government for a while and demanded accountability of the politicians before elections were held in the country. Their matching views on Bhutto brought them together as a measure of tactical necessity despite a vast divergence in their respective political philosophies. Their political honeymoon was over soon after the death of Bhutto in April 1979. Zia's utility for Wali Khan was on the decline. Their diverging ways became obvious after September 1979 when the strongman in Afghanistan, Mr Nur Muhammad Taraki, was killed in the People's Palace in Kabul. Wali claimed to have had good relations with Taraki. With Taraki dead, Wali's clout in Afghanistan was reduced. Wali Khan now became an open critic of Zia's Afghan policy.

At one time, Zia had been willing to appoint Wali Khan as the prime minister to prepare the country for elections. Wali Khan, aware of his limitations, marginal political following in NWFP and Balochistan, and none in Punjab and Sindh, had thought it prudent to stay away from a high profile responsibility. Besides, his secular credentials were in conflict with Zia's preference for an Islamic order in the country.

General Zia effectively employed the policy of 'carrot and stick' to keep his senior military colleagues in humour and in check. He promoted some already superceded officers belatedly and retired others to visibly demonstrate his authority and grip on the defence services. He kept others under control with hopes of promotion, and did not hesitate to retire them when their utility was over. Such acts occasionally created embarrassment for him, but a breach of promise was of no value for the General.

With a policy of 'philanthropy' at public expense, General Zia initiated the practice of granting small amounts of money to

soldiers who performed well during his visits to military units.
This was resented by many of the senior officers. He also
'compensated' some officers with ambassadorial and other
appointments. Others waited on promised hopes. There can
seldom be enough opportunities to accommodate all aspirants.
General Zia had many weaknesses, likes and dislikes and loved
to wield power.

Foreign journalists described Zia and his close associates as
they perceived them. The powerful international media
influenced readers, who were fed sometimes with juicy
concoctions, misleading conjectures and half-truths about the
military government in Pakistan. One example from an Indian
correspondent who wrote, in May 1982. 'If an accident overtakes
the General (Zia)... the successor could be President Ziaul Haq's
chief of staff, Lt. Gen. Arif, the strongest and perhaps the ablest
member of the Military Council of a dozen officers who function
as the President's super cabinet. In every decision that has been
made in Pakistan in recent years, the counsel of General Arif is
said to have been dominant. He was sent to New Delhi with
Agha Shahi to keep an eye on the foreign minister in the parleys
over the No-War Pact. It is claimed that General Arif commands
the respect, if not the love, of the majority of the fifty-two
officers of the armed forces, who are the effective parliament of
Pakistan. This strange, aloof, taciturn General gives credence to
the dictum "silent waters run deep".'[29]

Such a cocktail of half-truth and half-fiction was perhaps an
attempt to drive a wedge in the unity of Pakistan's armed forces.
Speculative reporting was also done within the country. In his
foreword written for my book, Mr Gowher Rizvi quotes an
anonymous, perceptive Pakistani analyst writing, 'It is Pakistan's
only regime in which a number two man is clearly identifiable
and allowed to function with considerable power without arousing
any feelings of insecurity in the top man. General Arif's role
since 1980 has been quite unique and probably without precedent
in our previous power structures.'[30] Needless to say that I knew
the limits of my power and maintained a steadfast course and a
deliberate low profile throughout the period that I enjoyed
considerable authority and Zia's confidence.

The Zia Papers

File work had a low priority for Zia. He was so patently lazy in this field that official mail remained piled up in his study for days, weeks and months and in some cases for years. Instead of clearing his mail at regular intervals, he adopted the unorthodox technique of getting his study room periodically expanded to place the fresh incoming files. In the twice-expanded study room the files were piled up on the floor with space just wide enough for one person to move around to search for the file that needed immediate attention. Zia was averse to any person disturbing the files lying in his study that resembled a junk yard rather than the office of the president of a country. Occasionally, he permitted his military secretary to wade through the sea of files to fish out a required document. And, it was a Herculean task to locate a file in a hurry.

General Zia's sudden death raised the question of dealing with the accumulated files and papers in his house. While some documents were of a routine nature, others were classified, and yet others were highly sensitive, dealing with his conversations held with foreign heads of states and governments. There were many 'Eyes Only' papers submitted by the intelligence agencies on individuals and events. Besides, the study contained tapes of some sensitive conversations recorded over a period of ten years. In short, the files formed a stack of highly 'explosive' reading material.

It is open to question why General Zia might have retained these papers—perhaps for writing a personal account of his rule. In fact, Mr Shahid Jamshed Burki, a Pakistani bureaucrat serving abroad had volunteered to write an account of the Zia years and the president had agreed to this suggestion. He was later talked out of such a venture by some of his advisers who argued that one Altaf Gauhar was more than sufficient for the country. The president could write his story or get it written after his retirement from the national scene. Fate determined otherwise. Zia never got a chance to say his piece in print.

Many claimants desired access to the Zia papers. Four main
contenders appeared on the scene. First, Lieutenant-General
Syed Refaqat, COS of General Zia, desired all the papers to be
sent to the president's office for their disposal to the concerned
ministries and other agencies. Secondly, the Prime Minister's
Secretariat made an attempt to get these documents, but it did
not pursue its demand because no prime minister existed at the
time to exert his authority. Thirdly, the Army Chief, General
Mirza Aslam Beg, showed interest in getting all the material to
GHQ. Fourthly, Begum Zia was keen to return the files but
retain the more sensitive material, classified papers and tapes.

Each claimant might have had his own reasons—official or
private—for wanting access to the wealth of official information
contained in the archives, that was, in fact, state property.
Whether such claims were legally justified or not was apparently
not considered. This was not the first time in Pakistan's history
when official correspondence was retained by a former policy
maker for private use.

Major-General Mahmud Ali Durrani, the former military
secretary of General Zia was detailed by GHQ, at the request of
Begum Zia, to look through the available records and
recommend their disposal. While leafing through almost 9,000
files, documents and other papers, he came across some highly
sensitive reports that incriminated some persons who were then
claiming custody of the records. He handed over such papers
directly to the new President, Mr Ghulam Ishaq Khan. Durrani
did a good job of the difficult task assigned to him, and this was
accomplished at a rapid pace. His work was successfully
completed and the bulk of the material was returned to the
respective departments. The more sensitive papers and tapes
remained in the custody of the Zia family and, as told to me by
Begum Zia, destroyed by her later.

NOTES

1. Interview Major-General Arshad Malik, Military Secretary to General Zia (1981-83), 18 September 1998.
2. Interview Air Chief Marshal Zulfiqar Ali Khan, Chief of the Air Staff (1975-78), 7 October 1998.
3. Interview Major-General Arshad Malik.
4. General K.M. Arif, *Working with Zia*, Oxford University Press, Karachi, 1995, p. 42.
5. M.P. Bhandara, 'Reflections and Recriminations', Dawn, 31 December 1999.
6. Conversation, Arif-Jilani.
7. Interview Lt-General Saeed Qadir, 22 August 1998.
8. Major-General Tajammal Hussain, *The Story of my Struggle*, Jang Publications, Lahore, 1991, p. 207.
9. Ibid., p. 209.
10. Ibid., p. 237.
11. Interview Major-General Arshad Malik.
12. Interview Air Chief Marshal Zulfiqar Ali Khan, Chief of the Air Staff (1975-78), 7 October 1998.
13. *American Foreign Policy Basic Documents* (1977-1980), No. 418, 248.
14. *International Herald Tribune*, 31 December 1979.
15. Interview Mr S.K. Singh, former High Commissioner of India in Islamabad.
16. Interview Air Chief Marshal Jamal A. Khan, Chief of the Air Staff (1985-88), 18 September 1998.
17. Interview Mr H.U. Beg, former Secretary of Finance (1979-87), 14 October 1998.
18. Interview Major-General Arshad Malik, 18 September 1998.
19. Interview Air Chief Marshal (ACM) Jamal A. Khan, Chief of the Air Staff (1985-1988), 18 September 1998.
20. Ibid.
21. Ibid.
22. Interview Air Chief Marshal Zulfiqar Ali Khan, Chief of the Air Staff (1975-1978), 7 October 1998.
23. Interview ACM Jamal A. Khan
24. Interview Admiral Iftikhar A. Sirohey, Chief of the Naval Staff (1986-88) and Chairman JCSC (1988-91), 17 November 1998.
25. Interview Mr H.U. Beg, 14 October 1998.
26. Ibid.
27. Ibid.
28. Interview Lt-General Saeed Qadir.
29. *After Zia, Who?*, S.N. Chopra in Islamabad, *PROBE INDIA,* May 1982.
30. Gowher Rizvi in his foreword to General Arif's book, *Working with Zia*, Oxford University Press, Karachi, 1995, p. xiii.

5

THE MOHAJIR QAUMI MOVEMENT

Historical Background

The Province of Sindh was separated from Bombay in 1936 for reasons of administrative convenience, and the claim of the Muslim majority that had demanded a separate province. Notwithstanding this change, the local Hindu population in Sindh retained their firm economic hold on the area. Their control on trade, commerce, and small scale industry was far greater than their population ratio. So was their influence in the field of education, technical expertise and politics. The province of Sindh had a wheat and cotton based agricultural economy and much of its cotton produce was consumed to keep the wheels of the textile industry in Bombay churning. Sindh had no industry of its own.

Renowned for its saints, *sufis*, soft music and soothing mystical lyrics, Sindh was, and is, a land of contrasts. On the one hand, the mighty *waderas* held vast tracts of lands largely gifted to them or to their ancestors by the British colonial masters, in recognition of services rendered by them to strengthen their imperial hold on India. The agricultural income generated by the state-gifted lands made the landlords rich, politically powerful, and arrogant. These rich masters looked down upon their *haris* who tilled their vast land-holdings, generation after generation, but continued to lead poverty-ridden lives. The *haris* obeyed the whims and dictates of their feudal lords and considered them sacrosanct and inviolable. Born in rags, they subsisted at a sub-human level and died in abject poverty. Sindh had a few ultra rich families but a vast majority of the population was poverty stricken and there was a very small and shrinking middle class. The rich-poor financial gap was wide, as was their social standing in society. The average Sindhi loves his home and dislikes being away from his ancestral surroundings and familiar landscape. To him, a place just across the river or even a couple of miles away from his home is *'pardes'* (foreign territory). Thus, in the declining decades of the *Raj*, many Sindhi landlords imported hardy and cheap agricultural labour for their lands from the neighbouring Punjab which had a surplus of farm-hands. These Punjabi tenants adopted Sindh as their home.

Sindh was conquered and annexed to the British *Raj* in India in 1843. Nine years later, in 1852, the Karachi municipality was established. 'The first mayor of the city, in 1933, when the Karachi Municipal Corporation was formed, was a distinguished Parsi gentleman, Jamshed Nusserwanjee who retired from public service in 1937. On the eve of his retirement, the doyen of Karachi's British community recorded: 'The city owes him an immeasurable debt of gratitude which I hope that each and every community will ungrudgingly recognize.'[1]

In 1947, Karachi, the capital of Sindh, was the 'sleeping beauty' of undivided India with a population of about 350,000 people. It was the cleanest city in Asia. It was a city of peace and tranquillity in which different communities lived in harmony with one another. The role played by the Parsi and the Bohra communities in the development and growth of this town was central and substantive over a prolonged period of time. Karachi was not the stronghold of 'rural Sindhis' even though it was the provincial capital.

Such was the political and the ethnic landscape of Sindh when Pakistan was born in August 1947. Despite some cultural differences between them, the Hindu *banias*, the Punjabi settlers and the native Sindhis happily co-existed with one another and Sindh was a peaceful province. It had taken a leading part in the freedom struggle, and it was a matter of pride and honour for the Sindhis that the father of the nation, Quaid-i-Azam Mohammad Ali Jinnah, was a scion of their soil.

The Partition Holocaust

The emergence of Pakistan bestowed on Karachi the unique distinction of becoming the capital of a new-born country. A sea of refugees migrated to Pakistan in the aftermath of the communal riots that engulfed northern India. People seeking shelter and security trekked across the international border in search of succour and relief. The migration across the turbulent border was two-directional, with the Muslims pouring into Pakistan, and the Hindus and Sikhs migrating to India.

The governments of India and Pakistan mutually decided to categorize the regions from where the trans-border migration took place under two heads—'Agreed Areas' and 'Non Agreed Areas'. The term 'Agreed Areas' was used with respect to East Punjab (India) and West Punjab (Pakistan). The 'Non-Agreed Areas' were UP, CP (India) etc.

Migration from India

The bulk of the refugees migrating to Pakistan belonged to the 'Agreed Areas' in India and they resettled in the province of the Punjab. They were quickly absorbed into the Punjabi milieu because of their close identity and affinity in language, culture, customs and traditions, dress and habits. They were initially called refugees but their mutual integration was so swift, smooth and effective that the use of this term soon became redundant. The distinction between the locals and the refugees disappeared, and most of the people who had migrated to Pakistan no longer looked towards their old ancestral homes except as a matter of academic reality.

The refugees that migrated to Pakistan from the 'Non Agreed Areas' in India—(UP) Utter Pradesh and (CP) Madhya Pradesh—were mostly urban dwellers and they largely resettled in the major cities of Sindh—Hyderabad, Karachi, Khairpur, Mirpur Khas, Nawabshah, Shahdadpur, Sukkur and Tando Adam. While most of them left their hearths and homes because of communal riots in their areas, many adopted Pakistan as their new home as a matter of choice. Unlike East Punjab, from where the transmigration of the Muslim population to Pakistan was complete and total, the movement of the refugees from the 'Non-Agreed Areas' was partial and divided families between India and Pakistan. This created many problems when the India-Pakistan border was closed, although family affiliations remained strong among the affected people.

The refugees from the 'Non-Agreed Areas' called themselves *mohajirs* in Pakistan. The more prominent among them hailed from the province of UP and considered themselves culturally superior to others. The past era of the Muslim Empire in the subcontinent gave them grandiose notions of their lost Delhi and Lucknow based cultural pre-eminence and they arrogated to themselves the role of the custodians of the vanished glory of Muslim Rule in India.

These people had settled in Pakistan but could not emotionally disengage themselves from the *Ganga-Jamni* culture. Instead of merging themselves with the social and cultural environment of Sindh to create a new and enriched blend of distinctive identity for Pakistan, they endeavoured to practice their UP culture in the desert of Sindh and hoped that their cultural identity would also be adopted by the old Sindhis. This attitude brought them into conflict with the local nationalist power centres who were themselves no less possessive and proud of their own ancient language, distinctive dress and rich cultural heritage.

Living in their once glorious past was painful for the *mohajirs*. The *mohajir* political leadership found themselves removed from their traditional and safe constituencies left behind in India. It was difficult for them to re-establish their roots and create new constituencies in Pakistan. Their task was made more difficult by local political minions who declined to share their constituencies with the incoming political giants.

Sindh became an economic haven for new investors. Karachi, the only seaport in West Pakistan, lured the *mohajirs* and entrepreneurs to resettle in Sindh in general, and Karachi and Hyderabad in particular. Their concentration in a few urban population centres gave them a sense of security and cultural unity. Some *mohajirs* hailing from Kathiawar and Rajesthan in India spread themselves throughout Sindh. The Memon and the Khoja communities, with considerable experience in business and trade, adopted these professions and achieved notable success in their efforts. Many of those migrating from Rajputana chose the army and the police services as their professional careers.

A fair number of the *mohajirs* enjoyed good financial status. This category included the Indian Civil Service officers and their dependents. In the post-independence era, these officers came to dominate the civil services in Pakistan. As the trauma of 1947 subsided, the *mohajirs* developed an air of supremacy supposedly enjoyed by them over the other segments of society and felt that their cultural heritage, dress, life-style, customs and traditions were superior to those of the native Sindhis. They also claimed that they had made more sacrifices for the creation of Pakistan than the local inhabitants. Urdu, their mother tongue and now the national language of Pakistan, was deemed to be superior to the regional languages, despite the fact that regional languages had deeper roots than Urdu in the areas that constituted Pakistan. Conversely, some locals taunted the *mohajirs* about their dress, living and eating habits.

The regional languages of Pakistan, developed over centuries, exercised a strong pull on the inhabitants of their respective areas, but they were not in conflict with Urdu, the national language. Both co-existed and flourished concurrently to the advantage of each and harm to none. It was to the mutual advantage of both that the regional customs and traditions continued to develop to enrich Pakistan's cultural heritage.

It is noteworthy that, notwithstanding their regional linguistic preferences and sensitivities, all the provinces in West Pakistan, Sindh included, unhesitatingly adopted Urdu as the national language and the *lingua franca* of the country. This was done despite the fact that Urdu was not a commonly spoken language in any of the provinces. However, Urdu enjoyed a distinct country-wide advantage, and no other language would have been acceptable to all the four provinces. The adoption of Urdu as the national language showed not only the foresight of the national political leaders but also the collective maturity of the people of Pakistan. The last fifty years have witnessed a phenomenal rise in the development of Urdu, a process in which Radio Pakistan and Pakistan Television have made major contributions.

Most of the old Sindhis gladly learnt Urdu and conversed in this language without any inhibitions. On the other hand, most *mohajirs* adopted a defiant attitude. They loved to live in Sindh but were averse to learning the Sindhi language. They also showed reluctance in adopting Sindhi dress and culture and this brought them into conflict with the nationalist Sindhi population.

While the local-refugee distinction disappeared in Punjab soon after 1947, it grew and eventually created serious ethnic problems in Sindh.

Sindh's Rural-Urban Population Ratio

The results of the 1998 Census in the country were released on 9 July 1998. The finance minister claimed this as the 'most authentic and fair population and housing census ever conducted in the country.' The 1998 Census showed that Pakistan's population had increased from 84.253 millions in 1981 to 130.578 million in 1998 with a population divide of 67.5 per cent in the rural areas and 32.5 per cent in the urban areas. As against this national average, the population in the Sindh Province increased from 19.029 million in 1981 to 29.991 million in 1998. In Sindh, 51.1 per cent people lived in the rural areas and 48.9 per cent in the urban areas. Karachi, the largest city in the country, had a population of 9.26 million. The close population ratio between rural and urban Sindh aroused rivalries between the old Sindhis, who dominate the rural areas, and the *mohajirs*, who constitute a majority in the urban centres.

Mohajir-Local Divide

The staunch nationalists—G. M. Syed, Comrade Hyder Bux Jatoi and Qazi Faiz Mohammad—feared that they might become a minority in their own province. In their perception, the *mohajirs* had usurped their rights and job opportunities, and the legitimate interests of the rural segment of Sindh's population were in jeopardy. They also resented the comparative affluence of the *mohajirs*, who dominated in the fields of business, trade and administration. The die-hard nationalists openly accused the *mohajirs* and the Punjabi settlers of being exploiters ravaging Sindh. Any local issue on which the *mohajirs* and the Punjabi settlers developed a consensus of interests and views became suspicious to the Sindhis, as the convergence of such bilateral interests was perceived by the old Sindhis to be at their cost. While not all these apprehensions were correct, and some were widely off the mark, Sindh festered with doubts and fears.

As usually happens in a developing society, the vocal urban population in Sindh, as elsewhere in the country, agitated for and often received more than its fair share in the field of development programmes. As a result, the education facilities, health services, industrial growth, job opportunities, and, consequently, the quality of life in the urban centres were better than those in the rural areas. The economic gulf between the rural and the urban belts increased to the disadvantage of the former. This created bitterness and resentment in the villages and small towns where civic facilities were outdated and inferior to those available in Karachi or Hyderabad. Such disparity reinforced the views of the nationalist elements that the old Sindhis were being discriminated against.

Mohajir View

The *mohajirs* claimed that Pakistan was created as a homeland for all Muslims in India and they had the right to settle in any part of the country without let or hindrance. They also argued that unlike the refugees, the local population of the areas constituting Pakistan was mercifully spared the trauma and the tribulations of uprooting from their ancestral hearths and homes in 1947. They felt that the sacrifices made by them deserved to be acknowledged.

The *mohajirs* believed that Karachi's rapid industrial growth was the result of the collective efforts made by the people of Pakistan, and rural Sindh had played only a small part in this development work. They demanded job opportunities on the basis of merit, knowing that such a criterion would favour the Urdu speaking urban population that had greater access to better education facilities in the large cities.

The *mohajirs* accused the locals of not accepting them without reservation, and for keeping them under psychological pressure or taunting them on one pretext or the other. They felt their silence in the early years had been taken as a sign of weakness. Gradually, they learnt to make their presence felt through the use of street power. They started asserting themselves when they realized that they were too many in number to be ignored or browbeaten. They became conscious of their inherent rights and of their power to agitate. A group of Urdu speaking civil servants secretly provided the intellectual input for creating such a realization.

Sindhi Nationalism

The people of Sindh actively participated in the freedom struggle and played a leading role in the creation of Pakistan. Their vote in the elections at the local, provincial and the national levels held since 1947 has consistently been in support of the broad-based political parties, following the centre-of-the-road approach. The Sindhi electorate has repeatedly rejected a parochial approach on issues of national importance. The regionalist and the extremist political parties in Sindh have been comprehensively rejected in all the elections held in the province so far.

This does not mean that regionalism is a dead issue or that nationalism lacks appeal among the people of Sindh. Many attempts have been made by Sindhi nationalist leaders to arouse local public emotions on regional issues. Such endeavors occasionally created difficulties and vitiated the political climate for a while but seldom influenced the voters to swing towards the extreme. This is a tribute to the maturity of the electorate and their political judgement. The Sindhi nationalists enjoy the support of a section of the local print media, that keeps them alive. This is in addition to the support amply provided to such elements from neighbouring India that occasionally uses the Sindh Card to promote its own vested interests.

The Sindhi nationalists display emotionalism but only a small fraction of them trekked across the porous Indo-Pakistan border to India during the movement for the restoration of democracy (MRD). In 1983-84, Prime Minister Indira Gandhi repeatedly threatened Pakistan that her country would not remain indifferent to the cause of the people of Sindh. A 'Sindhi *Sammelan*' (Seminar) was held in New Delhi under the chairmanship of the President of India in which it was demanded that Sindh be absorbed into the Indian motherland.[2] In 1986, General Sundarji boasted to Maj. General Nishat of Pakistan that India possessed the 'Sindhi Card'.[3] This card has been repeatedly used and 'India had been a major player in carrying out terrorism in Pakistan.'[4]

The nationalist Sindhi leaders, grudging the Punjabi settlers in Sindh, started a Sindhi Nationalist *Tehreek* [movement] to protect their 'regional interests'. They became vocal and active during the Ayub era for a variety of reasons, one being the creation of One Unit in West Pakistan which created fear in the minds of the people of the smaller provinces that Punjab would dominate them.

Some other developments added fuel to the fire. The establishment of One Unit necessitated bringing in officers from different provinces on a common roster. This was done in accordance with an agreed formula. Some Sindhi officers, finding their names down the ladder, blamed the Punjabi officers for this mischief. Also, the transfer of some Punjabi officers to

Sindh, as a part of the amalgamation of the officer cadre to various provinces, evoked criticism from the Sindhi nationalist elements, as well as from the *mohajirs*. They also censured the allotment of agricultural lands in Sindh to the Punjabi civil and military bureaucracy. Such measures provided fuel to vested interests to ignite regional sensitivities and emotions.

Karachi became the capital of Pakistan in August 1947 for reasons of administrative necessity. The heavy concentration of *mohajirs* in Karachi were provided economic opportunities generated in establishing a new capital city. They also received a generous share of job opportunities in the government and in its attached departments.

President Ayub, however, appointed a Site Selection Committee to select a new location for the capital of the country. The committee recommended the area now known as Islamabad as the most suitable location. Many considered the transfer of the capital from Karachi a prudent decision. Islamabad's location and climate made it an appropriate choice. However, the decision was not free from criticism. The people of East Pakistan desired that the national capital be located in their wing. A majority of the Sindhis, rural and urban, wanted Karachi to remain the capital, fearing that the importance and the distinctive status of Karachi would be compromised. Karachi was and still is the largest industrial and commercial city in the country.

The shifting of the capital became a major issue for the *mohajirs*. Their physical distance from Islamabad caused unease because they now became distanced from the national power base. Many *mohajirs* had come to regard themselves as an inseparable part of national power politics and the national economy. In their vision, Karachi was destined to be the hub of the country where the culture of the Urdu-speaking people would dominate to compensate for the loss of Delhi and Lukhnow.

Those who immigrated from India in 1947 to become permanent citizens of their newly adopted country, Pakistan, have now spent over fifty years here. A generation that migrated to Pakistan in 1947 cannot, by any stretch of logic or morality, claim to be perpetual *mohajirs*. And the generation that was born in Pakistan and grew up here cannot by any stretch of the imagination justifiably call themselves refugees or *mohajirs*. They would do well to promote national unity by fully integrating into the mainstream of Pakistan's national politics.

A perceptible social, cultural and linguistic integration is in progress in the country. Due to the decision taken by Pakistan's forefathers, and the yeoman service rendered by the print and electronic media, Urdu has rapidly developed as the link language of Pakistan. No other language in the country can fulfil this requirement. Urdu has made great strides in the last five decades. Its already rich vocabulary is gradually being enriched further with the regular absorption of many words from the regional languages of Pakistan, and this on-going process has helped in national integration. Urdu is a dynamic and a living language, and its impact is increasingly being felt in the whole of Pakistan. Likewise, a social and cultural identity of Pakistan has emerged as a happy blend of the regional and national mix. This trend is likely to strengthen further with the passage of time.

In the 1964 presidential elections, the combined opposition parties supported *Mohtarma* Fatima Jinnah against Field Marshal Ayub Khan. The *mohajirs* in Sindh, and the Pathan voters in Karachi generally voted in favour of *Mohtarma* Fatima Jinnah and Ayub Khan respectively. The votes of the old Sindhis and the Punjabi settlers were divided. The common perception was that the elections had been rigged in favour of President Ayub. The pro-Ayub supporters took out a victory procession in Karachi, and the political polarization intensified as the victory procession, led by Ayub's son, was largely attended by the Pathan supporters of the President. At this time, the victors used strong, irresponsible language that increased ethnic bitterness, led to many deaths in the resultant riots, and left deep scars on the body of Pakistan's nascent democratic order.

In 1967, Sindhi and *mohajir* leaders G. M. Syed, Qazi Faiz, Rasool Bux Palejo, Hafiz Qureshi and Nawab Muzaffar, held a convention at Hyderabad under the banner of Sindh United Front against the formation of One Unit and the 'domination' of the Punjab. Their unity, based on a common negative factor, proved abortive. The convention failed, although both the groups agreed to disagree on the interpretation of Islam and the ideology of Pakistan but failed to reach an agreement on the language issue. Later, the Sindh United Front split into two groups, the Jeay Sindh Tehreek and Mohajir, Punjabi, Pathan United Front.

These forces felt that the setback suffered by them was temporary. Their sympathizers and supporters provided encouragement to them to persist in their endeavors. Attempts continued to be made to create ethnic hatred and to spread violence. G. M. Syed pleaded with his supporters in Hyderabad that they could not fight the collective might of the Punjabi, Pathan and *mohajir* elements. He advised them that out of the three groups, the *mohajirs* were the most vulnerable and easy to deal with. Their number in the armed forces was small and their influence in the civil bureaucracy was also on the decline. Besides, it was easy to deal with them as they generally did not possess weapons. Such incitement negated a fair political course and suggested that the strategy had been prepared by experts in insurgency. Mercifully for Pakistan, and to the annoyance of the planners, the nefarious programme could not be implemented because the PPP had been voted to power which, on assuming control, treated the nationalists as well as the *mohajirs* even-handedly. At this time, both these communities adopted a low-key approach.

Prelude to the Power Tussle

Paradoxically, the honour of holding the first general elections in Pakistan since 1947 went to the military government of General Yahya Khan. Sheikh Mujibur Rahman's Awami League swept the polls in East Pakistan in the 1970 elections by capturing 160 seats in the Eastern Wing. The party position in West Pakistan was not much different with Mr Z. A. Bhutto's PPP, the largest single political party winning 81 seats in West Pakistan and none in the Eastern Wing. The PPP had its electoral strength mostly restricted to Punjab and Sindh.[5] Splinter groups emerged in the provincial assemblies in Balochistan and NWFP where no major party could single-handedly form a government.

The political follies committed by successive governments, both civil and military, since 1947 divided the country, and East Pakistan was amputated in December 1971. Pakistan's errors of omission and commission were exploited by India and with her covert support and overt military aggression, East Pakistan became Bangladesh. The Yahya government gave way to the PPP and Mr Bhutto took charge of what was left of Pakistan. Bhutto's cousin, Mumtaz Ali Bhutto, became the chief executive in his home province, Sindh, and worked to consolidate and strengthen the power base of the PPP.

Language Riots

Mumtaz Bhutto was a nationalist by conviction. His political instincts and nationalist leanings prompted him to win the support of the old Sindhi population in order to strengthen the PPP's grip on political power. Both Mr Z. A. Bhutto and Mumtaz Bhutto desired to go down in history as the champions of Sindh's interests and the saviors of its cultural heritage and traditions. This was a tightrope walk because over-playing the Sindh card ran the risk of creating political difficulties for Prime Minister Bhutto in Punjab, which had brought him to power. Z. A. Bhutto played his political trump card with finesse. While portraying himself as a leader with vision and national outlook, he left it to his 'talented cousin' Mumtaz Bhutto, the Chief Minister of Sindh, to woo the old Sindhi voters and to discipline the *mohajirs*.

On 7 July 1972, the Sindh Assembly passed the Sindh (Teaching, Promotion and use of Sindhi Language) Act, 1972 and it was assented to by the Governor of Sindh on 16 July 1972.[6] By this Act, both Sindhi and Urdu became compulsory subjects for class 1V to X11. Article 5 of the Act stated that the 'Government may constitute and set up Academies and Boards for cultural advancement and promotion of the Sindhi Language.' Article 6 of the Act said the 'Government may make arrangements for progressive use of Sindhi language in offices and Government departments including Courts and Assembly.' On face value it made sense that all Sindhis must learn the Sindhi language. However, the timing of the legislation was politically inappropriate, and the change was made in a hurry and without preparing the *mohajirs* for it psychologically. Legislation of a basic and permanent nature is best enacted after a consensus. This was not done.

The old Sindhis were jubilant over their 'victory'. However, the *mohajir* reaction to the Language Act was negative and severe. The province of Sindh was divided on ethnic lines, old versus the new Sindhis, both highly charged. The old Sindhis felt that the *mohajirs* had taken control of the two largest cities, Karachi and Hyderabad, in *their* province to the disadvantage of those who had lived in this region for centuries. The *mohajirs* argued that the Sindhi Muslims had been in a minority in both these cities even before independence. The exodus of the Hindu population from these urban centres in 1947 had created a vacuum that was filled by the incoming *mohajirs* from India. This was a natural phenomenon. Emotions over-rode logic on both sides.

The *mohajirs* became crusaders for the Urdu language forgetting that it was already the national language of the country and its development met the common needs of its people. Bruised emotions led to riots in which the *mohajirs* suffered. Out of the ashes of the language riots, as they came to be called, emerged the slogan of a 'fifth nationality' (*mohajir*). Some *mohajirs* were uprooted from Larkana and Shikarpur districts and they migrated to the safety of Karachi and Hyderabad. Larkana Colony in Hyderabad still presents a grim reminder of those troubled days.

Another point of contention was Article 27 in the Constitution of a ten year duration which reserved posts for persons belonging to certain areas to secure adequate representation in government jobs. This was a safeguard against discrimination in government services with respect to areas which were educationally underdeveloped. According to this law, called the 'quota system', all the public sector employment vacancies in Sindh were fixed between the rural and the urban areas of this province at a 40:60 per cent ratio respectively. Prior to the 'quota system', the vacancies in the public sector were filled, as in other provinces, on the basis of merit. The introduction of this system was supported in the rural areas and opposed in the urban areas that already enjoyed better educational facilities.

There were merits and demerits in retaining or discarding the 'quota system' and both the groups vehemently stated their points of view. The Constitution had visualized that this disparity in education between the rural and the urban areas would be eradicated in a decade. This did not happen. The successive governments kept the quota system in vogue by extending its duration through constitutional amendments.

The *mohajirs* called the 'quota system' in Sindh a discriminatory act because the remaining provinces did not adopt this system. However, the other provinces did not have the problem of a divided population prevalent in Sindh. The 'quota system' was an irritant for the urban-based, educated *mohajirs* because the more qualified and better educated candidates from urban Sindh were denied vacancies which they might have otherwise secured on merit. The language riots left behind ugly scars on the national psyche. Sindh was polarized.

Bhutto, a democrat in theory, was an autocrat in practice. His feudal approach, suppressive rule and harsh policies kept public wrath simmering under the democratic front of his elected government (1971-77). The 1977 rigged elections held by the Bhutto government led to a movement against this election fraud initiated by the Pakistan National Alliance in March, 1977. The *mohajirs* rose in revolt against Bhutto in all the cities in Sindh in concert with the people of other provinces who protested elsewhere in the country. The anti-Bhutto public avalanche led to the fall of his government when martial law was imposed by the army in July 1977.

The nationalist elements showed a mixed reaction. Some rejoiced at the fall of Bhutto because of his alleged failure to promote Sindhi nationalism. Others were grieved at the exit of a

'Sindhi prime minister' from the national seat of power. Taking advantage of the changed political scenario, G. M. Syed readjusted his tactics. He now expressed a desire to befriend the *mohajirs* and branded the Punjabi settlers as the sole exploiters. Later, Pathans were added to this list. Like a true politician, he adopted a dual approach. In public, he pleaded for Sindhi-*mohajir* unity, but in private he kept harping on the theme that all the three communities—*mohajirs*, Punjabis and Pathans—had exploited Sindh. At the other end of the political spectrum, in the late 1970s, some prominent Urdu-speaking intellectuals picked up the slogan of *mohajirism* and proclaimed the beginning of a struggle for achieving their rights. The failure of the major political parties to prevent the growing tide of polarization in Sindh opened avenues for other forces to fill in the vacuum.

Students in Politics

The Muslim Students Federation had taken an active part in the freedom struggle in India that led to the emergence of Pakistan. The goal achieved, the student community did not disengage itself from active politics and in the process it started lagging behind in the race for education and knowledge. The political parties added to the intellectual decline by exploiting the students as political pawns in their struggle for power. The student unions in the universities were affiliated with the major political parties and virtually became their militant wings. The students wasted their time and energy in wielding weapons rather than reading books. This phenomenon played havoc with the education system and often turned the citadels of learning into battlefields.

In the seventies, Karachi University was infested with the cancer of parochialism and ethnicity, and banners displayed in the university campus disclosed the presence of organizations like Jeay Sindh Students Federation, Pakhtun Students Federation, Punjabi Students Association, Baloch Students Organisation, Kashmir Students Federation, Gilgit Students

Federation and Qabaail Students Federation. While most of them were splinter groups, the university was essentially the stronghold of the Islami Jamiat Talaba, the student wing of the Jamaat-e-Islami. Nearly the entire panel of the student unions comprised Jamiat backed activists. After the fall of Bhutto and the imposition of Martial Law by Ziaul Haq, the *mohajir* students entered this arena and on 11 June 1978, the All Pakistan Mohajir Students Organisation (APMSO) was formed with Altaf Hussain as its president and Azim Ahmad Tariq as its secretary-general.

APMSO was initially more active in the faculty of pharmacy where Altaf Hussain and Azim Tariq were registered as students. The majority of students in this faculty were victims of the 'quota system' who had been denied admission in medical colleges. They protested because the students belonging to rural Sindh, with less marks than the urban students, had been admitted into the medical colleges of Sindh and Karachi purely on the basis of the 'quota system'. The urban students who rose up in arms to defeat the 'unjust' quota system from the platform of APMSO, a professedly non-political organization, sought enhancement in the number of seats for the Urdu-speaking population of Sindh. The youth of Karachi hailed the formation of APMSO, and the slogan of *mohajir* was raised for the first time from its platform.

The popularity graph of APMSO rapidly rose, and within months it became an effective organization not only in Karachi but also in Hyderabad. Its declared aims included:

a. Abolition of the quota system in Sindh.
b. Repatriation of Biharis from Bangladesh.
c. Increase in the grant of Karachi University and other departments.
d. Addressing the problems faced by the *mohajirs* in gaining admission into educational institutions.
e. Better employment opportunities for *mohajir* youth.

Universities Politicized

On 14 August 1979, Pakistan's Independence day, Altaf Hussain, Afaq Khan Shahid (later MNA) and Haseeb Hashmi (later MPA) staged a protest demonstration at the *mazar* of Quaid-i-Azam in Karachi demanding the repatriation of Urdu-speaking Biharis from Bangladesh to Pakistan. Much to the anger of every Pakistani, the national flag was torched on the occasion as a mark of protest.

Agitation-based politics in the universities was not confined to the students alone. University lecturers had also joined this bandwagon and indiscipline had crept into the university campus. The Vice-Chancellors and their administrative teams were too weak, ineffective and afraid of using their inherent powers to punish the defaulters. Instead, they adopted a policy of appeasement to earn the goodwill of the student community, to maintain peace and order, and to ensure their continuity in service.

So far the government had taken a lenient view of the students indulging in agitational activities in Karachi, but disrespect to the national flag by deliberately torching it was too serious an offense to be ignored. Altaf Hussain and his accomplices were arrested and tried in a court of law. Altaf Hussain was awarded a sentence of nine months imprisonment and fifteen lashes by the court. The sentence of lashes was later remitted. Altaf completed his punishment and was released from jail in April 1980. During Altaf Hussain's imprisonment, the secretary-general of APMSO, Azim Ahmed Tariq, stayed in India from where he returned just one month before Altaf Hussain was released. The reason for his visit to India remained unexplained.

Mr Altaf Hussain was influenced by Mr Akhtar Rizvi, a gentleman with leftist leanings, to work in harmony with Jeay Sindh. The politics of expediency brought G.M. Syed and Altaf Hussain so close to each other that Akhtar Rizvi was widely believed to be the ghost writer of the booklet, *Mohajir-Panchween Qaumiat* published in the name of Altaf Hussain.

The rapid rise in the popularity of APMSO among Urdu-speaking students in Karachi University made its impact felt not only within the university campus but also outside it. The student hostels in Karachi University became clandestine arsenals of arms and the hardware was frequently displayed to frighten the non-*mohajir* students, and to blackmail them to pay '*bhatta*' (extortion money). The weapons were easily available in the country as a result of the fall-out of the situation in Afghanistan. General Zia held a conference to analyse this phenomenon with the provincial governors and the vice-chancellors of the universities to devise a strategy to control the situation. They expressed their helplessness in enforcing the writ of law because the student unions had become too powerful for them to handle. The problem demanded firm handling and it was decided to ban student unions in all the universities.

Jamaat-e-Islami Influence in Karachi

The interregnum between 1977 and 1985 witnessed the rise of several rightist political parties in Karachi with the Jamaat-e-Islami leading the fray. The Mayor of the Karachi Metropolitan Corporation, Mr Abdul Sattar Afghani, belonging to the JI found the official Rules of Business too cumbersome to follow. High on protocol and keen on getting publicity, he sought prominence as an elected mayor of the largest city in the country and equated himself with the Lord Mayors of London or Paris. His style of work and his demand for the sharing of taxes and grants on a fair and equitable basis between the province of Sindh and the city of Karachi caused friction between him and the provincial government.

Abdul Sattar Afghani, a person with limited exposure in the administrative field and visibly obsessed with his official legal rights, came into serious conflict with Chief Minister Ghous Ali Shah, who was no less assertive in exercising his authority as the chief executive of the province. Ghous Ali Shah endeavoured to remove Afghani from his prized assignment. This political intolerance brought the chief minister into conflict with the JI, to which Afghani belonged. Eventually, Afghani was shown the door and Ghous Ali Shah indulged in political intrigue to placate the reaction from JI. He hobnobbed with the Mohajir Quami Movement to reduce the political influence of the Jamaat-e-Islami. The Sindh Governor, Lieutenant-General Jahan Dad Khan did not oppose the triple edged strategy adopted by the chief minister; disciplining Afghani, diminishing the influence of the JI and encouraging the MQM. In the MNA's conferences, the governor constantly pleaded that the situation in Karachi was essentially political in nature and it was being eminently handled by the chief minister. Such a shortsighted approach encouraged the MQM to spread its activist tentacles.

Initially, the JI had exercised considerable political influence in Karachi and its grip was strong. Its senior leadership had suspected Bhutto's motives and apprehended that he had sinister designs in creating an East Pakistan-like crisis in Pakistan, particularly in Sindh. Immediately after the fall of Bhutto's government, the JI complained that the favourite bureaucrats of the ex-prime minister in the administration were continuing to rule the roost, despite the imposition of martial law.[7] The JI joined the Zia government in August 1978 to consolidate its hold in Karachi, and to strengthen the party against the tide of Sindhi nationalism and the PPP. The Jamaat-e-Islami came to be regarded as General Zia's 'B' team, an allegation that harmed both Zia and the JI.

The Mohajir Qaumi Movement

The Mohajir Qaumi Movement (MQM) was established on 18 March 1984, as a non-political organisation out of APMSO with Altaf Hussain and Zahid Khan as its founder members. The concept of collective leadership, the hallmark of democracy, did not work in the MQM. Altaf Hussain kept the leadership of the party with himself and ensured that no one else could aspire for the top slot. Altaf and Zahid soon fell apart and the latter

formed the 'Mohajir Ittehad Tehreek'. Raees Amrohi, an elderly
and respected Urdu poet, laboured hard to unite the two factions.
He aligned himself with Altaf Hussain when his reconciliation
attempts failed to unify the opposing groups.

An attempt was also made by the MQM and the Jeay Sindh
to arrive at a political understanding. Both agreed on many
issues but no consensus was reached on the question of the
'fifth nationality', claimed by the MQM. In this emerging
political scenario, the Punjabi settlers became a convenient
punch bag for both these parties. While the MQM used its
influence and authority to isolate the Punjabi students in the
educational institutions, the Jeay Sindh activists committed acts
of terror against the Punjabi settlers to force them to flee from
their lands. Working in concert, the MQM and Jeay Sindh
became an extension of each other and their slogans showed
remarkable similarity. Inflammatory slogans were coined for
exerting pressure. Some examples. 'The Punjabi power
steamroller will not be permitted to crush the rights of the
Sindhis'. And, the 'proud Sindhis cannot be made the Red
Indians of Pakistan.' Altaf Hussain maintained a diplomatic
posture on the question of the 'fifth nationality', and restricted
its scope to the preservation of the Urdu language, *mohajir*
traditions, social environment and culture.

Movement for the Restoration of Democracy (MRD)

In February 1981, a conglomerate of twelve political parties,
with diverse political leanings, initiated a 'Movement for the
Restoration of Democracy.' The only major party in this
hotchpotch of centre, right and left—the PPP—technically joined
the MRD but in practice it remained on the sidelines as a keen
observer. The MRD remained ineffective till mid 1983 but its
leadership kept making political noises in their drawing-room
meetings. The MRD announced a plan to start protest rallies in
the country on Pakistan's independence day, 14 August 1983.

The Zia government adopted a pre-emptive strategy to seize the initiative and to deflate the MRD. On 12 August 1983, two days before the start of the MRD, it announced a three-tier action plan to hold local, provincial and national elections in the country spread over the next eighteen months. It was assessed by the government at the time that this announcement would derail the agitation. The opposition denounced this declaration as another ruse of the dictator to prolong his one-man rule.

Mr Ghulam Mustafa Jatoi spearheaded the movement against the government with the theme that Sindh faced a 'sense of deprivation'. This was a political blunder by the MRD as its own sponsors did not back it. The patently regional and emotive cry did not arouse public sympathy or interest in the provinces of Punjab, NWFP and Balochistan. Initially conceived as a nation-wide movement, the MRD became a non-event in three out of four provinces of the country. The public response in Sindh was divided. It gained reasonable momentum in some parts of rural Sindh, but urban Sindh did not display any interest in the agitation.

Mr Ghulam Mustafa Jatoi was arrested. His son emerged in London. Prime Minister Indira Gandhi was so sure of the success of the MRD that she issued a public statement threatening that India would not remain indifferent to the cause of the people of Sindh.[8] One Congress member in the *Lok Sabha* (Indian parliament) demanded that Sindh be absorbed in *Bharat-mata*. Pakistan formally protested to India at this offensive statement, to which the reply was that the member had expressed his personal view.[9]

With Jatoi arrested, the leadership of the MRD fell into the hands of inexperienced political minions who did not have a serious plan of action. They expedited the demise of the MRD by indulging in acts of terrorism and anti-social activities. Public property was burnt, banks were looted, canals breached, railway lines uprooted, and innocent citizens held hostage for ransom. Ironically, rural Sindh, that supposedly had felt a 'sense of deprivation' suffered most during the MRD misadventure. While the poor people suffered and faced hardships, those inciting them to agitate were comfortably lodged as the government's guests. Mr Jatoi faced a political setback, and the law enforcing agencies restored the writ of the government.

The MQM remained a silent spectator during the MRD agitation. It neither participated in the movement nor lent support to it. Peace prevailed in all the major cities of Sindh and the encounters between the miscreants and the law enforcing agencies in the rural parts of the province did not arouse the emotions of *mohajirs*.

Altaf Hussain's Stay in the USA

In 1984, Altaf Hussain went to the United States. His departure was not announced in advance, and the members of APMSO were given to understand that he had left the country to avoid arrest. This did not seem to be true because no case was pending against him to warrant his arrest or detention. Altaf stayed in the US for a long time which led to speculations in Pakistan. In view of his political background, the national intelligence agencies kept an unobtrusive watch on his contacts in America. The reports submitted by them to the government indicated that some family members were permanent residents of the US but his purpose in living there was not to renew family associations.

By the time Altaf Hussain returned from the US to Pakistan in November 1985, his inclination for active politics was obvious and he had decided to convert the MQM into a political organ. Unlike his quiet departure from Karachi, he was ceremoniously received by supporters on his return and was brought home from the airport in a motorcade of cars and scooters, and projected as the leader of a new MQM. The next few months were spent in organizing the MQM for its political role in provincial affairs. The planning was done with meticulous care. On 8 August 1986, the MQM held its first public meeting at Nishtar Park, Karachi. This well-managed, massive affair was a show of high discipline and painstaking effort.

The formation of the MQM could have been advantageous but led to tragedy. Because it was led by young and dedicated leadership from the middle class, it generated a hope that Pakistan might be able to 'get rid of the accumulated refuse of forty years, and throw up a fresh, vibrant, dedicated, and patriotic leadership.'[10] Much to the regret of optimists, this dream soon turned sour.

The tragedy was that the MQM was formed on an ethnic basis when the need for Pakistan was greater unity and national consolidation. Politics based on ethnicity and extremism could neither meet Pakistan's security concerns nor bring progress and prosperity to her people.

From Martial Law to Democracy

The government had conceived its triple-tier election plan of 12 August 1983 with care and it was implemented within the announced time frame. The local bodies elections took place on a non-party basis. The PPP boycotted these elections but allowed its members to contest them individually under the name of *Awam Dost* (People's friends). A referendum held on 19 December 1984 gave a vote of confidence to General Zia. It was planned to be conducted fairly but in reality, irregularities were committed that seriously affected its credibility. Zia's critics called it a hoax and ridiculed him for enacting a farce to entrench himself in power. The elections for the National Assembly were held on a non-party basis on 25 February 1985. Three days later, elections for all the four provincial assemblies took place, also on a non-party basis. The new Parliament held its inaugural session on 23 March 1985. Mr Mohammad Khan Junejo became the Prime Minister of Pakistan while General Zia retained his dual status as the President of Pakistan and Chief of the Army Staff. This situation was not popular within the army and was adversely commented upon in undertones. Martial law was lifted from the country on 31 December 1985.

The non-party elections had serious limitations. These were analyzed in depth and comprehensively debated. But General Zia was determined to commit the folly of holding them despite the advice given to him to the contrary by some of his close advisers, including myself. It may be stated that opinion on the issue was divided among his colleagues and Zia agreed with those who supported his own preference. His thinking was that this might be a half-way house to democracy, but it was a forward movement and a sea-change from the static position of martial law. Non-party elections were better than no elections. The incoming democratic order was institutionally superior to the one it replaced.

While the rest of the country prepared for elections, the MQM brooded and sulked. It had previously accused the Bhutto government of suppressing the political and economic interests of *mohajirs*. It now argued that Zia's 'Punjabi' martial law had favoured the old Sindhis.

Ethnic clashes in Karachi kept the city emotionally charged. In April 1985, a female student, Bushra Zaidi, was run over and killed by a mini-bus in a road accident. This unfortunate incident took an ugly ethnic turn because the bus driver happened to be a Pathan, and the victim a *mohajir*. The activists, wanting an excuse, any excuse, insinuated that the *mohajirs* were suffering (even in road accidents) because they were unarmed and powerless.

The mainstream political parties had failed to solve the growing needs of Karachi. The city kept expanding haphazardly and in an unplanned manner. While its population increased at a fast rate, the public utility services in the city were not geared to keep pace with the rate of population growth. Resultantly, the people of Karachi started drifting away from the mainstream political parties. This provided a tailor-made opportunity to the regional and ethnic groups to replace the old guard by presenting themselves as the guardians of the interests of Karachi in general and of the *mohajirs* in particular.

In the thick of emotions, absurdity took the better of good sense and even minor issues were stretched to ridiculous limits. For example, if an out of form *mohajir* sportsman lost his place in a national hockey or cricket team, it was projected as an act of discrimination against the community. On one occasion, Altaf Hussain suggested that the quota system might be applied in selecting the national sports teams!

The MQM Enters Politics

The MQM participated in the local bodies elections in 1987/88 under the banner of '*Haq Parast* Group' and achieved notable success. It took charge of the local councils in two important cities of Sindh—Karachi and Hyderabad. This gave the new party considerable confidence. In the 1988 general elections, the MQM captured twenty-nine seats in the provincial assembly of Sindh and thirteen seats in the National Assembly. A new political party triumphantly emerged on Pakistan's political horizon.

The PPP and the MQM formed a coalition in Sindh as well as at the federal levels. Doubts soon arose between them and the MQM accused the PPP of not honouring the deal in letter and in spirit.

The PPP, a broad-based national party with its roots in rural Sindh, was under the firm control of the Bhutto family. It was PPP's political compulsion to espouse the rights and aspirations of the people of rural Sindh in order to keep a hold on its base of power. It also needed the support of its regional rival, the MQM, which, on the other hand, opposed the 'quota system' that the PPP government had introduced in Sindh. Differences between them started showing from the very beginning of their shaky coalition and kept widening with the passage of time.

May-October 1988 was a period of intense political activity and ethnic unrest in Sindh. In the resultant ethnic riots, MQM displayed its street power that left many civilians as well as members of the law enforcing agencies, including the military, dead or wounded, and unable to ensure the writ of law.

The city of Hyderabad, that had simmered with tension in the past but had generally remained free from serious ethnic violence, suddenly plunged into chaos and suffered incidents of looting and arson. The Jeay Sindh leader, Dr Qadir Magsi was accused of propagating inflammatory and provocative slogans that ignited the already tense ethnic divide. On May 27, the police force, comprising police reserves and armed Eagle Squad, shot and killed more than sixty innocent civilians and many more were wounded. This led to a protest march by the people that included many women. The unarmed protesters were fired at by the police. The situation became highly tense and, as a measure of control Dr Qadir Magsi was arrested. The police force was replaced by the army. By the end of September 1988, over two hundred civilians, mostly *mohajirs*, had lost their lives due to indiscriminate firing in Hyderabad by political militants.

The reaction to the massacre in Pucca Qilla changed the complexion of life in Sindh. Karachi, the stronghold of *mohajir* militants, suddenly erupted and on 1 October 1988, about sixty persons, mostly Sindhis, were killed in what appeared to be a vengeful ethnic backlash. The unfortunate incidents at Hyderabad and Karachi divided the two communities in Sindh. The *mohajir* started to look upon every Sindhi—whether or not a supporter of Jeay Sindh, PPP or Muslim League—as an enemy. Likewise, nationalist Sindhis regarded every *mohajir*—whether or not a member of the MQM—a terrorist and an exploiter out to divide the province.

Such emotion-ridden feelings ignored the reality that the genocide of either community was, in fact, leading to the annihilation of their common interests as they were inseparable partners in the province of Sindh. The results of the 1988 general election reflected the political division of Sindh, with the *mohajirs* supporting the MQM and the Sindhis voting for the PPP. The resort to violence and militancy by the parties in power was a mockery of good governance and a blow to the coalition. The situation took an ugly turn many times, and specially when the PPP and the MQM activists physically clashed with one another during the elections of the Pakistan Steel Mills Workers' Union at Karachi. In this free-for-all operation, both the political parties kidnapped the activists of the other party and kept them in illegal confinement as if they were prisoners of war captured in the battlefield. That such a flagrant abuse of law was a serious violation of the constitution, mattered little to the political leaders of both the parties. Their political poverty showed when the hostages held by both the coalition partners were eventually exchanged through the good offices of Lieutenant-General Asif Nawaz, Commander 5 Corps at Karachi in whom both the parties had expressed confidence.

A point of no return was reached when the MQM voted against the PPP government on a no-confidence motion in the National Assembly in a deal with the opposition. This act led to the termination of the 'Karachi Declaration' on 5 January 1989. The coalition partners became arch rivals.

In May 1990, fresh riots broke out in Hyderabad, leading to wide-spread violence. Mr Altaf Hussain suddenly departed for London to undergo treatment for his 'renal' ailment. The violence in Hyderabad rapidly spread to Karachi where 130 people were killed within one week. Once again, army troops were inducted to take charge of the law and order situation.

The MQM blamed the PPP government for not meeting its following demands:

a. Accepting *mohajirs* as the 'fifth nationality'.
b. Repatriation of the stranded Biharis from Bangladesh.
c. Giving employment opportunities to the *mohajirs*.
d. Abolishing the quota system.
e. Only Sindhis and *mohajirs* be employed in the administration, police, educational institutions and technical institutions of Sindh.
f. Separate status for Karachi.
g. Revival of the powers of Mayor and Deputy Mayor of the Karachi Municipal Corporation.

The PPP could not accept all of these demands because of their likely repercussions in rural Sindh and elsewhere in the country. On the other hand, the MQM complained that in violation of established norms and institutions, the PPP government had started a Placement Bureau that had arbitrarily

employed a large number of 'old Sindhis' in the government to
the disadvantage of *mohajirs*.

1990 General Elections

With the MQM-PPP relationship ruined, the former concluded
a secret agreement with the PPP's arch political rival, the Islami
Jamhoori Ittehad (IJI), a coatition of parties led by the Muslim
League. Karachi became an undeclared battlefield where human
life was easily expendable and lawlessness prevailed. Banks
were looted, people kidnapped at gun-point for ransom and
innocent citizens killed or wounded by gun-wielding miscreants
on the roads and streets of the largest city in Pakistan. The writ
of the government dipped low. On 6 August 1990, the President
of Pakistan dismissed the government of Prime Minister Benazir
Bhutto, dissolved the National Assembly and all the four
provincial assemblies and ordered fresh elections to be held in
October that year.

In the fresh elections, the PPP suffered an electoral defeat
and the IJI formed the federal government. The MQM returned
to the Sindh assembly with almost the same mandate as it had
before (28 seats). As previously, its success was limited to the
urban areas of Sindh only. It won fourteen seats in the National
Assembly and became a coalition partner of the IJI at the centre.
In Sindh, the MQM shared power in the government of Chief
Minister Jam Sadiq Ali, an old colleague-turned bitter foe of the
PPP.

A ruthless ruler, Jam Sadiq Ali kept the PPP on the run in
Sindh and took sadistic pleasure in settling old scores with this
party. With the chief minister busy targeting the PPP without any
qualms, the MQM turned Karachi into a walled city with iron
gates fixed by civilians at street entrances who endeavoured to
safeguard themselves from the wrath of militant gangs spraying
bullets at random. The city became a state within a state. Political
terrorism tore apart the socio-economic fabric of society, and law
and order ceased to exist in the province. Car snatching, extortion

of money, blackmailing and vendetta killing assumed critical proportions. The army was asked to restore normalcy by the government of Nawaz Sharif, the new prime minister. The Constitution permits the civilian government to use the military as an aid to civil power.

The Fourth Estate

Freedom of expression is invariably enshrined in the constitutions of all democratic societies. It is a gift and a right that may not be denied to the people under normal conditions. For reasons of national security, however, this freedom may be curtailed during periods of emergencies and open conflict. Such are the accepted norms.

The word freedom is defined differently by different people and its universally accepted interpretation is open-ended. However, it is logical to assume that a free press can only be nurtured by free minds and no one can demand freedom to destroy freedom. Even a free media is governed by ground rules enshrined in the constitution or the law. The media may be funded by governments, syndicates or individuals, and the hands that pay invariably dictate its policy options.

Pakistan's state-controlled electronic media has an impressive record of destroying its many distinguished rulers through over-projection. However, despite the long fatality list, the incoming new faces in the corridors of power quickly catch this cancerous disease and insist that their 'captive maid' must always sing songs in their praise.

Since the death of Ziaul Haq, our print media is largely free and lively. It has had a chequered history but has made visible strides in the last couple of decades. Even so, barring some notable exceptions, the pendulum of its performance swings selectively. On a comparative basis, the English press in Pakistan is more responsible than the vernacular one. The Urdu newspapers, the most widely read segment of the print media, do not hesitate to print lies, half truths, misinformation and

disinformation in the name of freedom of expression. Although
we have many journalists of integrity, some resort to blackmail
and others develop unprofessional relationships with their
subjects.

Successive governments in the first four decades after
independence adopted coercive and punitive measures to
'discipline' those newspapers which consistently printed news
and views beyond the limit of tolerance of the power barons.
Now, despite freedom from government repression, the print
media in Karachi in general, and the Urdu press in particular,
was threatened and pressurized by MQM activists and militants
who demanded it publish only what they wanted the people to
read. Refusal to oblige earned the press the physical wrath of
party activists. Such brutal tactics negated the democratic
credentials of the organization.

Some sections of the Urdu press in Karachi played a partisan
role that added to the prevailing tension in the city. To plead for
the rights of one ethnic group does not give a license to anyone
to violate the rights of other ethnic groups. Ethnic slogans
polarize a society.

The MQM Splits

Democracy becomes the first victim of terror-ridden politics.
Many Third World countries, Pakistan included, have learnt this
bitter lesson at considerable cost. Militancy became a part of
MQM politics and those who opposed their path were soon
'neutralised'. By the end of 1990, some active party members
developed policy differences with the hitherto undisputed leader
of the MQM, Altaf Hussain. Afaq Ahmed, Badar Iqbal, Ashraf
Ahmad and Aamir Khan opposed the total concentration of
power in one person, and proposed changes in the top echelon
leadership. All the four dissidents were expelled from the MQM.

The four individuals went into hiding, resurfaced in Punjab,
announced the formation of a splinter group—MQM *Haqiqi*
(H)—and won over the support of some activists/workers of

their former party. Afaq Ahmad and Aamir Khan issued lengthy statements explaining the reasons for their falling apart with Altaf Hussain. These were carried in the national press. Excerpts: 'The ultimate aim of the MQM was not merely to be recognized as a fifth nationality...The ultimate had to be independence...to have our own state...The West was looking for an alternative to Hong Kong, and no city was better suited to fill this role than Karachi. The West would, therefore, be agreeable to any move which could bring this about, and so would India...Altaf was in touch with both India and the USA on this issue.'[11]

The prevailing perception was that the dissenting wing of the MQM was aided and abetted by the government. However, if the credentials of Altaf Hussain were dubious, his rivals in the MQM (H) were no saints either. The top leaders in both the groups had worked in concert with one another for a common cause over a prolonged period of time. They knew each other's respective strengths and weaknesses. Away from their base camp, Karachi, the MQM (H) leaders enjoyed the hospitality of an 'organization' in Islamabad that rehabilitated their confidence and raised their morale. Soon, they felt strong enough to return to Karachi and started supporting the government 'in restoring normalcy' in this city, a euphemism for settling old scores with their once parent body.

The government responded positively as it was looking for a 'thief to catch a thief'. The army played a less than even-handed role in this sordid affair. Its hands were soiled in petty and local politics, and in the process its image was defamed. The army top brass might have done a great service to itself and to the country by staying clear of both the factions of the MQM and dealing with them fairly and on merit. Alas, this was not the case. The army was accused of a bias and the criticism was not without substance.

Because of the split, the mainstream MQM became temporarily dormant but it continued to remain the more dominant and the more popular faction of the organization. The mutual alienation between the two groups developed into a bitter rivalry, and in the ensuing tug of war for power, a large number of opposing activists from both factions of the MQM were targeted and killed in Karachi.

In January 1992, Altaf Hussain left for London, ostensibly for medical treatment, and has not returned to Pakistan since then. He exercises control on MQM activities from London, addresses public meetings in Karachi through prolonged long-distance telephone calls, issues policy statements and negotiates with other political parties from his self-exile in Britain. His source of income for living abroad remains undisclosed. His grip on the MQM is firm. All the *mohajirs* are not supporters of the MQM but, all are mortally scared of the terrible retribution awaiting them if they express their opposition against the MQM in public or deviate from its declared policies. The people of Karachi subsist in a fear syndrome.

In May 1992, the government launched a cleansing drive in Karachi against the militants in which MQM(H) helped the law enforcing agencies. This was partially successful and a reasonable degree of peace was restored for a time.

General Elections 1993

During the 1993 elections, the MQM did not field its candidates for the National Assembly seats, an error in judgement that it came to regret later. The MQM complained that the government desired that they split the Karachi seats between their two factions. This interference being unacceptable, the MQM opted to stay out of the elections. However, it participated in the provincial elections in Sindh, winning twenty-eight seats. The PPP won a comfortable majority in the provincial elections in Sindh and formed a government.

An uneasy peace prevailed in Karachi where the army troops remained deployed till November 1994. Working under difficult conditions, they tried to restore normalcy in Sindh. After a prolonged tenure, the police, rangers and other para-military forces took charge of maintaining law and order in the province and the army reverted to its barracks.

With the exit of the military, low level insurgency resurfaced in Karachi. Besides prolonged disturbances, shutdowns and strikes stopped the wheels of industry from churning, causing considerable loss to the national economy. The MQM damaged national reputation by raising Pakistan's internal security issues in international forums held abroad.

Back home, Prime Minister Benazir Bhutto's government was dissolved on 5 November 1997, on charges of corruption by President Farouq Ahmad Khan Leghari, who had been hand-picked as head of state by Benazir from her own PPP. Fresh elections were declared once again.

Post-1997 General Elections Scene

In the 1997 general elections, assessed to be fair by international observers, the Pakistan Muslim League (N) routed the PPP and won a massive majority in the electoral contest. The PPP's traditional vote bank was reduced, but only marginally. The election results enabled the PML(N) to form the government at the federal level and in three out of the four provinces. In Sindh, the PML (N) and MQM formed a coalition in the government of Chief Minister Liaquat Jatoi. This was a shaky alliance as the coalition partners seldom seemed to agree. The PML(N)-MQM coalition spent much time in accusing and counter accusing against each other while the Karachi law and order situation, revival of economy and restoration of normal life, remained largely neglected.

The coalition partners looked more like political antagonists than mutual power holders. The MQM made demands from which it would be the sole beneficiary. Specifically, it asked for the withdrawal of all cases filed against its activists on charges of murder, abduction, kidnapping etc. Besides, it wanted the law enforcing agencies to look the other way to permit its activists to settle their political scores with MQM (H). It wanted the police to stay away when its workers collected *bhatta* (extortion money) from the trade centres, business houses and industrial units, even private residences. While much time was wasted in acrimonious debate, the uplift and development plans of the province, and the law and order situation remained on the back burner. To the misfortune of Sindh, MQM has not found it convenient to work in harmony with any of its coalition partners in the past.

Negative politics is a thriving business in Pakistan. In 1970, Maulana Abdul Hamid Khan Bhashani of the erstwhile East Pakistan once gave a twenty minute sermon on the ills of Pakistan to President Mohammad Yahya Khan. After hearing his monologue, Yahya asked the Maulana to enlighten him on how to correct the rot. Bhashani perked up to say, 'General Sahib, I am an agitator. My job is to agitate. You are an administrator. It is your responsibility to find the solutions.' Nawabzada Nasrullah Khan is a 'Grand Master' in negative politics. Benazir Bhutto, an effective leader of the opposition, proved to be a disaster as a prime minister during her two tenures.

The MQM-PML(N) coalition was a blessing for the MQM. During this time it consolidated its ranks, re-organized its party apparatus, rehabilitated its hard-core activists, improved its financial resources and replenished its weapon stocks. The field was open for it to silence MQM(H), and to caution the bureaucrats, the police and the people to remember that they were around.

In a healthy development, the Mohajir Qaumi Movement was renamed as the Muttahida Qaumi Movement. This would have made sense if the intention had been to convert the MQM into a broad-based national party. This does not appear to be the case. The word *muttahida* (united) was perhaps adopted in a limited way to cover only the unity of *mohajirs*. The top leadership and the membership in the MQM remains unchanged, and is exclusively drawn from the *mohajirs* only. Mr Altaf Hussain speaks in the name of *mohajirs* alone. He may enhance his image if structural changes are made in the MQM to make it a truly broad-based political party with a national outlook. Since the aims, objectives, policies and goals of the original MQM remain unchanged, the replacement of the word '*mohajir*' with '*muttahida*' is at best of academic interest.

Mr Altaf Hussain skilfully exploited the weakness of his coalition partners by extracting concessions from them piecemeal by threatening to ditch the wavering coalition arrangement. By his tightrope walk, he maintained contacts with both sides of the political divide. As a politician, he showed no inhibition in discarding one partner and getting a ride with another.

The MQM behaved more like an opposition party than a mutual power holder in the Liaquat Jatoi government in Sindh. It publicly complained that its ministers were powerless, and indulged in a barrage of criticism against the state and its organs, politicians, the armed forces, and the judiciary as well as the national security agencies. It accused the administration of corruption and other ills, but were silent about the fact that the ministries and the departments directly under the control of the MQM ministers were riddled with allegations of corruption just as all other non-MQM ministries were.

The parting of the ways between the PML(N) and MQM came in October 1998 when a senior and well-respected citizen, Hakim Saeed, was gunned down in Karachi. Initial police investigations revealed that the assassins were MQM activists. Prime Minister Nawaz Sharif announced that politics and violence could not co-exist and asked the MQM to surrender the suspected individuals for interrogation within seventy-two hours, failing which he would be constrained to end the coalition partnership. The following day, MQM opted out of the uneasy partnership. It remains unproved if the MQM was responsible for the murder of Hakim Saeed.

The *mohajirs* are an inseparable part of Sindh. They cannot be ostracized nor can the old Sindhis abandon their ancestral homes. Both these communities have to co-exist in the province in a spirit of give and take and brotherly cooperation. It was a national calamity that in the political and ethnic madness that engulfed Sindh, valuable and innocent lives were lost. The law enforcing agencies also fell victim to the bullets fired by the terrorists.

The army adopted a new operational strategy of becoming strictly neutral in the on-going internal security strife between the various political factions. It acted firmly and fairly in dealing with those who disturbed peace and tranquility in the province without tilting towards any group. The task was difficult and initially the people were hesitant in believing that the administration could be impartial. Their confidence returned gradually when the army repeatedly demonstrated its neutrality and firmness, and its patience and perseverance paid political dividends. Its image improved and so did its ability to quell disturbances and gain the sympathy and support of the people. Over a period of time, Sindh became a peaceful province, once again pulsating with life. This was despite the fact that a viable and practical political master plan for the province had not yet been negotiated through the collective effort of all concerned.

The Army and the MQM

'The army is the anchor of the country.'[12] The officers, the back-bone of the Pakistan Army, are selected from among the youth of the country on the basis of national merit. No quota system for any region restricts their entry. After their induction in military service they are trained to be broad-minded nationalists, free from regional biases and parochial prejudices. Their loyalty to their service and country demands that they hold political opinions without allowing politics to affect their loyalty to service or to the government in power. By and large, such service norms have been observed in letter and spirit, and military officers have invariably performed numerous internal security duties without fear or favour.

During its prolonged employment on internal security duties in Sindh, the army concentrated on maintaining law and order and adopted a non-partisan attitude in handling crises. The unrest in Sindh was generally attributed to the MQM agitation, with attempts by India to keep this province simmering. This is a simplistic view of a complex problem. The MQM did agitate. It also indulged in acts of lawlessness and violence. However, this did not imply that all *mohajirs* were members of the MQM or were guilty of any misconduct. Far from it, most *mohajirs* are peace-loving citizens. The MQM earned a bad name through the acts of miscreants and exploiters who tarnished the image of the majority. The vast majority of the people of Sindh were terrorized into silence for fear of reprisal and retribution.

MQM and General Zia

Was the MQM the creation of General Zia and a product of his patronage and support and did his government nourish its growth are questions commonly debated in Pakistan. Public interest on these issues is partly inquisitorial and partly accusational. The formation of the MQM was neither a sudden phenomenon nor one inspired by any outside influence. The trans-border migration of the population in 1947 created the urban-rural divide in the province of Sindh that caused concern to the old Sindhis and the *mohajirs* to protect their respective interests, heritage, culture, language and rights as perceived by them.

The language riots of 1973 strengthened the belief of *mohajirs* that the existing political parties—the Muslim League, JI and JUP—besides the PPP, had failed to protect their legitimate interests and rights. The *mohajirs* in general and the new generation of this community, its youth, in particular, lost confidence in the ability of the old guard political leadership to protect their rights. They felt that the 'fossils of the past', as Bhutto once called them, could not assess their problems and difficulties. A vacuum was created.

The MQM was born in this environment. The 'cause' was there; the vacuum was there; it only needed a spokesman. A demagogue, Altaf Hussain, filled the vacuum, and fitted into this role of the 'sole spokesman' of the *mohajir* youth quite comfortably. Within a short time, electoral success placed enormous power at his feet. But, he did not know, or would not

recognize, the limits of his power. The tragedy of a wrong man
for a somewhat right cause began.

Lieutenant-General S. M. Abbasi was the governor of Sindh
till March 1984. I once asked him to comment on the MQM. He
candidly replied that throughout his gubernatorial duties in Sindh
the MQM did not exist in the province and therefore the question
of patronising it did not arise.[13] Abbasi's departure from Sindh
coincided with my own elevation to the command of the
Pakistan Army. MQM was not a political factor in Sindh till
then either.

The situation underwent a substantial change in 1985, with
the induction of Mr Mohammad Khan Junejo as the Prime
Minister of Pakistan. Sindh politics came under the direct control
of Lieutenant-General Jahandad Khan, the Governor, and Syed
Ghous Ali Shah, the Chief Minister of Sindh. During the
conferences of the martial law administrators, which I used to
attend, it was mentioned more than once that the Jeay Sindh
nationalists and the Mayor of Karachi, Abdul Sattar Afghani, at
the behest of the JI, created hurdles for the Sindh government
which planned to discipline them politically by propping up
their political opponents.

At this point in time, Zia-Junejo relations were strained and
Prime Minister Junejo increasingly relied on the advice of the
Sindh government in handling provincial matters. The JI's
political decline in Karachi was already a fact of life and it was
engaged in a do or die political struggle to survive.

Neither the JI nor the Jeay Sindh were the monsters that the
provincial government had assessed them to be. Faulty
assessment led to flawed decisions by the provincial government.
Whatever game was played by the provincial government,
General Zia did not participate in it. One writer says thus, 'Weak
as an administrator with questionable integrity,' Syed Ghous
Ali Shah, 'is accused of deliberately allowing ethnicity to
emerge as a fault-line in Sindh politics.'[14]

NOTES

1. Ardeshir Cowasjee, *Dawn*, 29 November 1998.
2. General K.M. Arif, *Working with Zia*, Oxford University Press, Karachi, 1995, p. 221.
3. Ibid., p. 221.
4. Minister Javed Jabbar, *The News*, 21 January 2000.
5. General K.M. Arif, *Working with Zia*, p. 20.
6. *Gazette of Sindh*, 'Extraordinary', 17 July 1972.
7. General K.M. Arif, *Working with Zia*, p. 141.
8. Ibid., p. 221.
9. Ibid., p. 221.
10. Zwitterion, 'MQM: Portrait of an Ethnic Organisation', *Frontier Post*, 14 January 1992.
11. *Frontier Post*, 15 January 1992.
12. Field-Marshal Sir Claude Auchinlek, reproduced by Major-General Shahid Hamid, *Disastrous Twilight*, McKays of Chatham Ltd., Great Britain, 1986, p. 48.
13. Abbasi-Arif conversation.
14. Senator Shafqat Mahmood, 'The Sindh Imbroglio', *The News*, 7 November 1998.

6

EXERCISE BRASS TACKS

In the tension-filled months of January-February 1987, India and Pakistan came close to the precipice of another open conflict. The provocation was caused by India's large military exercise named Brass Tacks, held menacingly close to the border of Pakistan. India claimed that it was a war game to train its senior military commanders and staff in the planning and conduct of corps-size operations for its recently reorganized armoured divisions and freshly raised mechanized formations. Pakistan perceived it as a cleverly conceived attempt at military planning which gave India the option to speedily convert exercise Brass Tacks into Operation Brass Tacks at India's discretion.

For reasons considered sinister by Pakistan, India wrapped the exercise in a thick cover of secrecy and this created suspicions. Initially, Pakistan's General Headquarters did not suspect India's motives, and in good faith repeatedly sought information from its counterpart in India about the nature and scope of the exercise. India was reluctant to communicate with Pakistan on this issue. Despite the uppish behaviour of the Indian High Command, the GHQ avoided drawing any hasty conclusions. All available evidence was painstakingly analyzed by experts to rule out the possibility of Islamabad misreading New Delhi's military training activity. The possibility of India wishing to impose a military surprise on Pakistan could not be ruled out. In fact this appeared very probable to Pakistani intelligence.

India and Pakistan were known to have a weak crisis control mechanism, and failed in anticipating one that was brewing.

They also failed to defuse the crisis through political and diplomatic efforts before it assumed dangerous proportions in 1987. This brief narrative attempts to assess what went wrong, where, and why to benefit from the acts of omission and commission to promote peace and stability in South Asia in the future.

Prelude to the Crisis

In the mid eighties India embarked upon a modernization and development plan for its armed forces to be completed by the turn of the century. 'Plan 2000' aimed at enhancing the indigenous production capability of military hardware in the country; modernizing the main weapon systems held in all the three defence services, and inducting mechanized formations into the Indian Army. Specifically, it involved increasing the number of India's armoured divisions, raising mechanized divisions not hitherto held, and converting some infantry divisions into semi-mechanized (Reorganized Army, Plains Infantry Division—RAPID) divisions.

The raising of the additional armoured divisions and the introduction of the mechanized and semi-mechanized formations reflected India's military strategy for its land battles in the future. The friction of terrain in the mighty Himalayan mountain ranges located on the Sino-Indian border precluded the employment of such formations against China. India did not need these mobile offensive forces against her weak and small neighbours, Bangladesh, Maldives, Myanmar, Nepal, Sikkim and Sri Lanka. The armoured and mechanized formations could only be physically used in a military operational role against Pakistan. Such forces had been traditionally reinforced by India in the past in emergencies and in open hostilities by thinning out formations from its Eastern Command tasked to operate on the Sino-Indian border.

Being the largest regional country, India had a greater power potential *vis-a-vis* her neighbours and enjoyed numerical and technological superiority in conventional hardware. It had embarked upon acquiring a multi-dimensional missile capability to supplement its defence effort. This included medium and long range surface-to-surface, short range surface-to-air and the third generation anti-tank missiles. The missile arsenal included *Prithvi* (Earth), *Agni* (Fire), *Nag* (Cobra), *Trishul* (Spear) and *Akash* (Sky) missile systems. The missile race could not but inflame South Asia even further which had already been destabilized earlier by the explosion of India's nuclear-weapons in 1974. India's military euphoria posed a grave threat to Pakistan's national security and it demanded credible and effective countermeasures to protect her legitimate interests.

Concept and Plan

The declared aim of Exercise Brass Tacks was 'to test current operational plans *vis-a-vis* Pakistan and to practice the conduct of an offensive by a strike corps, incorporating a tank versus tank battle in a simulated operational environment.' The exercise was held in four phases:

1. *Brass Tacks 1.* This was a two-sided, semi-controlled war game-cum-map exercise to evolve concepts and systems for mechanized warfare. It was held at the national level at New Delhi in July 1986.
2. *Brass Tacks 2.* The concepts evolved in Brass Tacks 1 were debated in a semi-controlled war game in November 1986 at HQ Western Command. Additionally, the Indian Navy and the Air Force held their exercises separately to evolve techniques for inter-services integration.
3. *Brass Tacks 3.* Separate studies were held by arms and services to evolve drills, procedures and techniques in support of the ground-based offensive efforts at the division and corps levels. These study groups were held in November-December 1986.
4. *Brass Tacks 4.* This was planned for February-March 1987 for which 2 Corps (Blue Land) and 10 Corps (Red Land) were

concentrated in the areas of Jodhpur-Bikaner-Suratgarh in Rajasthan, close to the India-Pakistan international boundary.

Preparatory Grouping

The Indian military forces that directly participated in Exercise Brass Tacks included two armoured divisions (1 and 31), one mechanized division (33), three RAPID divisions (14, 18 and 36—one still under conversion), three infantry divisions (16, 22 and 24), and two independent armoured brigades (6 and 14). The details of the artillery, engineers, signals and logistic support elements are omitted. The quantum of forces made Brass Tacks the largest exercise held by India since independence in 1947. One Indian writer called it, 'Probably the largest land exercise in the world since the end of World War II.'[1]

Some other formations were also inducted in the close vicinity of the exercise area and within easy striking distance of Pakistan. These included 4 Division from Allahabad to Delhi and Bharatpur, 9 Division from Meerut to Gurdaspur, 23 Division from Ranchi to Amritsar, 54 Division from Secundarabad to the exercise area, and 57 Division from North-East to Punjab. Furthermore, 6 Mountain Division ex-Bareilly and 39 Mountain Division ex-Yol were inducted into Indian-held Kashmir.

The induction of additional troops in the Indian Punjab, Indian-held Kashmir and Rajasthan sectors was over and above the forces regularly employed in the defensive roles in these sectors. Such a massive concentration of forces, some directly participating in Exercise Brass Tacks while others stood readily available, provided India a four-fold military advantage.

First, the entire Indian Army was mobilized even though only a part of this mobilized force was to actually participate in the projected exercise. Secondly, the Indian Army was fully mobilized in its concentration areas under the cover of an exercise. In fact, her combat groups and logistic support elements were almost deployed in their launching pads for a real-time operational effort. Thirdly, while the Indian military had acquired an operational readiness status in the guise of an exercise, the bulk of the Pakistani forces were located in their peace time areas. This placed Pakistan at a disadvantage and the element of surprise favoured India. The operationally poised Indian Army could convert the exercise into an operation at short notice.

In addition there was the Punjab angle. The Sikhs had long been demanding an independent state, *Khalistan*, for themselves in the Indian Punjab and had launched an armed struggle to get their claim accepted. Their agitation had created turmoil in East Punjab and India wanted to induct additional military forces in the troubled areas to crush the unrest and tame the Sikhs. The Sikhs resisted this move. Brass Tacks provided an opportunity for India to induct military reinforcements in East Punjab in the garb of either using them for internal security duties or against Pakistan.

In June 1984, the Indian Army desecrated the Sikhs' holiest shrine, the Golden Temple in Amritsar, to militarily suppress the political demands of the agitating Sikhs for a separate homeland. Turning the holy temple into a battlefield was an unforgivable, offensive act, and an unacceptable insult to the self-respect of the passionate Sikhs and their religion. The indignity posed a challenge to the Sikhs. The world was stunned by the premeditated slaughter in the Golden Temple and it led to a vicious reaction. Prime Minister Indira Gandhi was gunned down in New Delhi by her own Sikh security guard in October 1984. In retaliation, the militant Hindus in 'secular' India killed many Sikhs in riots in New Delhi and elsewhere. The Indian government showed communal bias by slashing the quota of the Sikhs in India's armed forces to bring them at par with their population ratio in the country.

Logistic Support Arrangements

A comprehensive logistic infrastructure was made to support the field army. This included the establishment of logistic depots in the forward areas to meet the supply and ordnance needs of the forces. Significantly, all the formations carried their full authorized complement of the first and second line ammunition with them. This is normally not done in a training exercise in order to prevent the movement of the explosive cargo and to prolong its shelf life. Even more significant was the transfer of artillery and tank ammunition to the manoeuvre area.

In specific terms, two large ammunition depots were established in the forward area, one at Bhatinda and the other at Jodhpur. Petrol, oil and lubricants were carried to the exercise area at the scale of 500 kilometers for every A (tank and tracked) vehicle and 3,000 kilometers per B (cargo) vehicle. The ration stocks could last for a period of four months.

Some additional measures taken to increase the combat readiness of the Indian Amy included the recall of some reservist officers, cancellation of some courses of instruction and the activation of the territorial units in the Western Command.

The planning schedule of the movement time was:

a. Movement to the training area communes on 15 November.
b. Movement completed by 30 November 1986.
c. Concentration for Brass Tacks completed by 10 February 1987.

The Indian Air Force

The Indian Air Force was fully mobilized. Its regular and satellite bases, mostly located close to the border with Pakistan, were activated and made functional. Air defence measures were adopted and close support arrangements between the army and the air force, and the communication network for this task were made operative.

The IAF enjoyed a three-to-one advantage over the PAF in number and in the quality of the aircraft. In high altitude air surveillance capability, India's Mig-25R had unhindered freedom of manoeuvre in the entire air space of Pakistan. It did not fear any retaliation because these aircraft could fly well beyond the high-altitude capability of the PAF fighter interceptors. India's capability of photographic spying cover of the entire ground space of Pakistan gave her a marked advantage over an adversary who at best could cover only a limited border belt.

The Indian Navy

The Indian Navy was not directly involved in the exercise. Apart from carrying out its normal manoeuvres it participated in a brigade-size amphibious operation in the Gujrat sector.

India's Motives

Professional Benefits

India's desire to train its senior military commanders and staff officers in the planning and conduct of operations by its armoured divisions and its newly formed mechanized formations was clearly understood in Pakistan. The induction of such forces in the Indian Army justified the evolution of doctrines which were best tested in simulated operational environments. This universally accepted technique of training might not have raised any undue concern in Pakistan. Likewise, India's attempt to achieve greater inter-service integration was an inescapable training necessity and a non-provocative act.

An Indian writer goes beyond this. In his view, 'The Indian Army badly needed to learn to handle multi-corps forces, particularly to handle the two strike corps together. It is on the shoulders of these two corps that India's entire strategy against Pakistan rests. If those seven divisions do their work, Pakistan ceases to exist.'[2]

Exercise Brass Tacks went far beyond a routine conventional training exercise. It tested the national mobilization plans, the movement plans of each service, the logistics and the communication plans for combat and the integration of the civil-military war effort. The total mobilization of India's war effort made Pakistan wonder whether its combat readiness was being tested for a simple military exercise or if its intent was aggressive.

India might have achieved the full benefits of practicing its plans without eyebrows being raised in Pakistan if it had adopted an open-door policy. It should have announced and publicized her military manoeuvres to allay fears and eliminate the chance of being misunderstood in Pakistan and abroad. This was not done. Instead, a veil of secrecy was painstakingly woven to hide facts, conceal realities and pressurize Pakistan. Her extreme desire to mislead Pakistan and to play a game of hide and seek with her made her motives suspect.

The Pakistan Army's routine schedule of annual collective training exercises was well known to the Indian authorities. This was done in the months of November-December each year. The Indian planners carefully chose the manoeuvre period for Brass Tacks in February-March 1987 in the hope that, by this time, the Pakistani troops would have returned to their peace locations. Pakistan would thus be militarily unready at a time when the Indian forces were fully mobilized for combat.

Psychological Gains

The performance of the Indian Army had not been awe inspiring in the past and its attempt to refurbish its sullied image was not lost on Pakistan. In 1948, the Indian Army had failed to defeat a small group of ill-equipped and untrained civilian volunteers operating in Kashmir. It was humiliated by the Chinese in 1962. The 1964 Rann of Kutch conflict was a disaster. The 1965 war ended in a stalemate. The events of 1971 in East Pakistan were the result of treachery, not war. India's military misadventure in Sri Lanka ended in a fiasco, and exposed serious flaws in her political ambitions and military policies, both at the levels of planning and conduct of so-called peace keeping operations. For the military commanders in India, Brass Tacks offered an opportunity of raising the not-so-high morale of the Indian Army.

India had been carving a hegemonic role for itself in South Asia. Exercise Brass Tacks was also an attempt to test Pakistan's nerves under pressure and condition her to military concentrations on her border. Or, it was an implied warning or threat to Pakistan to stay away from the Sikh agitation that raged in East Punjab then.

Exercise Brass Tacks attempted to play on the psyche of India's small neighbours to subordinate their national identities and aspirations to the expectations of the largest regional country. The flexing of military muscle was a warning to them to either obediently float in the orbit of India's sphere of influence, or risk the wrath of the 'mother' country which possessed the military means and the political will to achieve her national goals. Specifically, India desired their internal and external policies to be harmonized with the objectives set for them by New Delhi.

This was also a signal to the major powers that India had come of age and her presence and military potential should be taken into consideration.

External Factors

With war raging in Afghanistan, Pakistan faced a two-dimensional threat to her national security, from the East and the West. Prudence demanded that Pakistan play it cool with India and avoid being caught in any unwanted conflict that might be imposed on her.

Islamabad's support to the Afghan freedom fighters in their struggle against the occupation of their country by Soviet military forces (1979-88) was an irritant to both Moscow and New Delhi. The Soviet military intervention was repeatedly condemned in the UN General Assembly for eight years. Throughout this period, India sat on the sidelines of the Afghan conflict and dutifully supported its strategic ally, the Soviet

Union, from a safe distance. At one time, the Soviet Union had proposed to the Indian Prime Minister Morarji Desai that a bilateral concerted military act be inititated to pressurize Pakistan, which he declined. Pakistan felt that India might be tempted to agree this time if the Soviet Union was to repeat that request to Prime Minister Rajiv Gandhi.

Notwithstanding its own large and multi-dimensional nuclear capability, India displayed a hysterical approach towards Pakistan's rather modest nuclear programme. It was known to have associated with Israel, with the idea to launch a punitive strike against Kahuta, a nuclear installation in Pakistan. The evidence was credible and a punitive attempt appeared imminent first in 1984 and then in 1985. Pakistan had then unambiguously conveyed to India that any such action would be taken as an act of war and replied accordingly. It seemed plausible that this threat could be repeated in 1987, at which time the Indian forces were already assembled on the border to prevent a riposte from Pakistan.

Internal Influences

Prime Minister Rajiv Gandhi suddenly catapulted into politics after the assassination of his mother Indira Gandhi. Soon, his earlier clean reputation was tainted and charges of corruption levelled against him. His kitchen cabinet included individuals whose primary qualification for the coveted assignment was their personal friendship with the prime minister. The Minister of State for Defence, Arun Singh, was the *de facto* defence minister though technically this ministry was under the direct charge of Rajiv Gandhi himself. Arun Singh developed a close rapport with General K. Sundarji who became the army chief of staff on 31 January 1986. This duo kept Rajiv Gandhi informed on defence issues on an 'as required' basis. Their intentions may have been aboveboard but the adopted methodology subordinated the institutions to personalities. For example, 'Communications within the defence apparatus were disrupted,

with the Ministry of Defence being kept on the periphery and
all of Brass Tacks-related decisions being taken between the
Minister of State and the Chief of Staffs Committee.'[3] As shall
be discussed later, the Arun-Sundarji team was widely accused
of creating the ugly situation *vis-a-vis* Pakistan in February 1987.

Kashmir was a simmering flash point that could trigger an
open crisis between India and Pakistan at any time. On face-
value, the Kashmir dispute remained on the back burner during
Exercise Brass Tacks. In reality this was not so. Much happened
on the Kashmir front directly and indirectly, openly and secretly.
'The political scenario accompanying Brass Tacks envisaged
the (Indian) military gaining substantial control over it
(Kashmir).'[4] This is further substantiated by a revealing narration
by an Indian author that:

> The Trident called for an (Indian) attack on 8 February 1987, at
> 0430 hours, with Skardu as the first objective and Gilgit as the
> second... If Pakistan chose to keep the conflict limited to the
> Northern Areas, this was fine with India. But suppose Pakistan
> wanted to retaliate and escalate, say by attacking Punjab. Then
> Brass Tacks, which was originally planned as a gigantic strategic
> deception to focus Pakistani attention on Sindh while we went for
> the Northern Areas, would have been converted into an actual
> operation ...[5]

The massive exercise held menacingly close to the
international border was a premeditated act aimed at intimidating
Pakistan. Strategic reasons, too, dominated the choice of the
manoeuvre area—a semi-desert belt, that offered good
operational opportunities in any conflict. But even a cursory
assessment of Exercise Brass Tacks in India would have led to
the inevitable conclusion that its diplomatic, political and
military fallout in Pakistan would be adverse. India did not take
any corrective measures to keep inter-state relations with
Pakistan tranquil. Instead, it adopted an offensive strategy and
played power politics in the belief that she held all the trump
cards in her hands.

India's political dilemma in East Punjab clouded its thinking. It was obsessed with the scenario that a Punjab-Kashmir nexus would unhinge her position in the disputed State of Kashmir. It habitually blamed Pakistan's intelligence agencies for committing acts inside India to cover up its own internal difficulties and fissiparous tendencies.

India's print media created an orchestrated war hysteria. The provocative headlines read: 'We need a small war', 'A pre-emptive strike...is not a bad idea', and, 'A war would work wonders for sagging Indian nationalism.' More important than the newspaper comments were the opinions expressed by eminent Indians. 'India will not be pushed around,'[6] said Mr Rajiv Gandhi. 'Informed Indians believed that there was going to be a major war with Pakistan (and) mechanized formations would be extremely useful for a quick thrust into Pakistani territory.'[7] Bhabani Sen Gupta, a journalist, commented that 'a tough stance against Pakistan is very popular with the Indian people.'[8]

The Political Input

Prime Minister Rajiv Gandhi emulated his ancestors in style and substance. His grandfather, Pandit Jawaharlal Nehru, India's mentor, philosopher and visionary, had drunk deep from the well of India's nationalism and played a key role in the freedom struggle culminating in independence.

In November 1985, during a routine morning meeting with his top military brass, Rajiv Gandhi, mooted the idea of holding a large scale, grandiose military manoeuvre to project India's power and status.[9] The meeting included Arun Singh, P. K. Kaul, the Cabinet Secretary, General A. S. Vaidya, Air Chief Marshal La Fontain and Vice Admiral K. K. Nayyer. The Indian Army proceeded to implement the wish of the prime minister and his political clearance set the stage for Exercise Brass Tacks. It decided to make it an all-time grand and memorable event. In so doing, the military took charge and gradually overshadowed other organs of the state in handling the exercise, the largest since 1947. Reportedly, even the Ministry of External Affairs was deliberately kept uninformed about key elements of Brass Tacks because 'they could not be trusted to keep a secret.'[10]

One Indian general maintains that Prime Minister Rajiv Gandhi had ordered Brass Tacks 'to achieve a total coordination of India's civil and military effort in combat. The prime minister expressed his unhappiness later when the exercise took a different shape at its conceptual level and said that 'ambitious general-ship and lack of political coordination created a difficulty for the country.'[11]

Plan in Outline

The exercise was between two conventional forces, Red Land (Pakistan) and Blue Land (India). The Blue Land was tasked to capture maximum territory of Red Land's heartland and to degrade her military potential. The Blue Land plan was in two phases:

a. *Phase 1.* Capture area up to Sutlej River between the towns of Hasilpur (Pakistan) and Fazilka (India).
b. *Phase 2.* Secure the Ravi-Sutlej corridor (in Pakistan) between the cities of Multan, Okara and Sahiwal (all in Pakistan).

The operational planning was completed, and a high state of combat readiness achieved to provide multiple options to India's military high command. If India could maintain the cover of secrecy and lull Pakistan into believing in the innocent nature of the exercise, then she could convert the exercise into an operation at short notice to take advantage of Pakistan's lack of operational readiness. Such was the professional assessment of the Pakistani intelligence agencies. On the contrary, should Pakistan get suspicious, then India could plead that her intention was limited to gaining professional experience in a training exercise.

Pakistan's Assessment and Response

Confidence Building Initiative

India maintains a flexible approach on many issues of substance. She acts with remarkable ease in shifting her political stance with changes in time and international environment. Pundit Jawaharlal Nehru explains thus, 'In any country, and especially in a large country like India with its complicated history and mixed culture, it is always possible to find facts and trends to justify a particular thesis, and then this becomes the accepted basis for a new argument.[12] Based on this philosophy, India now questions the disputed status of the State of Jammu and Kashmir, has become a *de facto* nuclear weapon power while maintaining in the past that her nuclear programme was only for peaceful purposes, and has become a strategic US partner after the collapse of the erstwhile Soviet Union in the early 1990s. The arrogance of power is manifest in her dealings with her small neighbours. India's diversity and internal conflicts are a legacy of her deeply rooted ancient history. In the post-independence era, she has endlessly meddled in the internal affairs of her close neighbours and invariably accused them for her own internal failures. Examples of this are seen in the political amputation of East Pakistan, aiding and abetting of the Tamil insurgency in Sri Lanka, and the absorption of Sikkim into the Indian Union.

The war hysteria created by Prime Minister Indira Gandhi in the early eighties was fresh in my mind when I took charge of the Pakistan Army in March 1984. I decided to break the barrier of silence that existed between the military commanders of India and Pakistan. Both sides maintained a status quo and did not take the initiative in breaking this deadlock. The hawks in both the countries were averse to a bilateral dialogue.

It was clear to me that the dispute between India and Pakistan could best be settled through political and diplomatic means. The military neither had the time nor the desire, or a government mandate to play any role in this process. Since 1947, troops from both sides had stayed perched on hill tops along the cease-fire line (CFL), later renamed the Line of Control (LOC), in the disputed state of Kashmir, within firing range. The casualties suffered by both sides were avoidable and unnecessary. I decided to take steps to save human lives and promote regional peace without compromising Pakistan's position.

Two military emissaries conveyed my suggestion to the Indian Army Chief, General A. S. Vaidya, for a bilateral agreement to maintain peace along the LOC. The Indian Military Attaché in Islamabad, Brigadier D. K. Khanna was given a verbal message to this effect, and Pakistan's Military Attaché in New Delhi, Brigadier Z. I. Abbasi had personally called on Vaidya with my proposal. Responding promptly, Vaidya wrote to me on 8 June 1984 saying, 'You would always find us meeting you more than halfway in any steps which may help in normalization of relations and building goodwill between the peoples of our two countries.'

The ice was broken, or so it appeared then. Taking advantage of the contact, I sent two concrete proposals to the Indian Army Chief through the Indian Foreign Secretary, M. Rasgotra, who had called on me during a visit to Pakistan. To his credit, General Vaidya replied immediately. His letter dated 3 July 1984, reads:

Shri M. Rasgotra has conveyed to me your suggestion for keeping the border tension-free and informing each other about movement of troops to the border...I would like to assure you again that we will only be too happy to reciprocate any steps taken in this direction. I am also agreeable to your suggestion for providing advance information regarding movement of troops close to the border. The modalities for this can be evolved by our Directors of Military Operations...

The change of emphasis from generalities to specifics was a positive development. Encouraged by this process, I wrote to Vaidya on 24 July 1984 saying, '...Perhaps the time has come for us to develop regular contacts at some agreed levels to promote better understanding...You will find us responsive to any practical measures that can help to generate light by removing the cobwebs of suspicion and doubt.' This proposal, made in good faith, failed to bring any response from New Delhi. I waited in vain and heard nothing. The honeymoon ended, as abruptly as it had started. Presumably the government of India took exception to the exchange of military correspondence becoming a regular feature. Perhaps the South Block got nervous that the generals might succeed where the diplomats had failed? In all probability, territorial imperatives took charge in India and Vaidya was forced into silence. But I heard him loud and clear despite a lack of reply from him.

The Arif-Vaidya understanding about providing advance information to each other with regard to the movement of troops close to the border, though not yet codified into a legal document, had a moral obligation that might have averted the Brass Tacks crisis. In international relations, such correspondence usually outlives the authors, and the mutual understanding reached and bilateral commitments made are invariably recorded, respected and honoured unless revoked. This norm was broken with the change of the army guard in India. The new Army Chief, General K. Sundarji, was more interested in a show of force than in honouring the letter and spirit of an understanding made by his predecessor. General Vaidya retired in January 1986.

Intelligence Assessment

Pakistan's intelligence antennas buzzed with the details of Exercise Brass Tacks picked up from India. The Inter Services Intelligence Directorate had its fingers firmly placed on the sources of information. The process of collection, collation and dissemination of information worked smoothly, in clock-like precision.

The president, the prime pinister and the relevant ministries were kept informed by the Inter-Services Intelligence Directorate about the details of Exercise Brass Tacks. The Chairman of the

JCSC and the services chiefs were given more than one timely and comprehensive briefing by the DGISI, Lieutenant-General Akhtar Abdur Rahman, about the details of the exercise. Akhtar maintained that the sources of his information were A-1, meaning highly reliable. Likewise, the operational and the intelligence staff at the services headquarters were provided the necessary information. All those officially responsible for safeguarding national security had the relevant data in their possession.

While the information provided by the ISI Directorate was generally accepted at face value, the conclusions drawn were invariably subjected to close professional scrutiny. The possibility of an intelligence agency projecting the worst-case scenario was debated threadbare, even at the cost of causing an embarrassment to it. The intelligence assessment was that the massive concentration of the Indian forces close to the border posed a threat to the security of Pakistan and the Indian planners had the hidden motive of initiating an armed conflict. Its conclusion was based on sound evidence and convincing logic.

The services headquarters had adequate time and warning to review the border situation and developments in Kashmir, and they had formulated their respective responses in terms of time and space. Such actions were discussed in the monthly JCSC meetings attended by all the services chiefs.

Chronology of Events

General Headquarters had expected that in the backdrop of the Arif-Vaidya understanding, India would convey to Pakistan its plan of holding an exercise by September 1986 to coincide with Pakistan's winter training schedule, October-December 1986. Despite the lapse of this time frame, there was no response from India. This created doubts in Pakistan about India's plans and motives. The Arif-Vaidya understanding remained operative because neither country had questioned its validity.

Come September, an uneasy calm prevailed as there was no communication from India. Late in the month, Pakistan's Military Attaché in New Delhi inquired from the Indian Army HQ about the impending Exercise Brass Tacks. He was given an evasive reply implying that no exercise was 'being' held, a phrase open to different interpretations. The doubts increased. Brigadier Abbasi made another attempt in October 1986 to seek a response from the Indian Army. This time he was seen by a lower level official, and the reply to his query was pointedly curt and the demeanor less civil. Abbasi was told that Pakistan's anxiety was misplaced and India had the right to actions inside its own territory. Pakistan was not naive to question this right. But India's arrogant reply showed that Pakistan's search for peace had perhaps been taken as a sign of weakness. India's military behaviour convinced Pakistan that her motives were suspect and her intentions untrustworthy.

A feeling of unease also gripped at least one general officer in India. Lieutenant-General Hirday Kaul, GOC Western Command, Indian Army, retired from military service on 30 September 1986. He told me on 14 October 1998, that soon after his retirement he met the cabinet secretary in India and asked him to convey to the prime minister that Exercise Brass Tacks might convey the wrong signals to Pakistan and suggested its cancellation. During his farewell call on Arun Singh he repeated this suggestion. Arun argued that it was too late to cancel the event. Later, during his farewell call he informed the prime minister that he had earlier conveyed to him his reservations about Exercise Brass Tacks through the cabinet secretary. Mr Rajiv Gandhi told this general officer that the cabinet secretary had not conveyed any message to him.

On 5 November 1986, on my orders, GHQ issued instructions on collective training to its own formations. They were also given a vigilance policy to keep their eyes and ears open. The next day, Brigadier Abbasi made a request to New Delhi for permission to call on the Chairman Chiefs of Staff Committee, Admiral Tahilani and the Vice Chief of the Army Staff. The request was processed by the Indian authorities at a leisurely pace, and Pakistan's Military Attaché was kept waiting.

Exercise Brass Tacks was discussed in the JCSC meeting which unanimously decided to apprise Prime Minister Muhammad Khan Junejo of the facts. Junejo was scheduled to travel to India to attend the SAARC summit at Bangalore on 16 November 1986, hosted by Prime Minister Rajiv Gandhi of India.

The Defence Committee of the Cabinet met under the chairmanship of the prime minister. The ISI Directorate made a comprehensive presentation to the DCC members with the services chiefs in attendance. It painted a bleak picture and cast doubts on Indian motives. In its assessment, India desired to disturb regional peace under the cover plan of an exercise. There was a moment of silence in the room. Prime Minister Junejo asked me a direct question, 'Is war imminent?' adding meaningfully, *'Baad mein jawab to aap ko dena parega.'* (subsequently you will be held answerable).

I replied that a comprehensive operational briefing could be given separately, if desired by the prime minister. For the present, I stated 'I have no reason to question the intelligence assessment, based on hard evidence, made by the ISI. The GHQ will initiate minimum and non-provocative defensive measures to safeguard our national security interests. Such precautionary steps will be taken despite the visible absence of any compelling reasons for India to engage in combat with Pakistan at this point of time. Logically, neither the global environment nor the regional situation or even bilateral relations indicate the imminence of an open conflict. But wars have defied rationality in the past and this phenomenon may be repeated in the future. Therefore, minimum essential defensive steps will be taken to meet our security needs.'

Junejo shot back, 'There is a contradiction in your statement,' adding, 'You intend taking protective measures even when you seem to rule out the outbreak of a war.' I replied that since I respected the intelligence assessment, the army would take minimum precautionary steps to prevent being surprised. But the ground realities did not yet suggest the imminence of an open conflict. The situation would be closely monitored in the weeks and months ahead.

Turn by turn all the other participants expressed their views freely, frankly and candidly and the prime minister was briefed by the services chiefs about the steps already taken or planned to be taken by them in the near future. The prime minister advised continued vigilance and approved the following measures:

a. He would discuss the issue with Rajiv Gandhi.
b. Services HQ were permitted to take minimum and non-provocative security steps.
c. ISID to keep Exercise Brass Tacks under observation.
d. Important diplomatic missions and the Military Attaches located in Islamabad were to be briefed.

This timely meeting seized the initiative from India and pre-empted its military adventurism in South Asia. Pakistan's apprehensions were promptly conveyed to the major powers on the international chessboard. New Delhi soon faced questions raised by different capitals, and was put on the defensive in the diplomatic and military fields. The replies given by India were conveyed back to Pakistan.

As a curtain raiser to the meeting between the two prime ministers, Pakistan's Foreign Secretary Abdul Sattar expressed unease on Brass Tacks and stated that his country would have to take precautionary measures because of the size and extent of the exercise. Addressing a press conference on 15 November 1986, he pointedly mentioned that India and Pakistan had an understanding to inform each other of troop movements in advance and India had not yet informed Pakistan of any such movements.[13] India did not contradict this statement.

Prime Ministers Junejo and Rajiv Gandhi met at Bangalore, India, on 16 November 1986, during the SAARC summit and discussed Brass Tacks. Junejo found Rajiv well informed and up-dated on the issue. In response to Junejo's concern about the large size of the exercise, Rajiv replied with a touch of humour that the Indian Army wanted to hold 'a *big tamasha*' (a grand show) but in view of the prohibitive cost involved he had directed the military 'to scale down' the exercise.[14] The remark showed that Rajiv not only knew what was planned but also relished the idea with visible pride. Subsequently, Junejo disclosed Rajiv's views to the press.[15]

While Prime Minister Junejo was still in India, the Pakistani Director-General of Military Operations (Naqvi) telephoned his counterpart (Mahajan) in New Delhi on 17 November 1986, who hesitated to engage in a discussion on the plea that 'the two Prime Ministers had already talked on the subject.' Mahajan claimed ignorance when Naqvi complained about an air violation in the Skardu region in Kashmir. Naqvi inquired about the need to carry ammunition by the formations moving for Brass Tacks. Mahajan stated that he would check on this aspect and promised to honour the understanding about reporting troop movements when they start.

This remark confirmed that the Arif-Vaidya understanding was well known to the military planners in India. It negates the arguments raised in India that the understanding might have been unknown to General Sundarji because the Arif-Vaidya correspondence was at the demi-official level. When Naqvi reported the conversation to me, I wondered if the evasive replies were prompted by secrecy or deceit.

Brigadier Abbasi's meeting with Admiral Tahilani took place at 1130 hours on 18 November. Abbasi was told that the army had planned to hold a corps level exercise with the participation of the air force while the navy would hold an exercise on the Western coast. But strangely, the Indian Army had no time for Abbasi. His request for a meeting with the VCOAS remained unanswered. Obviously, the priority of the Indian Army was conflict creation not resolution.

Two more events of some importance took place in the month of November. Pakistan sent an *aide-memoir* to India on Exercise Brass Tacks. This showed the extent of Pakistan's desire to promote peace in South Asia. Further, the Soviet leader Mikhail Gorbachev, on a visit to India, publicly stated that the neighbours should live in peace. This significantly pointed advice showed that the Soviet Union was against military adventurism in the region.

The concentration of the Indian Army close to the border of Pakistan started on schedule in November 1986, under a thick cover of secrecy unprecedented in normal peace conditions. Several express, mail and passenger trains were suddenly cancelled 'for unavoidable operational reasons.'[16] Denied the means of daily transportation, the Indian public in the affected areas faced hardship and their protests appeared in India's print media. One newspaper reported that 'issues relating to security, defence, and movement of food grains and *other commodities* (emphasis added) caused cancellation of the trains in the north.'[17] A railway spokesman retorted that, 'It is for the railways to decide whether to cancel goods train or passenger trains, or see if they can meet the defence requirements by running additional trains.'[18] The remark shows the domination of the establishment in democratic India.

What was known to every cab driver in Rajasthan two weeks earlier was finally conveyed by the Indian DGMO (Dias) to his opposite number in Pakistan on 2 December in the name of promoting 'bilateral confidence.' He stated that the troops had started moving to northern Rajasthan for routine collective training that will culminate in a large two-sided corps level exercise. The exercise area, he maintained, was far away from the border. Questioned about the fresh induction of formations in the non-exercise area of Kashmir, Dias tried to underplay them as 'relief movements.' Asked further about the carriage of ammunition and establishment of logistic depots in the forward areas, he stated that such arrangements were necessary as the formations were away from their peace locations. Pressed further for information on the proposed amphibious landing operation, he replied that it was a part of the army exercise. Dias inquired about the collective training schedule of Pakistan's military formations and this information was given to him.

The reality was that the war hysteria being systematically created by the Indian media coincided with the concentration of the Indian military forces to achieve a position of strength at the time and place of their own choice. An uneasy calm prevailing on the surface betrayed the war-like preparations secretly set in motion in India. Rajiv Gandhi's indication to Junejo about the scaling down of Exercise Brass Tacks was more symbolic than meaningful. It was so marginal that it made no material difference in the size, the scale and the scope of the exercise. On the contrary, it became increasingly evident that the 'Grand Show' planned to be staged on the border of Pakistan enjoyed the support and approval of the Prime Minister of India.

Pakistan took some military and diplomatic precautionary measures to safeguard her security interests. One such action was to increase the duration of the on-going collective training of the army formations in some selected areas. This decision was communicated to the Indian DGMO on 8 December.

Reaction in Pakistan

The print media in Pakistan expressed deep concern, but maintained a dignified stance. It showed restraint and avoided catchy headlines. On 10 October, Mian Tufail Ahmad, chief of the JI, called Exercise Brass Tacks a cause for alarm.[19] Three days later, one newspaper stated that the hard-liners in the Indian foreign office were attempting to convey that India would not tolerate Pakistani provocation in Kashmir, Indian Punjab or the nuclear issue.[20] Another comment was that India was employing Soviet advisers in Kashmir, Punjab and Rajasthan.[21] Senator Qazi Hussain Ahmad warned on 4 November of India's war preparations, particularly in the Rajasthan Sector.[22] One editorial indicated that India had not given up but just postponed an attack on Pakistan.[23] The official reaction in Pakistan was summed up by Prime Minister Junejo, who said in Dubai on 2 December that he was willing to meet Rajiv Gandhi anytime anywhere to decelerate tensions.[24]

The Crisis Deepens

The strategic army reserves play a central role in evolving the defence policies of countries and in their implementation at the decisive time and place. These are the trump cards held in the hands of the army chiefs to be used sparingly but decisively to achieve results of strategic dimensions. They are too precious an asset to be used in a fixed defensive mode. To commit them in this form is to deny oneself the inherent advantage of their immense power potential.

It is time consuming and expensive to move strategic reserves. For reasons of convenience and military necessity the army reserves of Pakistan were kept in the close vicinity of their training areas. It would have been naive to move them back to their permanent locations when the entire Indian army was threateningly poised on the borders. The initial deployment of the strategic reserves is as important as their subsequent employment in combat. It must radiate appropriate signals to all concerned to make their presence felt.

India claims that it detected the location of the Pakistani strategic reserves in the middle of January 1987, a full two weeks after their arrival in the locations. This inordinate delay in identification is intriguing and inexplicable because India possessed safe high altitude photo cover capability (Mig 25-Rs) which flew beyond the high altitude reach of the Pakistani fighter aircraft. During a group discussion on Exercise Brass Tacks held at Bellagio, Italy, in September 1994, I asked General Sundarji why India took so long in locating the strategic reserves of Pakistan despite the means at her disposal to do so within hours? He shrugged his shoulders, half-raised both his arms in the air and said with a raised voice, '*buss hum soe rahe*' (we just kept napping), a statement hard to accept from a person who indulged in brinkmanship. Sundarji's attempt to laugh-off a professional query confirmed my doubts that he was being deliberately evasive and reticent.

At about this time, Prime Minister Rajiv Gandhi was on holiday in the Andamans. Indian writers claim that the news about the displacement of the Pakistan Army reserves was not immediately conveyed to him for three reasons. It was considered precautionary and thus unexceptionable. Secondly, it was not judged important enough to disturb his well-deserved rest and recreation. Finally, the prime minister's premature return to the capital might have caused unnecessary alarm. This argument was hard to accept.

Exercise Brass Tacks was conceived by India as an instrument of coercive diplomacy. Its planners underestimated the resilience of Pakistan and convinced themselves that the concentration of 200,000 troops on the border, including the deployment of all the strategic reserves that India possessed, would intimidate and perhaps incapacitate the decision makers in Pakistan who would be compelled to react in the manner that India had predicted for them in its 'Forecast of Events'.

Much after the event, Rikhye wrote about the impact of the Pakistani move thus, 'In other words, instead of Pakistan getting coerced, India got coerced...' and, 'This simple (Pakistan Army) move so panicked the Indians that we immediately decreed general mobilization and simultaneously agreed to begin disengagement with Pakistan.'[25] General Sundarji's staff had reportedly rushed to the Indian Air Force, the Indian railways and the road transport authorities to help the army to re-deploy its units quickly to plug the vulnerability that had suddenly appeared across the Indian northern Punjab. It was reported that General Sundarji had been rebuked by Rajiv Gandhi for his failure to accurately anticipate Pakistan's reaction.

Pakistan's cool reaction, measured professional response and timely diplomatic initiatives exposed India's game and gave her a psychological setback. The plan to capture the Northern Areas misfired, and the pre-emptive steps taken by Pakistan grounded its operation. From an offensive and arrogant posture, India suddenly found herself relegated to a defensive groove. Her loss of face had to be prevented, and soon, to rehabilitate her battered image, a military drama was hurriedly enacted to extricate the Indian Army from its self-created quagmire.

The setting was skilfully laid. Pleading innocence, the Indian Army blamed its counterpart in Pakistan for threatening the security of India with the 'provocative and aggressive positioning' of her strategic military reserves within a striking distance of East Punjab. To give this preposterous accusation a touch of credibility the location of the Pakistani reserves was deliberately misreported to the government and to the media in an exaggerated form to justify raising alarm. The concentration of both the Pakistan Army reserves was falsely shown much closer to the border than they actually were. It was militarily absurd, almost comical, to accuse the Pakistani strategic reserves of being poised for an offensive against India when the Pakistan Air Force was only partially alerted and the bulk of the Pakistan army was located in its peace time barracks.

As if leaving nothing to chance, General Sundarji personally briefed the editors of important newspapers on 18 January 1987, to highlight the 'dangerous moves of the Pakistan Army.'[26] This was a significant departure from the norm. Such briefings are usually given in India by the Directorate of Public Relations. The fruits of their labour paid dividends and the 'desired' results were achieved next morning. As expected, the print media in India dutifully rose to the occasion with an orchestrated clamour of a military threat from Pakistan splashed in bold headlines.

Pakistan's then Chief of Air Staff says that:

The timely recognition by the Army Chief that while the intimidation motive of Brass Tacks was primarily political, its power to coerce derived entirely from the threatening deployment of the Indian Army close to Pakistan's border. Owing to the on-going Afghan war, the potential power of India's Soviet ally already stood counterbalanced by the American support for Pakistan. In this situation it was not possible for Pakistan to generate, through diplomacy alone, additional dissuasive power to deter India. The Pakistan Army needed, therefore, to neutralize the Indian threat, essentially an effective military counter-move. Since a force-against-force deployment would have seriously risked escalating the crisis, an exploitation of the Indian Army's vulnerability in the Punjab was chosen for creating the defensive deterrent effort. The unadvertised placement of the Pakistan Army's armour posed an unsolvable time-space problem for General Sundarji that compelled him to seek an

early retrieval of the situation. That the Pakistani GHQ's operational
staff was able to correctly assess the gravity of the threat as well as
to [offer a] telling response cannot but be attributed to the
imaginative leadership of the Army Chief, General Arif.[27]

Addressing a press conference on 20 January, Prime Minister
Rajiv Gandhi blamed Pakistan for creating tension along
the Indo-Pakistan border. Obviously his script had been
written by the military hawks. He surprised his fellow
Indians by announcing the removal of India's Foreign Secretary
A. P. Venkateswaran in a public statement. His fault was that
he had announced that Rajiv would be visiting Pakistan in his
capacity as the current President of SAARC. Publicly insulted,
the secretary lost his job.

India's Cabinet Committee on Political Affairs met on
22 January. It endorsed the panic scenario already painted to the
media by General Sundarji and adopted an 'act-tough' policy
with Pakistan. The armed forces in India were ordered into
immediate action.

At midday on 23 January 1987, Dr Humayun Khan,
Pakistan's High Commissioner in New Delhi, was summoned
to the Ministry of External Affairs at short notice. The Minister
of State for Foreign Affairs, Natwar Singh, conveyed to
Humayun India's deep concern on the presence of the army
contingents around the border areas despite the completion of
their annual military exercises. He demanded an immediate
withdrawal of the troops to their peace locations failing which
India threatened to take further retaliatory actions.

Natwar did not disclose to Humayun that in reality India had
already issued a 'red alert' to the army and her troops were on
the move to seal off the East Punjab border with Pakistan. The
Indian Navy had already been directed to 'keep its eyes open.'[28]

The External Affairs Minister, Mr N. D. Tiwari, briefed the
Soviet Ambassador and the Minister of State for Defence, Arun
Singh, met the American Ambassador to apprise him of India's
concern. India and Pakistan, the two traditional antagonists in
South Asia, were once again on the precipice of a conflict.

A *demarche* is a legitimate weapon in the armoury of diplomacy. Courtesy demands that the addressed country be provided time and opportunity to respond to a complaint. But India's gun-barrel diplomacy betrayed her claim of civility and in her perception the recognized rules of diplomatic behaviour were violable by her. India openly asserted her power potential.

Humayun Khan, a cool and experienced career diplomat, promptly conveyed India's *demarche* to the Foreign Office in Islamabad with his recommendation that General Arif might personally speak to General Sundarji to defuse tension. Hours later, he sent one more cipher telegram repeating his earlier suggestion. He had learnt during the day that without caring to wait for a reply from Pakistan, the Indian Army had already rushed to the border, and her air force and navy were placed on red alert.

Caught in a self-created quagmire, the Indian military High Command faced a nightmare and felt the tightening of the noose around its own neck. While exercising coercive diplomacy, the planners of Exercise Brass Tacks had adopted a proactive, provocative and aggressive approach to demonstrate India's will and power to browbeat Pakistan into submission, and subdue her armed forces if a suitable opportunity could be created for a decisive engagement. They had convinced themselves that the show of military might would compel Pakistan into adopting a meek response as assessed by them. This would fix the Pakistan Army Reserves in the areas of India's choice. This done, India would then be strategically poised to dictate military terms to Pakistan.

Pakistan's Cool Response

An emergency meeting of the Defence Committee of the Cabinet was held at the Prime Minister's residence at 2200 hours on 23 January. Besides others attending the meeting, the military commanders present were the Chairman JCSC, General Rahimuddin Khan, the Air Chief, Air Chief Marshal Jamal

A. Khan, the Naval Chief Admiral Iftikhar A. Sirohey and
General Arif representing the Pakistan Army. Foreign Secretary
Mr Abdul Sattar read out the two telegrams received from
Ambassador Humayun Khan and explained details of the
diplomatic initiatives taken during the day. He supported
Humayun's view that a personal contact between the opposing
army commanders could be useful in restoring tranquility and
peace.

General Akhtar beamed with confidence because the ISI
Directorate had accurately forecast Indian motives and its
intelligence assessment was proving correct. With a visible touch
of professional pride he argued that India had deliberately
created panic to cover up her own faults. A general discussion
ensued. The participants expressed the view that India had
deliberately politicised the military situation. She had over-
reacted in an unprofessional and arrogant manner. It was
proposed that Pakistan's response should reflect dignity with
firmness. Prime Minister Junejo asked me about Humayun's
suggestion to speak to the Indian Army chief on the military
hot-line. 'I am prepared to talk to General Sundarji if the prime
minister so desires,' I replied, adding, 'but given a choice I do
not support this proposal because it would be taken in India as a
sign of weakness.' Instead, he proposed that the Pakistani
DGMO might speak to his counterpart in the Indian Army as
per normal practice in the past. The hot-line could and should
be used.

Mr Junejo retired to an adjoining room for a few minutes and
on return announced that in view of the gravity of the situation
he had invited General Zia to join the deliberations. Zia, living
close by, arrived within minutes and virtually 'took over the
proceedings.'[29] The discussions continued till past midnight. I
reiterated his view that the hot-line be used to establish military
contact between the two DGMO's. A detailed analysis covering
the military, diplomatic, political, intelligence and media aspects
were examined and a working strategy evolved. All the concerned
agencies were tasked to take immediate steps to implement the
decisions taken in the meeting. The salient features were:

a. DGMO to speak to DGMO India on the hot-line and inquire about the Red alert imposed in that country.

b. Military vigilance to be maintained by all the three defence services.

c. ISI Directorate to monitor the India situation to the optimum.

d. A Press Note be issued about the latest developments proposing bilateral discussions between India and Pakistan. The major inputs for the text were identified but the drafting was left to be done by the Foreign Office.

e. Pakistan's High Commissioner in India to be suitably briefed.

f. All friendly countries to be kept informed.

Pakistan's measured response was in contrast to the angry alarm bells rung from across the border. A tit for tat approach might have prompted the decision makers in Islamabad to declare a state of emergency and order the military to take appropriate counter measures. This was avoided. Instead, despite the provocation, Pakistan adopted a cool and mature approach to ease tension. It was statesmanship of a high order.

ACM Jamal recalls that:

> The effective manner in which Pakistan's politico-military decision making structure functioned contributed to the successful defusing of the serious threat. President Zia and Prime Minister Junejo both allowed the structure to work freely and thus to become fully responsive. Junejo, understandably unsure in the midst of Brass Tack's high drama and complexity, listened attentively to the professional appraisals and the proposed political and military initiatives. The overall teamwork was so effective that throughout the crisis both the DCC and the JCSC met on numerous occasions, and at times at short notice. Junejo himself had the good judgement to invite Zia to join some crucial meetings. An atmosphere of free expression permitted the rigorous examination of every option and differing views were resolved through close scrutiny. Throughout the crisis the listening capacity, guidance and calming influence of President Zia played a central role in preventing an emotional or injudicious option being exercised. Above all, the wide-ranging participation that Zia encouraged helped in preventing the dangerous

syndrome of 'Groupthink' from taking hold within Pakistan's top security institutions and councils.[30]

Exercise Brass Tacks had been effectively handled in Pakistan from all politico-military and diplomatic angles over a period of time. This effort paid dividends. Pakistan not only seized the initiative from India but also made her react at critical moments. The decision-making institutions and mechanism worked like a well-oiled machine under the Zia-Junejo leadership. The inter-services effort at the professional level achieved notable success.

The DGMO India was busy supervising the movements of the Indian Army troops to the border areas when Major-General Naqvi spoke to him just after midnight. Naqvi complained that Dr Humayun Khan had been denied the courtesy of a reply to the Indian complaint and a Red alert was announced without even hearing him. The Indian DGMO called it a defensive step because the Pakistani troops had not reverted to their peace locations, and in particular the Army Reserves remained 'menacingly forward.' Naqvi replied that the collective training period of only some formations had to be, perforce, increased because of the unprecedented buildup of over a dozen Indian divisions in Rajasthan and the induction of formations in Kashmir and East Punjab. Despite this, Pakistan displayed considerable restraint and took only minimum and non-provocative defensive measures. The Indian DGMO stated that his country might have understood Pakistan's concern if it had taken defensive steps only in the close vicinity of the inter-state border. Naqvi replied that the hot-line could have been used by India to verify the facts in case of any doubt. Both the DGMOs agreed to maintain their telephone contact. The ice was broken. The conversation started the process of defusing tension.

Dr Humayun Khan said in a press statement that Rajiv Gandhi had informed Junejo at Bangalore that Exercise Brass Tacks would be curtailed to save expenditure.[31] Humayun argued that his country would not initiate a military conflict because the power equation was against it.[32] Pakistan issued a press note on 24 January denouncing tension and proposing dialogue to put the peace process back on the rails. Foreign Minister Zain Noorani suggested immediate negotiations with the Indian High Commissioner in Islamabad, Mr S. K. Singh, to decelerate tension. Such visible initiatives, along with the moves made by foreign powers through diplomatic channels, had a sobering impact on the tense situation and provided an opportunity to restore regional normalcy. Prime Minister Rajiv Gandhi had a brief impromptu exchange of views with Humayun Khan whom he met at New Delhi airport on 24 January. He expressed the desire to restore normalcy expeditiously. The remark helped in improving the regional political climate.

Prime Minister Junejo addressed a joint session of the Parliament on 25 January. He spoke about the concentration of Indian troops and eulogized the Pakistani armed forces for acting with restraint in protecting the security interests of the country. He expressed his willingness to hold consultations with India to restore normalcy. He went a step further and telephoned the Indian prime minister. The two heads of the governments agreed to convene a meeting at the Foreign Secretaries level to restore normalcy. The details were left to be settled through diplomatic consultations. The tension eased but it did not end. Both the countries claimed that the steps taken by them were defensive, precautionary and necessary to safeguard their respective national interests. Zia maintained his public posture of being on a peace offensive with India. He remained calm, vowed to defuse Indo-Pakistan tension, and departed on a previously planned visit to Kuwait. This was his manner of indicating that the storm was over, and he had confidence in Junejo's leadership qualities in handling the situation.

The delegations from the two countries led by Foreign Secretary Mr Abdul Sattar from Pakistan, and Mr A. S. Gonsalves, Secretary in the Indian Ministry of Foreign Affairs, met in New Delhi between 31 January and 4 February 1987. Both the delegations agreed to disagree on the genesis of the conflict and held a series of meetings to evolve a mutually acceptable compromise to defuse tension. They traded allegations with counter-allegations and the going was less than smoothen the situation. The Pakistan delegation presented a twelve-point proposal for consideration to which the Indian delegation responded with an eight-point agenda. After prolonged discussion, a sector by sector approach was adopted for the pull-out of troops deployed on the border by both sides. The minutes of consultations were recorded on 4 February in Document 1 that listed 'immediate measures to defuse present tension, to prevent escalation, and to de-escalate the situation along the Indo-Pakistan border.' This was a victory of bilateral diplomacy. A settlement on the immediate measures eased the tense political and military climate.

A second round of consultations between the delegations was held in Islamabad from 27 February to 2 March 1987, to wrap up a settlement on the remaining stumbling blocks. It was relatively easy this time. The minutes were recorded in Document 2. The crisis ended.

In the final analysis, Exercise Brass Tacks was held only as a training manoeuvre. India's military arrogance had been effectively reduced by Pakistan's vigilant, calm and professional response. Starting on a high note, the exercise ended in low key, void of the 'big *tamasha*' planned to be held on the borders of Pakistan.

Hidden Motives

Few in India knew then of the existence of the wheels within wheels in its senior bureaucratic hierarchy. Besides, the Ministries of Defence and External Affairs worked as exclusive mini-empires. One retired Indian army general disclosed on the basis of anonymity that 'the Ministry of External Affairs was deliberately kept uninformed because they could not be trusted to keep a secret.'[33] This serious accusation indicates that the military hawks and their collaborators in this hush-hush drama had worked on a hidden agenda.

The Indian Army has a long history of adventure which became a part of its psyche early in its post-independence life. Military exuberance enjoyed the patronage of its top political leadership. The military occupation of Junagadh, Manawadar, Hyderabad, Kashmir, Goa, the forward policy against China in 1962, the Rann of Kutch dispute in 1965, and the Indo-Pakistan wars in 1965 and 1971 are some examples of the flexing of India's military muscle.

In keeping with the style of her administration, the decision-making process in the prime minister's office was centralized during the government of Prime Minister Indira Gandhi. Rajiv Gandhi not only continued with this practice but also further tightened his personal grip on the decision making process. 'Nobody, except a small group in the prime minister's office and an equally limited group of officers near the army chief, was aware of the crisis.' This lends support to the belief that the military madness in 1987 was a pre-meditated act.

In a sudden decision that caused surprise in India, Prime Minister Rajiv Gandhi made changes in the portfolios of his cabinet ministers. In a late night announcement, Finance Minister V. P. Singh was shifted to the Defence Ministry and Rajiv Gandhi himself took charge of the finance portfolio. The defence portfolio was till then held by Rajiv, with Arun Singh as Minister of State. Arun retained his post but his authority was diluted by the appointment of a full time minister to take charge of the Ministry of Defence.

If the changes made on 24 January were significant, the timing was even more striking. Some Indian analysts argue that the move killed two birds with one stone—V.P. Singh was shifted from the Ministry of Finance and Arun cut to size because both 'had started asserting themselves.'

A section of India's print media later blamed its defence establishment for exceeding the norms and acting without political sanction. A senior bureaucrat working in the prime minister's office writes, 'The most critical of these moves and counter-moves (in Brass Tacks) were effected without the knowledge of our Prime Minister.'

Prime Minister Rajiv Gandhi, assertive and dynamic, knew the ground realities. He personally 'opposed the inter-state contacts at the DGMO level.'

Prime Minister Rajiv Gandhi adopted a multi-track approach. He approved the coercive diplomacy behind Exercise Brass Tacks but personally maintained a political distance from its actual conduct. His actions kept his options open. An informed Indian writes thus, 'Pakistan feared Brass Tacks was just a ruse before a full frontal attack. It is now an open secret that the then Chief of Army Staff, K. Sundarji, had advanced the forces to a point that was several kilometers ahead of what Prime Minister Rajiv Gandhi had sanctioned.'

The Nuclear Angle

India and Pakistan were potential nuclear powers in 1987. While India had conducted one nuclear test in 1974, both these countries were known to possess fissile materials and the technical ability to convert them into nuclear-weapons at short notice. India's nuclear establishments were larger in number and multi-dimensional in nature as compared to those in Pakistan. Despite this status, the nuclear factor remained conspicuously absent throughout the crisis. Neither country threatened the use of nuclear weapons during the open arms conflict. This phenomenon was perhaps based on the fear of retaliation, a mutual fear of self-destruction, and the maturity of the decision makers in both the countries.

The foreign powers in general and the US in particular viewed this issue differently. The American analysts apprehended, without giving any cogent reason, that a regional conflict had the potential of taking a nuclear turn and posed a threat to the safety of large population centres in India and Pakistan. This was a hypothetical and academic argument. Their purpose was to deter a nuclear war and encourage a nuclear non-proliferation regime.

NOTES

1. Ravi Rikhye, *The Militarization of Mother India,* self-published, 1991, p. 21.
2. Ibid., p. 21.
3. Stephen P. Cohen (and four co-authors), *Brasstacks and Beyond,* Manohar Publishers and Distributors, New Delhi, India, 1995, p. 12.
4. Ravi Rikhye, *The War that Never Was: The Story of India's Strategic Failures,* Chanakya, New Delhi, India, 1988.
5. Ashok Kapur 'Nuclear Deterrence in the Developing World: India and Pakistan, 1987 and 1989-90 Crisis', paper presented at the American Association for the Advancement of Science, Chicago, 11 February 1992, p. 9.
6. Conversation General Arif, Lt-General Hirday Kaul, former GOC-in-C Western Army Command, Indian Army on 14 October 1998 at New Delhi.
7. *The Times of India,* 15 November 1986.
8. Junejo-Arif conversation.
9. *Indian Express,* 26 January 1987.
10. Jawaharlal Nehru, *The Discovery of India,* p. 241.
11. *The Times of India,* 10 November 1986.
12. Ibid., 11 November 1986.
13. Ibid.
14. *Jang,* 11 October 1986.
15. Ibid., 13 October 1986.
16. *Nawa-i-Waqt,* 21 October 1986.
17. *Dawn,* 4 November 1986.
18. 'Maghribi Pakistan', *Brass Tacks and Beyond,* p. 160.
19. *The Times of India,* 3 December 1986.
20. Ravi Rikhye, *'The Militarization of Mother India'*, self-published, 1991, pp. 22-3.
21. *Brasstacks and Beyond,* p. 33.
22. Interview Air Chief Marshal Jamal A. Khan, 25 October 1998.
23. *Pakistan Times,* 24 January 1987.
24. Interview Admiral Iftikhar A. Sirohey, 17 November 1998.
25. Interview Air Chief Marshal Jamal A. Khan, 26 October 1998.
26. *The Times of India,* 25 January 1987.
27. *Reuters North European Service Report,* 24 January 1987.
28. *Brasstacks and Beyond,* p. 43.
29. Ibid., p. 44.
30. G. K. Reddy, *The Hindu,* 30 January 1987.
31. Mani Shankar Aiyar.
32. Ajoy, Bose, *The Sunday Observer,* 8-14 February 1987, and *The Times of India,* 18 November 1986.
33. Kuldip Nayar, *Dawn,* 26 May 1998.

7

THE ROLE OF THE JUDICIARY

Arbiters in Power Politics

The geographic separation between East Pakistan and West Pakistan and disparity between them in their population strength, economic wealth and political power created difficulties for Pakistan from the very beginning. Although 56 per cent of her population resided in East Pakistan, the base of political power was located in West Pakistan and separated by 1600 kilometers of an unfriendly India. Pakistan's internal difficulties suited India which she exploited to her own advantage. Jinnah's death (1948) and Liaquat's assassination (1951) catapulted lesser people to dizzy political heights and many of them proved themselves unequipped for the tasks they faced.

A power struggle at the centre between the president and the prime minister created a crisis. Prime Minister Khwaja Nazimuddin, dismissed in April 1953, silently sulked. He bore the pain of insult but did not seek justice in a court of law. The emboldened governor-general struck again and on 24 October 1954, dissolved the Constituent Assembly and dismissed the central government. In the resultant scenario, the superior courts became arbiters in the distribution of political power. Their judgments, tempering law with political expediency, came to be bitterly criticized in judicial and political circles.

Justice Munir, a judge in the colonial mould, upheld General Ayub's military takeover in 1958 on the basis of the doctrine of 'successful revolution being legal'. Be it judicial prudence, as claimed by some, or a judicial surrender, as criticized by others, the country paid a hefty price for granting judicial legitimacy to a draconian act.

8

The 1956 Constitution was abrogated by the martial law authorities without getting a fair chance to function. Ayub, emerging on the national centre-stage, acted fast to tame the judiciary. The executive branch introduced the practice of interviewing the candidates before appointing them as judges in the higher judiciary, a measure that compromised the dignity of the judiciary. In 1973, the Supreme Court held General Yahya Khan a 'usurper' for imposing martial law in 1969. This belated judgment, without even hearing Yahya Khan, did not enhance the image of the judiciary. By then, East Pakistan was lost and Yahya, out of power, was under detention following Pakistan's defeat in 1971.

The geography of the country changed. A homogenous but shrunken Pakistan emerged, with Bhutto at the helm of its affairs.

Bhutto Takes Charge

A small group of dignitaries witnessed the oath-taking ceremony held at the Presidency, Rawalpindi, on 20 December 1971. Those present included Mumtaz Bhutto, J.A. Rahim, Air Marshal Rahim Khan, General Abdul Hameed Khan (COS), Lt.-Gen. S.G.M.M. Peerzada, and the two bureaucrats Ghulam Ishaq Khan (Cabinet Secretary) and Roedad Khan (Secretary Information). Bhutto had invited Lt.-Gen. Gul Hassan Khan to attend his oath-taking ceremony. Gul Hassan had excused himself from attendance. The low-key ceremony was in contrast to the gaiety and glamour usually witnessed in a conventional transfer of power. The oath of office was administered by Mr Justice Hamoodur Rahman, the Chief Justice of Pakistan, whose visible calm betrayed the anguish deep within his heart. He hailed from the fallen East Pakistan.

India's military attack against East Pakistan in November 1971, demanded that Pakistan make vigorous attempts in the United Nations Security Council to stop the aggression quickly. Surprisingly Pakistan remained silent. Her lack of effort in the

UN Security Council remains a mystery. The Security Council resolution of 4 December calling for a cease-fire was vetoed by India's strategic ally, the Soviet Union. The General Assembly's 'Uniting for Peace'Resolution passed on 7 December by a wide margin of 104 votes to 11 with 10 abstentions was not pursued further. Pakistan's diplomatic hibernation astonished even her friends. The Soviet veto gave time to India to achieve her objectives in East Pakistan.

Pakistan's Deputy Prime Minister and the Foreign Minister, Bhutto, were in New York then. With Dhaka collapsing, Yahya asked Bhutto to return to Pakistan. After his last address in the Security Council on 15 December, Bhutto stayed in the US for three additional days, 'to clear his path to power with Nixon... explaining to him that he was not anti-US.'[1] Enroute to Islamabad he stopped at Rome where, as confidentially pre-arranged, he received an all clear green signal from his confidante Ghulam Mustafa Khar to return home without fear. Bhutto had feared that Yahya might arrest him.

This was Bhutto's hour of glory. His rise to the pinnacle of power as the head of state came at a time when the national morale was low. Despite the dubious role played by him in the dismemberment of the country, his personal image soared high and the people expected him to lift the country from the depths of defeat. Though Bhutto was a major player in this sordid drama, the stigma of surrender was also shared by the government, the military and many political leaders. On the invitation of General Yahya Khan, the leaders of political parties from West Pakistan had travelled to Dhaka to participate in the talks held between the government and the Awami League. Yahya had wisely associated them in the failed negotiations that preceded the military action on 25 March 1971.

In December 1971, the loss of her Eastern wing converted West Pakistan into Pakistan. But, contrary to Jinnah's vision of creating a plural, democratic and egalitarian state, Pakistan remained under the umbrella of martial law. It would have been politically prudent, morally praiseworthy and legally appropriate to seek a fresh public mandate before enacting a constitution for the residual Pakistan. Besides, it would have set a healthy democratic tradition. Sheikh Mujibur Rahman adopted this course in Bangladesh before enacting a constitution for the new country.

Constitutional Amendments

Bhutto had the 1973 constitution amended eight times, primarily to tame the judiciary. Among other issues, the First Amendment (8 May, 1974) curtailed the freedom of expression and allowed the Federal Government to ban political parties formed or 'operating in a manner prejudicial to the sovereignty or integrity of Pakistan', subject to a final decision by the Supreme Court. The axe fell on the National Awami Party, which, after being banned, was renamed the Awami National Party.

The Second Amendment (21 September, 1974), declaring Qadianis as non-Muslims, enjoyed a national political consensus. The Third Amendment (18 February), *inter alia*, empowered the government to detain a person without trial for three months and facilitated the continuation of a Proclamation of Emergency. The Fourth Amendment (25 November, 1975) curtailed the writ powers of the High Courts under Article 199 in respect of preventive detention and further restricted the systematically curtailed freedom of association.

The Fifth Amendment (15 September, 1976), (a) further reduced the writ powers of the High Courts; (b), fixed the tenure of five years and four years respectively for the Chief Justices of the Supreme and High Courts. This empowered the government to ease out the Chief Justice of the Lahore High Court, Sardar Iqbal, and the Chief Justice of the Peshawar High Court, Safdar Shah, and appoint Aslam Riaz, who stood eighth in the order of seniority, as the Chief Justice of the Lahore High Court; (c), empowered the executive to transfer a judge to any High Court up to a period of one year without his consent or consultation with the Chief Justice concerned; (d), enabled the executive to appoint a High Court judge as a puisne judge of the Supreme Court and in case of his failure to accept such appointment he 'shall be deemed to have retired from his office'; and (e), permitted the executive to appoint 'any one of the judges', and not the senior most, to act as Chief Justice. This curtailed the independence of the judiciary.

The Sixth Amendment (4 January, 1977), allowed the Chief Justices of the Supreme and High Courts to hold office for tenures of five and four years respectively even if they had attained the retirement age of 65 and 62 prescribed for them. The beneficiary was the Chief Justice of the Supreme Court, Yakub Ali, who publicly lavished praise, 'I can say from personal knowledge that the prime minister, by conviction, has great respect for the judiciary from the lowest to the highest rung.'[2] Yakub's certificate of appreciation to Bhutto did not enhance the image of the judiciary. The Seventh Amendment (16 May, 1977) was enacted after the people had risen in revolt against the Bhutto government as a result of the rigged elections held in 1977. It provided for a referendum to escape from re-election. It also prohibited the High Courts from exercising jurisdiction over people and property of an area where the armed forces had been brought in aid of civil power.

These Amendments weakened the fundamental rights of the people and compromised the independence of the judiciary. These were made when Bhutto's popularity was high and the military was still recovering from the shock of defeat in 1971. The army held Bhutto in high esteem and did not comment, in public, on the amendments made. The Army Chief, General Tikka Khan, was supportive of the prime minister and, as a matter of policy, did not comment on political or legal issues.

Successive governments played politics with the judiciary and denied it its rightful place as a pillar of the state. Their oft-repeated commitment for the separation of the judiciary from the executive was a facade, mere political rhetoric and a vote-catching election gimmick. All governments retained coercive powers with the executive branch for reasons of administrative convenience. These powers were often used to pressurize and weaken the opposition, to misuse the police force and to hide administrative excesses.

For reasons of administrative convenience, military rulers also failed to separate the judiciary from the executive. Their primary concern was to maintain peace and to have a healthy law and order situation in the country. Unlike elected rulers, they did not have a public mandate to promote a democratic order in the society. And, they took refuge behind this position.

Throughout Bhutto's five year rule, a state of emergency remained operative in the country and the fundamental rights of the people were suspended. Those critical of the government's arbitrary and harsh policies soon felt the coercive instruments of the state closing in on them. Bhutto demanded subservience and those daring to differ with him were firmly 'fixed'.

Opposition Hounded

In 1973, the provincial government in Balochistan was dismissed by the federal government for political reasons. Bhutto's authoritarian attitude was matched in good measure by the passion of the tribal *Sardars* (leaders) in Balochistan to safeguard their traditional tribal rights. The *Sardars* took to arms to restore their 'honour'. An internal security situation erupted that kept parts of Balochistan unstable and volatile for five years. The Bhutto government directed the army to restore normalcy in Balochistan, a euphemism for strengthening the loosening writ of his government. The opposition leaders alleged that Bhutto desired that the military crush the Baloch 'insurgency' with force. Normalcy returned to Balochistan when, after the exit of the Bhutto government, Zia ended military operations in Balochistan, withdrew troops from the area, and granted general amnesty to all dissidents.

The dismissal of the government in Balochistan led to the resignation of the provincial government in the North-West Frontier Province in protest. This made the government indulge in political 'horse-trading'. Soon, it was easy for Bhutto to win over a working majority in the provincial legislature by offering lucre to legislators who put their conscience on the back seats.

Agencies Misused

A Federal Security Force (FSF) was created in 1972, ostensibly to supplement the police effort in maintaining law and order in the country. In reality, it disrupted the political meetings organized by the opposition and committed acts of sabotage and terrorism in the country. Such misdeeds were then falsely attributed to Bhutto's opponents to keep them under check and pressure. The FSF was created as a parallel force in the country to weaken the image of the Pakistan Army. It was equipped with rifles, automatic weapons and rocket launchers and plans were made to equip it with tanks and helicopters. It had its own intelligence cell and secret service fund. The FSF, a mini army, was created at a time when the military was down and recovering. Bhutto took advantage of the situation and established a para-military force for political purposes. He used it as a weapon of terror to discipline and silence his critics. It was an act of the FSF that took Bhutto to the gallows.

Judiciary Harassed

Between the years 1947-71, the judiciary in Pakistan maintained a reasonable degree of freedom of action and asserted its statutory powers in deciding issues on legal merit. It did not hesitate in setting aside those decisions given by the executive branch that infringed on laws or were *ultra vires* of the constitution. The court judgments enjoyed respect and the executive branch implemented them in letter and in spirit.

The judiciary kept a low profile in public life and took pride in speaking through its judgments. However, not all judgments were free of criticism. Some showing political streaks in them, like Justice Mohammad Munir's 'Doctrine of successful revolution being legal', earned public ire. Constructive criticism was tolerated as a *sine qua non* of a democratic dispensation.

The situation underwent a visible change during the Bhutto rule. The people, expecting enlightened leadership from him, wanted justice and fair play. Bhutto started well. He skilfully pieced together the broken spirit of a dejected nation and promised a bright future for a reinvigorated Pakistan.

A Judge Arrested

In 1973, there was a political dispute in Sanghar District that resulted in the arrest of some persons. On August 23, an FIR (first information report) was filed by an opposition leader. The government frustrated the process of law. On August 24, the District and Session Judge, Sanghar (Mr Mohammad Owais Murtaza) was arrested. He was released on August 27 after a bail application had been filed on his behalf in the Sindh High Court. The same day his telephone was disconnected and he was 'advised'by the government to leave Sanghar immediately for a couple of days in his own interest.

The Chief Justice of the Sindh High Court, Mr Tufail Ali Abdul Rahman, protested against the arrest of the district judge. In a letter addressed to Bhutto on 4 September, he complained that he had been kept in the dark about the circumstances leading to the arrest and requested an interview. The prime minister neither conceded to the request nor cared to respond to the letter. Instead, he marked it to the chief minister of Sindh with the remarks, 'For heaven's sake, meet this *old woman* (emphasis added) and keep him happy, otherwise deal with him. You are duly...'[3] This attitude of ridicule towards a chief justice showed Bhutto's 'respect' for the judiciary.

Rule by Ordinances

The Bhutto government enjoyed a comfortable majority in the Parliament to meet the legislative needs of the country. It had the legal and the moral responsibility to administer the country on democratic lines. Law-making by parliament is a democratic process. Instead, the Bhutto administration adopted the technique of legislation by ordinance, at the average rate of one ordinance per week. It is conceded that ordinances were also promulgated during the army years, but during those periods legislatures did not exist. Besides, it is futile to judge military rule by democratic standards—martial law is a negation of democracy. The annual breakdown of ordinances passed was as under:

1972	66
1973	30
1974	24
1975	31
1976	44
1977 (up to 5 July)	24
Total	219

Amendments in the Constitution

A constitutional amendment demands serious reflection by the government, consultation with the opposition, and an informed public debate on the issue in the media. A discussion in the parliament is then held with adequate time and opportunity provided for a comprehensive debate.

Rhetoric dominated Bhutto's political agenda. During his tenure eight constitutional (amendment) bills were passed in the National Assembly, in quick succession. In five cases, the bill was introduced in, and passed by, the National Assembly on the same day or the next. Such haste showed the parliament's subservience to the executive branch in the law-making process.

Judiciary Targeted

The constitution forbids any 'discussion in Parliament with respect to the conduct of any judge of the Supreme Court or of a High Court in the discharge of his duties.' During the debate on the Fifth Amendment Bill, Bhutto declared in the National Assembly on 4 September that:

The judiciary cannot become a parallel executive by wholesale misapplication, misrepresentation and misinterpretation of the laws. This must be very clearly understood.....and anyone who does not understand it does so at his own peril...

...each organ must remain in its sphere of influence, in its own orbit. It cannot transgress into the orbit of others. The judiciary cannot transgress into the executive function, into the executive organ.

...it has been necessary to introduce this Fifth Amendment as a result of the transgressing by the judiciary of its functions into the executive branch.

The tone and tenor of Bhuttto's language were insulting to the judiciary.

Zia's Martial Law

The imposition of martial law by General Zia on 5 July 1977, was neither a sudden development nor did it surprise the people. Zia had informed Bhutto of the army's contingency plan and Bhutto was too sharp a person to miss the ramifications of this loaded hint. Yet Bhutto did nothing to reach a political compromise with the opposition. Their on-going negotiations moved at a snail's pace. A compromise had all but emerged. The Pakistan National Alliance adopted delaying tactics to extract additional concessions from a cornered government. They had nothing to lose. The PNA intensely distrusted Bhutto and feared that he might outsmart them to their disadvantage.

The clock kept ticking. There was too much at stake for Bhutto and he should have known that he alone would suffer if the talks failed. It was vital for him to strike a deal, and quickly, to pre-empt a point of no return. The sycophants in the PPP did not comprehend that the more Bhutto wasted time haggling on trivial issues the more the noose was tightening around his neck. The military takeover was a double jeopardy for Bhutto. He squandered away his electoral victory and his adversaries escaped a sure defeat were elections to be held once again in 1977.

Some political rats left his sinking ship. Others distanced themselves from the fallen Bhutto and looked for greener pastures. The sycophants took shelter behind cover. In the final analysis, Bhutto faced the ordeal alone, along with his relatives and some of his party loyalists during the prolonged agony of his trial and execution. Later, with Bhutto dead and the crisis over, some political minions reappeared to get on board once again for reasons easy to fathom.

Zia had sensed intransigence and rigidity in both the camps and the gulf of their mutual distrust was wide. The military contingency plan was prepared to cater for a political deadlock. The political scenario was so fluid and uncertain that in early July, the army chief and its corps commanders were uncertain if a political settlement would be achieved. The corps commanders left the choice and timings of the military option to their chief.

General Zia decided on 3 July 1977, to implement operation 'Fair Play'. Commander 10 Corps, at Rawalpindi, was ordered to implement the plan on the night of 3/4 July 1977, and the remaining corps commanders were so informed. Chishti gave the green signal to his already selected team. There was a glimmer of hope on the afternoon of 3 July that a political settlement might be in the offing. Zia ordered Chishti to stand down just before the final orders were to be issued. The optimism proved short-lived. On 4 July, the political pendulum swung decisively when Nawabzada Nasrullah Khan told a press conference that the talks had failed. Zia decided to act on the night of 4/5 July 1977. Martial law was imposed.

At the time, neither the PNA leaders nor Bhutto and his cabinet colleagues ever claimed that an agreement had been reached before the military intervention. On the contrary, the PNA leaders repeatedly and jubilantly endorsed the military takeover and a little later eagerly joined the Zia cabinet.

However, soon after the execution of Bhutto in April 1979, some PNA leaders began to whisper about a mythical agreement supposedly reached between the PNA and the Bhutto government. With Bhutto out of their way, these minions found it politically expedient to mend fences with the PPP. They coined a bogus story to distort reality. Never once did they tell Zia about the agreement that was supposedly reached. Nor did Bhutto claim clinching an agreement during his lifetime. Why the PNA kept mum on this vital issue between July 1977 and April 1979 remains unexplained. A bash-Zia allegation suited the politicians for whom he had become a symbol of hatred.

The Judiciary during the Zia Era

Pakistan's judiciary co-existed with the high profile executive branch led by democratic and autocratic rulers under the parliamentary, presidential and military forms of government. The legal system in the country is lengthy, expensive and nerve-racking, but the judgments given by the superior judiciary in civil and criminal cases enjoy respect and credibility. On the other hand, judgments on constitutional matters have, on occasions, received mixed responses from the political parties, for reasons more political than legal.

The judiciary has had to frequently adjudicate on constitutional issues emerging out of the quagmire of dirty politics. Some such judgments earned the courts the stigma of judicial weakness. In one case, an extra-constitutional act was upheld (in 1958) on the plea that 'a successful revolution destroys a constitution'. On another occasion a chief martial law administrator was belatedly declared a 'usurper' in 1972 after he was already out of power.

Martial law is a negation of civil law. The military takeovers of 1958 and 1969 put the judiciary under pressure. On these occasions, the military brass claimed to intervene because the civil system was corrupted by the political rulers, the national institutions had weakened, politics had become a lucrative business and the courts, weak and hesitant, were silent spectators unwilling or incapable of correcting the rot. Ayub and Yahya had not imposed martial law to strengthen the democratic process. Had the legal writ been firm and effective in the country, they would have had no excuse to intervene in civil affairs. That the military had no legal and constitutional right to take charge even when the civilian rulers had failed to govern efficiently, is a valid observation.

Zia's martial law had a smooth start. The anti-Bhutto agitation instantly ended without firing a single bullet. All the four chief justices of the four provincial high courts became governors in their respective provinces. The 1973 Constitution was not abrogated. The Chief Justice of Pakistan, Mr Justice Yaqub Ali, when contacted, advised Zia on 5 July that the constitution might be held in abeyance. This formulation was adopted.

Zia's primary legal experts were Mr A.K. Brohi and Mr Sharifuddin Pirzada. Both served him long and well with distinction and dedication. They gave sound and well considered legal advice on all issues. However, being professional rivals, they were not the best of friends and this occasionally caused problems in their official work. Brohi, a constitutional expert, had a philosophical approach to life. Seldom brief in conversation, Zia had lengthy post-dinner meetings with him on legal issues and Islamic jurisprudence.

Sharifuddin Pirzada, pragmatic and factual, had learnt in his early years, 'know thy law, know thy facts and know thy judge.' His vast experience enabled him to sense the mood of the courts and the sensitivity of its judges. He had the knack of synthesizing law with politics and he knew the art of expressing his views on sensitive issues mildly and tactfully. He shared his general views in the cabinet meetings but the more controversial discussions were held privately. His advice on touchy issues helped the administration in weathering many a storm.

Differences between Brohi and Pirzada on handling legal issues provided a welcome opportunity to hear both their views. A patient listener, Zia quickly grasped the essentials of a point and used it to good advantage in handling crises.

The legal luminaries and political pundits cautioned Zia that his takeover was a violation of the constitution, and the issue might be agitated in the courts. The constitutional experts felt that in the final analysis, political considerations would outweigh legal aspects. If Zia was worrried on this account he did not show it. Acting firmly, he amended the constitution which, under the sixth amendment, had extended the tenure of Justice Yaqub Ali. The matter was not agitated in the courts. Zia hosted a dinner in honour of the outgoing chief justice who reciprocated the gesture by inviting Zia to a return dinner at his residence. Mr Justice Anwarul Haq became the Chief Justice of Pakistan.

The expected happened. Mrs Nusrat Bhutto, the wife of the deposed prime minister, challenged the imposition of martial law. On 10 November 1977, a nine-member Bench of the Supreme Court, headed by Chief Justice Anwarul Haq, upheld Zia's intervention under the 'law of necessity.' One day before the announcement of the judgment, the Chief Justice met Sharifuddin Pirzada at a party and told him that the judgment would be announced the next morning, at 9 a.m., adding that the court had decided to hold the promulgation of martial law as legal. He enquired from Pirzada if he would be attending court. Pirzada asked if the power to amend the constitution was also being conceded to the chief martial law administrator. Justice Anwar replied in the negative. 'In that case,' replied Pirzada, 'the government would have to swear in a new chief Justice.' 'What do you mean?', asked an inquisitive Anwar 'You will be removing yourself from the appointment of the chief justice', replied Pirzada, adding, 'your predecessor will have to be sworn in once again as he had retired through an amendment made in the constitution by the CMLA.' Anwar inserted the words, 'including the power to amend it (the constitution).'[4] in the sentence in his own hand. This conversation was narrated to the author by Mr Pirzada.

The Case of Justice Ghulam Safdar Shah

This narrative is about a judge who obtained the basic academic qualification through forgery and deceit, then rose to dizzy heights and retired as a judge of the Supreme Court of Pakistan.

The Zia administration is often accused of being unfair to the judge in question, and for 'hounding him out' of the country. What follows will reveal the truth.

While seeking admission in the Sind Muslim Law College, Karachi, Safdar Shah stated in his application dated 24 June 1950, that his date of birth was 15 June 1920, and that he had passed the Intermediate Examination from the Holker College, Indore, India, held in March/April 1941. Both these contentions turned out to be false. Qualification in the intermediate examination was mandatory for admission to the Sind Muslim Law College, Karachi. It transpired, however, that Safdar Shah had, in fact, never taken the Intermediate Examination. He had, in fact, forged a certificate and misled the college authorities. Safdar Shah gained admission in the college on the basis of false evidence, and succeeded in passing the LLB examination from the Karachi University in 1952.

Safdar Shah then joined Lincoln's Inn, England, from where he was called to the Bar on 20 June 1955. On 17 July 1956, he applied at the Karachi Bench of the West Pakistan High Court for admission to the Roll of Advocates of the High Court of West Pakistan. The formality completed, he practiced law at Karachi till 5 November 1966, and was then appointed as Additional Advocate General, West Pakistan, Lahore.

Safdar Shah was elevated to additional judge of the High Court of West Pakistan and he assumed charge at Karachi on 4 September 1967. This was a sad day for the judiciary. Here was a judge who took the oath of office to uphold the constitution and maintain the writ of law in the country but had himself committed a fraud. Subsequently, Mr Justice Ghulam Safdar Shah was transferred to the High Court at Peshawar where he rose to become the Chief Justice of the Peshawar High Court.

On becoming a judge of the High Court, he altered his date of birth to 15 June 1922 without adopting the prescribed procedure laid down for making such a change. If the date of birth had been incorrectly recorded earlier, he should have written to the Chief Justice of the West Pakistan High Court, requesting him to get the error corrected.

Thereafter, Mr Justice Safdar Shah became a judge in the Supreme Court.

On 18 March 1978, a five member bench of the Lahore High Court presided over by the Chief Justice of the Lahore High Court awarded capital punishment to all the five accused facing trial in the Nawab Muhammad Ahmad Khan murder case. The judgment was unanimous. The accused included Mr Zulfikar Ali Bhutto, the Prime Minister of Pakistan at the time when the victim was gunned down by the officials of the Federal Security Force. The family of the deceased accused Bhutto of masterminding the murder, and his name was included in the First Investigation Report. The remaining four accused were officials of the Federal Security Force.

The appeals filed by the accused were heard by the full bench of the Supreme Court presided over by Mr Justice Anwarul Haq, the Chief Justice of Pakistan. Mr Justice Safdar Shah was one of the nine members of the bench.

The appeals were rejected on 2 February 1979, with a majority of four to three votes. Mr Justice Safdar Shah was one of the three dissenting judges.

All the five accused filed review petitions which were heard by the full court. These were unanimously rejected on 24 March 1979, by all the judges, including the three who had dissented at the level of appeal.

Then a strange development took place. Two days after the rejection of the review petition, Safdar Shah told some press correspondents that the observations made by the Supreme Court in the Nawab Muhammad Ahmad Khan murder case, and the arguments submitted by the defence council during the course of the trial, could not be disregarded by the executive while deciding the question of implementing the verdict of death.

He also stated that all the seven judges of the Supreme Court held a similar view.

Under the circumstances, on 29 March 1979, the Supreme Court issued a Press note saying:

The attention of the Chief Justice of Pakistan and the remaining five judges constituting the Bench which dismissed Mr Zulfikar Ali Bhutto's review petition against the appellate judgment of the Supreme Court dated the 6th February 1979, has been drawn to some remarks reported in the press today as having been made by Mr Justice G. Safdar Shah, in relation to certain observations contained in the order made by the learned judge to the BBC correspondent and two others whom he came across while walking on a road in Islamabad. It is not the practice of the Supreme Court to issue statements explaining the import of their judgment or orders, or of any observation contained therein, as they speak for themselves. Whatever Mr Justice G. Safdar Shah has said reflects his personal views only and he had no authority to speak on behalf of the other members of the Bench. As the remaining judges would not like to depart from this settled practice, they would refrain from making any comments on this behalf.

After this event, an unsigned 'non-paper' providing evidence of misconduct by Safdar Shah was received by General Zia. Mr M. Aslam Hayat, the Director General, Federal Investigation Agency (FIA) was directed to conduct inquiries to verify three facts:-

(1) The date of birth of Mr Justice Safdar Shah.
(2) The circumstance under which he left his service with Burmah Shell, Karachi, in the early fifties.
(3) Details about the Intermediate Examination certificate received from the Board of High School and Intermediate Education, Rajputana (including Ajmer Marwara), Central India and Gwalior, based at Ajmer.

Investigations revealed that Mr Justice Safdar Shah had allegedly been guilty of misdeeds, and a deeper and fuller inquiry was warranted. In view of the sensitivity of the matter, the government thought it prudent to place all the available facts before the Chief Justice of Pakistan before proceeding further. After examining the evidence, Mr Justice Anwarul Haq said that *prima facie* it was a fit case for further investigation.

The FIA investigations revealed that:

Mr Justice Safdar Shah's date of birth was 15 June 1920, as recorded (1) in the admission register of the Middle School, Siri Kot: (2) in the admission register of the Islamia High School, Peshawar city; (3) in the Gazette notification of the Punjab University containing the results of the Matriculation Examination held in March 1939; (4) in the Army service record; (5) in the register of Burmah Shell; (6) in the application for admission to Sind Muslim Law College, Karachi; and (7) in the application submitted to the Karachi Bench of the West Pakistan High Court, for the grant of a license to practice as an advocate of the said court.

However, Mr Justice Safdar Shah changed his date of birth to 15 June 1922 while forwarding his particulars to the Comptroller, Southern Area, Karachi on 17 February 1969. This new date was also endorsed in his application for pension and gratuity, dated 26 October 1976, addressed to the Chief Secretary, Government of NWFP. This leads to the inevitable conclusion that his intention was to gain two extra years of service as a member of the superior judiciary.

Mr Justice G. Safdar Shah had joined Burmah Shell, Karachi, on 25 July 1947, as Assistant Fuelling Superintendent and was assigned duties at Karachi Airport. He was dismissed from Burmah Shell on 10 September 1951, and the fact of his dismissal is recorded in the register of the firm without indicating detailed reasons for dismissal. Mr Justice Safdar Shah secured admission in the Sind Muslim Law College, Karachi, for his law degree on the basis of a certificate showing that he had passed the Intermediate Examination as a student of Holker College, Indore, from the Board of High School and Intermediate Education, Rajputana in the year 1941. This was a false claim. The certificate in question, in fact, belonged to another person, Muhammad Amin Khan, and had been forged.

Safdar Shah's assertion that he had studied at the Holker College between April 1939 and March 1941, was found to be patently false because during the period 24 August 1940 and 3 June 1942, he was, infact, serving as a sepoy in the Frontier Constabulary in NWFP.

It was also discovered that Muhammad Amin Khan, who had actually passed the Intermediate Examination from the Ajmer Board in 1941, against Roll Number 815, as a student of Holker College, Indore, had migrated to Pakistan in 1948, and was living in Karachi. Amin joined the Police Department, as an Assistant Sub Inspector of Police, and was posted in the Immigration Department at the Karachi Airport when Safdar Shah was also serving at Karachi Airport as the Assistant Fuelling Superintendent of the Burmah Shell Company Ltd. This proved that the intermediate certificate was secured by Safdar Shah and fraudulently abused and forged by him to seek entry in the Law College. The forgery was detected when the FIA obtained a duplicate copy of the certificate of Intermediate Examination, 1941, from the Central Board of Secondary Education, Ajmer, India, through official channels. The certificate No 445 showed that Roll Number 815, Muhammad Amin Khan of the Holker College, Indore had passed the Intermediate Examination held 1941, in the third Division.

This documentary evidence was examined by legal experts including Mr Sharifuddin Pirzada, the Attorney General for Pakistan. They held the case fit for trial in a court of law as the conduct displayed by Mr Justice Safdar Shah in changing his date of birth without recourse to proper procedure, and in securing admission to a Law College on the basis of a forged document rendered him guilty of misconduct.

The FIA submitted its investigation report concerning Mr Justice Safdar Shah on 2 February, 1980, to the Attorney General of Pakistan with a copy endorsed to the President's Office. This was forwarded to the Chief Justice of Pakistan on 21 February, 1980, to apprise Mr Justice Safdar Shah of the allegations against him and to enable him to offer comments, if any. Justice Anwarul Haq sent the report to Safdar Shah on 23 February, 1980, who did not reply. The Chief Justice then issued a reminder to the judge indicating that if no reply was received from him by 8 April 1980, it would be assumed that he had nothing to say in the matter, and that further action according to the law shall be taken. Mr Justice Safdar Shah replied to the Chief Justice on 8 April, 1980.

In his eight page reply, Mr Justice Safdar Shah maintained that the inquiries conducted against him by the FIA were 'uncalled for' and 'misconceived' and had 'missed the point that the only conduct of mine which was relevant was my conduct as a judge of the Supreme Court.' '...Under the provisions of the Constitution, a judge is answerable to the Supreme Council only for his conduct as a judge, and not for his conduct which has no nexus with his office as a judge, or for that matter with his conduct before he was appointed a judge.' '...As a result of the wide, penetrating and searching inquiries ...going back in point of time to my cradle, the FIA has failed to find anything against me as a lawyer, or as an Additional Advocate General of the then West Pakistan Government, or as a judge,...as well as the Chief Justice of the Peshawar High Court, and finally as a judge of the Supreme Court.'

Mr Justice Safdar Shah, in his defence, did not directly contest or deny the specific charges framed against him and expressed the view that these were technically inadmissible because they pertained to a period prior to his elevation as a judge of the High Court.

Significantly, Mr Justice Safdar Shah, in his reply, also passed inflammatory insinuations against his own brother judges without directly naming them. He complained, 'I have been discriminated against as to the best of my knowledge there are serious charges and allegations against some members of the superior judiciary, all related to the period when they were judges. If the scope is extended to a period prior to their appointment as judges, the charges against some of them may be even more serious. I only wish that a stage may not come when I have to refer to the concrete instances.'

Finally, Safdar Shah briefly dealt with the issue that had made him overtly controversial. He said that, 'During the hearing of late Mr Bhutto's appeal in the Supreme Court, I had, owing to reasons which I wish I would never have to explain, caused

annoyance to many people. I had conducted myself correctly
with the sole object of maintaining the independence and the
dignity of the Highest Court of the country. The type of inquiries
conducted against me have to be seen in this perspective.'

On 21 April, General M. Ziaul Haq addressed a letter to
Mr Justice S. Anwarul Haq, the Chief Justice of Pakistan
authorising him to enquire into the matter.

The Supreme Judicial Council, presided over by Mr Justice
S. Anwarul Haq, the Chief Justice of Pakistan, met on
16 October 1980, to hear the case. Instead of defending himself,
Mr Justice Ghulam Safdar Shah submitted his resignation as a
judge of the Supreme Court.

Tussle for Power

Working under the CMLA Order No. 1 of 1977, the country
was administered by various martial law orders and regulations
issued by the CMLA. Likewise, provincial martial law
administrators had issued martial law orders and regulations
within the jurisdiction of their respective provinces. The
elections initially promised for October 1977 were postponed,
debilitating Zia's credibility. Initially, the military hierarchy was
divided on the issue as it adversely affected the credibility of
the army. However, General Zia's judgement prevailed and a
consensus was reached. On 23 March 1979, he rescheduled the
elections for 17 November 1979. The announcement was made
to dampen the impact of the impending execution of Mr Bhutto.
Zia's image was seriously denigrated when the elections were
indefinitely postponed on 16 October 1979. Having burnt his
fingers twice, Zia became overtly cautious and declined to
announce a fresh election schedule.

A judicial dichotomy soon surfaced. The co-existence of the
military courts and civil courts in the country started creating
tension soon after the initial impact of martial law declined. The
twice-postponed election schedule put the government on steep
declivity. Bhutto's execution raised political dust even though

the public reaction was milder than anticipated by the administration. Gradually, the courts started asserting their authority and making the operation of military courts difficult. The power of judicial review was liberally exercised by them, which created administrative hurdles for the provincial governments.

The political pressure started rising and the judges, an inexorable part of the national milieu, increasingly intervened in the military courts to redress the grievances of the oppressed. They granted stay orders liberally in respect of cases tried or under trial in the military courts. Such orders took a long time to vacate because, under the law, no time limit was prescribed for the courts to complete the process. The lacunae in the legal system were fully exploited. The concept of one-government two-systems was misused by the litigants. Those convicted by the military courts rushed to the High Courts to get stay orders to the chagrin of the administration.

The administrators argued that the impact of martial law must be maintained through speedy trials and quick justice. Pakistan's legal system was slow and expensive even under normal conditions. An abnormal situation existed in the country that demanded firm and quick handling of the cases under trial in the military courts. The law and order requirement justified awarding quick, deterrent and inexpensive judgments to the delinquents to revert the country onto the rails of normalcy. The military courts felt they should be able to function without undue interference from the High Courts.

Article 212-A

The martial law administrators unanimously demanded that the jurisdiction of the judiciary from the operation of the military courts be ousted. Conversely, the judiciary guarded its constitutional right to interpret all laws, notwithstanding the fact that the constitution itself was held in abeyance. In October 1979, the Law Minister was asked to evolve a mechanism to keep the functions of both the courts mutually exclusive within their respective jurisdictions. On the suggestion of Sharifuddin Pirzada, General Zia sought the advice of the Chief Justice of Pakistan, Mr Justice Anwarul Haq. A meeting was held in Zia's house. The Chief Justice and Mr Justice Maulvi Mushtaq Hussain, after mutual discussion, suggested that an additional Article 212-A be incorporated into the constitution. Both the judges scrutinized the draft and further modified it before the Constitution (Second Amendment) Order, 1979 was issued on 18 October, 1979.

Article 212-A stated that no civil court, including a High Court 'shall grant an injunction, make any order, or entertain any proceedings in respect of any matter to which the jurisdiction of the military court extends.' General Zia and Justice Anwar felt that the amendment would serve the purpose.

Provisional Constitution Order 1981

The legal imbroglio remained unresolved. One bench of the Sindh High Court dealing with a large number of petitions, held that the petitions before it had not abated, and the High Court continued to have the power of judicial review notwithstanding the incorporation of Article 212-A in the constitution of 1973. This judgment was passed on 14 April 1980. Another Full Bench of the same High Court, comprising a chief justice and four other judges, held the opposite view in the judgment passed on 30 June 1980. It supported the view that the Supreme Court had never claimed to be above the Constitution nor to have had the right to strike down any provision of the Constitution. It had accepted the position that it was a creature of the Constitution, derived its powers and jurisdiction from it and confined itself within the limits set by the Constitution. The court also observed that it was outside its limits to enter upon an inquiry to determine the correctness or validity for holding or striking down the amendments.

The confusion compounded when, unlike the Sindh High Court, the High Court of Balochistan came out with a diametrically opposite judgment declaring that notwithstanding the amendment in the constitution through the insertion of Article 212-A, it had the jurisdiction to set aside the convictions and sentences awarded by the military courts. The day to day setting aside of various orders of detention, trial and punishment awarded by the military courts became a routine affair, particularly in Balochistan, and this was done with some sarcasm and in open affront to the administrative authorities. The weakness of the martial law showed rather prominently, and Zia came under intense pressure from the provincial administrations to either lift the martial law or enforce it firmly. He opted for the latter.

Two sets of rulings of the High Courts were operative in the country. This brought the military courts to a virtual standstill which adversely affected their performance besides placing the state administration in an embarrassing situation. Interestingly, the Supreme Court did not make any effort to resolve this dichotomy despite the fact that appeals from the judgments of the Division Bench of the Sindh High Court setting aside and remanding cases of martial law for retrial, and the judgment of the Balochistan High Court were pending before the Supreme Court. This created an *impasse* and a conflict situation emerged.

The hamstrung provincial administrators felt that the judicial difficulty had been created with a purpose. Initially, Zia did not suspect any motives and felt that the delay was more procedural than intentional. But slowly he began to sense trouble. The Law Secretary, Mr Justice S. A. Nusrat approached the Chief Justice of Pakistan, Mr Justice Anwarul Haq and requested him to consolidate the two appeals and hear them expeditiously or at least stay the judgment of the Balochistan High Court. The Chief Justice did not order an early hearing of the appeals under the pretext that the Court was too busy with other important cases. This did not appear a convincing argument to the government.

The administration came to the conclusion that the delaying tactics had been adopted as a matter of policy. This also created an impression that, given a chance, the judiciary did not hesitate to dabble in politics. It was with this background of facts and events that the Federation was compelled to promulgate the Provisional Constitution Order (PCO), on 24 March 1981. This order virtually and effectively put the Constitution of 1973 in abeyance. The PCO required the judges of the Supreme Court and the High Courts, and the judges of the Federal Shariat Court to take a fresh oath which provided that a judge will discharge his duties and perform his functions to the best of his ability in accordance with the PCO and the law. The judges were to take the oath at the expense of losing their jobs in case of their refusal to do so. This was a hard decision to take but it was consistent with the abnormal conditions that had resulted after the imposition of martial law. The statistics of the oath-taking act are summarized below:

Court	Oath taken	Oath not taken	Oath not given
Supreme	8	3	—
Shariat	—	—	1
High	40	—	14
Total	48	3	15

A weak and indecisive administrator is a liability for himself and for the state. Power politics demanded, therefore, that Zia should not only retain authority, but also demonstrate it occasionally, to administer the country smoothly. He kept his options open to ensure that he remained in charge. He respected the judiciary but it is simplistic to assume that he had risked his own life to be dictated to by others. His patience, enormous as it was, had its limits. He had a small but mature and competent team of advisers on diplomatic, political, administrative, economic and legal matters. They had the vision to see beyond the obvious and prepare contingency plans to meet unforeseen developments.

The PCO was one end-product emerging out of such a process. It was carefully conceived and prepared in secrecy to prevent its premature leakage. The summary for the cabinet was prepared in the Ministry of Law with such confidentiality that it took the Law Secretary, Mr Justice S. A. Nusrat by surprise. He recorded on the file, 'This is not my draft. It may be shown to the author.' The author, Sharifuddin Pirzada fully trusted Nusrat. His intention was to save Nusrat from embarrassment from his brother judges.

Justice Usman Shah Dissents

The Indus Basin (Rivers Indus, Chenab and Jhelum) is the lifeline of Pakistan. The water from these rivers is used for hydroelectric generation in the upper regions of the country, and for irrigation purposes in all the four provinces. The demand for water exceeds its total availability, and the distribution of the Indus Basin water between the provinces has invariably created a keen rivalry, with each claimant wishing to get a greater share for itself. The provinces use their allocated share through a vast network of canal systems to meet their agricultural needs. The fixing of the water share for the provinces has always been a sensitive and emotive political issue in which the provinces usually exaggerate their water claims and express grave concern that their interests will suffer if their demands are not accepted in toto by the water distribution authority. A political approach towards deciding a technical problem made a fair settlement more complicated.

President Ayub Khan and Prime Minister Pundit Jawaharlal Nehru signed the Indus Basin Treaty between Pakistan and India in 1960 through the good offices of the World Bank. Thereafter, it became technically possible for Pakistan to deal with the inter-provincial water issue. However, internal and external developments—the Sino-Indian border conflict (1962); the Rann

of Kutch dispute (1964); the Indo-Pakistan War (1965); political
agitation against Ayub Khan (1968-1969); martial law (1969);
and the East Pakistan crisis (1970-1971)—kept the issue
unaddressed.

The rigidity of provincial positions did not permit Bhutto's
government to apportion the distribution of the Indus water to
the provinces on a permanent basis during his rule (1971-77).
Instead, water was provided to the provinces on an *ad hoc* yearly
basis on the understanding that this would not prejudice the
interests or claims of any province. The Zia government
inherited this situation. The yearly ritual of an *ad hoc* decision
on water was clearly unsatisfactory. Additionally, the fate of the
proposed Kalabagh Dam on the Indus River, urgently needed
for the storage of water for irrigation and power generation to
meet the increasing needs of the country, hung in the balance
because it's construction was linked with the distribution of the
water system on a permanent basis.

The Water and Power Development Authority (WAPDA) had
the technical data on the issues of water apportionment to the
provinces, and the construction of the Kalabagh Dam. By-passing
bureaucratic channels, HQ CMLA requested its Chairman
Lieutenant-General Ghulam Safdar Butt to meet all the four
provincial governors and achieve a consensus on an inter-
provincial water distribution formula. Safdar met all the
governors, shared the technical data with them and made
presentations to the provincial teams. He found that while some
provincial misgivings were genuine, others were based on
unsupported evidence and a fear of the unknown. In the
interregnum, a considerable volume of water flowed into the sea
un-used.

While the governors of Sindh and Balochistan argued for an
enhanced share for their provinces, their counterpart in the North
West Frontier Province, Lieutenant-General Fazle Haq adopted
an uncompromising approach. He challenged the accuracy of
the WAPDA data without providing the evidence to prove it
otherwise. He arbitrarily demanded eleven million acres of water
as the share of NWFP but without having any plans for its

utilization. Fazle Haq acknowledged that the province could not use this volume now or in the foreseeable future but argued that an advancement in technology might render some projects in the future technically and economically viable.

With Safdar Butt's efforts not succeeding, the government decided, in 1984, to appoint a judicial commission to give an award on the water distribution issue. Mr Justice Mohammad Haleem, the Chief Justice of Pakistan, was its chairman and the chief justices of the four provincial high courts were its members. The Haleem Commission, after hearing all the technical, administrative and political views of the four provinces, prepared its report. The judges retired to read this report before affixing their signatures on it. The Commission fixed a date and decided to meet in Lahore to complete its report.

On the appointed date, the member from NWFP, Mr Justice Usman Ali Shah, arrived a couple of minutes late and looked visibly tense. Anxiety was writ large on his face. As the proceedings of the Haleem Commission started, Justice Usman Ali Shah abruptly submitted a note of dissent to the Chief Justice of Pakistan and quickly left the room, as if in a huff. This was not the Usman his brother judges present in the room knew him to be. The incident surprised the judiciary and soon became public.

I asked Fazle Haq if he was aware of what Justice Usman Ali Shah had done. With a mischievous smile on his face, he replied that, 'He did what I wanted him to do,'and went on to confide that he had dictated what Usman had submitted to the Commission, after putting it in legal language. About the brusque attitude of Justice Usman, Fazle Haq said, 'The intention was to avoid a discussion in the Haleem Commission on the contents of the note of dissent.'It was a startling revelation that the premeditated acts of the general and the judge had frustrated the commission report. Who the prime mover in this drama was might be irrelevant at this stage to establish. If Usman was influenced by the strong man of the NWFP to dissent in his judgment, he violated the law. If it was his personal decision to submit a note of dissent then he was quite capable of personally drafting his judgment, which he did not do. Also, it was perhaps an unprecedented case in the judicial history of the country when a member of a Commission disclosed the judgment before the Commission had announced it.

What General Fazle Haq told me at the time appeared in print a decade later, contributed by an eye witness. Fazle Haq's secretary writes thus, 'I remember, the Governor was on a tour of Kohat. Justice Usman Ali and his team of experts (Irrigation Department) came to Kohat and briefed the Governor. The Governor himself dictated the "note of dissent", to Justice Usman Ali Shah and asked him to put it in the proper legal language.'[5]

The water distribution problem remained unresolved because the Zia government did not pursue it seriously enough to evolve a provincial consensus on the issue. An opportunity was lost. The issue was settled during Nawaz Sharif's first tenure as the prime minister, when a distribution formula evolved by him was unanimously accepted by all the provinces. Nor was the construction of the Kalabagh Dam decided during the Zia era, a project of vital importance for the country. In one cabinet meeting, General Fazle Haq said that in case the government decided to go ahead with the construction of this dam, he would have to offer his resignation because he could not sell this project to his province. A technically viable project became a victim of emotionalism when the people in the Mardan-Swabi belt were made to believe, by their political leaders, that the town of Nowshera would be submerged in water and their fertile lands would run the risk of being waterlogged.

Zia did not relish the choice of over-ruling the provincial sensitivity of NWFP on the Kalabagh Dam issue. Perhaps he did not wish a split in his military team either. He paddled a soft course that relegated the project to a back burner.

Fazle Haq, a strong-willed extrovert, was a great communicator and a pleasant conversationalist who could keep his audience engaged on a variety of topics for hours. He anticipated problems, planned for the worst, firmly exercised authority, and had developed a taste for politics. His foul unbridled tongue was his main liability. 'Chiding politicians, tribal *maliks*, bureaucrats and even *maulvis* used to have fun, with him.'[6]

In September 1991, Fazle Haq spent two hours in my house reminiscing over our long association. He had already warned his family members that he had fully enjoyed his life, and they should not be surprised if he came to a sudden and violent end. When he shared his concern with me, I asked him the likely sources of danger, as anticipated by him. He named two persons; Mir Afzal Khan, a politician from NWFP who had maintained links with him, and a fugitive from the law who, in the assessment of Fazle Haq, was plotting to eliminate him. I advised him to take additional personal security measures and share his security anxiety with Prime Minister Nawaz Sharif. He promised to do so. I felt uneasy when Fazle Haq left me. Three weeks later, he was gunned down in broad daylight by a hired assassin about 200 yards from his residence at Peshawar. It was a cleverly planned ambush at a blind turn in the road. Fazle Haq died on the spot.

Seething Samdani

Mr Justice S. M. A. Samdani, a judge at the Lahore High Court was not administered the oath of office under the PCO. His case needs explaining. A bureaucrat-turned judge, Samdani worked as the Federal Law Secretary from February 1978 to June 1980 in the Zia administration. A sophisticated and eloquent man, he presented advice on legal matters in a businesslike manner. Despite his soft-spoken manner, the rough edges of the bureaucrat occasionally surfaced in him. Two incidents illustrate this point.

President Zia was presiding over a conference, attended by ministers and secretaries, in the Planning Division auditorium in Islamabad. While expressing unhappiness over administrative lethargy, he became excited, and used inappropriate language. 'If things don't improve', said Zia raising his voice, 'I will hang

the secretary concerned by the first available pole.'There was a
hush of silence in the auditorium. If Zia had gone too far,
Samdani took a leap further still. 'Instead of hanging the
secretaries', said a visibly bruised Law Secretary, who had
shown no hesitation in serving under a military dictator, 'You
should hang the generals for imposing martial law.'The
atmosphere became even more tense. For a few moments silence
prevailed. Zia kept cool and business continued. No action was
taken against Samdani.

The President's Secretariat had asked the Ministry of Law to
give their legal opinion on an official summary submitted by
another ministry. The summary shuttled between the President's
Secretariat and the Ministry of Law a couple of times, but the
legal scrutiny remained incomplete. To avoid further delay, I
suggested to Mr Justice Samdani over the telephone that both of
us could meet to identify the un-addressed parts to enable the
legal experts to examine the case. An offended Samdani said
curtly, 'I am a judge of the High Court. You cannot call me for
a meeting.' Taken aback, I replied, 'I see no reason why the
Law Secretary cannot be requested for a meeting to discuss
official business.'

The status-conscious Samdani took offense at my words. With
an arrogant tone he said firmly, 'interpretation of law is my
responsibility and on all legal matters the government is bound
by my advice. In my opinion, I cannot be called by you for a
meeting because I hold the status of a judge of the High Court.'It
was my turn to respond. 'Mr Law Secretary,'I replied, 'I will
not argue any further. And, since you have invoked law, we
shall now proceed legally. I shall address you a letter today
fixing a date and time for our meeting in my office to discuss
the case under reference. I hereby pend further disposal of this
issue till after the appointed time is over.' To his credit,
Mr Justice Samdani was punctual for the projected meeting. It
was my turn to be embarrassed. The Minister for Law,
Mr Sharifuddin Pirzada also magnanimously accompanied the
Law Secretary.

This unfortunate incident caused anguish. I felt sad because it was the only time in over seven years as the Chief of Staff to the President, that I had an unpleasant conversation with a government official on a matter of state. Perhaps it was my misfortune to catch Samdani in a rasping mood.

By the time the PCO was promulgated, Mr Justice Samdani had reverted to the Lahore High Court. The oath to the judges of the Lahore High Court was to be administered at the Governor's House and General Zia directed Governor Jilani not to include Samdani in the group. This showed his reservation about the judge presumably because of the incident recorded earlier. I was unaware of this development. A communication error at Lahore created an awkward situation. Jilani was surprised to learn that Samdani had arrived at the Governor's House along with the other judges to take the oath. He tried to contact Zia on the Green telephone but the President was not available. I was taken aback at Zia's decision when Jilani contacted me with the recommendation that Samdani be given the oath. This started a race against time. The oath-taking ceremony at Lahore was minutes away, Samdani was present and ready to take the oath but Zia was not available to approve his candidature. Eventually, I contacted Zia and pleaded Jilani's recommendation be accepted. By the time I managed to get Zia's approval to give the oath to Samdani, the oath-taking ceremony at Lahore was over and Samdani felt insulted at being left out. Jilani conveyed the President's affirmative decision to the Chief Justice of the Lahore High Court, Mr Justice Shamim Hassan Qadri. As a gesture of goodwill, Qadri personally went to the residence of Samdani, explained the confusion, and conveyed the government's desire to administer the oath to him. A bruised Samdani declined the offer.

Apathy of the Courts

President Zia invoked Article 58 (2) (b) of the constitution on 29 May 1988, and dismissed the Junejo government. The army was not consulted on the issue, as martial law had since been lifted. Zia, had, however, informed the Vice Chief of the Army Staff, General Mirza Aslam Beg, half an hour earlier about his decision. Concurrently, the National Assembly and all the Provincial Assemblies were dissolved. None, including the sacked prime minister, challenged the dismissal order in a court of law. Ten weeks later Zia was killed in an aircraft crash. The dismissal order was then agitated in the Lahore High Court which held it 'not sustainable in law.' The court did not restore the dissolved assemblies and ruled that fresh polls be held in November 1988, as announced by the Zia administration earlier. The Supreme Court upheld this ruling.

Cashing in on sympathy votes, the Pakistan Peoples Party came to power in 1988, and the young and inexperienced Benazir Bhutto became the Prime Minister. Working with the zeal of youth, she simultaneously opened many fronts against her government and soon landed herself in a mess. Her most striking quality was to prefer PPP over Pakistan. In her official business she behaved more like a party leader than the Prime Minister of the country. The inevitable happened. Her inverted priorities led to the fall of her government. In her view, her illustrious father was incapable of doing any wrong. Consistently and vigorously she bitterly criticized the judiciary inside the Parliament and in public for the 'judicial murder'of Bhutto by the 'kangaroo'courts. That the Bhutto case was heard in the Lahore High Court and in the Supreme Court of Pakistan was of no consequence to her.

Benazir Bhutto's inflammatory oratory and her derogatory tirade against the judiciary was tolerated by the courts for reasons hard to fathom. The custodians of law in the country kept silent and meekly swallowed the insults frequently and rudely hurled at them. No judge took *suo moto* notice of the insulting statements and no court issued a notice of contempt of court. By showing such insensitivity the higher judiciary compromised its own image and prestige and showed its weakness. That a constitutionally elected democratic Prime

Minister had ridiculed the courts so much and so frequently was perhaps rare if not unprecedented in Pakistan's history.

The ten years between 1987-97 were a decade of political convulsions. Pakistan muddled through nascent democracy in which the prime ministers were dismissed five times by the presidents, and fresh elections were held on four occasions—all prematurely. Power politics became a game of musical chairs and the courts, becoming arbiters in political matters, ruled if the dismissal of the governments by the president were legal and constitutional. The judiciary became a promoter of democratic culture with its judgments evoking a mixed response.

Judiciary Subdued

In her second tenure (1993-96), Prime Minister Benazir Bhutto launched a premeditated plan to dominate the judiciary. In 1994, the Chief Justice of the Sindh High Court, Nasir Aslam Zahid, was consigned to the Shariat Court because of his 'uncooperative'attitude. He was replaced by Abdul Hafiz Memon 'who holds the record of having been sworn in as a judge six times.'[7]

Justice Sajjad Ali Shah became prominent in 1993, when he dissented with the majority judgment in the Supreme Court that had restored the government of Prime Minister Mohammad Nawaz Sharif. The following year, Benazir Bhutto appointed him the Chief Justice of Pakistan, superceding three senior judges. This was the second time in the history of Pakistan when the senior most judge in the Supreme Court was not made the Chief Justice of the country. The appointment evoked loud public criticism and a quiet resentment within the judiciary.

The emboldened executive branch struck again. Benazir packed all the high courts with judges of her own choice, mostly loyalists of the ruling PPP. The political motives of this palpably arbitrary act were so transparent that the judiciary showed its unease. The criticism increased when some of the elevated luminaries were found to have tainted pasts. One newly appointed judge to a high court bench was facing trial on a murder charge. Another was an inexperienced advocate virtually dormant in his profession. Yet another gentleman was 'compensated'for his perseverance in losing three elections contested by him under the PPP flag.

Such disclosures put Benazir on a low moral ground. The judiciary silently grudged executive interference in its professional domain. Gradually this resentment started showing in public.

Judicial Activism

It distressed Benazir to learn of Justice Sajjad Ali Shah's reluctance to compromise for she had taken his obedience for granted.

The prime minister showed her bitterness by passing an inappropriate and contemptuous remark against the chief justice in a kitchen cabinet meeting. Her outburst leaked out and buzzed in the corridors of power in Islamabad. The chief justice also learnt of it.

On the night of 27-28 February 1996, the house of Syed Pervez Ali Shah, the son-in-law of the chief justice, a bureaucrat serving in Hyderabad, was raided by police officials who broke open the lock and threw out his furniture and belongings onto the roadside. The incident was widely reported in the print media.[8] A press note issued by the local administration asserted that the individual had occupied the house without lawful authority. Days later, the car of the chief justice was fired at in Karachi. Mercifully, the chief justice was not travelling in the car when the firing took place. Such acts were meant to convey a message.

Justice Sajjad expressed concern about his personal security to President Farooq Leghari. In response, a police official met him, but the Chief Justice lacked confidence in the police department. He approached General Jahangir Karamat, the Army

Chief, through an intermediary and sought protection. An intelligence agency started overseeing his security arrangements. Such incidents adversely affected the health of Justice Sajjad who was a cardiac patient. In 1996, he was admitted to the Armed Forces Institute of Cardiology with angina pain. Also under treatment in this hospital at the time was Lieutenant-General Saeed Qadir, a victim of the Bhutto vendetta. While visiting this general officer I noticed Justice Sajjad, went over to him and wished him a speedy recovery. He was courteous and thankful. I inquired if the Hyderabad incident had been accurately reported in the media. He smiled and pointing to a young person present in the room said, 'He is my son-in-law who faced the hidden hands.' I was pained to hear his story.

Justice Sajjad Ali Shah not only believed in judicial activism but also politicized the judiciary. He loved being heard in public and seeing himself in the print media. He claimed that he would get the judiciary firmly established as a pillar of the state and separate it from the executive. His inflexibility created difficulties for him.

In November 1996, the Benazir government was dismissed by President Farouq Leghari on charges of corruption and maladministration under Article 58 (2) (b) of the constitution. This Article had been invoked for the fourth time in one decade by the third successive president. The president's decision was hailed by the public as the cancer of corruption was widespread and accusing fingers were increasingly raised against the 'First Family'. The dismissal was upheld by the Supreme Court.

Zia spent a fair amount of his post-Referendum (1984) time in preparing constitutional amendments. While the most conspicuous architects of the amendments were Mr Sharifuddin Pirzada and Mr A.K. Brohi, he consulted many other experts and scholars on the issue. The president had the proposed changes discussed in the MLAs meetings on two occasions. In so doing he adopted a clever technique. He took it upon himself to verbally explain the proposed changes but carefully avoided showing the written text to the members. Perforce, the ensuing discussion was in generalities and specifics remained unaddressed. Obviously, General Zia did not take his colleagues in total confidence when he had something to hide. Zia's military team had earlier been suggesting to him that the amendments package should be small and the constitution should not be excessively tampered with. The president had different views. In the final analysis, the full text of the proposed constitutional amendments were made known to his military colleagues only when they appeared in print in the Press. They were excessive and lacked military unanimity. Article 58(2)(b) of the constitution was one of the controversial amendments.

On 24 March 1996, a bench of the Supreme Court headed by Chief Justice Sajjad Ali Shah held that:

(a), the senior most judge in the High Court has legitimate expectancy to become Chief Justice and Additional Judges in the High Courts have legitimate expectancy to be made permanent judges. Transfer of a Judge of the High Court without his consent and induction in the Federal Shariat Court is violative of Article 209. A Judge of the Supreme Court may not be sent as Acting Chief Justice of a High Court. (b), the consultations held by the President with the Chief Justice of Pakistan and the Chief Justices of the High Courts on the appointment of judges should be effective, meaningful, purposive, census-oriented leaving no room for arbitrariness or unfair play.[9]

The president was also required to record his views in writing in case he differed with the recommendation made by the Chief Justice. The court would then adjudicate the issue. This judgment, *ipso facto*, curtailed the executive authority of making judicial appointments in superior courts and reversed all the decisions made by the Benazir government except the controversial appointment of the Chief Justice of Pakistan, which was to be decided separately. This case was never taken up.

The judgment in the 'Judges Case'was called 'historic'and praiseworthy. Judicial activism was supported by the intelligentsia and analysts, as filling up the courts with political nominees ran counter to the administration of justice. Mr Justice Sajjad Ali Shah and his other brother judges were happy.

The landslide public mandate inflated Prime Minister Nawaz Sharif's ego and he started giving sermons about the supremany of the Parliament, inside and outside the House. Justice Sajjad retaliated by pointing out in a seminar that all the three pillars of the state had their respective functions clearly defined in the constitution. This broad hint clearly implied that the interpretation of the constitution was the task of the judiciary.

It became mutually difficult for President Farooq Leghari and Prime Minister Nawaz Sharif to co-exist. Leghari had already dismissed two prime ministers. Nawaz Sharif did not wish to become the third victim. He speedily clipped the President's constitutional wings. The 13th Amendment bill was passed by the Parliament which deleted Article 58 (2) (b) of the constitution. This disputable provision had been inserted into the constitution by President Zia. By this amendment, the President was divested of his powers to dismiss the government or the Prime Minister. The amendment bill was passed unanimously in the parliament. The President assented to the bill but its *vires* was challenged in the Supreme Court. Leghari supported this amendment publicly but he might have been deeply hurt. A weakened President, dreaming of a second term in office, became a wounded tiger. The stage was set for intrigue.

On the legal front the 'Yes Sir' ministers convinced Nawaz Sharif that an effective method of combating terrorism was to burden the country with an Anti-Terrorism Act (ATA) that may prohibit the grant of bail to the accused and disallow the right of appeal in the High Court and the Supreme Court. The Prime Minister discussed the proposal with Justice Sajjad, who opposed the idea. Nawaz initially agreed with the Chief Justice that to create a parallel judiciary would be an undesirable step. However, he changed his mind later. This brought the judiciary and the executive on a collision course.

A war of nerves began between the judiciary and the executive. In August 1997, Chief Justice Sajjad recommended the elevation of five high court judges to the bench of the Supreme Court, one each from Sindh and Peshawar and three from the Lahore High Court. There was no difficulty with regard

to the elevation of the two judges from the Sindh and Peshawar
High Courts. However, for personal and official reasons, Nawaz
Sharif desired to retain the LHC Chief Justice Sheikh Riaz at
Lahore and was not in favour of elevating the other two, Munir
and Arif, who seemingly did not enjoy his confidence. An
impasse ensued. Justice Sajjad insisted that the rule of seniority,
as laid down in the 'Judges Case' be observed in letter and
spirit. He also demanded a written reply to his request if the
recommendations made by him were not acceptable to the
government. The Prime Minister neither wished to elevate the
two judges nor initiate a written report opposing their elevation
fearing that the court might over-rule the government. The
recommendations made by the Chief Justice were neither acted
upon nor was a written reply given to him on the subject. An
irritated Sajjad fussed and fumed.

The polarization intensified when the government
circumvented the issue and arbitrarily reduced the strength of
the Supreme Court Bench from seventeen to twelve. This made
Justice Sajjad's recommendations infructuous. But it also put
the government under moral pressure as it had reneged on its
obligation. A series of meetings were held between Justice
Sajjad on the one side and the Prime Minister and his emissaries
on the other. The intermediaries included the Army Chief,
General Jahangir Karamat, the Chairman of the Senate and the
Speaker of the National Assembly. All the three acted in good
faith and for the well-being of the country. The last two jointly
met the Chief Justice. Justice Sajjad demanded the cancellation
of the notification as a pre-requisite for easing tension with the
government, and went on to add that such a step would settle
70 per cent of the problem and immediately thereafter, there
would be a sea-change in improving judiciary-government
relations. This was bargaining, pure and simple.

Both the emissaries, Wasim Sajjad and Soomro, jointly met
Nawaz Sharif at 1000 hours next morning and the Prime
Minister agreed to cancel the notification. They apprised Justice
Sajjad of Nawaz's decision. In their presence, Justice Sajjad
spoke to the President over the Green telephone on this subject.

This confirmed the public belief that Justice Sajjad Ali Shah was not the lone crusader in this high drama. Nor was the President an innocent spectator in the judiciary-executive tug of war. Both worked in unison for a common cause—sacking Nawaz Sharif. A cornered Nawaz Sharif acceded to the demand in a statement made by him in the National Assembly. 'This was a victory for the Chief Justice and a humiliation for the Prime Minister.'[10] Nawaz Sharif was under pressure because a case of contempt of court was pending against him with a bench of the Supreme Court headed by Justice Sajjad.

Fourteenth Amendment

Both the houses of the Parliament passed the Constitution (Fourteenth Amendment) bill on 1 July 1997 in haste, without any debate and with no dissenting vote by any legislator. The bill that was assented by the President two days later, prohibited floor-crossing by the parliamentarians, a menace that had assumed alarming proportions, particularly in recent times. The change fully reflected the aspirations of the people who felt ashamed that their chosen representatives carried invisible price tags on their heads. The bill received the President's assent and the Amendment Act came into force. It's validity was challenged in the Supreme Court.

On 29 October 1997, a three-member bench of the Supreme Court headed by the Chief Justice admitted a petition against the 14th Amendment, and after hearing the petitioner's lawyer the amendment was suspended through an interim order passed the following day. Strangely, this was done without even hearing the government council. The decision raised eyebrows because it was announced in the morning of the same day on which the National Assembly was to be in session. The government considered it a wilful attempt to instigate the members of the National Assembly to criticize Prime Minister Nawaz Sharif or revolt against him.

The attempt boomeranged. The Members of the National Assembly severely criticized the suspension order in strong language that at times exceeded parliamentary norms. The Speaker expunged the objectionable portions of the members' statements from the official record.

The Chief Justice ordered that the portions of the statements expunged from the National Assembly records be produced before him. The Speaker had these presented. Days later, the Prime Minister also criticized the suspension orders in language to which the Chief Justice took exception. A legal battle ensued in the Supreme Court when the Chief Justice issued contempt of court notices to Prime Minister Nawaz Sharif and to other members of the Parliament who had made statements in the house considered objectionable by the Chief Justice.

Nawaz Sharif was summoned by the Chief Justice to appear in person before his court. He did so. He expressed his regret but it was not accepted as an apology by the court. The contempt proceedings continued. This led to the impression in the executive that Nawaz Sharif might be held guilty of contempt to set the stage for the fall of his government.

In self-defence, the government took a pre-emptive legal course. While the contempt proceedings were still in progress, the law of contempt was amended by the Parliament. The amended bill provided for an appeal in a contempt of court conviction to be heard by all the remaining judges of the Supreme Court who had not been party to the conviction. The sulking Chief Justice was now visibly infuriated.

The constitution required the President's assent to convert the amendment bill into an act. Before the President had granted the assent, the Chief Justice sent a directive to the President restraining him from signing the bill, and went on to add that if he had done so already the Chief Justice would declare it unconstitutional. This order was strange and unprecedented in the legal history of the country. It was a violation of the Constitution and a serious deviation from the established norms of legal procedure. The constitution required the courts to determine the validity, or otherwise, of an act in accordance with the laid down procedure but they had no authority to pass a judgment on an amendment bill which was not yet an act. It was now widely believed that the President and the Chief Justice were working in concert to topple the elected government through a 'legal *coup d'état*.'This created insecurity and emotions ran high. So did the intrigue. In this charged environment, an incident of enormous calamity hit the country like a thunderbolt. A rowdy group, organized by the party in power, staged a noisy demonstration in front of the Supreme Court and stormed the premises. This act brought shame to the country. No one was physically hurt but the grievous cut left a deep scar on the body politic of Pakistan.

The Chief Justice wrote to the Chief of the Army Staff seeking military protection. Was it an attempt to drag the military into the on-going tussle for power? The President took the opportunity of writing a stiff letter to the Prime Minister saying that, 'The Chief Justice is more than justified in expressing his total lack of trust and faith in the ability of your administration to provide security in Islamabad.' One can debate if it was an expression of concern or an exposure of a nexus.

It became an open secret that three emissaries of the President maintained constant links with the Chief Justice. These troubleshooters or trouble creators played an unsavoury part in this sad drama. The President and the Chief Justice appeared to operate on an identical wavelength. The Army Chief told the President in a meeting that Khawaja Tariq Rahim, Malik Allah Yar Khan and Younis Sethi were using his name frequently in the on-going tussle. As told to the author by Karamat, Leghari sheepishly replied that these gentlemen were no more than his informers.

The military got pulled into this triangular tug of war. The Prime Minister requested General Jahangir Karamat to intercede. The General met the Chief Justice, pleaded for constitutional sanity and obtained a two-week adjournment of the contempt case. The President tried to woo the military in a different way. He threw in feelers to Jahangir Karamat to win over his support against the Prime Minister. The Army Chief made it known that he would play straight without entering the political arena and the army would not be a party to any wheeling-dealing.

The Climax

It may be recalled that the validity of the 13th Amendment had been challenged and this petition was kept pending before a bench of the Supreme Court headed by the Chief Justice. This issue came under sharp focus and one senior bureaucrat in President House, in a surge of emotion, hinted at the imminent fall of the Nawaz Sharif government and measures taken for induction of an interim cabinet. This could happen in two ways, either through a military take-over which was not possible because the army was against any extra-constitutional act or through revival of the deleted Article 58 (2) (b) in the constitution which would empower the President to dismiss the government.

The Chief Justice of the Supreme Court and the Chief Justices of all the High Courts, senior among their other brother judges in the respective courts, are like commanders. Justice Sajjad failed to lead from the front. Because of his love of publicity and eagerness to speak from a public platform, he disregarded judicial ethics. A judge speaks only through his judgment. His confrontation with the executive branch, and his political statements created unrest among the judges of the Supreme Court. They also resented the fact that despite the Supreme Court judgment in the 'Judges Case', the issue of the seniority of the Chief Justice himself had remained unaddressed.

In November 1997, seven judges of the Supreme Court wrote a joint letter to Justice Sajjad Ali Shah requesting an in-house meeting of all the Supreme Court judges to discuss 'internal matters', a euphemism for the on-going crisis. They took care to release the letter to the media and, as anticipated by them, it made bold headlines the next morning. The shattered unity of the court and its tattered image posed a challenge to the leadership of Chief Justice Sajjad.

The Chief Justice promptly retaliated. He immediately transferred all the seven judges from the seat of the Supreme Court at Islamabad to the Supreme Court circuit benches working at Karachi, Quetta and Peshawar. It was now the Chief

Justice versus the 'exiled' judges of the Supreme Court. It was a no-holds-barred legal tug of war.

A government supporter submitted a petition to the Supreme Court Bench at Quetta seeking the suspension of the notification dated 5 June 1994, that had appointed Justice Sajjad as the Chief Justice of Pakistan, on the ground that this was a violation of the rule laid down in the appointment of the 'Judges Case'. The Quetta Bench entertained the plea and issued an interim order on 26 November 1997, restraining Justice Sajjad from acting as the Chief Justice of Pakistan.

A Bench presided over by Justice Sajjad Ali Shah, sitting at Islamabad, immediately held that this order was passed without lawful authority and was of no legal effect. Another salvo was immediately fired by the Bench of the Supreme Court sitting at Peshawar. It reiterated the order of the Quetta Bench and also restrained Justice Sajjad from functioning as the Chief Justice of Pakistan.

On 2 December 1997, Chief Justice Sajjad did what had been long anticipated. He suspended the operation of the 13th Amendment without hearing any arguments from the government side, an act that showed bias. The stage was legally set for President Leghari to take charge. The revival of Article 58 (2) (b) had removed the only lingering legal hurdle to sack the government. The ball was now in his court to deliver a final *coup de grace* to Nawaz Sharif.

There was a legal lacuna. The President could not constitutionally dismiss the government, even under the restored power, when the National Assembly was in session. Nawaz Sharif had kept the National Assembly in session and it could, on short notice, start proceedings to impeach the President, should a necessity arise.

Simultaneously, minutes after the Chief Justice had suspended the operation of the 13th Amendment, a rival ten-member bench of the Supreme Court met in an adjoining room under the same roof and immediately held the order issued by the Chief Justice in abeyance and restrained the President from acting on the ruling. Going a step further, it also held that Justice Ajmal

KHAKI SHADOWS

Mian, the senior most judge, should immediately assume the administrative powers of the Chief Justice.

Justice Ajmal Mian was sworn in as the acting Chief Justice of Pakistan. Justice Sajjad went on long leave. Sanity returned to the Supreme Court. On 23 December 1997, a ten member bench of the Supreme Court declared the appointment of Justice Sajjad as Chief Justice void. This order, a mere formality, put the seal of authority on the fate of Justice Sajjad. The dissenting judges could not have decided otherwise.

One former Chief Justice of Pakistan writes, 'Judicial activism which soared to such dramatic heights...got mired in controversy in 1997...Some described it as "judicial despotism" rather than "judicial activism."...Judicial review was used more for meddling in political matters rather than for furthering the social and public rights of the community.'[11]

The judicial and constitutional crises shook the country, exposed hidden intrigues, weakened President Farooq Leghari but strengthened democracy in Pakistan. The rule of law prevailed and a crisis of great magnitude was constitutionally averted. The cornered President facing the threat of impeachment or resignation opted for the latter. He resigned against the 'unconstitutional' demands of the government.

A bruised and humbled Justice Sajjad retired from service on 16 February 1998. It was a painful end to his otherwise illustrious professional career. It was made worse when he was denied the courtesy of a full-court reference by his brother judges in his honour on the eve of his retirement.

This judicial crisis was avoidable. Justice Sajjad was caught between the conflicting requirement of judicial activism and his self-interest as the Chief Justice of Pakistan. He politicized the judiciary and hob-nobbed with the political power centres. As the Chief Justice of Pakistan he compromised the dignity of the judiciary and disrupted the unity of the Supreme Court.

The remaining judges of the Supreme Court did not set a worthy example by revolting against their own Chief Justice. The tilt in their approach, particularly during the closing stages of the final act, was too obvious to miss.

The Benazir government politicized the judiciary. It appointed Justice Sajjad, a junior judge, as the Chief Justice of Pakistan and elevated several political loyalists, some with questionable credentials, to the superior courts. The 20 March judgment was a reaction to such arbitrary appointments. The fact that Benazir's hand-picked President and Chief Justice eventually turned against her, illustrates that the route to power is hard to predict.

Nawaz Sharif came close to meeting his Waterloo because his initial decisions were half-baked and subsequently he took inflexible stands on minor issues. By such acts he antagonized the judiciary as in the case of the anti-terrorist laws and appointment of judges recommended by the Chief Justice. The assault on the Supreme Court was an ill-conceived and abominable act.

President Farooq Leghari played a clever role in the dismissal of the Benazir government. His links with Justice Sajjad on the 13th Amendment and his vain attempt to drag the military into the political quagmire against Prime Minister Nawaz Sharif exposed his wheeling-dealing tactics.

The military enhanced its image by its sobering influence on the development of events. It kept aloof, declined to participate in the intrigues and did not interfere in the political interplay. In the process, it indirectly helped in strengthening democracy in the country.

Finally:

The crisis became a naked manifestation of ugly power politics. The judicial process became only a means to an end. Everyone— the President, the Prime Minister and the Chief Justice—got into a blind race to strengthen their own individual positions, to concentrate power in their own hands...The judiciary, in its activism that bordered on adventurism, did itself immense harm. It has lost its credibility in the public eye. It now stands vulnerable before the executive and the Parliament.[12]

324 ·KHAKI SHADOWS

NOTES

1. Rafi Raza, *Zulfikar Ali Bhutto and Pakistan 1967-1977*, Oxford University Press, Karachi, 1997, p. 136.
2. *Dawn*, Karachi, 9 December 1976.
3. *White Paper on the Performance of the Bhutto Regime,* Vol. 11, Government of Pakistan, January 1979, Annexure-16, p. A-45.
4. PLO, 1977, S.C. 657.
5. Brigadier Fahimullah Khattak, 'Fazle Haq as I Knew Him', *Muslim,* Islamabad, 6 October 1995.
6. Ibid.
7. Ardeshir Cowasjee, 'Dishonesty-from Day One', *Dawn*, Karachi, 9 November 1997.
8. *Dawn*, Karachi, 1 March 1996.
9. PLO 1996, S.C. 324 (commonly known as the Judges Case)
10. Islam Shaikh, 'The Anatomy of a Conspiracy', *Dawn,* 20 August 1998.
11. Dr Nasim Hasan Shah, 'Impact of Judicial Activism', *Dawn,* Karachi, 12 March 1998.
12. Hamid Khan, 'A Drama with no Heroes', *The News,* Islamabad, 15 March 1998.

8

THE LURE OF POWER

Introduction

Pakistan emerged through a political and constitutional process, the result of a legal and peaceful struggle that eminently depicted the passion of its founding fathers, led by Quaid-i-Azam Mohammad Ali Jinnah, for the rule of law and the aspirations of her people for a free society. The final lowering of the Union Jack on 14 August 1947, at Karachi, then capital of Pakistan, and the inaugural hoisting of the green and white flag of the new country bid adieu to the British *Raj* and welcomed independence. Pakistan was visualised as a democratic plural polity and a progressive country.

The price paid for freedom was heavy. Massive communal disturbances engulfed Northern India in which one million people[1] lost their lives in a savage orgy of violence. Another writer estimates that, 'One million dead would be a conservative figure.'[2] In addition, fourteen million refugees migrated[3] across the newly created Indo-Pakistan border in search of safety and honour. In the annals of human history this was the single largest trans-border migration of population in peacetime. This human carnage and suffering might have been averted, or at least its magnitude reduced, if the Viceroy, Lord Louis Mountbatten, had not practically abdicated his constitutional responsibility to ensure a smooth and orderly transfer of power in India. His inexplicable callousness and patently partisan performance was shameful. So also was the indecent haste in which he dismantled the Indian Empire, 'built over three hundred years in just over seventy days.'[4]

During the crucial transition phase Mountbatten played an assertive pro-India role in persuading, luring and coercing the rulers of undivided India's Princely States to accede to India. Geographical proximity and other factors had offered opportunities to some of the affected states to join either India or Pakistan. Mountbatten's compelling advice to them was to join the dominion of India. In critical cases, political expediency dominated his decisions. The accession of Bikaner to India is one example.[5]

Mountbatten's bias for India was nevertheless transparently visible. One such act planted the seeds of the Kashmir dispute, perhaps deliberately. An Indian scholar argues that it was to promote the 'British strategic interests in the post transfer of power era.'[6]

Four martial laws in Pakistan in over fifty years is a record of dubious distinction that demands an in-depth analysis of the country's power politics and the role played by the Pakistan army in national affairs. The military interventions need to be critically analysed to record history and to learn lessons for the future.

The Genesis

What went wrong, where and why is the burden of this narration. Some questions pique the inquisitive mind. For example, how robust was the democratic system inherited in 1947? Why did it fail? What was the state of the political institutions inherited at the dawn of freedom? Were they strong, weak or mediocre? Why did they not function properly? Did bureaucracy play its role in Pakistan as expected in a democratic society? Or, did it become an active participant in the power game played on the national political chessboard? What factors influenced the military to sideline civil rule? Has the army become a permanent pillar of power? Is this role reversible? How have the military take-overs affected the army's own professional performance and thinking? What does the future hold? The list is long.

It is an unpleasant reality that flawed democracy and self-serving dictatorship frequently alternated in Pakistan during the first fifty years of its independent life. In the process the roots of real democracy, and democratic norms were not strengthened. But, as truth cannot remain hidden for long, democracy cannot be indefinitely chained. Its slow emergence like a phoenix out of the ashes of authoritarian rule, gives hope for a democratic future for Pakistan.

The military dictators were not the sole spoilers of the democratic order. Many elected leaders in the country were in fact only democratic in name but autocratic in their conduct and behaviour. They promoted a brand of sham democracy to further their personal interests and for reasons of political expediency. Such persons contributed no less in eroding Pakistan's nascent democratic order.

A quick look at history may reveal why the military was lured into forbidden political waters at the first instance. This is followed by a brief discussion of military interventions in Pakistan during the period 1947-1997. The narrative then analyzes the factors that led to the interference of the army in national politics. And finally an effort is made to synthesize the role of the military in Pakistan.

Political-Military Background

Political Experimentation

Pakistan has had four martial laws, three imposed by military dictators (Generals Mohammad Ayub Khan, Mohammad Yahya Khan and M. Ziaul Haq) and the fourth by an elected civilian (Z.A. Bhutto). The fifth military take-over by General Pervez Musharraf in 1999—briefly mentioned—is outside the scope of this narrative. Collectively, the country remained under martial law for about sixteen years. In addition, martial laws were imposed in portions of the country twice, first in March 1953 and then in April 1977. Ironically, both the mini martial laws were clamped by elected civilian governments to extricate themselves from their self-created political quagmires. No less tragic is the fact that civilian governments earned the stigma of introducing martial law in the country.

In the first fifty years, six out of eleven Heads of State were either soldiers or bureaucrats. Their cumulative tenure came to thirty-six years. Their performance in the power saddle included the 'dismissal of eight out of fifteen prime ministers; dissolution of seven out of ten national assemblies; and banning five out of seven political parties that were outlawed.'[7]

Pakistan variously tried four different forms of political systems—parliamentary, presidential, military, and a half-breed between the parliamentary and the presidential form. This cycle depicts her political desperation and search for a durable democratic order. It may be recalled that the Indian Independence Act, 1947, established two independent dominions—India and Pakistan—both with a parliamentary form of government. While India quickly framed a constitution, Pakistan's attempts in this field were less than laudatory.

The Dominion of India had a head-start over Pakistan as she inherited an established central government with all the paraphernalia of a functioning state. Her electoral mill had groomed the Indian National Congress into an established political party with a large reservoir of leadership at different tiers—from the local to the national levels. The Congress Party played a long and leading role in the political affairs of post-independence India. Prime Minister Pandit Jawaharlal Nehru, the political guru and philosopher of modern India, guided his nation's destiny for seventeen long years. His wisdom and vision gave stability to India and laid its democratic foundations on an even keel.

On the contrary, Pakistan inherited a country split into two wings geographically and without the infrastructure of a state. The federal government and its numerous institutions did not exist and a functional arrangement for administration of the new state started from scratch. The immediate influx of refugees from India and the death of her founding father added to her monumental difficulties. India played a Machiavellian role, exploiting Pakistan's internal difficulties and creating hurdles for her in the economic and other fields.

India's effort failed because, notwithstanding the hurdles in her way, public morale in Pakistan was high and her people had confidence in the ability of the founding fathers to weather the storm. Soon, however, trouble brewed. Within one decade (1947-58) Pakistan's nascent political system crumbled and her inefficient and quarreling politicians made a mockery of democracy. This caused a vacuum and an opportunity for the other organs of the state to fill it.

Presidential Form Introduced

General Ayub Khan's Martial Law government introduced a presidential form of government under the 1962 Constitution. He was accused of doing so for getting a stamp of legitimacy affixed to his personal rule. This constitution became a non-starter as it was imposed on the people under 'khaki shadows' by a person who had personally shown the door to a democratic order. To be acceptable and durable, the constitution must enjoy the support of its people. This was not the case.

Under the 1962 Constitution, the president was not directly elected on the basis of adult franchise. Instead, Ayub was indirectly elected president by 80,000 Basic Democrats who had themselves been elected earlier on the basis of one-man one-vote. This indirect election was perceived to be held unfairly because it was easy for a sitting incumbent to win over the support of the Basic Democrats. The 1962 Constitution was consigned to history with the exit of Ayub Khan.

Street agitation against Ayub caused the collapse of his government and he was forced to resign in 1969. He did so by transferring power to the Army Chief instead of handing it over to the Speaker of the National Assembly, as provided in the 1962 Constitution. In so doing, Ayub violated his own given constitution. Besides, the collapse of his government proved that the constitution was too serious a document and too sacred a trust to be left to the dictates of a single individual, howsoever patriotic he might be. In addition, an indirectly elected President, with the vast powers of the head of state and the head of government combined in him, was not acceptable to a majority of the Pakistani people. People demanded a system with built-in checks and balances.

In their respective tenures in office Ayub, Yahya, Bhutto and Zia wore two hats each, one, that of the chief martial law administrator, and the second, of the President of Pakistan. It was an administrative, legal and diplomatic requirement for the country to have a head of state. However, in the spirit of law this designation was a misnomer. The four Presidents were in reality absolute military rulers who did not derive their authority either from the constitution, which was abrogated or suspended, or from the Parliament, which did not exist. They ruled by the gun and wielded absolute power without any institutional system of accountability.

Quasi-Parliamentary Form

Following the non-party election held in 1985, General Zia's martial law gave birth to a semblance of democratic order. He hand-picked Mr Mohammad Khan Junejo as the Prime Minister and the National Assembly gave him a vote of confidence as the Leader of the House. Junejo, an unpretentious politician was an honourable but quietly assertive person, a leader with integrity and moral courage. A stickler on money matters, he exercised his constitutional authority and refused to function as a puppet prime minister. Such 'independence' annoyed Zia who publicly declared that he was 'not transferring power, he was sharing it.' Their differing perceptions created difficulties for both. Cracks appeared between them and mutual distrust increased. Their respective advisers added fuel to the fire and the working arrangement between the President and the Prime Minister became tense and brittle. The inevitable happened. Zia dismissed Junejo. In the process, like Ayub Khan, he also dismantled the constitutional system he himself had sought to erect.

The 1973 Constitution had been restored with major amendments but with one vital exception. President Zia, in addition to being the Head of State, continued to hold the office of the Chief Martial Law Administrator and remained the Chief of the Army Staff. This was an undemocratic and self-serving arrangement. Zia retained the source of power and kept its reins under his personal control. Not surprisingly critics called it a quasi-democratic order, taunted Zia and castigated Prime Minister Junejo for being constitutionally hamstrung by the omnipotent President.

Constitution Making

The Constituent Assembly, established in 1947 to frame the constitution, took seven years to produce the draft. The ill-fated 1956 Constitution, parliamentary in form, was abrogated two years later. It was based on the parity formula that compromised the democratic rights of East Pakistan by placing it at par with West Pakistan, despite its larger population. The parity formula was assessed differently in the two wings of the country. Generally supported in West Pakistan, it was viewed with reservations in the numerically dominant, economically weak and politically sensitive East Pakistan. President Iskander Mirza lamented that the 1956 Constitution was 'unworkable.'[8] An opposite view was that he himself put it under the guillotine within two years without giving it a fair chance to work.

In a parliamentary system, the head of state is the symbol of the nation, and the powers entrusted to him are symbolic and ceremonial, largely to be exercised only in an emergency. In effect, all powers are exercised by the cabinet through the parliament. The powers of the Indian President are close to that of the President of Pakistan under the 1973 Constitution. The British Sovereign is another example of a parliamentary system, where the King or Queen only perform ceremonial functions and have no executive authority. Division of authority between two independent power centres creates a conflict.

The perceived or real conflicts stemming from the 1956 Constitution prompted Ayub Khan to impose martial law and introduce a presidential form of government. He then set about to frame his own constitution, passed in 1962, then violated it himself in 1969 by asking the Army Chief, General Yahya Khan, to assume control of the country—an act that was legally and morally untenable. General Yahya Khan abrogated the constitution and imposed martial law. Pakistan's search for a constitution again got a setback.

East Pakistan felt alienated because its due share in power was denied to it. Besides, provincial governments were imposed on it by the distant centre. This created local grievances that were fanned and exploited by a hostile India. A concerted effort of internal subversion and external aggression eventually cut Pakistan into two.

The amputation of Pakistan in December 1971—creating euphoria in Bangladesh and joy in India—caused sadness among the people of Pakistan who had attained freedom only two decades ago. To them it was a national tragedy. Mr Zulfikar Ali Bhutto now became a hero who pulled Pakistan out of the debris of war. An interim constitution was passed in 1972 which was replaced by the 1973 Constitution enacted by the Parliament on the basis of near unanimity of the legislators.

Parliamentary in form, the 1973 Constitution was so heavily tilted in favour of the prime minister that any constitutional act of the president required the counter signatures of the prime minister to become law. An omnipotent head of the government and an impotent head of the state were the two striking features of the 1973 Constitution. The constitutional pendulum swung from one extreme to the other. Once again it was the turn of the feudal lords to flirt with the constitution under the guise of democracy. Pakistan had yet to learn the virtues of moderation, tolerance and balance of power in statecraft.

Mr Bhutto's rule (1971-77) was a civilian dictatorship. While claiming to be a democrat, he weakened the institutions of the state, converted Pakistan to serfdom and employed the coercive instruments of the state to 'fix up' those who dared to cross his path. The ruling Pakistan People's Party became a cult and Bhutto a high priest, a messiah, answerable to none in the country except himself. Intoxicated with power, the 1977 elections held under his government were so patently rigged that the people rose in revolt.

The 1973 Constitution was put to the test during the country-wide anti-Bhutto agitation in 1977, President Fazal Elahi Chaudhry 'virtually twiddled his thumbs'[9] and helplessly watched the paralyzed state administration do nothing. The Constitution did not permit the Head of State to act except on the advice of the Prime Minister. Bhutto was too proud to accept his faults and seek a compromise with the opposition. The end result was a foregone conclusion. Bhutto destroyed the democratic system and himself with it.

The Gallup Polls at the time had predicted an easy victory for Mr Bhutto's PPP in a fairly held election. Bhutto's overkill election strategy boomeranged and the opposition capitalized on the opportunity offered to it. The anti-Bhutto agitation soon took a religious turn. The polarization between the Right and the Left paralyzed the country and presented to the military a difficult option—watch a drift towards civil war or intervene. The Chief of the Army Staff, General Ziaul Haq who took charge of the country claimed that the army had been sucked into the political quagmire created by the politicians. A section of the print media called him a reluctant ruler. His act of seizing power was upheld by the Supreme Court. However, once in the driving seat General Zia showed just how much he liked power and displayed considerable tenacity in retaining it much beyond the expectations of most analysts.

Initially, it was claimed that martial law would be imposed for ninety days only, and the 1973 Constitution was held in abeyance. However, eight years passed before the constitution was revived, in 1985, with the addition of the 8th Amendment which included Article 58(2) (b). It empowered the president to dismiss the prime minister and the national assembly if the situation so warranted. The president was also given discretionary powers, besides others, to appoint the services chiefs and the Chairman of the Joint Chiefs of Staff Committee. The enhanced powers of the President created two power centres. The seeds of conflict were planted.

During the period 1985-1997, three successive Presidents invoked Article 58(2)(b) on four different occasions and dismissed four elected prime ministers. The repeated use of the President's discretionary powers created uncertainty in the country and started a national debate on whether Article 58(2)(b) was legally valid, politically justified, and institutionally appropriate. The issue was agitated in the Supreme Court of Pakistan under the Constitutional Petition No 60/1996. The Supreme Court held that this article had 'in fact shut the door on martial law which had not been imposed since 1977.'[10] The Supreme Court further stated that 'the 8th Amendment, including Article 58(2)(b), was a valid piece of legislation and it was open to the Parliament to amend it, if so desired.'[11] The controversial parts of the 8th Amendment were subsequently deleted from the statute book by the Parliament after a unanimous vote.

Political Landscape

Pakistan's thorny journey through history is a panorama of political inefficiency, military chauvinism, bureaucratic arrogance, constitutional failure, feudal over-lordship and democratic frailty. The executive domination, judicial docility, legislative feebleness and the media weakness showed rather prominently in this vista. The first five decades witnessed some noticeable achievements but the disappointments weighed heavy. Despite the progress made in some fields, by and large, the hopes and expectations nourished by the people in 1947 remained unfulfilled, casting a pall of gloom in the country. However, this is not a balance sheet of national achievements and follies.

At the macro level Pakistan's geography changed. Who was more to blame for the errors made is a matter of opinion but none of Pakistan's power groups had clean hands. Sadly, since 1947, twenty-nine out of the thirty-eight elected provincial assemblies were prematurely dissolved. During this period forty-four out of seventy-seven chief ministers were dismissed by the federal government, and another thirteen resigned because they failed to win support in the provincial assemblies.

Pakistan took twenty-three years to hold her first national elections. It is a rebuke to her political sagacity that these were held by a military dictator, General Yahya Khan. The elections, held in the backdrop of the Six Points Programme and in the aftermath of the worst cyclone that had hit East Pakistan in her history, were perceived by the people to be fair and free. But they failed to inject political sanity into the system. Or, perhaps sobriety was deliberately discarded at the altar of the personal whims of those who called the major political shots then. The post-election period witnessed a polluted struggle for power between two egoistic leaders and an administrator who precipitated the national collapse. Pakistan sunk low, very low indeed, in 1971. The Quaid's Pakistan was broken. And yet, none were held answerable. Those who ruled what remained of the country did not dare to hold accountability because they were also among the destroyers of Pakistan.

Seen with hindsight, democracy made a trying start. The absorption and resettlement of eight million refugees in 1947 was a herculean task. Jinnah's death in 1948 was a serious blow to the young state. The people had great faith in Jinnah's ability to steer the country out of her troubles. His exit placed Prime Minister Liaquat Ali Khan at centre stage. He tried hard to build a nation state but despite his considerable qualities of head and heart he lacked the charisma and authority of the Quaid. The Muslim League, facing petty intrigues, lost public contact and regional issues started clouding the national horizon.

Liaquat's assassination in 1951 by a hired Afghan agent was a telling blow. Stunned by the tragedy, the nation absorbed the shock with commendable courage. However, this was the beginning of a steep slide. Coming to the fore, political pygmies grabbed positions of eminence and authority. Their tunnel-vision could not solve the macro problems faced by the country and their political poverty and administrative innocence showed rather prominently.

The landed aristocracy and feudal lords, in and outside the legislatures, dominated the national political scene. This large, powerful and assertive group was opposed to reforms—legal, political and agricultural—that would have weakened its social and political domination of the rural areas inhabited by more than seventy per cent of Pakistan's population. So dominant is the influence of this lobby in the legislatures that agricultural income has remained tax free ever since 1947. The dichotomy of taxes paid by the urban and rural sections of population is striking.

Most political parties are undemocratic from within. Only a few hold in-house elections at all tiers on a regular basis. Some others perform election rituals nominally. Family-controlled and autocratic parties are a norm. Genes and means dominate the prevailing political culture in which the accident of birth provides a sure and secure ladder for top leadership. 'The feudal system negates the concept of democracy in the same way as military rule does. Consequently, the political system that has taken root in Pakistan is the antithesis of democracy. It is feudal in character and practice and democratic in name only.'[12]

In 1947, 'The intelligentsia was Westernized, completely urban, partly unemployed and mostly frustrated.'[13] The situation has not changed much since. Gains and greed dominate the political culture in which moral decline is visible. Political horse trading is a lucrative business. The search for greener pastures takes precedence over political ethics.

During the period 1985-97, the curse of corruption in the administration, though prevalent previously, became so rampant that the few honest politicians and bureaucrats were laughed at. The policy makers were accused of making shady deals and the distinction between public money and private property lost relevance in the national political culture.

Islam, an enlightened religion, has a remarkable flexibility in happily co-existing with other religions and cultures. A modern and moderate state, Pakistan has consistently abhorred extremism as an instrument of state policy. The country has enjoyed a fair measure of freedom of expression. The rightist political parties are vociferous and they attempt to arouse religious sensitivities on controversial issues. However, their vote-catching ability has never exceeded five per cent in the national and in the provincial elections.

A corrupt, weak and semi-democratic political order co-exists with a disciplined, cohesive and well organised defence structure based on a pyramid of hierarchy. Senior bureaucracy plays an inconsistent role in the administration. While some civil servants excel in professionalism, others are neither civil nor servants. They are arrogant to the public and submissive to their political masters in power who do not draw the distinction between public servants and private servants. A few dance to the tunes played by the ruling political parties. Such weaklings make some worldly gains but lose respect and impair the institutions. While some bureaucrats know the art of self-survival, others suffer the agony of being principled in their profession.

Muslim League Decays

The Muslim League, formed in 1906, was a party of the upper middle class, elite, and landlords. Conservative in outlook, its manifesto was more intellectual than inspirational in content. It was not a party of the masses when Mr Jinnah became its president in the mid-thirties and led it in the 1937 elections with results which were not very encouraging.

The demand for Pakistan (1940) turned the Muslim League into a people's movement. Suddenly its popularity surged. The Pakistan Movement raised a fierce political storm that shook India. This was proved in the 1945-46 elections when the Muslim League achieved stunning electoral success. 'It captured hundred per cent Muslim seats for the Indian Central Legislative Assembly and won 446 out of a total of 495 Muslim seats in the provincial (state) assemblies.'[14] The massive margin of victory—

86.6 per cent of the votes in the Muslim constituencies in the provincial elections—shocked Congress. Nehru had boasted earlier that, 'There are only two forces in India today, British imperialism and Indian nationalism *as represented by the Congress*' (emphasis added).[15]

The Muslim League's rapid success disguised a weakness. Political parties develop vitality and experience from the knocks and shocks of the electoral process. Electoral gains and losses enrich the party and make it robust. The League's rapid rise denied it a grooming and maturing opportunity. The League, 'began to rule Pakistan by the right of occupation: it was the only party in existence.'[16] Others were weak and ineffective.

The demand for Pakistan was phase one of the struggle. The emergence of Pakistan, the second phase, required a consolidated effort to transform public expectations into reality. It needed statesmanship of a high order. The first three years of the League rule were on the whole unobjectionable. Thereafter drift ensued. The League's doctrine, ideas and style lost touch with the march of time and complacency overshadowed its performance.

Simmering Provinces

The Congress ministry in North West Frontier Province dug its own grave by declining to honour the national flag. It was dismissed in August 1947. A judicial tribunal found the Chief Minister of Sindh guilty of corruption and maladministration. He was dismissed in 1948. His successor was involved in cases of jobbery and nepotism. Governor's rule was imposed in the province of Sindh.

In 1949, a power tussle in the Punjab led to the dismissal of its ministry, the dissolution of the provincial legislative assembly and the imposition of Governor's rule in the province. Four years later, anti-Qadiani riots in Punjab created policy differences between the province and the centre. Lahore was put under martial law. Normalcy instantly returned to the troubled city without a single shot being fired. But peace carried a big political price tag. The politicians stood exposed. Kalat, a princely state in Balochistan, had acceded to Pakistan. Emboldened by the prevailing unrest in the country, the former ruler demanded restoration of his state and defiantly replaced Pakistan's flag at Miri Fort with that of his own emblem. Snap military action restored the writ of the government.

In 1948, some students in East Pakistan demanded that Bengali be declared a national language along with Urdu. In his address to Dacca University on 24 May 1948, the Quaid-i-Azam said, 'There can be only one lingua franca, that is, the language for inter-communication between the various provinces of the State, and that language should be Urdu and cannot be any other.'[17] The students' agitation subsided but only temporarily. Bengali was a developed and rich language and regional sentiments for its adoption were high. Besides Bengalis were not known for their emotional docility. Not too long afterwards, language riots broke out. India added fuel to the fire and created a big gulf between East and West Pakistan, which only widened over the subsequent years.

Provincial elections for the East Pakistan Legislative Assembly were due in 1953. The Centre, fearing the defeat of the Muslim League in an electoral contest, postponed the polls for a year. However, even in the delayed elections held the following year, the ruling Muslim League was routed—winning no more than ten seats in a house of 309.[18] The peoples verdict was violated by the arrogant power barons at the centre and East Pakistan was punished for defeating the ruling party. A bureaucrat-turned politician, Iskandar Mirza, was appointed Governor of East Pakistan to discipline the province which was placed under the direct rule of the centre. The Governor's rule in East Pakistan was resented by the people. It caused alienation and planted the seeds of separation.

In 1955, the East Pakistan Legislative Assembly declared its own Speaker insane and, in a shameful display of frenzy, beat to death its Deputy Speaker inside the house.

The provinces alone were not in disarray. The malaise ran deeper and there was also trouble at the centre.

Scheming Centre

The Quaid-i-Azam was the peoples' icon not only because he was the first Governor-General, but because he was the Founding Father of the nation. His reverence and eminence in public eyes could not have diminished whether he had become the Prime Minister or remained a plain citizen.

Those succeeding Jinnah as Governors-General, earned respect because of the office held by them but none matched Jinnah's popularity in public. Their arrogance was great. They harmed the country by violating the constitution that they had taken oath to protect.

Governor-General Ghulam Mohammad indulged in arbitrary acts. On 18 April 1953, he dismissed Prime Minister Khwaja Nazimuddin. Later, differences arose between him and Prime Minister Mohammad Ali Bogra. In 1954, a bill was moved in the Constituent Assembly that bound the governor-general to act on the advice of the prime minister.[19] The fuming Governor-General pre-empted the bill. Ghulam Mohammad dismissed the Central Cabinet, dissolved the Constituent Assembly and declared a state of emergency in the country on the plea that the institutions could no longer function. In October 1954, Bogra formed another cabinet in which the Army Chief, General Mohammad Ayub Khan, was included as Defence Minister. This was a formal acknowledgment of the rise of Ayub in national affairs. He joined the cabinet on terms dictated by him and retained the power-wielding post of Commander-in-Chief.

Ethics and morality were removed from Pakistan's political culture. Legislators changed their loyalties with such gay abandon that between the years 1953 and 1958 seven prime ministers were nominated and removed through internal intrigues. Each of them got a vote of confidence from the rubber-stamp Constituent Assembly. The drama of musical chairs played in the corridors of power was almost laughable if it had not been so pathetic. The political system was weakened by the overnight creation of the officially sponsored Republican Party. The legislators changed their party labels with stunning speed.

Military Interventions

Power Game

Pakistan's peculiar geography—two wings separated by more than a thousand miles of hostile Indian territory—demanded vision, foresight and character from her political leadership. From the beginning the country faced, among others, five serious problems. Firstly, while East Pakistan had a majority population (56%), West Pakistan enjoyed the monopoly of power. This dichotomy created regional bitterness and caused constitutional constraints. Secondly, the massive communal riots and influx of eight million refugees placed a heavy burden on the meagre resources of the new state. Thirdly, the early death of Mr Jinnah in 1948 and the assassination of Khan Liaquat Ali Khan in 1951, created a leadership vacuum which their political successors failed to fill. The ruling Muslim League wrapped itself in a cocoon and got distanced from the masses. The gap between the rulers and the ruled widened. Fourthly, weakening political control lured the civil and military bureaucracy into the game of power. And finally, the Kashmir dispute, an unresolved item of the independence agenda, created a conflict of national interests between India and Pakistan that overshadowed their policy options.

At independence, the armed forces inherited the British tradition of non-involvement in politics. Professional and disciplined, they found career satisfaction in defending the territorial integrity of Pakistan. Soon after Liaquat's death, the senior civil servants and the military brass were alarmed to see the decaying political behaviour of the ruling elite. Some cabinet ministers lacked ability. Others lacked integrity. Few made a positive contribution to the policy making process. For years no constitution was framed. Prime Minister Khawaja Nazimuddin was noble but ineffective and provided weak leadership. Governor-General Ghulam Mohammad, a civil servant, and his successor, General Iskandar Mirza, also a civil servant, indulged in political intrigues and manipulated politicians to serve their personal ends.

The mess created by the inept civilian rulers and inefficient politicians brought them into popular contempt and eroded the foundations of the state. Ayub lamented in 1958 that the country had become 'the laughing stock' of the observers. President Iskandar Mirza advocated 'controlled democracy'[20], presumably under his personal 'control.'

In October 1958, the *de facto* power duo—President Iskandar Mirza and General Ayub Khan—acted in concert to derail the democratic order. The Army Chief, Ayub Khan, was made the Chief Martial Law Administrator. In so doing, Iskandar Mirza misjudged the political calculus and the chemistry of power. If his own ambition was high, as was obvious, Ayub loved authority no less. Within three weeks Ayub, the king-maker, himself became the king and Iskandar Mirza, the initial front man, was forced into exile. Not an innocent victim, Iskandar Mirza 'had been an intriguer of mammoth proportions, was untrustworthy, and was unfit to be the President of Pakistan.'[21] With his forefinger placed on the trigger, Ayub felt that he was the most qualified person to lead the country. Shifting democracy backstage, the Pakistan Army occupied the centre stage of national political power.

So discredited were the politicians that the public at large heaved a sigh of relief and hailed the imposition of martial law. The process of transition was peaceful and smooth. Ayub—a handsome, tall and imposing Pathan—a modern and a moderate person, introduced a wide range of reforms that brought economic prosperity to the country.

However, Ayub's love for power showed. The constitution he gave to the country displayed its weakness when it was manipulated by him to get himself elected as President. His victory over the revered *Mohtarma* Fatima Jinnah in 1964 was widely believed to have been rigged. Besides, he was seen to be preparing for dynastic control with his brother performing the role of the leader of the opposition in the National Assembly and his son, released from the army, becoming a politician.

In 1965, India and Pakistan blundered into a war over Kashmir. The deadlocked conflict weakened Ayub's grip on the administration. A UN-sponsored cease-fire ended the war and the Soviet Union-brokered Tashkent Declaration of 1966 restored a measure of normalcy between Pakistan and India. Ayub's popularity graph dipped low as the people felt that the Tashkent Declaration was against the national interests of Pakistan. A coronary thrombosis attack in 1968 left Ayub feeble and in poor health, unable to function effectively as President. His protégé, Z. A. Bhutto, groomed in politics under martial law, exploited his benefactor's waning control on the administration to gain power for himself.

Unable to handle the political storm raging against him, Ayub quit power in March 1969 in favour of the Commander-in-Chief of the Pakistan Army, General Yahya Khan. Another view is that Yahya demanded the transfer of authority to him and Ayub was too weak to resist and happy to oblige. This bilateral arrangement was mutually beneficial to the generals. Ayub Khan ensured his personal safety and Yahya Khan got into the saddle of power. Years later, the Supreme Court held Yahya's martial law as unconstitutional without giving him a chance to be heard.

Yahya did not impose martial law to promote democracy in the country. To his credit it has to be said, however, that he held general elections in 1970, the first in the country since 1947. Unfortunately, the flawed post-election strategy of the Yahya Government and the political intrigues of Sheikh Mujib-ur-Rahman and Zulfikar Ali Bhutto denied the country a democratic government. The internal security situation in the eastern wing took an ugly turn and Pakistan's internal follies were exploited by India. With her covert subversion and overt aggression, East Pakistan was converted into Bangladesh.

The fall of Dhaka and the ignoble military surrender was a nightmare for the people of Pakistan. It tumbled the Yahya government out of power and the subdued military reverted to its barracks.

General Yahya Khan died some years later after a prolonged illness. President Zia was then away on a tour of Turkey. By that time, General Zia had taken over the reins of the country after removing Bhutto through a *coup de état*. The acting CMLA, General Sawar Khan, arranged the burial with full military honours. The acting President, Chief Justice Anwarul Haq advised Sawar to hold a quiet and low key family funeral in view of 'General Yahya Khan's role in the East Pakistan crisis and the opinion expressed about him in the Hamoodur Rahman Commission Report.' Sawar told Anwarul Haq that General Yahya Khan was not only a retired Army Chief but also a highly decorated general-officer who had neither been tried in a court of law nor convicted on any charge. Besides, the Hamoodur Rahman Commission Report was not a public document and its contents were unknown. General Sawar discussed the issue with President Zia in Turkey who approved Sawar's decision.

With Mr Z. A. Bhutto assuming power in what remained of Pakistan, the country started afresh with its power potential altered. Sadly, Bhutto allowed his dictatorial ambitions to overwhelm his judgement. Although it goes to his credit that he had the 1973 Constitution framed, he convinced himself that he would remain an irreplacable player in the power game for a long time. Bhutto was blinded by power and, in the later stage of his rule, he saw only what he wanted to see.

A feudal by birth, a socialist by his own declaration but a capitalist at heart, any system that kept Bhutto in the power saddle was considered democratic by him. His tyrannical acts victimized his opponents—politicians, bureaucrats and out-of-step colleagues—who did not submit to his egotistical dictates and dared to criticize him or cross his political path. Under his harsh personalized rule the institutions of the state weakened.

One example. In October 1972, Bhutto created a Federal Security Force without prior parliamentary approval (an Act of

Parliament was subsequently passed in June 1973). This quasi military force was raised with the twin objective of diluting the influence of the Pakistan Army and keeping his political opponents on the hop. The personnel of the FSF were drawn from among the former members of the police and military services who had mostly been retired for reasons of professional failing. The FSF earned public notoriety for allegedly committing state-sponsored acts of terrorism which were dutifully attributed by the state-controlled media to the opposition. One such act committed by the infamous FSF later took Bhutto himself to the gallows. That the Army Chief did not oppose the raising of the FSF, a force parallel to the military in some ways, shows how Bhutto exploited the military, humbled in the 1971 war.

Mr Bhutto invited disaster by rigging the 1977 elections. By so doing he lost his credibility, his government and his life. But for the fall of his government, the already hushed up murder inquiry that eventually took him to the gallows might never have seen the light of day. The people rose against the rigged elections and demanded fresh polls. The opposition parties united in a protracted agitation against him. Hundreds of people were killed and Bhutto's cabinet minister confessed that the economy had been 'bled white'. Bhutto imposed a mini martial law in Karachi Division and in the Districts of Hyderabad and Lahore. It proved counterproductive. Once again the country was paralyzed by street agitation. Once again it was internally polarised and its disputes were not settled politically. Once again the politicians created a power vacuum that lured the military in to fill it. Soldiers indoctrinated to fight the enemy, normally hate to train guns on their compatriots. The armed forces find it easier to dislodge an unpopular leader than to defend him.

General M. Ziaul Haq, the Army chief, imposed martial law in July 1977. His act had the support of his corps commanders. Once a charismatic leader, Bhutto's public image was so tarnished that his overthrow was acclaimed by the public and the country witnessed scenes of jubilation. Disturbances ended, peace was restored and national activities revived.

On 18 March 1978, Bhutto, and four others were sentenced to death by a full bench of the Lahore High Court. They had been charged with conspiracy to murder Nawab Mohammad Ahmad Khan, the father of one of Bhutto's bitter political opponents, Ahmad Raza Kasuri. The Supreme Court upheld the sentence on 2 February 1979, and Bhutto was hanged on 4 April 1979. His execution divided the country into those who justified the decision and others who strongly looked upon it as a vindictive act.

Looming large on Pakistan's political horizon, Bhutto's death influenced Zia's options. He wanted public legitimacy for himself but without personally facing the rigours and risks of an electoral contest. The protraction of his rule was criticised by many as a subterfuge to remain in power. Nothing earned him greater discredit than the national referendum in 1984 in which a vote for an Islamic system was equated with endorsement for Zia to remain in power for a further period of five years.

Non-party elections were held in February 1985, and Mr Mohammad Khan Junejo was nominated by Zia as the prime minister. Democracy was restored but the opposition chided Junejo for being a nominated head of the government, working under the shadow of martial law even after it was lifted in December 1985. This was a precarious time for Junejo. His friends, admirers and critics wanted him to assert his constitutional authority. Zia expected docility from his nominated prime minister but Junejo was a man of integrity. The inevitable happened. Zia lost patience and dismissed Junejo in May 1988. His honeymoon with democracy ended on a sour note.

Junejo was not the sole victim. General Zia followed an even-handed approach and trusted others only to the extent necessary. Although it was improper in a civilian and democratic dispensation for the head of the state to remain the Chief of Army Staff, for Zia it was an ingenious arrangement.

Three issues dominated the first post-Zia decade. First, the 8th Amendment in the 1973 Constitution and its invocation on four occasions. Second, the Bhutto phenomenon. And, third, the Zia factor. That the ghosts of both—Bhutto and Zia— dominated

Pakistan's political scene for so long, reflected the nation's political impoverishment.

The military was directly responsible for the national policy making process during the decade 1977-88. Zia had a firm grip on national affairs and the opposition, weak and fragmented, did not pose a serious challenge to his rule. Barring one or two years, the three major crops—wheat, rice and sugarcane—had bumper yields and the national economy did reasonably well. Industrial performance was commendable too. On the external front, some opportunities of geo-strategic importance presented themselves and the Zia Government took advantage of them. These included the Soviet military intervention in Afghanistan, the Iranian revolution, the Iraq-Iran war, India's war hysteria against Pakistan, including Exercise Brass Tacks and the US-led Western tirade against Pakistan's nuclear programme.

General Zia's sudden death in August 1988 created a 'power troika' comprising the President, the Prime Minister and the Chief of Army Staff. The army chief was consulted by the other two on matters of substance before taking decisions. General Headquarters became a port of call for national decision-makers and foreign dignitaries visiting the country. By such acts the president and the prime minister exposed their weaknesses and damaged the image of the high offices held by them. They also violated military norms. The Chairman of the Joint Chiefs of Staff Committee, senior to the army chief, was bypassed and frequently ignored on issues of substance creating doubts about the usefulness of this office.

The army chiefs selectively and subtly meddled in politics. This was against military tradition and a violation of the constitution. This proclivity led to speculations about the military having political ambitions.

Political polarization increased during 1988-1998. Successive governments lacked a working equation with the opposition. Their mutual distrust created political uncertainty and retarded the growth of healthy democratic traditions. Rampant corruption at the top became a malignant disease and economic mismanagement came under severe criticism internally and by the international aid giving agencies.

Politics became a quick-buck business. Democracy was compromised by the greed of worldly-wise politicians who indulged in a mad race to amass their personal wealth by dicey means that earned them disrespect and notoriety. The dismissal of four governments in rapid succession exposed the frailty of the democratic institution. Successive governments sought the support of the Chief of the Army Staff to survive in power. At the same time, the opposition looked towards the military to save it from the brutal excesses of leaders in the power saddle.

Military intervention in political affairs is not a new or rare phenomenon in Third World countries. While the reasons for this differ from one country to another, the underlying factors of the malady are common: a low literacy rate, weak democratic institutions, state sponsored repression, corruption, sustained political unrest, internal security difficulties, biased accountability and excessive ambition on the part of the military brass. Experience shows that once derailed, a political process takes considerable time and effort to get back on track. The fear syndrome and the dynamics of power delay the process.

The genetics of military intervention also differ from a blood bath to a completely peaceful transfer of authority. The psyche of the people and the nation's experiences set the course. All military *coups* in Pakistan had a common factor. These were all peacefully implemented and were preceded by a period of political unrest and chaos that polarized the country. On each occasion, the public felt that the military was justified in doing what it did. Therefore, people generally supported the military take-overs.

Some military brass nourished political ambitions. Ayub is an example. At other times, the military got sucked into the political whirlwind by circumstantial pressure created and abetted by the politicians. Zia is a case in point. On yet another occasion Ayub did what Yahya wanted him to do and a deal was struck. Power intoxicated all the three commanders and, once in power, the Sword of Damocles hung on their heads.

The disengagement process was invariably burdensome. Ayub violated the constitution drafted and passed by him and the constitution died when its author lost power. Yahya failed to comprehend that the game was over for him. He floated a draft constitution to remain in power when East Pakistan was on the verge of collapse. Zia wanted to scrap the 1973 Constitution but his military team prevailed on him to retain the consensus document. He agreed, albeit reluctantly, but in the final analysis amended it substantially and went ahead to sack a prime minister on the biased advice of his sycophants.

It is naive to expect a martial law administrator to run a country in a democratic manner. The military rulers risk their necks in up-turning the constitution either for reasons of ambition or for a higher cause. National unity and military integration have been the primary reasons for the unpleasant acts of Pakistan's military rulers. While some might have had political ambitions *ab initio*, others could not remain silent spectators to the systematic erosion of national security from within. Whether their acts were legally valid and morally correct are issues worth analysing but are best left to the judiciary to decide. All the affected generals claimed to be staunch nationalists. Repeated military rule in Pakistan has, nevertheless, created a growing realization within the top defence hierarchy that the army is not a panacea for all disputes, and political issues are best settled politically.

A change in thinking is discernible. The military realizes that its repeated interventions in civil affairs neither cured the ills of society nor produced economic, social, legal and administrative miracles. Military rule achieved some short-term gains only. However, hindsight reveals that in the long run, their disadvantages outweighed their advantages. Among other losses, the debit balance includes a bruised national image, frailty of democracy and accumulation of rust in the military's own professional performance.

The defence services are neither organized nor trained to fight in the political arena. The psyche and suitability of their respective players are very different. Some politicians have had a sinister agenda in politicizing the armed forces. They have

manipulated the army for selfish political ends. Also, apart from
the well known faces, a couple of military commanders since
1988 overstepped their position and indulged in political
manoeuvering. However, their acts exposed them. This reflects
a growing maturity of the system.

By and large, the military gradually receded into the
background since 1985, and visibly adopted a posture of
neutrality and non-interference in political controversies. This
discernible change was publicly applauded by the political
leadership. Prime Minister Nawaz Sharif's actions—the 13th
and the 14th Amendments in the Constitution and the premature
retirement of four services chiefs—two from the Pakistan Navy
and one each from the Pakistan Air Force and the Pakistan
Army—demonstrated the growing political supremacy in the
country.

Security Game

Most Pakistanis perceive a threat to their national security from
a numerically superior and hegemonic India. The role played by
India in 1971 strengthens their thinking. India desires a
subservient Pakistan, too weak to defend herself and too fragile
to pursue a foreign policy independent of the regional big
brother. She wants to be the master of her own destiny but
denies this right to her neighbours in South Asia. This raises
doubts about her reliability and intentions.

It is seldom comfortable for a weak country to live with a
large and aggressive neighbour. Pakistan has the unenviable
distinction of having three giant-size neighbours, the erstwhile
Soviet Union (now Russia), China and India. Pakistan's bilateral
ties with two of them, that is Russia and India, have been less
than smooth. Her location—proximity to the Gulf, Central Asia
and South Asia—provides her with great geo-strategic
importance. Given internal unity, national cohesion and economic
stability, this advantage can be a force multiplier. Pakistan has
largely failed to harness such gains. Instead, it is disturbing that

Pakistan's internal polarization, institutional vulnerabilities and crises in leadership have retarded the growth of democracy besides weakening the country from within. The erosion of unity and loss of power potential poses a threat to her national security. And yet, the political masters continue with their business as usual, unconcerned with the fate of the state.

Was the national downhill slide exploited by the military as an alibi to grab political power? This doubt stems from the fact that national security is a taboo, a hush-hush affair, closed for public discussion and debate. Such a situation creates doubts and gives birth to speculations. National security covers a wide spectrum of which the military aspect is just one component. The issue is too vital to be left to the wisdom of a selected few. No sane person can object to the security of classified material. But a lot can and should be discussed publicly for the common good of the country.

The military leaders take an oath under the constitution for preserving and protecting the territorial integrity of the country from internal subversion and external aggression. Their charter of responsibility does not include reformation of society, moral rearmament and national character building, notwithstanding the importance of such measures. Their primary task is unambiguously defined in the constitution and by the government. The penalty for deviating from the prescribed constitutional path is heavy. And yet, Pakistan's military has dismissed elected governments. Those doing so were people holding the high office of great responsibility. They took the extreme step for cogent reasons, and were conscious of what they did. With an odd exception, others claimed to be reluctant intruders in the political domain, acting under the burden of responsibility and preservation of national integrity. Generally, the superior courts upheld the military interventions and declared their acts to be legal.

It is difficult to foretell if the era of extra-constitutional rule is finally over. It is not possible to predict the future with a reasonable degree of surety because political developments defy quantification. However, it can be prognosticated with reasonable surety and conviction that the chances of military take-overs in future will decrease or disappear with the passage of time, once a truly democratic system gains vitality and maturity in the country and the national literacy rate substantially improves. Pakistan's political masters may do a great service to the country and to themselves if they discharge their national and political responsibilities democratically, transparently and impartially with a clear distinction drawn between public and private money. And finally, the feudal system has to be extirpated.

The military institutions in Pakistan have been painstakingly nurtured and they enjoy a healthy respect from all sides of the national political divide. The military is seen by the people as a symbol of pride and the harbinger of national unity, stability and integrity. A national consensus demands that this institution be strengthened further to enable it to meet its constitutional obligations of safeguarding national freedom and sovereignty. An attempt to politicize the military draws contempt and reaction. And, any effort to create a division within its ranks would be unacceptable. General Zia had publicly admitted that the looming fear of a division within the army had influenced his decision to remove Mr Bhutto's government in July 1977.

Beg Tastes Power

President Zia dismissed Prime Minister Junejo's government in May 1988, and ordered fresh elections to be held in November that year. With General Zia's sudden death in August, barely three months later, the army also lost its Chief of Staff. The Constitution had the necessary provision for filling in the vacant posts. This was done. The Chairman of the Senate, Mr Ghulam Ishaq Khan, took over as the Acting President and his first act was to appoint General Mirza Aslam Beg, vice army chief, as the Chief of Army Staff. Days later, the acting governor of Sindh and the chief ministers of Balochistan, Punjab, and NWFP jointly met General Beg at GHQ. Beg gave them a long political sermon. 'The Muhajir Qaumi Movement,' said Beg, 'is in my pocket. The PPP must not win the forthcoming election and

Benazir Bhutto will be unacceptable to the Army as the Prime Minister.'[22] Beg also publicly announced that General Zia's official military residence would be converted into a museum. The MQM continued to function effectively under its own party leadership. Benazir Bhutto became the prime minister. The Army House was not converted into the Zia Museum.

The Lahore High Court held the dismissal of the Junejo government as 'not sustainable in law'. However, it did not restore the dissolved assemblies and held that fresh elections, as announced by the Zia administration earlier, be held on schedule in November 1988. An appeal against this judgment was made in the Supreme Court. On 5 October 1988, General Beg met the Minister for Law, Mr Wasim Sajjad, in his office at GHQ and requested him to convey his message to the Chief Justice of Pakistan that the already declared election schedule might not be changed in the Supreme Court judgment, when given. This constituted an interference in the process of law which remained unreported in the media at the time.

On 4 February 1993, General Beg, then retired, created a political-cum-legal storm in the country by publicly admitting that in 1988 he had sent a message to the Supreme Court asking it not to restore Junejo's dismissed government and to permit the elections to be held as scheduled.[23] He was charged for contempt of court. During the trial, Beg admitted that he had sent a message to the Chief Justice of the Supreme Court in good faith and in the public interest. Wasim Sajjad denied acting as an intermediary or conveying Beg's message to the Chief Justice. The third vital witness, the then Chief Justice of Pakistan to whom the message was addressed, was spared the trouble of entering the witness box to confirm or deny the receipt of the communication addressed to him. Why he was not called remained unexplained.

The Supreme Court took into consideration the mitigating circumstances, discharged General Beg, but held him guilty of contempt.

A feeling prevails in the country that the whole truth did not surface. One of the judges of the Supreme Court Bench that heard the case met me soon after his retirement. When I asked him if the then Chief Justice had taken his remaining brother judges into confidence about the receipt or non-receipt of a message allegedly sent by Beg, he answered in the negative. But he said that 'a strange development' took place in the courtroom on the final day of hearing of this case. Mr Mohammad Khan Junejo, the dismissed prime minister, had been summoned by the Court to appear as a witness and he was waiting for his evidence to be recorded. The Chief Justice completed the case without hearing him. One member on the Bench whispered to the Chief Justice, that Mr Junejo was present and his evidence had not yet been recorded. 'It is no longer needed', replied the Chief Justice to the 'amazement' of my guest.

General Beg's three-year term as the army chief, displaying his taste for politics, ended on 17 August 1991. During his command he did not hesitate to express his views on national affairs and on major policy matters with conviction and authority. On 28 January 1991, he predicted that the Gulf War, that had started two weeks earlier, would last for several months and create for the US a Vietnam-like quagmire. Beg publicly advised Iraq to adopt a 'strategy of defiance', whatever that meant, and this statement created diplomatic difficulties for Pakistan. His support for Saddam Hussain was in conflict with the officially declared policy of the government.

During the Gulf war, a meeting of the Defence Committee of the Cabinet, chaired by the prime minister, was held in Islamabad. In this meeting, General Beg loudly criticized Pakistan's policy on the Gulf War in a tone and style unexpected of a man in his position. The outburst was officially reported to President Ghulam Ishaq Khan who later 'talked' to the general about the issue. Under the Constitution, the president at that time had the discretionary power to appoint and retire the services chiefs. General Beg's statement and President Ishaq's weak handling of the complaint did not please the prime minister. In subsequent years, the President's discretionary power was withdrawn by an amendment made in the Constitution by the Parliament.

After the retirement of General Beg, General Asif Nawaz Janjua was appointed as the Chief of Army Staff. Sensitive by nature, Asif spoke little, avoided meeting the gentlemen of the press, and was not publicity crazy. During his tenure of command, the MQM split and its faction, MQM (H), emerged. This development provided opportunities to a secret organ of the state to fish in the troubled waters of Sindh. The army was accused of being partisan, and Sindh simmered with unrest. The army claimed to be a neutral party but a segment of the public felt to the contrary. Disturbances in Karachi and Hyderabad kept the troops engaged in internal security duties in the Province of Sindh. On 8 January 1993, General Asif died of a sudden, massive heart attack.

The selection of Asif's successor created a controversy. The president and the prime minister disagreed with each other on the panel of candidates and unfortunately, their differing views became public knowledge. Soon, however, better sense prevailed and they unanimously selected General Abdul Waheed Kakar who was then commanding a corps at Quetta. His command assignment coincided with an action-filled political climate in the country in which the government and the opposition expected the army chief to get involved. Waheed advised both to spare the military and allow it to attend to its professional work. This turned out to be a futile hope.

In the continuing political intrigues, the president and the prime minister fell apart, for reasons not pertinent to this narration, and the army was compelled into playing the role of intermediary. That both showed confidence in the army chief reflected his neutrality. This scenario came under public criticism. As if the tension between the head of state and the head of government was not enough, the Prime Minister, Mr Nawaz Sharif, started flexing muscles with the superior judiciary. In so doing, he converted his 'heavy parliamentary mandate' into a liability and a threat to real democracy. In a painful development, two vital pillars of the state—the executive and the judicial branches—were caught in a syndrome of confrontation. Once again, the military played a part behind the scenes, and the role played by it soon became public property.

On his retirement General Waheed was replaced by General Jahangir Karamat on 12 January 1996, as the army chief. Karamat steered a professional course but his time and effort were occasionally diverted attending to the problems created by the feuding non-military pillars of power. He was asked to use his good offices in the on-going tussle for supremacy between the Chief Justice and Prime Minister Nawaz Sharif. He counseled moderation to both. The political pendulum swung in the Prime Minister's favour when the Chief Justice was left with no option but to quit. Details of this tussle are discussed elsewhere in this book. The political hurdles cleared from his way, General Karamat became dispensable to the Prime Minister. General Karamat's publicly expressed recommendation for forming the National Security Council became the proverbial last straw. Prime Minister Nawaz Sharif expressed his unhappiness, Karamat took the hint and sought premature retirement. Nawaz was quick to oblige. General Jahangir Karamat was denied the courtesy of bidding a formal farewell to the army that he had commanded—a tradition developed over centuries.

Supremely confident, Nawaz Sharif rode high and took pride in weathering the political storms that blew around him. One after the other, he had successfully taken care of all the big-wigs who had either earned his displeasure or crossed his path. Those fallen included one president of Pakistan, one chief justice of Pakistan and four services chiefs. Additionally, the leader of the opposition in the parliament, Benazir Bhutto, had been convicted by the court and disqualified from holding public office for seven years. A pliable parliament and a docile federal cabinet placed Nawaz Sharif in an envious position that no other prime minister had enjoyed in Pakistan's history. Humble in words and impetuous in action, he scarcely consulted parliamentarians and cabinet colleagues and rarely met senior bureaucrats. He relied heavily on the advice of a selected few who were more personally loyal to him.

Politically, Prime Minister Nawaz Sharif was in an unassailable position. But his striking ability to destroy himself took the better of him. His inefficient associates, who had put him on the warpath with President Ghulam Ishaq Khan in his first term, and expedited the doom of his government in 1993 with the inappropriate remark he made in his address to the nation on the electronic media, 'I shall not take dictation' (from the President), once again helped to dig his political grave. On 12 October 1999, Nawaz Sharif, in an intrigue-filled drama, announced the retirement of the Chief of the Army Staff, General Pervez Musharraf and the promotion of promoted Lieutenant-General Ziauddin in his place. This was done at a time when Musharraf was returning home from an official tour of Sri Lanka. Nawaz Sharif ordered that the PIA commercial flight in which he was travelling alongwith 200 other passengers be prevented from landing in Pakistan. However, the army intervened, and the plane landed at Karachi with just seven minutes worth of fuel remaining. Nawaz Sharif was arrested, General Pervez Musharraf took over, and emergency was imposed in the country.

Intelligence Agencies and Politics

Pakistan has two federally controlled intelligence agencies. The Intelligence Bureau (IB) covers political intelligence and works under the head of the government. The IB draws its officers from the police department, and the provincial governments are usually reluctant to part with their better police officers for federal intelligence work. The IB works in conjunction with the Special Branches in all the provinces.

The Inter-Services Intelligence Directorate (ISI) is the second federally controlled intelligence agency. It largely covers external intelligence. Until 1975, the ISI was responsible to all the three services chiefs for counter-intelligence and strategic operational intelligence. In theory, it operated under the Joint Services Secretariat. However, in practice the ISI worked under the head of the government and maintained a close link with the Chief of the Army Staff on matters of professional intelligence.

The ISI draws its manpower from the three services on a *pro rata* basis and a bulk of its field manpower is recruited from the civil market. It is invariably commanded by a serving army officer. The only exception to this practice was during Prime Minister Benazir Bhutto's first government in 1989, when Lieutenant-General Shamsur Rehman Kallue, a retired general officer, was appointed DG ISI. He relinquished his assignment when the Benazir government was dismissed in 1990.

The tasks of the IB and ISI overlap to a degree, but in a democratic rule the dominant intelligence agency for political work is the IB. In practice, this position underwent a change during the 1958, 1969 and 1977 martial laws because the army chiefs-turned presidents had greater confidence in the professional ability of the ISI Directorate and were more comfortable in dealing with it.

In 1975, Prime Minister Zulfikar Ali Bhutto created a political cell in the ISI Directorate through an executive order and assigned it a role in the field of national and political intelligence. This act showed Bhutto's confidence in the ISI's professional competence but involved the organization in domestic politics, with long-term serious consequences. The successive governments after Bhutto including Ziaul Haq, did not change this arrangement, though some of them criticized Bhutto for involving the ISI Directorate in internal politics.

The intelligence agencies, established for the purpose of protecting the State against external aggression and internal subversion, were perverted to promote the personal interests of the head of the government. In the process, the institutions were debased and their personnel, selected on the basis of personal loyalty, abused their powers and resources to advance the interests of the rulers as well as their own.

The induction of Soviet military forces in Afghanistan, in December 1979, destabilized the region and caused a fundamental change in the geopolitical environment. Pakistan was seriously affected. The ISI Directorate became the channel for funneling covert military support to the Afghan freedom fighters from the US and from other countries and agencies. During the Zia era (1977-88) the Pakistan Army was not directly involved in the Afghan struggle, although it was generally aware of what was happening inside Afghanistan. Pakistan's Afghan policy was made by a select group and implemented by the ISI and the ministries concerned on the orders of General Zia. General Zia's death changed the situation. In early 1989, Prime Minister Benazir Bhutto requested President Ghulam Ishaq Khan to assume the role played by Zia in Afghanistan. Ishaq declined. She then tasked the Army Chief, General Mirza Aslam Beg, to coordinate the implementation of the Afghan policy, a task that was till then performed by the ISI. This involved the Pakistan Army in the Afghan war.

In 1990, the Benazir government was dismissed by President Ghulam Ishaq Khan and fresh elections were announced. Under General Beg's orders, the ISI pieced together an anti-PPP electoral alliance of some political parties. Such active politics on the part of serving general officers earned them, and the army, public criticism that tarnished the military's image.

The Election Cell working in the President's secretariat influenced Mr Younis Habib, of Habib Bank Limited, to 'donate' funds for the 'election intelligence' work during the 1990 elections. Promptly, a sum of Rs 140 million was deposited in the cover accounts of the DG ISI. Out of this amount, about Rs 6 million was doled out to various politicians for election related intelligence work, a euphemism for political corruption. The remaining amount (Rs 8 million) enriched the Special Funds of the ISI Directorate and its subsequent utilization remained undisclosed. President Ghulam Ishaq Khan, the Army Chief, General Mirza Aslam Beg and the Chief of Staff to the President, Lieutenant-General Syed Refaqat, were privy to the transactions and they became political puppeteers committing an act that was illegal, unethical, undemocratic and undignified.

Four years later, this hush-hush transaction became public and a case was initiated in the Supreme Court against General Beg by Air Marshal M. Asghar Khan (retired), for bringing 'the

Armed Forces of Pakistan into disrepute and (for being) guilty of undermining the discipline of the Armed Forces.' The case is pending in the court. Quick justice is not the hallmark of Pakistan's judicial system.

Extraneous Influencing Factors

Moral Decline

A distinguished statesman of enviable character, impeccable integrity and tremendous strength of conviction, Muhammad Ali Jinnah, the founder of Pakistan, gave his countrymen a triad slogan of Unity, Discipline and Faith and urged them to 'work, work and work' for making their motherland a model of democracy, good governance and prosperity. He practiced what he preached, and was held in high esteem even by his contemporary political critics who praised his qualities of character, honesty and probity in superlative terms. At the time of his death he left behind a will that gave generous donations out of his worldly assets to Sindh Madrassa, Karachi, Islamia College, Peshawar and Muslim University, Aligarh. This is an example of his love for knowledge. This enlightened visionary with high moral and intellectual integrity had converted a political dream into a reality.

Jinnah, the statesman, was ably assisted in his crusade for freedom, and the creation of Pakistan by a group of honourable politicians, who lacked his awe and authority, but were sincere and dedicated, scrupulously honest in public financial transactions and individually as well as collectively enjoyed a high reputation of moral integrity. This shining political constellation comprised of, to name a few, Mr Liaquat Ali Khan, Khawaja Nazimuddin, Mr Shahabuddin, Mr Nurul Amin, Mr I.I. Chundrigar, Sardar Abdur Rab Nishtar, Mr Abdul Qayyum Khan, Khan of Mamdot, Mr M. M. K. Daultana, Mr Firoz Khan Noon, Mr Yusuf Abdullah Haroon, Mr Muhammad Ayub Khurro and Qazi Issa. To the misfortune of her people, the country failed to replace such respected luminaries with a younger group of enlightened political leadership that could speak with conviction and pride from a high moral pedestal. Pakistan's political poverty started showing soon after the exit of its top echelon leaders from the national scene.

The evacuee property left behind in Pakistan by the Hindu and Sikh population that had migrated to India during the communal riots in 1947 became a source of corruption in the country. This property, comprising houses, shops and land, was allotted to the refugees who had migrated from India to Pakistan. The allotment procedure, fair on face value, was circumvented by vested interests to get undue personal gains. The claimants were required to provide documentary evidence of the property left behind by them in India. Those doing so had their claims settled. Such people were few in number. Others claimed that their property documents had either been burnt in disturbances or lost in transit or left behind in India. In such cases, a verification process evolved that was often misused. One heard instances of some genuine claimants suffering because of the fraudulent tactics adopted by others. Some worldly wise people managed to acquire evacuee property by hoodwinking the law. This inflicted an invisible but severe blow to the country.

The Ayub government promulgated the Elective Bodies (Disqualification) Ordinance 1959 (EBDO) under which some politicians were charged with misuse of power and corruption. Many of them accepted the offer of retirement from public life for a number of years fixed under the law instead of contesting the charges framed against them in a court of law. The Yahya government (1969-71) repeated a somewhat similar process in which 303 politicians and civil servants were proceeded against on charges of corruption and for living beyond their known sources of income. This reflected that a process of moral decay had set in and the disease was spreading. The Bhutto administration (1972-77) took an arbitrary step. A very large number of bureaucrats was, unceremoniously and without prior notice, suddenly dismissed or retired under Martial Law Regulation 114. A few years later, some bureaucrats were also retired during the Zia government (1977-85). Additionally, a few politicians were debarred from holding public office for a given number of years.

Such negative disciplinary and punitive measures failed to check the menace of corruption and misuse of authority. Many of those disqualified from holding public office for some years resumed their nefarious practice with a vengeance to speedily compensate for the lost time. The Junejo government (1985-88) enjoyed a healthy reputation. But thereafter, during the period 1988-99, corruption and non-return of public-sector bank loans became a widespread practice that reached alarming proportions. Quaid-i-Azam's Pakistan faced a crisis in political leadership.

While the allegations of corruption and amassing wealth by unfair means were largely against the politicians and bureaucrats, some accusing fingers were also raised against the military. President Ayub's decision of inducting his sons into politics was criticized. Public disapproval increased against Ayub Khan when the financial prosperity of his young children became obvious. To his credit, General Yahya Khan avoided this temptation. No one accused him or his children of financial wheeling-dealing. During the Zia era also, some allegations were made against senior military officers. Even after Zia's death, some senior military officers and the scions of others continued their extravagant lifestyle unhampered.

Military Sensitivity

Macaulay writes in his poem 'Horatius':

> *And how can man die better*
> *Than facing fearful odds,*
> *For the ashes of his fathers*
> *And the temples of his gods.*

In combat, a soldier prefers death over defeat. To him no sacrifice is too great for defending territorial integrity and preserving the dignity and honour of his motherland. The impulse that motivates him to enter the valley of death is painstakingly instilled by military training. Character, knowledge and application—the hallmarks of military leadership—chisel raw soldiers into professional and disciplined individuals with confidence and *esprit de corps.*

The military is an apolitical organization with a national outlook. It is voiceless till its advice is sought on professional issues. In a democratic dispensation its interests are defended, inside the parliament and outside it, by the government and the opposition, alike. Being a national asset, the military belongs to both. Its pride, image and high morale serve the national interest. They are accountable and open to fair and constructive criticism but they must not be dragged into political wheeling-dealing. In our context, national unity and the cohesiveness of the armed forces are inseparable entities. A disunited country compromises its military's effectiveness in safeguarding its territorial integrity. Likewise, a divided or politicized defence effort becomes a liability to the State.

When in power, some of Pakistan's political rulers were less than circumspect in military matters and their acts created negative implications for the country, for the military and also for themselves. These incidents, minor on face value, touched military sensitivity and were often perceived by it to be directed against its unity of command and public image. Some illustrations:

In December 1971, Mr Bhutto took charge of Pakistan with East Pakistan amputated and the military humbled. He seized this opportunity as a defining moment to establish himself as a national hero and a populist leader. His agenda included disciplining the armed forces. He took steps to improve the national defence effort but also ridiculed and humiliated the army as a matter of state policy. To quote some instances, the military brass was retired in Bhutto's inaugural address on the electronic media; a film on the surrender ceremony at Dhaka was telecast on the plea that it was necessary 'to tell the truth' and barely three months later, the army chief, General Gul Hassan Khan, was prematurely retired. This was Bhutto's style of exerting authority and proving that he was the boss. There was no need for this public display of anger. He was the accepted leader of all, military included.

In 1988, Ms Benazir Bhutto became not only the first female prime minister of Pakistan, but also the youngest and most inexperienced. She proved herself to be a disaster for the country. Working with political flexibility, she opened too many fronts against her government and showed gross deficiency in crisis-management ability. Benazir failed to comprehend that statecraft was far more than playing with the sentiments of unsuspecting people. President Ghulam Ishaq Khan told me in those days, '*Mohtarma bahut jhoot bolti hain*' (The [Prime Minister] is a big liar).

Benazir inherited the immediate post Geneva Accord Afghanistan and found it an arduous task to handle. On their part, the Afghan leaders desired Pakistan's support but faced a gender problem. They were ill at ease in dealing with a woman politician. Pakistan's Afghan policy was relegated to lower levels, and the army started overseeing developments in Afghanistan. In the process, Pakistan's Afghan policy lost consistency and direction.

In June 1989, Prime Minister Benazir Bhutto appointed retired Lieutenant-General Shamsur Rahman Kallue as Director General Intelligence, a military assignment, without consulting the army chief. This was a violation of the norm. Her act was premeditated. The official announcement of the appointment was timed to coincide with the absence of Benazir who had just left for a visit to Turkey. This was the first time when a retired general officer was appointed to command the prestigious ISI Directorate. This change and the arrogant style of its implementation created mistrust between the government and the army. General Beg quietly strengthened the Military Intelligence Directorate within GHQ and started ignoring the ISI Directorate in important matters. This was a national loss and those short-sighted people who advised Benazir to take this measure harmed the country, the institution and Benazir herself.

On Benazir Bhutto's desire one particular brigadier was appointed as her military secretary. She had this officer, previously superseded by the Army Selection Board, promoted to the rank of major-general. This was against the prescribed rules. The Prime Minister's interference in the internal functioning of the officers promotion system was resented by the army.

Benazir's political expediency also came in the way of administering military justice. During the Zia era, one army officer absconded from duty and showed up in London publicly claiming himself to be in self exile. His act, causing embarrassment to the government, earned him the sympathy of the Pakistan Peoples Party. A decade later, with the PPP back in power, this officer decided to return home but he apprehended arrest by the military authorities. He approached Benazir for help who in turn asked the army chief to withdraw the case against the absconding officer. The army chief advised the prime minister to let the law take its normal course. The officer returned home. He was arrested, tried in a military court, convicted and later his sentence was commuted by the army chief.

After the dismissal of Benazir Bhutto's government, Mr Nawaz Sharif became prime minister amidst great public hopes and expectations. In March 1992, Prime Minister Nawaz Sharif told the army chief, General Asif Nawaz, that he desired to make a top level change in the ISI. Asif responded that he would send a panel of names for final selection by the government. 'There is no need for this', said Nawaz Sharif, adding, 'I have a person in mind. Appoint Lieutenant-General Javed Nasir.' A stunned Asif did not wish to argue on the choice. He later narrated this conversation to all the corps commanders who criticized the selection for cogent reasons, but by then Javed Nasir was already in the saddle.

Brigadier Imtiaz Ahmed, serving in the ISI Directorate, became a controversial personality. On the recommendation of GHQ he was retired from military service. The Nawaz Sharif government showed a pro-Imtiaz bias and in December 1990, he was re-employed in the coveted assignment of Director Intelligence Bureau. The military felt aggrieved and resented the favour shown to the retired officer. The officer was selected without consulting GHQ and the appointment given to him raised many eyebrows.

General Asif Nawaz died of cardiac failure on 8 January 1993. Months later his wife publicly alleged that Asif had been poisoned. The print media speculated that she was instigated by an opposition party to put the government under pressure. On the request of Mrs Asif Nawaz, the body of Asif was exhumed and medical authorities had a chemical examination conducted by a team of foreign experts of her choice. Falsehood could not endure as nothing objectionable was detected. The issue ended but not without exposing the attempts of political parties to drag the military into their internal political squabbles.

In October 1998, Prime Minister Nawaz Sharif, appointed Lieutenant-General Zia-ud-Din as head of the ISI Directorate without consulting the army chief. That the nomination was for reasons other than professional, became apparent when on 12 October 1999, the Army Chief, General Pervez Musharraf, was suddenly retired and replaced by General Zia-ud-Din. This attempt to divide the army failed but not without a heavy price. Once again the country was placed under military rule.

In the decade 1988-1999 major political parties made efforts to win over the loyalties of senior military officers by offering incentives and job opportunities to them. Such subtle moves were aimed at politicizing the military and in some cases creating a division within its ranks. In many cases military discipline and service allegiance came in the way. Notwithstanding this, minor inroads were made, here and there, particularly in the army and a few senior officers earned the label of being pro this or that party. For example, Lieutenant-General Farrukh Khan, the president's preferred choice to become the army chief in 1993, was denied promotion because he was not politically acceptable to the prime minister. The allegations against this competent and apolitical general-officer were based on some misunderstanding but he suffered all the same.

Such incidents adversely affected the military and lowered their morale. They also reflected the immaturity of political parties that showed lack of vision in politicizing the defenders of the country.

Blossoming Bureaucracy

The British *Raj* gave to the subcontinent a largely honest, fairly efficient and visibly stiff-necked cadre of civil servants excelling in professionalism and code of conduct. Corruption existed in the lower tiers of the administration but was trivial in scope and petty in volume. Instances of corruption and misconduct against senior bureaucrats were rare. Conspicuous, though, was the behaviour of the anglicized Indian civil servants who arrogated to themselves a superior status as compared to the 'uncivilized' native public they dealt with. The colonial aura had been painstakingly built on the edifice of the 'superiority' of the ruling elite over the public. The gulf between the rulers and the ruled was awesome and wide and the system was tailor-made to portray the dominance of Imperial rule. Pakistan inherited a number of such civil servants in central and provincial governments.

Since the politicians lacked administrative experience, some bureaucrats were inducted into lucrative posts and they dominated the national political scene for many years. These bureaucrats-turned politicians included luminaries like Mr Ghulam Mohammad, Chaudhri Muhammad Ali and Colonel Iskandar Mirza.

In subsequent years and decades many more civil servants played politics, some directly but largely indirectly, and became controversial. Mr Aziz Ahmed, Mr Altaf Gauhar, Mr Saied Ahmad Khan, Mr Masood Mahmud, Rao Abdul Rashid, Mr Waqar Ahmad, Mr Agha Shahi, Mr Ghulam Ishaq Khan, Mr A.G.N. Qazi, Mr Roedad Khan, Mr Ijlal Haider Zaidi, Mr Sartaj Aziz, Dr Mahboob-ul-Haq, Mr V. A. Jafri, Mr Salman Farooqi, Mr Ahmad Sadiq, Mr S. K. Mahmood, Mr Khalid Ahmad Kharal, Mr Anwar Zahid and Mr Saeed Mehdi are notable examples. The more fertile of these dignitaries blossomed in their careers, wielded extensive powers, excelled in personal loyalty and showed great flexibility in their conduct and behaviour. The lucky ones among them got adequately compensated for their services or for sycophancy rendered to the government in power, and achieved dizzy heights.

The bureaucrats holding important posts and high profile assignments came in contact with the ruling elite. While some confined themselves to the professional field, others showed political flair and caught the eyes of the rulers. This helped the bureaucrats to further tighten their grip over the levers of governance and wield authority.

Bureaucracy is omnipotent and omnipresent in Pakistan. Its hold on administration is so firm and perennial that nothing moves without its approval. Governments come and go but the real and hidden power lies in the Rules of Business expertly tailored by the bureaucrats with a stamp of political approval affixed on them.

Extensive discretionary powers are held by many public servants and ministers. These are interpreted selectively. For example, many governments have announced a 'One-Window Operation' to promote the growth of industry in the country. This dream remains a distant target. The power-wielding departments do not close the avenues of corruption on which they thrive. Instead, those trying to break this vicious circle are accused of violating the 'biblical' procedure for 'ulterior motives.' Such a corruption-ridden system frightens away foreign investors from Pakistan.

The bureaucrats complain that they lack job security which is exploited by their political masters to extract undue favours and slanted decisions from them. Those who succumb to the pressure protect their future and become party loyalists.

Barring exceptions, a great majority of civil servants normally resist undue political pressure exerted on them by the party in power, but in some cases they become willing instruments in the hands of favour-seeking power barons. Many civil servants faced punishments under different administrations on charges of corruption, misuse of authority and possessing wealth beyond their known sources of income. The respect and honour that civil servants once enjoyed stood substantially eroded.

Four bureaucrats—Ghulam Mohammad, Iskandar Mirza, Ghulam Ishaq Khan and Farooq Ahmad Leghari—became Heads of State. They had distinguished careers. Ghulam Mohammad was, 'a conservative financier, a strong believer in private enterprise and ruthless in keeping down expenditure.'[24] Iskandar Mirza, a military officer-turned civil servant, was a distinguished administrator. Ghulam Ishaq Khan, a down-to-earth civil servant, was renowned for his integrity, hard work, phenomenal memory and stubbornness. Farooq Leghari, a feudal lord-turned-bureaucrat-turned politician started with a clean reputation but ended up with obloquy. All the four individuals made serious errors in judgement as Heads of State and earned for themselves unenvious reputations in history. The reasons for their failure were many. Perhaps, while their bureaucratic backgrounds had trained them to synthesize problems, produce papers on viable options and prepare lucidly written summaries, the more complex high level decision-making tasks were usually performed by others. Yet another possibility could be that they chose weak advisers who misjudged events and got their bosses inextricably involved in political cobwebs. However, it may be said that if the bureaucrats failed Pakistan, so did the politicians and generals.

Judicial Pacifism

The executive, parliament and judiciary are the three pillars of a democratic state. In Pakistan, the executive branch, taking advantage of the Official Secrets Act, Law of Libel and other coercive instruments of state, has traditionally dominated the other two. The second pillar of the state—parliament—meekly claims undefined privileges, and has generally looked towards the government for a lead. The Committee System, government-opposition relationship and the law-making performance of Parliament are not anything to boast about. Most governments have largely ruled through ordinances promulgated at their behest by the president.

The judiciary, the third pillar of the state, has occasionally brandished the whip of contempt but has usually been a docile partner, playing a low key role in judicial matters. Subordinate courts have been only half-free. While some magistrates employed on executive duties go by the mood of the government in power, others conduct their judicial functions with a sense of responsibility. The performance of the lower judiciary has been neither envious nor free from allegations of corruption and criticism. The 1973 Constitution had fixed a date for the total separation of the judiciary from the executive branch. This was not implemented on various pretexts till 1996.

Some judgments given by the higher judiciary on important constitutional matters were controversial and faced severe criticism. Upholding the October 1954 dismissal of the central government by Governor-General Ghulam Mohammad by the Federal Court is one example. So was the judgment under which the abrogation of the constitution in 1958 was declared legitimate by the court.

General Yahya was belatedly declared 'usurper' by the Supreme Court after his retirement from service, however, the martial law of General Ziaul Haq in 1977 was held valid by the Supreme Court.

Pakistan's constitutional journey might have been smoother if her superior judiciary had interpreted the constitution differently. Political streaks running in judicial judgments on vital constitutional issues have seriously affected Pakistan's constitutional history.

Martial laws were not the only constitutional headaches faced by the country. Three successive Presidents since 1985—Zia, Ishaq and Leghari—used their discretionary powers under Article 58(2)(b) on four occasions—1988, 1990, 1993 and 1996—to dismiss four Prime Ministers—Junejo, Benazir, Nawaz Sharif and Benazir again. This started a debate on whether an elected government could be prematurely dismissed under the law. One constitutional expert, Khalid M. Ishaq, writes, 'It is often claimed that whatever mistakes an elected government makes and whatever its other forms of misconduct, it should be allowed to complete its term. This is an absolutely spurious claim. In a democracy no individual has a birthright to rule. Nor has any person or group a right to public trust. They get power to take decisions in the public interest; vesting of power is justified only so long as their decisions are fair.'[25]

Since 1996, Pakistan's higher judiciary has adopted an assertive mood. Judicial activism has substantially replaced judicial pacifism. The Benazir government provided justification. This is discussed in a separate chapter.

Military Performance

Pakistan inherited the British tradition in which the military forces did not engage in active politics. And yet, barely eleven years after independence, the Pakistani military imposed martial law and has subsequently repeated this act more than once. The reasons for this phenomenon are many. The more important ones are narrated below.

Rapid Promotions

The joy of independence brought a bonanza of promotions. A few junior officers got high military assignments at a rapid pace. The quick promotions denied these officers progressive professional grooming at successive levels in higher command. One case illustrates the point. Ayub Khan, a colonel in 1947, became a four-star general in January 1951 commanding the Pakistan Army. Such a rapid rise in the professional ladder is rare in peacetime military history.

There was a reason for it. As a matter of colonial policy, initially the Indian military units had only British officers posted in them. The process of inducting Indian officers into the Indian Army started in 1932, when the first Indian cadets joined the Indian Military Academy. This included a very small number of Muslim cadets, a trend that persisted in the subsequent courses as well. Some of these officers acquired combat experience during World War II but they were mostly from the lower ranks.

The bulk of promotions on independence went to those who had maximum service to their credit in 1947. By and large, in promotion matters seniority took precedence over other considerations.

Statistics tell the story. Officers form the backbone of an army. The officer rank structure in 1947 was so unbalanced that out of 2,310 available officers, only 154 officers held pre-war regular commissions. Another 400 were post-war regulars. The remaining army officers, that constituted the biggest chunk, held emergency commissions and generally lacked command experience. There was a pronounced shortage of staff-trained officers in the higher ranks. The Pakistan Army inherited only one major-general, two brigadiers and six colonels in 1947.

Teething Difficulties

The dawn of independence saw the Pakistan Army in a skeleton form. Only 40 per cent of its share of 150,000 personnel was physically located in the territory of the new state. The balance was either still in India or serving abroad in distant locations, Japan, Hong Kong, South East Asia, West Asia and North Africa. The state of Pakistan's military hardware, equipment and stores was deplorable. The country had to accommodate, and rehabilitate eight million refugees who migrated from India. The army actively participated in the challenging task of their resettlement with distinction and élan. Fighting erupted in the disputed State of Jammu and Kashmir. It compounded Pakistan's national and military worries. Added to this was the consistently negative role played by India in its attempts to suffocate or cripple Pakistan at birth. The army was thus involved from day-one not only in its much needed professional reorganization process and defence commitments but also in civil tasks assigned to it by the government. Its role in the national consolidation effort was appreciated by the public and it became a force to contend with.

Decline in Discipline

'Swift promotions from junior to senior ranks' raised 'expectations' and 'perfectly sensible people, brigadiers and generals, would go about bemoaning their lot. Each one of them was a Bonaparte, albeit an unhappy one.'[26] So lamented Ayub Khan.

Military culture is built on a moral foundation and indiscipline erodes the base. An incident in 1951 started this process. Some 'young Turks'[27] getting impatient of the government's performance, showed their frustration. They became critical of the government for doing too little too late in handling matters of state in general, and in respect of the on-going operations in Kashmir in particular. Emotions got the better of Major-General Akbar Khan, Brigadier Siddique Khan, Colonel Arbab Niaz etc. and they got involved in what came to be called the Rawalpindi Conspiracy case. A well-known poet, Faiz Ahmad Faiz, editor of a leading English language daily of Lahore was also one of the conspirators. These persons were tried in a special tribunal. On conviction they received sentences of imprisonment. This unprofessional indulgence and lenient punishments awarded to them set an unhealthy precedent. Harsh punishments awarded in this first case might have imposed greater caution on those who subsequently imposed supra-constitutional rules.

Political Exposure

Military involvement in civil affairs became transparently evident when the Army Chief, General Ayub Khan was made the federal minister for defence in 1954. The cabinet post gave him a taste of politics and a chance to judge the weakness of the civilian leaders from an internal vantage point. It set a process in motion that repeatedly sucked the military into a political quagmire.

Extensions in Service

A senior military commander, in a democratic polity, transfers the baton of his assignment to the next selected incumbent at the end of his fixed tenure. This system promotes the supremacy of civilian government and rejects the myth of indispensability of the serving officers. This norm was violated. The tenures of the services chiefs were generously extended, presumably to provide stability in the senior rank structure. Such extensions had their ill-effects and promotions were denied down the ladder.

Besides, prolonged assignments generated non-professional ambitions in the minds of favoured commanders.

The Commander-in-Chief had a term of four years. The first Pakistani incumbent, General Ayub Khan, served in this post for seven and a half years. He placed the country under martial law. General Muhammad Musa, the second Army Chief, superseded two professionally respected Sandhurst trained lieutenant-generals, Sher Ali Khan and M.A. Latif—who both sought and got premature retirements. Musa served in this appointment for eight years. Soon after his elevation to the four-star rank, General Musa developed a personality clash with his chief of staff, Lieutenant-General Habibullah Khan. Ayub retired the latter. Musa remained steadfastly loyal to Ayub and had blind faith in his ability to guide the destiny of Pakistan. With military support fully assured by Musa, his patron and benefactor, Ayub, had a field day to play politics and rule Pakistan. An Army commander other than Musa might have acted more firmly and perhaps averted the 1965 war with India. The third Army Chief, General Yahya Khan, left behind a shrunken country, a bewildered nation and an army labelled with the stigma of defeat.

The next Army Chief, General Gul Hassan Khan, had a short tenure of only three months. A personality clash between him and Prime Minister Z. A. Bhutto resulted in his premature retirement. Gul Hassan was too firm a person to co-exist with Bhutto despite their personal friendship. The new incumbent, General Tikka Khan, was a loyal and down-to-earth person blessed with a phenomenal memory and enviable perseverance. Notwithstanding these sterling qualities, he was not known as an original military strategist with vision and imagination who could inject innovation into military doctrines, concepts and philosophy. Tikka Khan joined Bhutto's PPP after his retirement from the army. General Ziaul Haq, the next army top brass, pushed Bhutto out of power in 1977 through a *coup de état* and remained the army chief throughout his unprecedented rule of eleven years. Similarly, some naval chiefs and air chiefs were also given extensions in service. No army chief following Zia received an extension in service.

The grant of extensions to the army chiefs was a political blunder. The country might not have faced the pain of the 1958 martial law had General Ayub Khan been retired from military service in 1955 after completing his full term of four years as prescribed. The history of the country might have then followed a different course.

Political Favours

Some politicians cultivated military officers as their friends with petty favours like hunting, bird shooting and invitation to parties etc. This was their investment for the future. Some military extroverts accepting such invitations fell prey to temptations and such friendships matured with time. Their number was small but the seeds planted had serious, long-term consequences. Such political inroads made in the defence services were detrimental to military discipline.

Aid to Civil Power

The constitution permits the deployment of troops in aid to civil power on the demand of the government of the day. In practice such tasks are best given to soldiers as a last resort when other police and para-military forces have failed to rectify the situation. In Pakistan, army troops have been deployed extensively, at times for years at a stretch, on internal security duties. They were thus kept away from their primary task.

Martial Law and the Judiciary

In theory, martial law is an antithesis of the judicial system. Where one is present the other is absent. However, although it may appear paradoxical, in practice, military governments in the country usually co-existed with the higher judiciary reasonably well. Their mutual relationship was neither cozy nor antagonistic and both acknowledged the ground realities while functioning in their respective fields. The Supreme Court and High Courts continued to function during martial law and exercised the right of judicial review of all military trials. The lower civil courts also functioned as usual. Offenses that could be tried in military courts were specified in law. The system caused occasional pinpricks to both sides but such rough edges were normally amicably smoothened through bilateral dialogue.

At times, difficulties arose and unrest surfaced here and there between the judicial and executive branches but the predicament faced by both sides was mutually understood and the government took suitable damage control measures to diffuse tension. The country needed speedy justice to make its impact felt. Had normal laws been adequately and effectively implemented, Pakistan might have been spared the agony of being placed under supra-constitutional rules.

Gains and Losses

Unless declared otherwise by the courts, the martial law governments were legal but undemocratic. The martial law administrations had deliberately introduced a system of checks and balances to prevent administrative excesses. For example, every martial law initially imposed press censorship that was progressively liberalised and eventually lifted. The private sector print media was fairly vocal, almost critical, of government policies and its criticism was tolerated by the administration. But journalism had its own woes. Many journalists developed personal relationships with their subjects—politicians, bureaucrats and businessmen—for worldly reasons. The electronic media dutifully supported government policies because it had and still remains under state control since 1947.

Its fairness to all governments is reflected by the reality that in the final analysis it destroyed them all through over projection.

Political freedom was curtailed. Initially the political parties were either banned or curbs were imposed on their functioning. Gradually restrictions were removed and political campaigning was permitted before elections were held.

The country made economic progress particularly during the Ayub era. Islamabad emerged as the permanent capital. The Karakoram Highway (KKH) constructed at the time linked Pakistan and China by road. Industrial growth took a giant leap. Defence preparedness improved and all the three military services were reorganised. Ayub's achievements in foreign affairs included the conclusion of a border agreement with China and signing of the Indus Basin Water Treaty with India under the good offices of the World Bank. The latter set a precedence for third party involvement in settling bilateral disputes with India.

The Zia rule witnessed a decade of peace in South Asia despite the Afghanistan war, Soviet threats and repeated provocation from India. Normalization of Indo-Pakistan relations is a story of missed opportunities—some due to errors of judgement in Islamabad and others by New Delhi's consistent arrogance. It is a rebuke to their political sagacity that India and Pakistan remain prisoners of their geography. The type of statesmanship needed by this region has been conspicuous by its absence.

Despite serious technological barriers created and the intense pressures exerted by the US and its strategic allies, the Pakistan government relentlessly persisted with Pakistan's nuclear programme started many years earlier and gave it a quantum jump against monumental odds. What was demonstrated on 28 May 1998, in the Chaghai hills in Balochistan was an example of what and how a determined nation can achieve miracles in a highly complex field despite intense external pressures.

The withdrawal of Soviet forces from Afghanistan was a unique achievement that shall be remembered in history. General Zia played a leading role in achieving this significant success. Never before had Soviet defence forces withdrawn so tamely from a country occupied by them. The strategic initiatives taken

by his government were timely, well conceived and skilfully
implemented. Their full import has not yet been impartially
evaluated primarily because of the internal polarization in
Pakistan and the prevailing prejudice against a military ruler.
Successive martial laws eroded State institutions from within.
They retarded the growth of democracy and democratic
traditions. Already weak in 1947, they failed to develop and
mature. Pakistan's political system promoted cults in political
parties and diluted their democratic culture. The constitutional
crises caused in the country might have been avoided had the
political parties been robust, democratic and accountable under
an institutionalized system of checks and balances.

Institutions Weakened

A democratic order does not guarantee good government. Moral,
material and intellectual corruption is not an uncommon
phenomenon in democratic societies. Despite this drawback, a
democratic dispensation is superior to military rule because it
has an in-built and institutionalized process of accountability. A
representative government is perceived to function on the
concept of collective wisdom and joint responsibility, unlike
martial law which is a one man rule.

Accountability promotes progress. Parliamentary debate on
the defence budget and the question hour in legislatures on
defence related matters promote the supremacy of civil rule and
identify errors of omission and commission. In the absence of a
fully functional democratic institution, the military became
excessively sensitive to criticism on defence matters. It also
resented the slow decision making process in a civilian-
dominated political system and insisted that decisions on
defence-related issues should always be taken on terms
acceptable to them.

National Psyche

A democratic order needs patience and perseverance, qualities that are scarce in Pakistan. Here political culture is debased by polarization, political instability and politics without principles. The feudal gentry preach democracy in public but in private plead that the military is a panacea for all the country's problems. The army is encouraged and often provoked to intervene in political issues. The wily political pundits wish the military to clear up the muck created by them and return to its barracks at the time of their choice. They ignore the fact that the growth of democracy is a time consuming process. They would help the country better if they cultivated political patience.

On balance, military indulgence in national affairs weakened not only the country and the political system but also the military itself. Pakistan's national security demanded a full-time commitment on the part of the military services. The additional burden of administering the country under martial law taxed their already heavy professional work schedule. In the process military work frequently suffered. They were blamed for what they did and also for what they did not do.

The Military's Positive Contribution

Military performance during natural calamities and national crises has earned the respect of the people. The military has provided security, medical assistance, transportation facilities and humanitarian aid to eight millions refugees that migrated to Pakistan in 1947. Its disaster relief operations in adversities like floods, earthquakes, anti-wild boar operations, droughts and other such calamities are timely and effective. So, also is its performance on tasks like census work, election duties and keeping all essential services operative during periods of labour strikes.

The military has silently acted as a harbinger of national integration. Its officers are drawn on a competitive, country-wide

basis that promotes efficiency and national cohesion. The rank
and file of the three defence services are recruited from all parts
of the country. The military restored law and order at the request
of the government in Kalat (1958), Bajaur, Balochistan (1973-78),
Swat, twice in Sindh during the MRD agitation (1983-85) and
the MQM agitation (1990-97), and assisted in anti-drug operations
in the Tribal Belt. Additionally, it detected and dealt with the
Al-Zulfikar Organization (1981-88) and the RAW-aided London
Plan (1984).

Pakistani military contingents employed in the United Nations
peace-keeping and peace-enforcing operations in hot spots,
around the globe—Angola, Bosnia, Kampuchea, Congo, Eastern
Slavonia, Georgia, Haiti, Indonesia, Kuwait, Liberia, Namibia,
Rwanda, Sinai, Somalia, Western Slavonia and Yemen—
acquitted themselves with credit. Their performance was of
international standards. Their contribution in achieving peace
and maintaining an enviable standard of discipline under difficult
working conditions earned them global respect.

The defence services also participated in the national
development efforts by building roads, airfields, dams, canals
and power plants worth Rs 35 billion approximately. Their
contribution in the national social sector included running
schools, colleges, hospitals, and participating in the national
afforestation efforts.

Military contribution in the fields of industry and welfare is
not insignificant. Fauji Foundation, the Army Welfare Trust,
Shaheen Foundation and Behriya Foundation 'contribute more
than two per cent to national GNP annually'[28] through taxes.

Military Influence

In a democratic dispensation, military advice on professional
matters is given to the civilian government when asked for.
Decisions taken by the government are then implemented by
civil and military agencies to the best of their abilities.

Generally, this system worked reasonably well in Pakistan but, occasionally, with a sense of unease on both sides.

Political supremacy in the country got eroded, among other factors, by the delay in framing a constitution and its implementation; frailty of the judiciary; meekness of legislatures; weaknesses in the Political Parties Act; and prolonged domination of national politics by feudal bigwigs. The low literacy rate in the country meant a lack of public awareness about people's rights and obligations and the distinction between them. Politics turned into a business where self-service took precedence over serving the people and those preaching ethics were laughed at. Good governance became a dream. The accountability process either did not exist or it was sporadic and one-sided. The democratic political culture thus became fragile.

A couple of dozen feudal families dominate major political parties and legislatures. They impede progress and change. Irrespective of their political divide, the members of Parliament and provincial assemblies normally act in unison when it comes to protecting their own powers, privileges and perks. They oppose reforms that may curtail their influence and control in rural areas where more than 70 per cent of their voting population lives. Successive governments have failed to weaken the feudal influence on power.

Moral Decline

The media is not free from misinformation planted by the government and the opposition, and neither is it an innocent agent in this game itself. This erodes public confidence in the political system and the media. Such factors, besides others like corruption, have tarnished society and degraded human conduct and behaviour.

Impartial Bureaucracy

Good governance needs an efficient and impartial bureaucratic cadre to inspire public confidence. A section of Pakistan's bureaucracy has been politicized by the various governments in power which has caused great damage.

Summary

Ironically, martial law was first introduced in Pakistan by an elected civilian government in 1953. A heavier axe was used in 1958 when President Ayub upturned the civilian government and announced to the quarreling politicians 'enough is enough. Out you go. Henceforth, I control the national political centre stage'. Whether Ayub and those army chiefs who took charge of the country later, were legally and morally justified in making such announcements is a matter for the historians to judge. The military rulers claimed that they intervened to prevent 'the disintegration of Pakistan.' They succeeded because they held the guns. Napoleon Bonaparte once said, 'He who saves the nation violates no law.' The vital question is, did the military rulers save the nation or put it on a different course for their own reasons?

It is a historic reality that the military rule imposed by Ayub Khan, Yahya Khan, Ziaul Haq and Pervez Musharraf was initially welcomed by a vast majority of the public who were frustrated with the political intrigues that had polluted politics on every occasion. Nevertheless, public reaction gradually turned against the military dictators when the duration of their governments exceeded reasonable limits.

Further, on all four occasions, the military take-over was bloodless, peaceful and, by and large, benign in nature—to whatever extent martial law rule can be benign.

Also, except on one occasion, political activity was initially banned by the military governments. These restrictions were later lifted and political parties were permitted to perform their political work and participate in the elections when held. The Zia government, however, held the elections on a non-party basis.

It is a fact that Ayub, Yahya and Zia showed a preference for a presidential form of government. There could be three reasons for this. One, they did not wish to reinforce failure by persisting with a system that had failed before. Two, the presidential system removes one major source of corruption—it denies executive appointments to power-seeking parliamentarians. Besides, the head of government can serve for his/her fixed tenure without worrying about gratifying the parliamentarians.

It must be kept in mind that the military *coups* succeeded because the planners were themselves in command of the Pakistan Army and had accurately predicted the sequence of events and public reaction to their take-over. Their intelligence was perfect. So also were the timings of their intervention. The secrecy of the plans were maintained, and the ousted governments failed to anticipate or prevent the military steamroller from its operation.

The Pakistan Army, a disciplined professional force, has been ably led and all ranks have reposed confidence in the judgement and skill of their army chiefs. In return, the army chiefs have led a well-knit and united military team and taken their senior formation commanders into confidence on their impending plans. Their trust has always been honoured.

As against this phenomenon, all *coup* attempts or acts of indiscipline at the lower military levels have failed. The leakage always came from within the establishment. The Rawalpindi Conspiracy case (1951), the Attock Conspiracy case (1972), attempts by Tajammal Hussain (1976) and (1981), and the Zaheer-ul-Islam Abbasi case (1996) are examples. This indicates that the Pakistan Army obeys the Chief of the Army Staff, follows his decisions in letter and spirit and exposes those who try to undermine military command and national unity.

Finally, Pakistan demands an impartial postmortem of its past at the academic, professional and public levels to enable it to record its history and to evaluate the performance of its history makers. The performance of its leaders might be wanting in some fields, but in many others their achievements have been commendable. It is also important to remember that, but for the artificial hurdles created by foreign vested interests, Pakistan's journey to democracy and economic prosperity might have been less arduous.

NOTES

1. The Partition of the Punjab in 1947, (privately distributed paper).
2. Transfer of Power 1942-47, Vol. X, no. 371.
3. H.M. Seervai, *Partition of India: Legend and Reality*, Emmenem Publications, Bombay, India, 1989, p. 190.
4. Alastair Lamb, *Kashmir—A Disputed Legacy*, Oxford University Press, Karachi, Pakistan, 1942, p. 101.
5. Andrew Roberts, *Eminent Churchillians*, Weidenfeld and Nicolson, The Orion Publishing Group, London, 1994, pp. 100-101.
6. Dr H.L. Saxena, quoted by Alastair Lamb. Ibid., p. 17.
7. Dr Inayatullah, 'Fifty Years of Democracy', *Dawn*, Karachi, 12 April 1997.
8. Mohammad Ayub Khan, *Friends not Masters*, Oxford University Press, Karachi, Pakistan, 1967, p. 246.
9. General K. M. Arif, *Working with Zia*, Oxford University Press, Karachi, Pakistan, 1995, p. 93.
10. *Dawn*, Karachi, 13 April 1997.
11. Ibid.
12. Javed Hussain, 'Anatomy of the Crisis Syndrome', *Dawn*, 15 May 1997.
13. K. K. Aziz, *Party Politics in Pakistan 1947-1958*, National Commission on Historical and Cultural Research, Islamabad, 1976, p. 228.
14. Chaudhri Muhammad Ali, *The Emergence of Pakistan*, Wajidalis, Lahore, Pakistan, p. 48.
15. Ibid., p. 29.
16. K.K. Aziz, *Party Politics in Pakistan 1947-1958*, p. 227.
17. Chaudhri Muhammad Ali, *The Emergence of Pakistan*, p. 366.
18. K.K. Aziz, *Party Politics in Pakistan*, National Commission on Historical and Cultural Research, Islamabad, 1976, p. 16.
19. Altaf Gauhar, *Ayub Khan*, Sang-e-Meel Publications, Lahore, Pakistan, 1993, p. 92.
20. *Dawn*, Karachi, 31 October 1954.
21. Brian Cloughley, *A History of the Pakistan Army*, Oxford University Press, Karachi, 1999, p. 50.

22. Interview Lt-General Fazle Haq, Chief Minister NWFP.
23. *The Muslim,* Islamabad, 5 February 1993.
24. Chaudhri Muhammad Ali, *The Emergence of Pakistan,* p. 361.
25. 'Demise of Article 58(2)(b)', *Dawn,* 22 April 1997.
26. Mohammad Ayub Khan, *Friends Not Masters,* p. 38.
27. Ibid., p. 35.
28. M. Ziauddin, *Dawn,* 28 April 1997.

9

GLIMPSES—FOREIGN
RELATIONS

Emancipation

The Cabinet Mission Plan was accepted by both the Congress and the Muslim League in 1946. It envisaged a free and united India under the trilaterally negotiated power sharing formula painstakingly pieced together between Britain and both the principal political parties in united India. This was a major breakthrough. Or, so it seemed to impartial observers. The political package had paved the way for the transfer of power from colonial hands to a free India. At this critical juncture in India's history, Pandit Jawaharlal Nehru intervened. On 10 July 1946, he dropped a political bombshell by declaring in Bombay that the Congress would enter the Constituent Assembly 'completely unfettered by agreements and free to meet all situations as they arise ... Congress has agreed only to participate in the Constituent Assembly and regards itself free to change or modify the Cabinet Mission Plan as it thinks best.'[1] It was backtracking from a fully negotiated agreement even before it was signed. A crisis of confidence sabotaged the deal. It became obvious that the Hindu-dominated Congress, as implied by Nehru, planned to dictate terms to the Muslim minority in India during the post independence period in flagrant violation of the terms of the transfer of power.

An independent India, in the vision of Nehru, would be free to alter the negotiated constitutional structure, as considered appropriate by it, with the brute communal majority that the population divide gave to the Congress. While the Hindu majority would be free to achieve its own goal, the post-independence Muslims in India would merely change their colonial masters from the British to the Hindus. Nehru demanded an impossible price that the Muslims in India were not prepared to pay. His arrogance disillusioned even the chronic optimists within the Muslim League and the parting of the ways became inevitable. The U-turn made by the Congress forced the Muslim League to rescind its earlier acceptance of the Cabinet Mission Plan. A united India became a dead issue. The Muslim League demanded and got a separate homeland for the Muslims—Pakistan.

To the people of Pakistan, India's motives were suspect from the first day of independence. A strategic uncertainty, created by India's arrogant and devious behaviour, influenced the thinking of Pakistan's policy planners and a quest for security dominated the national agenda. Logic demanded that the emerging dominions of India and Pakistan shed the fetters of slavery and coexist as friendly neighbours to achieve their common goal, the welfare and prosperity of the teeming millions of their poverty-stricken people.

In international relations the powerful rely on their muscle power to promote their self-interests. India adopted this route. Her hostility threatened Pakistan's security at a time when this newly born state faced serious difficulties. The dilemma of strengthening Pakistan's strategic capability caused anxiety because she lacked the resources to provide for her credible security. To compound her worries, quick on the heels of independence, came the crisis in the State of Jammu and Kashmir which locked the armies of India and Pakistan in a conflict that has defied a settlement since 1947.

Free India was obsessed with the passion of choking new-born Pakistan during her infancy, weakening her security, isolating her in the comity of nations and converting her into a satellite state. India's Pakistan policy was built on the pillars of military chauvinism and hegemonic aspirations.

Pandit Nehru, the mentor and philosopher of modern India, provided the conceptual framework for hegemonism. This policy has been generally implemented by all governments succeeding Nehru, at times with minor adjustments. On 25 August 1952, Nehru wrote to Sheikh Abdullah saying:

> We are superior to Pakistan in military and industrial power. But that superiority is not so great as to produce results in war or by fear of war. Therefore, our national interest demands that we should adopt a peaceful policy towards Pakistan, and at the same time, add to our strength. Strength ultimately comes not from the armed forces but the industrial and economic background behind them. As we grow in strength, as we are likely to do so, Pakistan will feel less and less inclined to threaten or harass us, and a time will come when, through sheer force of circumstances, it will be in a mood to accept a settlement *that we consider fair, whether in Kashmir or elsewhere* (emphasis added).[2]

Foreign Policy Options

It was in such an environment of uncertainty and regional hostility that in 1947 Pakistan had to formulate her foreign policy options to safeguard her security. Four choices were open to her. One, to build a congenial, if not a cooperative relationship with India, on the basis of sovereign equality of states as enshrined in the United Nations Charter. India's hegemonic designs and Pakistan's reluctance to submit to the dictates of New Delhi prevented adoption of such a course. Pakistan's own inherent weakness and India's adversarial attitude compelled the policy makers in this country to seek security from elsewhere.

The second option was to turn towards the erstwhile Soviet Union. It may be noted that Pakistan was admitted as a member of the UN by a unanimous resolution of the Security Council on 18 August 1947. The Soviet Union supported the resolution which constituted Moscow's recognition of Pakistan. Despite this, the Soviet Union did not send a congratulatory message to

Jinnah on the birth of Pakistan[3] and moved slowly to extend formal diplomatic recognition to her. She did so on 2 May 1948. Mr Shoaib Qureshi, the first Pakistani ambassador to the Soviet Union, presented his credentials in Moscow on 31 December 1949, twenty eight months after the emergence of Pakistan. The first Russian ambassador took charge of his appointment in Karachi still later—on 22 March 1950. Such a delay implied that the process of formal recognition apart, both the countries had reservations about each other. Their different ideologies might have imposed caution on them. However, it is relevant to mention that Pakistan did not show any inhibitions in establishing a friendly relationship with communist China.

As against this leisurely pace, Mr Habib Rahimtoola, Pakistan's first High Commissioner had assumed charge of his assignment in London in August 1947 and Mr M.A.H. Isphahani had reported in Washington on 7 October 1948.

It is also relevant to recall that Nawabzada Liaquat Ali Khan undertook a tour of the USA in May 1950. He had received an invitation from Moscow much earlier but no dates for the visit were fixed. For reasons beyond the scope of analysis in this narrative, the bilateral ties between the Soviet Union and Pakistan were not on the priority lists of either of these countries. Under the circumstances, the second option was of academic interest only and it was not seriously considered.

The third option was to rely on the Islamic countries and adopt an arrangement with them on the issues of security, economy and technology etc. This was an ideal, more emotive than real, easy to preach but hard to achieve objective. Many Islamic countries faced their own peculiar security and economic problems, and had security relationships with some third countries. Besides, they were internally divided and seldom spoke in unison on world issues. They had little in common except perhaps their common submission to Islam in a broad and general way. Their economic strengths (the oil wealth came later) and their technological know-how were limited and Pakistan could not hope to get much help from this bloc except for diplomatic, moral and political support.

The fourth choice was to seek a cooperative security arrangement with the United States, a country that revered India because of its democratic credentials, sheer geographical size, and massive population which offered lucrative opportunities for trade and investment.

The Cold War

With the end of the Second World War, some war-time allies turned into adversaries, proving the oft-repeated dictum that their were no permanent friends or foes in politics. The US and the erstwhile USSR led the two opposite camps. Whereas the Soviet Union kept the West busy with bush-fires in various troubled spots around the globe, the US adopted the policy of containing the two communist giants, the Soviet Union and China, with a ring of alliances to prevent the spread of communism. In this scenario, Washington tried to win New Delhi over to its side but was disillusioned when Prime Minister Nehru, on an official visit to the US, turned down the offer.

After Nehru's visit, President Harry Truman invited Prime Minister Liaquat Ali Khan to visit America in May 1950. The pro-West speeches made by Liaquat Ali Khan during his visit to the US annoyed the Soviet Union, 'Liaquat Ali Khan has been transformed into the Pakistani variety of Chiang Kai-shek or Syngman Rhee.'[4]

Liaquat provoked diplomatic grievance by visiting the USA first despite an invitation received by him earlier from the Soviet Union. Consequently, Pakistan waited for sixteen years before its head of state, President Ayub Khan, visited the USSR in April 1965.

The policies of Pakistan and India during the Korean War (1950-51) and at the time of the signing of the Japanese Peace Treaty (8 September 1951) aligned them distinctly. Nehru was called a 'lost leader' and Liaquat praised as 'America's one sure friend in South Asia.'[5] As Pakistan got closer to a distant US, she distanced herself from her neighbour, the USSR.

The fears nourished by Pakistan were compounded when India threatened her national security twice in quick succession, first in 1950 and then in 1951. On these occasions, military forces in both the countries were put on red alert and hostilities looked imminent. While these were averted through diplomatic initiatives, they left behind a deep and lingering impression on Pakistani policy makers that national security was required to be upgraded on a priority basis to safeguard against repeated blackmail by our aggressive neighbour in future.

The Ayub Era (1958-1969)

Military Influence

General Muhammad Ayub Khan had the honour of becoming the first Pakistani Commander-in-Chief of the Pakistan Army in 1951. He entered his office with the passion of building a powerful and hard-hitting army to meet its challenging professional obligations of defending the territorial integrity of the country. As a student of military history, Ayub knew that the Mughals had failed to build a strong military force in India and had paid the penalty for this error. He reorganized the Pakistan Army, trained it well but could not make much headway in equipping it with modern hardware because of the paucity of national resources.

At first, Ayub worked within the limits of his professional charter of responsibilities. His contacts with the outside world, particularly with the senior military and intelligence hierarchy in the USA, were at the professional level. At home, he had a strong personal equation with Iskander Mirza, defence secretary, whose ascending stars made him more powerful than the appointment he held. Later, he was to hold the appointment of home minister, 'dominating the proceedings of the cabinet'[6] and finally he became Governor-General in 1955. Gradually, General Ayub's image and stature grew and so did his ability to influence and often overshadow the foreign policy of the country substantially, on security-related problems.

The Foreign Office was eclipsed when General Ayub Khan played a dominant role in negotiating a Mutual Defence Assistance Agreement with the USA in May 1954. It paved the way for the provision of US military assistance to Pakistan. His immense contribution in this regard was acknowledged, among others, by Iskander Mirza who respected Ayub for his persuasive logic and depth of vision. General Ayub Khan actively supported Pakistan's joining the US-sponsored South East Asia Treaty Organization (SEATO) in 1954, and the Baghdad Pact in 1955, later, in 1958, renamed the Central Treaty Organization (CENTO).

Pakistan, the only Asian country to have joined both SEATO and CENTO, earned the dubious distinction of being 'America's most allied ally in Asia.' Dubious, because as Henry Kissenger once told Agha Shahi, 'It is dangerous for any country to oppose the US, and fatal to befriend it.' Pakistan has learnt at her cost the veracity of Kissenger's caustic comment.

Pakistan joined SEATO and CENTO purely for reasons of her own national security and she had neither the intention nor the capacity to have aggressive designs against any country, least of all against the Soviet Union, a superpower, or against China, a friend. The United States, on the other hand, had conceived these Pacts with a different motive.

Pakistan, an Islamic state, did not have any inhibitions in conducting political business with other countries and with peoples having allegiance to other religions, beliefs or ideologies. A religion of peace, Islam preaches that its followers respect all faiths and tolerate the sentiments of those who may differ with it on principle. A modern and moderate Muslim would not personally preach communism but neither would he deny the right of others to adhere to this philosophy, if they so desire of their own free will. This is amply illustrated by the reality that Pakistan has had an enduring, cooperative and very cordial relationship with communist China dating back to the time when China was a pariah for the Western world.

No single event caused as much misunderstanding and suspicion in Soviet minds about Pakistan as her joining SEATO and CENTO. Soviet retaliation was quick and harsh. In November-December 1955, Premier Nikolai Bulganin and First Secretary Nikita Khrushchev visited India and courted their hosts by saying that the Soviets 'were grieved that the imperialist force had succeeded in dividing India into two parts.'[7] Khrushchev pointedly visited Srinagar and declared that Kashmir formed a part of the Indian Union as decided by its people.[8]

Pakistan's permission to the USA to establish a military base at Badaber, near Peshawar and her clumsy approach during the 1956 Suez crisis further annoyed the Soviet Union. Pakistan also criticized the Soviet invasion of Hungary a little too loudly for her size and power. The Soviet Union retaliated in February 1957, by casting her first veto on the Kashmir question in the UN Security Council.

Ayub Dominates

Pakistan-US relations ultimately turned sour because of the conflicting interests of the two countries. By 1956, strains began to appear in their relations. Pakistan's serious concern about India's domineering behaviour with her was underplayed in America. The US administration also accused Pakistan of being too demanding. On the other hand, Pakistan complained to the US of tilting towards India and equating a legally committed friend with a freelance India who was hobnobbing with both the superpowers. The growing US economic aid to India enabled New Delhi to divert its internal resources for boosting its defence capability still further to the detriment of Pakistan.

A domestic struggle for power in Pakistan between quarreling and inefficient politicians weakened her bargaining position with foreign countries. A debate ensued about the efficacy and reliability of the pacts negotiated with the US administration. Such criticism irked the US Congress and the Administration. Under such conditions, General Ayub once again became the main trouble-shooter and negotiated with the US administration for the supply of hardware not only for the Pakistan Army but also for the Pakistan Air Force. Iskander Mirza, now the Governor-General, seemed to have greater confidence in Ayub Khan than in the Foreign Minister and the Foreign Office in handling such delicate talks. In the process, politicians got sidelined. They were not considered worthy of handling this sensitive issue. On their part, they were too weak to complain and too deeply involved in their political intrigues and infighting to worry about external developments. This situation continued till 1958 when the national democratic cart was upturned by the duo, Mirza and Ayub. Soon, Iskander Mirza was shown the door and Ayub Khan emerged as the unquestioned supremo. A vast majority of the politicians quickly flocked around Ayub Khan and felt honoured in assisting him in administering 'Basic Democracy' which, in the assessment of Ayub suited the 'psyche of the people of Pakistan.' The military reaction to Ayub's political diagnosis is difficult to judge at this belated stage, in the absence of official records (as none were maintained). However, on the intellectual plane, the concept of 'Basic Democracy' was self-serving for the author of the concept.

Cost-Benefit Ratio

Assessed logically, Pakistan's choice of seeking a strategic relationship with the US in the fifties was both appropriate and justified. India's arrogant behaviour limited Pakistan's viable options. Pakistan's vital security needs justified a quick induction of modern hardware to restrain an aggressor. Her own domestic economic resources could not bear the cost, even if the weapons were available in the world market. The choice of relying on the US was almost inevitable, but not without serious flaws. Pakistan's size and power potential vastly differed from that of the US, and the stronger partner in this unequal, bilateral, strategic relationship could always tilt the situation against Pakistan at critical times. Pakistan perhaps took this risk in good faith and, years later, paid the penalty when her worst fears were proved right. The US showed no hesitation in promoting her own self-interest at critical moments even when such actions went to the gross disadvantage of Pakistan. Pakistan paid a heavy political and diplomatic price for receiving economic and military aid from the US. Pakistan's top priority was her own security. For the US, the containment and defeat of communism was at the top of her global strategic agenda. Pakistan's pro-US policy was severely criticized by many countries, including some in the Islamic world. While many accused Pakistan directly, others blamed her for not seeing through the 'hidden' motives of the US.

Predictably, India's tirade was strong and persistent. She bitterly criticized Pakistan for augmenting her limited military capability by getting hardware from any quarters, be it a tank, a gun, an aircraft or a radio set, on the plea that it endangered her own security, notwithstanding the reality that she already enjoyed a considerable numerical and qualitative superiority in the military field over Pakistan.

The Soviet reaction was hostile. A Soviet Foreign Office statement declared that, 'SEATO was directed against the security interests of Asia and the Far East and, at the same time, of the Asian peoples.'[9] In Moscow's perception, the Baghdad Pact constituted a threat not only to the Soviet Union but also 'to all the peace loving countries of Asia and Africa, and especially to those defending their national independence and opposing colonialism.'[10]

Pakistan's Bilateral Defence Agreement with the US in March 1959, and the shooting down of the American spy plane, U-2, after it had taken off from Peshawar and was on its way to Bodo in Norway, created further tension and severely strained Pakistan-Soviet relations. Pakistan felt deceived because the US had kept her in the dark about such clandestine spy operations launched from Pakistan's territory.

Mending Pakistan-Soviet Fences

President General Ayub Khan was a political realist. His pro-West stance was influenced by Pakistan's security needs to give a fair opportunity to his people to live with dignity and honour. Ayub, a shrewd statesman, was too clever to ignore the harsh realities of the game of power and, despite his leaning towards the US, he had a healthy respect for the superpower neighbour, the Soviet Union. During Ayub's rule (1958-69) Pakistan-Soviet relations began to improve. Ayub saw no reason why Pakistan could not do business with the Soviet Union.[11] This hope began to bear results with the conclusion of the Pakistan-Soviet Agreement of 4 March 1961, by which the Soviet Union agreed to provide technical assistance and equipment for the exploration of oil in Pakistan.

Dialogue replaced isolation. Ayub visited the Soviet Union between 3-11 April 1965, the first Pakistani Head of State to undertake such a journey. This was not an easy visit as both sides had much to complain about. The bilateral talks, extensive and exhaustive, helped in removing many doubts that had created difficulties for both the countries in their inter-state relationship. During their meeting, the Acting Chairman, Anastas Mikoyan, told Ayub, 'We are aware of your own great role and we recognise you as the architect of an active foreign policy.'[12]

Ayub's visit yielded positive results. The Soviet Union responded by remaining neutral during the India-Pakistan military skirmishes in the Rann of Kutch in 1965, and expressed the hope that the dispute would be settled by peaceful means, with consideration for the interests of both sides.[13] Moscow's balanced stance did not go unnoticed in Islamabad. In the aftermath of the India-Pakistan War of 1965, the Soviet Union played the role of an intermediary in piecing together the Tashkent Declaration. This was a tribute to Soviet diplomacy. Some Western observers at the time expressed grave doubts saying that the Soviet Union 'was trying to open a lock that has no key.'[14] The Tashkent Declaration was considered in Pakistan a reasonably balanced deal at the official, academic and intellectual levels. However, at the popular platform it was thought to be an agreement that was biased in favour of India. Such a view prevailed in the military as well. The Ayub-Bhutto differences that emerged in the wake of this Declaration made it all the more controversial.

The Pak-Soviet relations took another forward step when, despite Indian protests, the Soviet Union signed an agreement with Pakistan in June 1968, for the sale of some military equipment to Pakistan. This was a significant development, the first of its kind in Pak-Soviet relations. Pakistan received a small quantity of equipment under this agreement. But later, New Delhi succeeded in prevailing upon Moscow to decline any further supply of hardware to Pakistan.

Pak-China Relations

Pakistan recognized the People's Republic of China soon after it was established in October 1949. The Chinese action in Tibet in 1950 was handled by Pakistan with a great deal of political finesse. It did not go unnoticed in Beijing when Pakistan abstained from voting on the US-sponsored resolution in the UN accusing China as aggressor. Pakistan's membership of CENTO and SEATO injected an element of strain in Pakistan-China bilateral ties. If China had any suspicion of 'double-dealing' from Pakistan, her doubts were soon put at rest by Pakistan through diplomatic channels. China was assured that Pakistan's membership of SEATO was not directed against her. The clouds of doubt gradually disappeared and both the countries began to develop healthy ties.

Chou En-Lai, playing a significant role, showed statesmanship of a high calibre and laid a sound foundation for Pakistan-China bilateral ties. From the Pakistani side, Prime Minister Muhammad Ali Bogra's role at the historic 1954 Bandung Conference and the first ever meeting between the prime ministers of China (Chou En-Lai) and Pakistan (Bogra) broke the ice between the two countries. This saw a turning point in Pakistan-China relations.

The year 1956 was a leap forward year in the Pak-China relationship when the Prime Ministers of Pakistan and China visited each other's country in quick succession. The joint statement issued at the end of Prime Minister H.S. Suhrawardy's visit to China stated that the visit had, 'contributed greatly to the strengthening of friendly relations already existing between the two countries.' The return visit of Chou En-Lai cemented the ties still further. On 23 October Chou En-lai, addressing Pakistani newsmen, said that, 'there was no reason why China could not be friends with Pakistan.' This diplomatic remark was an implied declaration that Pakistan's membership of CEATO was no longer a major stumbling block in Pak-China bilateral ties. Leaders of both countries paved the way for developing a harmonious relationship between them by ensuring that they did not interfere in the internal affairs of each other.

President General Ayub Khan, on assuming power in 1958, took a bold strategic decision to blend Pakistan's foreign policy with the dictates of her geography. Earlier, he had played a significant role in establishing Pakistan's friendly ties with the US. Ayub understood the importance of Pakistan's location in the hub of a politically sensitive and strategically important area, and proceeded to balance relations with her two big neighbours—the Soviet Union and China. In November 1959, Ayub informally proposed to China to demarcate the common border between their respective countries to eliminate any chance of misunderstanding or dispute on the issue. The proposal was formally conveyed to China in March 1961.

The initial response from China was ambivalent, neither supporting the initiative nor rejecting it. It was not difficult for Pakistan to comprehend the reasons for the slow response from China. Kashmir, for one, was a disputed territory and the Chinese desired to reflect on the implications of demarcating the border. China also wanted an early and peaceful settlement of her border dispute with India. A border agreement with Pakistan first, in the assessment of China, might have hindered the conclusion of the boundary talks with India. Chinese pragmatism, however, saw through India's game and soon reached the conclusion that India's tactics were to prolong negotiations on the border dispute without opting for its early settlement. The delay helped India to use the China card with the West to earn Western sympathy and support against China that was *ab initio* a suspect in the Western capitals.

Notwithstanding Chinese reservations, Ayub persisted with Pakistan's carefully timed initiative. While in Washington, he declared that Peking should occupy its legitimate place in the United Nations and Pakistan would in the future vote for China's admission to the world body. This singularly bold policy statement significantly made on US soil announced Pakistan's China policy loud and clear. Days later, at the luncheon given by Chancellor Adenauer in Bonn in his honour, Ayub Khan declared that Pakistan had normal ties with China and negotiations were taking place between the two countries to define the border in certain areas.[15]

The Sino-Pakistan agreement on the demarcation of their common border was announced on 27 December 1962. It shocked the US, that was then busy wooing India after it had received a drubbing from the sharp and swift Chinese military reaction provoked by Nehru's aggressive forward policy in the Himalayan border. Ayub was perturbed with the quick U-turn in the US foreign policy. Pakistan, an ally, was ignored and abandoned and a consistently bitter critic of US policies, India, was lavished with political support and substantial military aid, airlifted in quick time, to shore up India's sagging morale. This also exposed the hypocrisy of Pandit Nehru, who quickly shed his cloak of neutrality and bent backwards to receive the US-led Western military aid. This was a wake-up call to Pakistan that convinced Ayub of the danger of putting all the Pakistani eggs in one basket. The sincerity and reliability of US friendship towards Pakistan stood eroded.

President Ayub Khan claims in his book 'Friends Not Masters', that he reflected a lot on the regional security environment. With India spreading venom against Pakistan, and Afghanistan suspected of being willing to play second fiddle against Pakistan, Ayub weighed the options open to the country.

While both these adversaries enjoyed the support of the USSR, Pakistan's Western allies had unhesitatingly joined the US, almost in indecent haste, to appease India, and reward her with massive military assistance, as if to 'compensate' her for criticizing them in the past. That this hardware might eventually be used against Pakistan was of little significance to them.

Pakistan's China policy during the Ayub era was pragmatic and well conceived. It was based on Ayub's vision and realism. The prevailing realities had strengthened his resolve to lay a sound foundation for Pak-China ties and build on it an edifice of a bilateral structure, durable and mutually beneficial, to serve the interests of both the countries. The conclusion of a boundary agreement with China was a tribute to his political sagacity.

On 29 August 1963, Pakistan and China signed an Air agreement in Karachi that gave the latter the first air link with the world that did not go through Moscow. A surprised US called it 'an unfortunate breach of free world solidarity.' To Washington, 'The unthinkable had happened and Ayub had opened a window on the world' for the air-locked Chinese.[16] Such a negative response was ironic from a country that claimed pride in preaching freedom to the world. The US displeasure was quick and sure. In retaliation, Washington backtracked from a loan agreement with Pakistan for the improvement of Dhaka Airport.

The public reaction in Pakistan was firm, spontaneous and supportive. The people endorsed the process of strengthening bilateral ties with China. As it is, they had been disillusioned by the US tilt towards India during the 1962 India-China border skirmish in the Himalayas.

America and Britain, seeing an opportunity to woo neutral India, were over-eager to boost India's military power. Pakistan felt shocked and betrayed. Whereas China demonstrated her peaceful intentions by accepting a cease-fire, and immediate withdrawal from disputed territory and return of Indian prisoners of war and military equipment, Indian hostility toward Pakistan was unrelenting.

Under the circumstances, the military aid received by India from the West could only further endanger the security of Pakistan. The aid donors to India had thus in reality added to Pakistan's perception of the threat to its security, even if this might not have been their intention.

President Ayub Khan has faced criticism at home for not immediately de-freezing the Kashmir dispute by taking advantage of India's military weakness in the 1962 conflict. It is alleged that he had succumbed to American pressure and in the process Pakistan lost a chance to benefit from Indian military preoccupation. The US pressure on Pakistan is well documented and it was a relevant factor. But, no less significant are the weighty reasons that the duration of the conflict was short, and China, for her own reasons, did not consult Pakistan either while starting the military action or while unilaterally halting its operations. The military takes time and effort in changing policy. The time factor alone precluded a meaningful intervention by Pakistan on the Kashmir front.

The joint demarcation of the Pakistan-China boundary was an act of high statesmanship and political vision displayed by the senior leaders in China and Pakistan. It amicably settled an explosive and emotive issue that might have otherwise caused friction between the two countries. China and Pakistan did not have any other bilateral dispute between them to worry about. Both fully understood each other's compulsions about their differing social systems and wisely decided that these will not be allowed to create a hurdle in establishing a close and mutually beneficial relationship between them.

A firm foundation had been laid by the two countries to build their inter-state ties on a durable basis. During the next five decades Pakistan-China relations grew in strength and dimension despite the vicissitudes of time, numerous global upheavals, regional developments and internal changes in both the countries. This remarkable success story explodes the self-serving bogey of the so-called 'clash of civilizations' coined by some vested interests. The credit largely goes to the founding fathers.

Bilateral ties between Pakistan and China were carefully cemented with the passage of time. President Ayub Khan added great strength and vitality to these relations by peacefully settling the inter-state boundary issue between them. The continuous and unwavering efforts made by successive governments in both the countries consolidated and strengthened the initial decision.

Bhutto Becomes Foreign Minister

Pakistan's Foreign Minister, Muhammad Ali Bogra died suddenly on 24 January 1963. This created an opening for the young, impressive, articulate and ambitious Zulfikar Ali Bhutto to be appointed as the foreign minister. Bhutto was then engaged in talks with the Indian foreign minister, Swaran Singh, for seeking a settlement of the Kashmir dispute. The talks were aborted after six rounds because, by then, India had recovered from her shock defeat in the Himalayan border conflict, and President Kennedy had given a formal undertaking to Pandit Nehru that the US would assist India in the case of aggression by China.[17] With the threat from China removed and the US assurance given, India hardened its stance on the Kashmir dispute.

India-Pakistan War—1965

The 1965 India-Pakistan war was triggered unwisely and in an ill-prepared manner. The roles played by President General Ayub Khan and Foreign Minister Z. A. Bhutto in the war are discussed at some length in a separate chapter. Suffice to mention here that, strange as it may appear, Foreign Minister Bhutto and his trusted Foreign Secretary Aziz Ahmed, kept the Foreign Office officials out of the picture throughout the war on issues of substance. Ayub's trust in Bhutto was abused by the Foreign Minister.

Ayub's Influence on Foreign Relations

President Ayub Khan did not rush into the national political arena without doing his homework. He had thoughtfully conceived his intervention over a prolonged period of time and painstakingly prepared the blueprint of his plan of action to introduce a wide range of administrative reforms in the country. He launched his multi-directional plan in quick-time and with visible gusto and drive. His forward-looking policies, broad vision and economic achievements earned him the respect and admiration of his people, of the outside powers and of neutral observers. His impressive performance on the domestic front improved his stature externally.

General Ayub's intervention in national civil affairs subverted the process of nourishing democracy in the country and established an unhealthy tradition. It remains undisclosed if the scheme was his own brainchild or whether the army played a role in preparing a blueprint. Ayub claims that in 1954 he prepared a document 'A short appreciation of present and future problems of Pakistan.'[18] This shows that the conceptual input came from himself. He took his senior military commanders into confidence before be decided to intervene and carried his military team with him, who fully supported Ayub by their acts and words.

Unlike the instability that Ayub inherited in 1958, Pakistan could boast of political stability a decade later. No political rival of comparable status and stature seemed to challenge Ayub's hold on power. The economic development and growth of the country were internationally quoted as success models for other developing countries to follow. Market economy was practiced and industry became buoyant. The electoral system that Ayub introduced in Pakistan was experimental, semi-democratic and tailor-made to affix a stamp of public legitimacy on his candidature for election as the President of the country without facing the pains and pitfalls inherent in a conventional electoral process. The bulk of the politicians in the country helped Ayub to make it a success. The parliamentarians had

such 'democratic' credentials that the loyal opposition in the
House chose Sardar Bahadur Khan, Ayub's brother, as the
Leader of the Opposition. In contrast to the chaos and confusion
that prevailed in 1958, peace and tranquillity reigned supreme.

In the field of external affairs, Pakistan's honeymoon with
the US in the fifties had helped her in the economic and in the
military fields, but the intensity of their early relations had
subsequently tapered down. The United States did not view the
growing ties between Pakistan and China with understanding
and magnanimity. Pakistan's relations with the Soviet Union
had been pulled out of the freezer. They were not as warm as
those with China, but both the countries had developed a
forward-looking, working relationship between them. The Indo-
Pakistan war in 1965 dampened Pak-US relations, but President
Ayub's visit to Washington in December 1965 partially repaired
the damage. On the whole, Pakistan was respected, internally
and externally. Her international standing and prestige were high
commensurate with her size and power potential despite the
1965 war. The country had a progressive outlook and a balanced
approach on internal and external affairs.

The internal scene changed after President Ayub's cardiac
ailment in 1968. His hitherto firm grip on events, institutions
and personalities loosened. Once a forceful and decisive leader,
Ayub became a shadow of his once domineering and impressive
personality. His bubbling confidence was replaced by his
subdued posture. His illness mellowed him down considerably.
Increasingly, he came to rely on the advice of a few close
associates who excelled in the art of pleasing their once powerful
boss. His sons, Gohar Ayub Khan and Akhtar Ayub Khan,
indulging in industry and politics earned the ire of the people.
The hitherto dormant opposition rallied together to sink their
internal differences and challenged Ayub to topple his
government in the twilight of his political career. The turn of
the tide came quickly for Ayub. A minor incident triggered a
storm and an anti-Ayub agitation started all too suddenly but
decisively. Perhaps Ayub had dominated the political landscape
of Pakistan for too long and the people wanted to see a new

face in authority. In the final stages he blatantly blundered, on the advice of his sycophant 'well-wishers', in transferring power to the Commander-in-Chief of the Pakistan Army instead of the speaker.

The Yahya Interregnum (1969-71)

General Yahya Khan appeared on the national political horizon with essentially a domestic agenda. Immediately yielding to the 'popular demand' he announced a package of political proposals the details of which are listed in the chapter on the East Pakistan crisis. He gets the credit for holding the first ever nation-wide elections in the country. These were held under a 'Legal Framework Order' because the constitution was not operative.

Foreign Office Dilemma

With the solitary exception of President Fazal Elahi Chaudhury, all the heads of State of Pakistan from Ghulam Muhammad to Muhammad Farooq Leghari dismissed prime ministers and federal governments and ordered premature elections in the country. Their arbitrary acts harmed Pakistan internally and lowered her external image. It then fell to the lot of the Foreign Office and to the Pakistani ambassadors serving abroad to correct or limit the damage and to explain to the world the reasons for such actions. Foreign countries rely on reports from their own ambassadors as also media reports.

Pakistan's Foreign Office faced a greater quandary when, on three occasions, the army commanders—Yahya and Zia directly and Ayub working in partnership with Iskander Mirza—took charge of national affairs and placed the country under martial law. On such occasions Pakistan's diplomats could not take refuge behind the constitution and relied heavily on the thesis that the actions were entirely the internal affairs of the country.

The foreign policy and the internal policy of any country,
including Pakistan, are two inseparable facets of the same coin.
Both should be debated in the Cabinet, in the National Assembly
and in the media to evolve a national consensus on them. Such
scrutiny helps policy makers to take well considered decisions
to harmonize the internal and external elements of national
policies.

Instead, the Yahya government functioned on a need-to-know
basis in which the external and internal developments were
handled separately by the ministries concerned to the exclusion
of each other. The lines were so drawn that at times the right
hand did not know what the left hand did. This serious handicap
became quite apparent when the internal scene in East Pakistan
took an ugly turn in 1970-71, and Indian involvement in
Pakistan's internal affairs became covert as well as overt in
form.

A conference of about nineteen Pakistani envoys from
important countries was held at Geneva in July/August 1971.
All the assembled ambassadors advocated a political rather than
a military solution to the on-going crisis in East Pakistan.
However, the powerful bureaucratic trio, Secretary Information
(Mr Roedad Khan), Secretary National Security (Major-General
Ghulam Umar) and the Foreign Secretary (S. M. Yusuf), asserted
that the situation in East Pakistan was well under control and
the current difficulties would soon smoothen over. The
ambassadors serving abroad did not agree with the home based
official's optimism and expressed grave concern about Indo-
Soviet collusion in their coordinated objective of separating East
Pakistan from Pakistan.

The proceedings of the envoys conference were tape
recorded.[19] Later, these tapes mysteriously disappeared from the
official record. Obviously, those who wanted to hide their sins
of omission from public exposure knew the art of suppressing
facts.

The Rabat Episode

The Conference of the Muslim Heads of State held at Rabat (Morocco) in 1969 exposed General Yahya Khan to international diplomacy. Prior to this Conference, a delegation of Indian Muslims visited Saudi Arabia at the initiative of their government and pleaded with King Faisal that they be represented in the Conference. King Faisal agreed to help without taking into confidence other Islamic countries. This development was in the knowledge of the Foreign Office.

The participation of genuine representatives of Indian Muslims in deliberations on so evocative an issue as the Israeli occupation of the Holy City of Jerusalem, could have been understandable. But the entry of India, a self-proclaimed secular state opposed to the formation of an Islamic organization, was sure to undermine and destroy the emerging solidarity among Muslim states.

At that time the Foreign Office was headed by a non-career Foreign Secretary (Yusuf), an officer of the Civil Service of Pakistan (CSP), having no personal experience in managing foreign relations.

The brief for the Summit delegation was approved by the Foreign Secretary who amended the recommendation of the Foreign Office officials that Pakistan should strongly oppose any move by India or any member of the OIC to give observer status to the Indian Muslims at the OIC meeting. The Foreign Secretary overruled the Foreign Office officials and amended the brief against opposing the proposal for an observer status. The Foreign Office officials noted their strong reservation on the file.

It so happened that Foreign Minister Sharifuddin Peerzada and Foreign Secretary Yusuf did not trust each other. Foreign Office officials had been instructed to submit all the files by them only to the Foreign Secretary, who in turn decided which files were to be sent to the Foreign Minister. This particular brief, containing the recommendations of the Foreign Office officials, was not submitted to the Foreign Minister, who ironically became the Secretary General of the OIC. General Yahya attended the Summit meeting without knowledge of this matter.

At the Conference, King Faisal proposed that India be included as a member in recognition of the services rendered by its eighty million Muslims towards Islam. No objection was raised by any country and the proposal was taken as accepted.

India had worked hard for the occasion. Its Ambassador to Morocco, a Sikh, already waiting in the wings, was invited to occupy a seat till the arrival of an Indian Minister, Mr Fakhruddin Ali Ahmad, the next day. The OIC then witnessed a scene unprecedented in its Summit meeting. The Muslim minority in India, a country where *Hindutva* and Hindu culture ran supreme, was being represented by a bearded Sikh wearing a traditional turban richly bright in colour. The delegates from different countries curiously glanced at one another with suppressed emotions writ large on their faces. India succeeded in committing a diplomatic coup against Pakistan.

During the break, some members in the Pakistani delegation quickly conveyed to General Yahya to be prepared for a hot public reception on his return to Pakistan, and advised him that the situation might become too ugly for the government to handle. Foreseeing trouble Yahya sent an urgent message to the host, King Hassan of Morocco, the Chairman of the Conference, that if India became a member, he would not participate in the conference any further and initiated plans to return home. This raised a diplomatic furore. Yahya remained firm in his resolve despite the persuasive efforts made by King Hassan, King Hussain of Jordan and the Shah of Iran to change his mind particularly when he had not raised any objection to the proposal when it was first mooted in the Conference. Yahya did not yield. Eventually King Faisal was approached to withdraw the proposal, which he did to maintain Islamic unity. The crisis was averted. Yahya returned home claiming diplomatic success.

General Yahya's Foreign Secretary claims that the President 'relished his meetings with the heads of government and state (but) he took little interest in foreign policy formulation.'[20]

Dr Kissinger's Visit to China

For two decades, Washington had sought to contain and isolate China. By the late 1960s this policy was beginning to become counter productive. Support for restoration of China's legitimate rights in the United Nations was gathering momentum. President Nixon, though reputed an anti-communist, was a realist. He decided to open a dialogue with China.

The US had earlier sent numerous proposals to this effect to China through a number of different countries but none had been reciprocated. During Yahya's visit to the US in October 1970, President Nixon requested President Yahya to act as an intermediary and arrange a secret meeting between his emissary and a Chinese leader, preferably Chou En-lai. Yahya agreed. Nixon knew then that his guest was scheduled to visit China a month later. Yahya kept Nixon's request confidential and did not share it even with Pakistan's Foreign Office.

General Yahya received a tumultuous welcome on his arrival in Beijing on 10 November 1970. Chou En-Lai personally received his guest at the airport and the reception reflected the close and deep ties between the two friendly neighbours. Yahya personally conveyed Nixon's proposal to Chou En-Lai during their *tete-a-tete*. Chou En-Lai promised to respond later after informing Mao Tse Tung. This he did with a characteristic personal grace and a high quality of diplomatic statesmanship. He informed President Yahya that previously the US had sent similar messages through other sources 'but this is the first time that the proposal has come from a Head (of State) through a Head, to a Head. The United States knows that Pakistan is a great friend of China and, therefore, we attach importance to the message.'[21] Chou En-Lai indicated that a special envoy of President Nixon would be welcome in Beijing to discuss the subject of the vacation of the Chinese territory called Taiwan.

General Yahya was relieved to hear the response, even though it was qualified in content. The ice was broken. Yahya knew that it had been difficult to make a breakthrough but once the negotiations started other issues would inevitably come under

discussion. Foreign Secretary Sultan M. Khan claims that
General Yahya Khan took him into confidence on 22 November
soon after his return from China and directed him to personally
handle the issue on a highly confidential basis, which he did.

During the next few months, messages were exchanged
between Beijing and Washington through Islamabad for which
a special channel was established to preserve the secrecy of the
mission. Perhaps other channels were also used. According to
Henry Kissenger, he spoke on the matter to Agha Hilaly. Later,
Hilaly told Ambassador Abdul Sattar[22] that he wrote a note in
long-hand to Yahya, not to the Foreign Secretary. After
painstaking effort, finally, an agenda for the China-US talks
was mutually agreed. It was decided that each side might raise
issues of concern to them during the talks. All the preliminary
spadework was completed in total secrecy and not a word leaked
out to the world media. The stage was set for the first Kissinger-
Chou En-Lai meeting through Pakistan.

Dr Kissinger arrived in Islamabad on 8 July at the end of his
hectic tour of South East Asia. His circuitous arrival in Pakistan
was a part of his unannounced secret travel plan from Islamabad
to Beijing. A carefully staged drama was played by Pakistan to
cover up Kissinger's absence from the public eye for the
duration of his 'stay' in Pakistan. As if to provide him relief
from the heat and humidity of Islamabad, he was taken to the
cool serenity of the 8,500 feet high picturesque hill resort of
Nathiagali for a rest. To give credence to this news a fake
Dr Kissinger drove to Nathiagali with full protocol. At
Nathiagali, 'Kissinger' complained of acute stomach pain after
consuming mangoes at lunch and the doctors advised him
complete rest and light diet. So the world media was told about
Kissinger's arrival in Pakistan and his indisposition.

In reality, in the early hours of 9 July, a PIA aircraft took the
real Dr Kissinger from Islamabad to Beijing across the mighty
Karakoram Range on a secret historic visit to meet Chou En-Lai.
The aim was to establish direct high-level contact between China
and the USA. Kissinger returned to Islamabad on 11 July with
his mission successfully accomplished. Hours later, he took off

for Paris in the US aircraft that had remained parked in Islamabad for three days. Pakistan had thus played an important role in providing a communication bridge between two powerful countries with distinct cultures and different philosophies on life. In so doing, Pakistan in general and General Yahya in particular earned the gratitude of President Nixon and Dr Kissinger.

Diplomatic Isolation

Pakistan's internal situation was not enviable when General Yahya Khan took charge of the country. The blunders and errors committed by successive governments in the past in administering the two widely separated wings of the country had produced fissures in Pakistan's nationhood. Right or wrong, an unease was perceived in East Pakistan that was both visible and clearly heard. It was Yahya's misfortune that the political debris and the accumulated follies committed by all the previous governments were dumped at his door and the mistakes made by the Yahya administration itself added to this mess.

The politicians were to blame for the follies committed in the first decade of Pakistan's independence as they were at the helm of national affairs during the period 1947-1958. From 1958 onwards General Ayub Khan administered the country—first under martial law and then under a constitution tailor-made to put a stamp of legitimacy on his quasi democratic rule. His decade-long rule, longer than that of any of his predecessors, witnessed the widening of the gulf of mistrust between East and West Pakistan. The process of Pakistan's diplomatic isolation in the comity of nations started in the closing stages of his rule. He has to be assigned the responsibility for this downward trend. Pakistan was in a state of disarray when General Yahya Khan was tasked to lead it.

Internal developments dominated General Yahya's actions throughout his tenure as the Head of State/Government. The internal policy options of his government emerged out of the discussions held with those who were intimately involved with affairs in East Pakistan. Yahya often relied on their advice because he was himself physically removed from the East Pakistan scene. Those rendering such advice had their own views, preferences and limitations.

External affairs remained on the back burner. The Foreign Office was marginally aware of the ground realities in East Pakistan despite the fact that the portfolio of Foreign Affairs was under the control of the President. Thus, at a time when the country gradually drifted towards an unprecedented crisis, its domestic and foreign policies operated in different gears. Resultantly, the internal policy and the foreign policy were conceived and implemented in isolation of each other and the wisdom of evolving them collectively and synchronizing them did not dawn on the policy makers. The country became a rudderless ship sailing in a turbulent sea. Those at the helm of its affairs lacked the moral courage to speak the truth, take the nation into confidence and foresee the diplomatic disaster towards which it was heading.

General Yahya Khan gets a major share of the blame. He was personally handling the situation in East Pakistan and was also totally involved in diplomatic efforts as Foreign Minister. The burden of responsibility rests on his shoulders.

At a critical time when diplomacy should have been at the height of its efficiency, Pakistan was diplomatically isolated in the comity of nations. Some countries, China, Britiain, USA and Iran, to name a few, did advise her to take a quick and meaningful political initiative to defuse tension. The US through its naval ships made some half-hearted diplomatic and symbolic moves as if to lull Pakistan and scare India. That these efforts proved fruitless once again revealed the historic truth that internal disunity invariably invites external aggression and he who relies on external crutches during a crisis situation normally ends up the loser. Pakistan's foreign policy might not have, by itself, performed a miracle or averted the disaster that hit the country but it deserved a fair and full opportunity to play its role and prove its worth. Diplomacy did not get a fair chance at the most critical juncture of Pakistan's history. Who were to blame for this tragedy remains clouded and undetermined in history.

The Zia Years (1977-88)

Unlike Generals Ayub Khan and Yahya Khan, General Ziaul Haq started with a handicap. He had stepped into the office of a charismatic and once populist Bhutto, who would have certainly won at least one more term as prime minister had elections been held in a fair and free environment. Zia neither possessed the charisma of Bhutto nor did he have the support of a public mandate behind him. Nor, indeed was he an intellectual. Initially, the foreign media called him a 'reluctant military ruler' but Zia shed his reservations, if he had any, when he quickly developed a taste for power and authority.

Salient Issues

The list of external developments facing Zia was long in 1979. These were the international reaction to the trial, sentence and execution of Mr Bhutto; the Afghan *Jihad* against the induction of Soviet military forces in their country in 1979; the global condemnation of Soviet intervention in Afghanistan; the migration of over three million Afghan refugees to Pakistan and their temporary location in the country; the Geneva Accord on Afghanistan; the collapse of the Shah of Iran and the success of the Islamic Revolution in Iran; the Iraq-Iran War; the successful diplomatic efforts made by Pakistan to join the Non-Aligned Movement at the NAM Summit held at Havana; Zia's peace-offensive with India in the face of consistent provocation; the seemingly friendly but internally bruised and uneasy Pakistan-US relations; the US aid package to Pakistan and the US-led Western tirade against Pakistan's nuclear programme. The succeeding paragraphs list, in a broad outline, the troubleshooting techniques adopted by the Zia Government in response to these external developments that impinged on Pakistan's national interests.

Foreign Policy Formulation

General Zia took a visible personal interest in the formulation of Pakistan's policy responses in respect of the global and the regional developments that affected the country. A typical plan of action was that the initial option papers were invariably prepared by the Foreign Office. These were discussed amongst the special committees by all concerned including the security and intelligence experts. On occasions a special committee was created for an independent assessment of the situation by the military experts. At each stage Zia spent long hours listening to the opposing views on the situation and the recommendations made by the sponsors. He gave freedom of expression to every speaker and never interrupted a presentation. All along he took copious notes. Finally, after all had spoken the General would take considerable time in summing up the discussion and giving directions for the future. The initial draft was then improved by the Foreign Office in the light of the discussions held. Normally recommendations emerged in a tentative form. These were then discussed, first in the Martial Law Administrator's Conference and finally in a cabinet meeting. The options were further refined to evolve the national policy plans.

Involvement in Foreign Relations

General Zia spoke to the Foreign Minister and the Foreign Secretary almost daily, sometimes more than once, to remain abreast of the external issues and frequently issued orders on the telephone for implementation. Additionally, he met them at least twice a week in respect of issues that needed his attention. Despite his massive dislike for clearing his file-work he regularly read the cypher despatches received from the Pakistani missions abroad and wrote lengthy instructions on the sidelines for the Foreign Office to act upon. All the important meetings on external and internal affairs were invariably attended by the Foreign Minister as well as by the Foreign Secretary.

Manpower Training

The President was surprised to learn in 1977 that the concept of in-service training did not exist for the officers in the Foreign Affairs Group (FAG) and civil service officers in the administration. They gained experience through the process of trial and error and by working under the guidance of their seniors. Most of the FAG officers were not familiar with the problems of the 'other' ministries and, with some exceptions, were almost reluctant to learn about them. Not surprisingly, most of the senior FAG officers holding ambassadorial assignments were generally more effective in their diplomatic work and their handling of economic, technical and military matters was largely left to the respective attachés posted in the missions. The Zia administration attempted to rectify this shortcoming by institutionalising a system of in-service training of officers and delegating additional responsibilities to all ambassadors in respect of their total work load. The attempt succeeded, but only partially. Territorial imperatives posed in-built hurdles and the system functioned in a rut, impervious to change.

Administration in Missions Abroad

Most of the political appointees in diplomatic assignments and the career ambassadors were new to the specialized field of administration. To them, the cumbersome financial rules and regulations and the bureaucratic delays inherent in the decision-making process were irksome. Those trying to circumvent the system committed financial irregularities. A system of the annual administrative inspection of all missions was introduced to enhance administrative efficiency. This was not popular with most ambassadors who considered it yet another sword hanging over their heads.

President Zia was not favourably disposed towards posting female FAG officers abroad in Pakistani Missions. Later, when the implication of this ban on the careers of the affected persons was explained to him, he abated this ban on a case to case basis. In practice, all restrictions were removed. In most cases, the female members of the FAG have proved to be more hardworking and successful as diplomats than their male counterparts.

Envoys Conferences

The government periodically held conferences of Pakistani ambassadors either in Islamabad or at some central regional location for a review of the situation. This provided an opportunity to up-date the ambassadors on domestic issues and to listen to their assessment of the situation as seen from different capitals. Each conference, usually spread over two days, was invariably presided over by the President himself. Such exhausting sessions were beneficial though repetitive and boring.

Meticulous in written work and articulate in presentation, Agha Shahi was a model of diplomatic perfection. Deeply dedicated to his profession, he was sensitive to criticism of foreign policy and often complained about those newspapers which indulged in sensationalism to promote their sale. Foreign Secretary Shah Nawaz showed his Afghan tribal trait with an enviable knack of conveying unpleasant views in a congenial and jovial style. A few envoys were 'talking encyclopedias', never short of words and ever eager to inflict their opinions on others. Some others spoke at length to justify their 'brief comments.' Yet others visibly suffered from 'localitis' in their assessment of events.

Postings and Transfers

General Zia involved himself in the process of the posting and transfer of ambassadors and senior diplomats. Normally such sessions were held in the Foreign Office and the deliberations took the better part of a day. On such occasions he would occasionally make teasing inquiries like, 'which Mafia group does this individual belong to?' or, 'the favoured blue boys of the Foreign Office monopolize the lucrative assignments while the underdogs move from one hard posting to another,' or, 'doesn't he love to serve Pakistan from a distance?'

The career planning rules required each FAG officer to serve abroad for two consecutive terms and then return to base for an assignment in the Foreign Office. Such a balanced mix of foreign and home assignments was aimed at grooming the diplomats for their tasks besides keeping them updated with domestic affairs and national policies. The rules were generally followed but with some notable exceptions which drew adverse criticism from within the FAG officers. For example, in the early eighties one senior officer, Mr Iqbal Akhund, made a request that he might not be considered for the prestigious post of the foreign secretary because of his personal family considerations. His foreign wife preferred to stay abroad on the assignment he then held.

Some FAG officers working in the United Nations agencies quietly promoted their own candidature for absorption in those agencies to earn in-service monetary advantages and post retirement UN pension benefits. The initial spadework silently done, cogent reasons were then coined requesting the government to agree to the UN request for the nomination of the officer concerned in the supreme 'national interest'. The argument was almost invariably the same. If Pakistan lost this vacancy, some other country, particularly India, would grab it to the disadvantage of Pakistan.

One FAG officer, Abdul Waheed, had the privilege of serving in Western Europe, a region of his choice, on three successive assignments, an exception to the rule. He was a close relative of

Ziaul Haq. Prime Minister Muhammed Khan Junejo asked Foreign Secretary Abdul Sattar to submit to him the names of all the FAG officers who were overdue for home assignments. The name of this ambassador was included in the list submitted to the Prime Minister. President Zia did not intervene in the matter but he did not take this development kindly. Junejo, a stickler for principles, stood his ground. The diplomat was ordered to return to Pakistan. Instead, he submitted his resignation and joined politics to become a parliamentarian.

Foreign Policy Achievements

In a civil society, military rule is not a preferred form of government. Pakistan suffered this trauma more than once. Pakistan's military dictators defended their intervention claiming it was done to preserve national unity and to rid the country of its prevailing chaos. With the exception of Yahya's rule, the prolonged tenures of Ayub Khan and Zia were blends of successes and failures. For reasons of political expediency, their critics tend to underplay their achievements and highlight their failings. The censure is magnified in the emotionally charged environment that prevails in Pakistan.

The Zia Government mended fences with the United States, received US aid and participated in the UN-sponsored Geneva Accord which resulted in the withdrawal of the Soviet forces from Afghanistan. An impossible mission was achieved. This was the first time in Soviet history that her armed forces had withdrawn from a country once occupied by them and it was a tribute to diplomacy. The people of Afghanistan and Pakistan and those of the free world deserve credit for this achievement. Pakistan played a critical role during this long and turbulent period under the firm and unflinching leadership of General Zia. The end result of the Soviet occupation of Afghanistan might have been more bitter and unpalatable had Pakistan buckled under Soviet military provocation and diplomatic pressure.

For reasons of domestic expediency, Prime Minister Junejo lost patience in the Afghan dispute at a time when a UN-sponsored settlement was close to conclusion. The opposition joined hands with Junejo in eclipsing Zia from the international limelight and the Prime Minister became a victim in their game. The Zia-Junejo differences of opinion on the final modalities of the proposed settlement plan were cleverly highlighted. The erstwhile Soviet Union exploited this situation. The Geneva Accord failed to address the issue of forming a government of national consensus in Afghanistan in the immediate post withdrawal period. Zia had advocated such a course. And the senior military commanders supported him on this issue. Mr Junejo, however, felt differently and his views finally prevailed. With the signing of the Geneva Accord an opportunity was lost.

India's 1974 nuclear test created an unacceptable strategic imbalance in South Asia that forced Pakistan to adopt the nuclear weapons route. Prime Minister Z.A. Bhutto called upon Pakistani nuclear scientists to counter the threat and meet the needs of Pakistan's national security. The uranium enrichment process adopted by Pakistan was in an elementary stage when the Bhutto government fell in 1977.

The Zia government faced intense diplomatic, economic and political pressures and veiled threats from the US-led Western countries to abandon Pakistan's nuclear programme. The greater the external pressures exerted on Pakistan the more firm became Zia's determination to complete the on-going nuclear effort. The US non-proliferation concern against Pakistan was patently partisan, discriminatory and grossly unfair. India had first committed the so-called nuclear sin in South Asia. Despite this she kept shopping around the world obtaining sensitive technology, training facilities, materials and high technology computers from the US, France, Britain, the Soviet Union and other countries.

On the contrary, all technology, material and equipment of dual-purpose use were denied to Pakistan by the cartels formed by the developed states. The foreign powers had underestimated the tenacity of Pakistan, the firmness of its policy and the ability of its demographic resources in mastering nuclear technology. Working under Western imposed restrictions, Pakistani scientists and technologists rose to the occasion. One after the other all the technological hurdles were successfully surmounted. To the disappointment of her distracters and to the satisfaction of her own people, Pakistan acquired nuclear capability.

South Asia had a decade of peace (1977-88) despite the chorus constantly chanted by Prime Minister Indira Gandhi that 'the clouds of war' were looming on the horizon. General Zia calmly ignored the threats and countered the provocative slogans by advocating a 'peace offensive' with India. During this period a *jihad* waged in Afghanistan against Soviet aggression and India sat on the sidelines attempting to bail out her benefactor and strategic ally, the Soviet Union. Strategic compulsions guided Zia to ensure that Pakistan did not get unwittingly caught in an open conflict on two fronts simultaneously at a time of her adversary's choice. He desired to settle one issue at a time and gave first priority to the settlement of Afghanistan.

President Zia's decision, despite opposition from some of his cabinet colleagues and other political leaders, to attend the funeral rites of Mrs Indira Gandhi, was an act of considerable diplomatic acumen and foresight. It was for the first time in India-Pakistan relations that a Pakistani Head of State had attended the funeral of an Indian leader—an act that did not go unnoticed in India.

General Ziaul Haq carried forward his diplomatic offensive with Prime Minister Rajiv Gandhi when, in a meeting on 6 December 1985, the two leaders agreed to sign an accord against attacking each other's nuclear facilities. The second major agreement on that occasion was to disengage in the Siachen Glacier area.

The other noteworthy foreign policy achievements during the Zia era included the conclusion of two aid packages with the US; the constructive role played by Pakistan during the war between Iran and Iraq; General Zia's personal efforts to get Egypt re-admitted in the Organisation of Islamic Countries;

Pakistan's admission in the Non-Aligned Movement and clearing of the decks for Pakistan's re-admission in the British Commonwealth of nations. Above all, General Zia subtly re-adjusted the foreign policy orientation of Pakistan from the socialist tilt given to it earlier by the Bhutto regime to bring it in the centre of the road with a leaning towards the right. Good relations with China, the US and the Muslim bloc formed an important triangular core in Pakistan's foreign policy.

NOTES

1. Rajender Sareen, *Pakistan—The India Factor*, Allied Publishers, New Delhi, 1984, p. 3.
2. Pandit Jawaharlal Nehru, *Selected Works of Jawaharlal Nehru*, Vol. 19, New Delhi, p. 322.
3. S.M. Burke, *Pakistan's Foreign Policy - A Historical Analysis*, Oxford University Press, 1973, p. 98.
4. Moscow Literary Gazette, quoted in *Hindu*, India, 28 July 1950.
5. *New York Times*, 15 September 1951.
6. Altaf Gauhar, *Ayub Khan*, Sang-e-Meel Publications, Lahore, 1993, p. 112.
7. N.A. Bulganin and N.S. Khrushchev, *Visit of Friendship to India, Burma and Afghanistan*, p. 111.
8. Ibid., pp. 107, 112.
9. Pravda, 15 September 1955.
10. *New York Times*, No. 50, 1955, p. 19.
11. *New York Times*, 27 June 1960.
12. Altaf Gauhar, *Ayub Khan*, p. 302.
13. *Asian Recorder*, 1965, p. 646.
14. *The Times*, 3 January 1966.
15. Altaf Gauhar, *Ayub Khan*, p. 236.
16. *Dawn*, Karachi, 24-26 August 1963.
17. Altaf Gauhar, The Nehru Letters, quoted in *Ayub Khan*, p. 232.
18. Mohammad Ayub Khan, *Friends Not Masters*, Oxford University Press, 1967, p. 186.
19. Interview Mr Niaz A. Naik, former Foreign Secretary.
20. Sultan M. Khan, *Memories and Reflections of a Pakistani Diplomat*, The London Centre of Pakistan Studies, 1997, p. 237.
21. Ibid., p. 242.
22. Interview Ambassador Abdul Sattar, 17 August 1999.

10

ADIEU

The Pakistan Army is a disciplined, professional and reputable institution. It offers a life of challenge, daring, honour and respect to all able-bodied youth in the country on a competitive basis, without discrimination. Military service offers a career of adventure, struggle, hazards and job satisfaction. It demands good character, courage, education and professionalism from its officers who form the backbone of the army. It is a privilege for a citizen to become an officer in the Pakistan Army and a pleasure to retire from it with dignity and honour after completing one's tenure of service. Those wearing khaki uniforms, like their colleagues in their blue and white outfits in the Pakistan Navy and in the Pakistan Air Force, are required to uphold the high and noble military traditions of soldiering with their sweat and blood.

The uncertainty in the profession of soldiering stems from the reality that those in uniform forego some of their fundamental rights for the time-tested reasons of national security. These include denial of collective bargaining and trade unionism, prohibition on political activity, and the trial of military personnel in military courts. Every military officer serves at the pleasure of the Head of State. This 'pleasure' may be abruptly withdrawn without assigning any reason when his 'services are no longer required.'

Fully aware of the military traditions, I was mentally prepared for retirement from the time I reached the rank of a major. Thereafter, all promotions in the selection grades were on a competitive basis. My family was prepared also to be ready for my early retirement. However, the opposite happened. My promotions came at regular intervals. The army's promotion system was fair. I treated every successive rise in my rank as a bonus but persisted with my life style. My promotion to the rank of a four star general took me to the zenith of my career and a process of countdown began in my thoughts. I silently prayed for an honourable fading away from the pinnacle and worked towards this goal. My first act in the office as the army commander was to offer *nawaafil* seeking retirement with honour, dignity and respect.

Soon after my appointment, I understood the meaning of the old saying, 'Uneasy lies the head that wears the crown.' One *maulvi*, while delivering a religious sermon in flowing oratory in a mosque in upper Sindh, accused me of being a Qadiani, a strong abuse for a Muslim in Pakistan. Feeling hurt, I brought this allegation to the notice of General Zia and told him that he might have put a wrong person in a highly sensitive appointment. Zia laughed heartily. He dismissed the mischievous allegation as a 'hazard of command' and asked me to ignore the falsehood. 'You were my Chief of Staff from 1977 to 1984', said Zia and 'in this long period no one made such an allegation. How has this *maulvi* suddenly discovered about your religious belief immediately after your promotion?' I could not determine if the *maulvi* was a free agent or someone had put the words in his mouth.

Then there was yet another intrigue. From late 1984 onwards the ISI Directorate started reporting to the President in confidential whispers that General Arif was acting too fast and too independently in running army affairs. This was a subtle attempt to create a misunderstanding between the President and myself. This rumour spread to such an extent that General Fazle Haq, the Governor of NWFP, inquired from me if I was aware of this sinister development. Fazle Haq, an insider, used to keep his eyes and ears open and had good reason to call it a sinister development. I reported the prevailing rumour to General Zia including Fazle Haq's inquiry. As usual, he smiled and remarked that speculative reporting was a part of the 'power game' and did not deserve serious attention. It is best ignored. Nosy people look for scoops, he added. Significantly, General Zia did not specifically confirm or deny the allegation that the source of the report was a secret agency of the state. A couple of months later the President's Military Secretary, Brigadier Mahmud Ali Durrani, casually hinted to me that some persons close to General Zia had become 'extra active' and I might watch their activities. It confirmed my doubts but I pretended to ignore the remark.

It soon became apparent that, notwithstanding their visible cordiality, all was not well between President Zia and Prime Minister Junejo. The sharing of power was a painful process for both of them. Zia wanted to play the senior role and influence, if not dominate, the decision-making process on issues considered important by him. He wanted to be consulted on important matters and kept informed about the affairs of the state. He considered Junejo as his nominee, his creation, and desired him to play a role with his own visible support. General Zia's close advisers and the ISI Directorate created problems between the President and the Prime Minister on minor issues and constantly but uncharitably painted Junejo as an ungrateful person who had become too big for his boots. Zia's personal staff was not free from blame either in this tirade. They always found some flaws in whatever Junejo did, or failed to do, in the performance of his responsibilities as the executive head of Pakistan.

Prime Minister Junejo, a stickler for details and, unlike Zia, frugal in public money matters, wanted to exercise full authority vested in the chief executive under the constitution without any strings attached. He considered the President's patronizing attitude as undue interference in his clearly defined constitutional domain and expected him to follow the constitution in letter and spirit. On constitutional and protocol matters he wanted to imitate Bhutto to demonstrate his hold on the government. Junejo's kitchen cabinet was over-sensitive to the Prime Minister's rights and authority and resented the President's involvement, if not interference, in such matters. The issues under debate were usually trivial in nature but their cumulative effect created a great psychological impact on the Prime Minister. Junejo wanted to dispel the public impression (mischievously) created by the opposition that being a nominated Prime Minister he was hamstrung and lacked the courage and the authority to take independent and crucial decisions. It goes to the credit of Junejo that he took some difficult and bold decisions during his prime ministership. The lifting of emergency from the country was one such act.

To be fair to Zia, he usually impressed on his military colleagues to fully support Junejo in nourishing the democratic setup that his martial law government had planted in the country. He wanted the army to help the civil administration in maintaining law and order in all troubled areas, particularly in Sindh which then faced a serious law and order problem. Personally, Zia claimed to stay in power to 'act as a bridge' between the civil and the military bodies and he wanted all others to leave it to him to decide for how long this 'bridge' would be necessary. This self-serving arrogance earned him the criticism of the people and of many parliamentarians to whom Zia had once specifically pledged to retire from military service by a definite date. Zia went back on his firm commitment on the advice of his sycophant subordinates who convinced him that he was indispensable for the country. Besides, he was cautioned not to take the risk of shedding his uniform and appointing someone else as his relief. That he accepted this logic showed that he did not have total confidence in any of his senior serving generals to replace him as the Army Chief.

The fault lay more with Zia than with Junejo. Zia claimed to his military colleagues and parliamentarians that he wanted to promote the growth of democracy, but he was hesitant to dilute his personal authority and power to enable the head of government to function under the constitution. Interference by Zia in matters of state administration was resented by Junejo for justifiable reasons and their mutual alienation kept growing.

The Zia-Junejo power tussle created obstacles in running the army smoothly. My visits to the President on matters of national security or on issues of the army's interests quickly buzzed

intelligence antennas carried by the Prime Minister's inner
supporters. They started speculating about my 'frequent visits' to
the President and drew self-serving and baseless conclusions from
them. Likewise, motives were hypothesized by the self-appointed
supporters of the Presidency whenever I met the Prime Minister.
Knowing such a proclivity, I avoided discussing political issues
with both of them and restricted my conversation to professional
matters alone. Additionally, by way of abundant caution, I
invariably kept both the President and the Prime Minister
informed about my discussion with the other person. The system
worked reasonably well, on face value, and I did not get any
complaint from either the President or the Prime Minister.
However I did not know if they nourished any undeclared
reservations against me. My tight-rope walk was precarious and
I knew the pitfalls of simultaneously serving two masters who
were engaged in a tussle for power.

I had reached the pinnacle of my profession and felt proud
about it. With no political ambitions in my genes, I did not have
to please either the President or the Prime Minister to earn a
berth in the political hierarchy of the country. I had seen and
handled politics from close quarters during the Yahya and Zia
eras and the more I saw the more distant I wanted to be from
them. Politics is a fascinating game but those in uniform are not
psychologically and institutionally groomed to excel in the art
of double-talk barring exceptions.

My personal relations with Zia and Junejo were balanced and
correct and I maintained a distance from both of them in the
time-tested traditions of the Pakistan Army. Both, I felt, had
confidence in me and I did not betray this trust. I gave them due
respect and they reciprocated appropriately. I was aware of their
growing mutual unease and was concerned about it. While I tried
to smoothen a rough edge or two, I never took advantage of
them. My sole ambition was to retire from the army with respect,
dignity and self-satisfaction.

Lieutenant-General S. R. Kallue retired from the Army in
mid 1986. Just before his retirement I asked General Zia if he
had any particular general officer in mind to replace Kallue.

I also reminded the President that I was myself due to retire in March 1987 and urged him that, keeping the dignity of the appointment, my retirement might be announced at least two months before the due date. An army chief should retire from military service with grace and be given a reasonably long notice to bid farewell to his command in the well-established tradition of the Pakistan Army. The early nomination of a successor also provides sufficient time to the new incumbent to reflect on his priorities before assuming his new assignment. Besides, it shows to the world that the decision making process in the country is institutionalized and effective. General Zia agreed with my views. But, in a half reflective and half jovial mood, he said, 'All the service chiefs before you had tenures of four years or more. We shall not part company in a hurry. I do not foresee your early retirement.' The discussion remained inconclusive.

The 17th Corps Commander's Conference was held in Rawalpindi on 20-21 December 1986. During the two days that he spent in the General Headquarters, I again reminded General Zia of my impending retirement and impressed on him to select my relief and announce the date of my retirement at the latest by early February 1987. Zia told me that General Rahimuddin Khan, Chairman of the Joint Chiefs of Staff Committee, had also made a similar request to him about his own retirement. Then, talking aloud he said, 'Rahim would retire in March next year as he would be over sixty years of age by then. Your case falls in a different category. You will be under fifty-seven then.' It became apparent that Zia had done his homework and was aware of the relevant facts. Then, with a deliberate pause he looked at me in confidence and said, 'I have been thinking about my own retirement from the army. This is a difficult decision to take because there is so much at stake beyond myself. I have to think of the country and of the future of the recently inducted democracy. Should I decide to shed my uniform, you shall replace me as the next Chief of the Army Staff. But if I opt against my own retirement, then I intend to keep you in your present post for another two years. You have prepared a plan to reorganize the army. I want you to implement it before you retire.'

I told Zia that I had an official invitation to visit China but I had deliberately kept it pending as I did not wish to be away from the country till after the completion of India's Exercise Brass Tacks due to be held early next year. Zia urged me to accept the invitation in principle and quickly communicate the dates of the visit to China. 'Pakistan has excellent relations with China', said Zia, adding, 'and it will be diplomatically inadvisable to delay your response to this friendly country.' 'I agree with you Mr President', I replied, adding, 'but since my retirement is due in March 1987, it may be more prudent for the next Vice Chief to avail this invitation.' A smiling Zia insisted, 'I had told you earlier that come what may you will not be retiring in March 1987. So accept the invitation and plan your visit'.

General Zia discussed the proposed plan of his own retirement with one or two of his close advisers. This set in motion an intrigue-filled campaign in which Zia was told by them that he alone could nourish the sapling of democracy that he had laboured hard to plant in the country. They also told him what Zia wanted to hear from others. He must neither retire himself from the military service nor appoint anyone else as the army chief. The system was working well and 'needed continuity.' Why upset it, they argued? It was also subtly conveyed to Zia that General Arif had lately become pro-Junejo and this important factor might be kept in view. This wilful fabrication was patently false. I was neither pro-Junejo nor against him. However, I gave due respect, as demanded of my official position, to the Prime Minister of the country.

The 18th Corps Commander's Conference was held at Rawalpindi on 14-15 February 1987. General Zia was not in his usual exuberant mood on this occasion. He took lukewarm interest in the conference agenda, and unlike his routine practice in the past he did not address the participants on political developments in and around the country. As usual, he hosted a dinner at his house to which the VCOAS, all the corps commanders, and the DG ISI, Lieutenant-General Akhtar Abdur Rahman Khan, were invited. These invitees were asked to meet the host in an exclusive pre-dinner meeting. The PSOs, not invited to the pre-dinner meeting, joined the group just before the dinner.

As the invitees sat around the table in the President's office that evening, General Zia gave an hour long monologue on internal developments in Pakistan. At first he talked at length about generalities but finally came to the specifics. His main theme was that whereas he had fulfilled his promise of holding elections in the country and democracy stood restored, the democratic system was meek, weak and corrupt. The Prime Minister spent considerable time in humouring the National Assembly members in an attempt to get their support, and the demands of the parliamentarians for concessions and favours were unending. The nascent democracy needed military support and uninterrupted patronage to strengthen and flourish.

After a lengthy preamble, General Zia came to the heart of the matter. He paid warm tributes to the army for remaining steadfast despite facing stresses and provocation. He then said, 'We owe it to our country to complete the task started by us. We must not leave it half way. Continuity of effort and leadership is our utmost requirement at this critical juncture of our national history. We must reach our goal. The government needs the military support to do so. We shall help the government in achieving its objective.'

President Zia had borrowed the words 'continuity of effort and leadership' from the intelligence briefs prepared by the ISI Directorate. General Akhtar Abdur Rahman (DGI) had used this formulation countless times during the intelligence briefings given by him to the general officers. With Zia still speaking I meaningfully focused my eyes on Akhtar. He quickly shied away. General Zia's decision to remain in uniform and retain authority under his personal control did not surprise his audience. They had all worked with Zia long enough to know his idiosyncrasies and to see through his game plan. The intoxication of power is a disease easy to acquire and hard to shed. Besides, Zia's advisers had their own interests linked with the President's decision to stay in authority.

General Zia's broad hint was loud and clear to me and I waited for his next move. Instead, there was silence. The month of February slipped into history without the announcement of my retirement. In early March, I reminded him again to nominate my relief. I found him evasive. He claimed that Prime Minister Junejo's pre-occupation with other issues had prevented him from discussing this matter. On 12 March I spoke to the President once again and failed to get a decision from him.

On 13 March 1987, General Zia and I attended a dinner in Lahore. He inquired from me if I planned to spend the night at Lahore to which I replied in the negative. 'In that case why shouldn't we travel together on our return flight to Rawalpindi,' he said, adding, 'We can talk enroute.'

During the presidential flight, General Zia expressed regret that the nomination of the new Chairman of the Joint Chiefs of Staff Committee and the Vice Chief of the Army Staff had been delayed. The reason for the delay was the Prime Minister's pre-occupation with the National Assembly work. General Zia said that he had a brief talk on the subject with Junejo but it was an inconclusive discussion. His tone and stance were different to his normal self and his mind appeared pre-occupied and unprepared for an in-depth discussion.

With hesitation writ large on his unsmiling face he asked for my recommendations. I told him that it would be imprudent for me to suggest my own relief as he knew the general officers as well as I did. His reticence caused anguish to me and I told him quite firmly that I would appreciate it if the government's decision was definitely conveyed to me by the following day, 14 March 1987. Zia must have sensed the change in my tone but he remained quiet. He then divulged that he was due to meet Junejo the next day, and asked me to telephone him after 9 p.m. He also apprised me that because of his age, General Rahimuddin Khan would be retiring, but he wanted me to stay in my appointment. This prompted me to inquire who was replacing Rahim. General Zia pretended that he had not yet finally made up his mind. Both of us knew that Zia was hiding the obvious. Not wishing to embarrass him, I changed the topic of our discussion.

I called the President on 14 March as desired by him. He told me that while a decision had been taken, it needed 'some explaining' for which he would meet me in the General Headquarters at 0930 am on 15 March 1987.

General Ziaul Haq arrived at General Headquarters at 10 am on 15 March 1987. We shook hands but Zia avoided direct eye contact. The absence of his congenial style showed that he was under strain. As we settled down in the office, I found his eyes blank, face glum and for once, he was short on words. He was aware that I was scheduled to visit the School of Armour, Nowshera, immediately after our meeting.

I sympathized with General Zia when he began to talk. In an amiable monotone he said that he had discussed the subject with Junejo on three or four occasions in the past six weeks and regretted that the decision was delayed. He told me that he found Junejo well prepared on issues of facts and law about the appointment of the services chiefs. He had shown to the President documentary evidence to prove that under the constitution, whereas the appointment of the Chairman of the Joint Chiefs of Staff Committee fell within the discretionary powers of the President, the appointment of the Vice Chief of the Army Staff was the prerogative of the Prime Minister, even when the Vice Chief had been delegated full powers of the Chief of the Army Staff for the duration that General Zia held the dual appointments of the President and the COAS. I interjected to say that Junejo had interpreted the legal position quite correctly and there was no ambiguity on this issue. Junejo felt, so said General Zia, that as a matter of policy, tenure appointments should not be extended and a new Vice Chief of the Army Staff should be appointed with effect from 22 March 1987. I told General Zia that I shared the Prime Minister's views.

General Zia eulogized my services as his Chief of Staff and as the Vice Chief of the Army Staff. He complimented me for revamping the spirit of professionalism in the army and for the sobering role played by the army during the transition of power from martial law to a democratic order. He praised the operational, training, motivational, logistical and welfare measures adopted during my tenure of command. 'You would be remembered,' said Zia, 'with respect and gratitude for your contribution in improving the defence capability of the Pakistan Army.' He strongly appreciated the strategic role played by the army during India's Exercise Brass Tacks in early 1987. The well-conceived, timely and firm response, said Zia, had won the admiration of the people of Pakistan. He commended the large military construction programme initiated by me, and concluded by saying that I had given a new sense of direction and leadership for which I would be remembered.

It was generous of General Zia to make such complimentary remarks. How many of them reflected his real sentiments was hard to guess. If it was an attempt to prepare me psychologically for my retirement, the explanation was unnecessary. I knew how to give and take orders.

General Zia struggled to conceal his embarrassment. This was not the first time that he had created a problem for himself. His command technique was to keep his subordinates under suspense till the end to get maximum work out of them and to demonstrate that he was the boss. It was the President's prerogative to appoint commanders and change them when due. Since I had completed my prescribed tenure of assignment, a change in command was due and logically desirable. There was no need for Zia to be apologetic about it.

General Zia took pains to convey to me that while he wanted me to stay, Junejo desired that the sanctity of the tenure assignments be observed and it was the Prime Minister's privilege to have the last word on the subject. According to him, Mr Junejo personally held me in high esteem. He felt sorry that the matter had taken a shape different to what he had earlier planned. I told him that I did not seek an extension in service and was happy to retire after completing the prescribed tenure of my assignment.

Visibly relaxed, General Zia now spoke with greater ease. He praised Lieutenant-General Akhtar Abdur Rahman Khan for the

services rendered by him as Director General of Intelligence for
the last eight years and felt that 'he deserved to be compensated.'
He had, therefore, nominated him to replace General Rahim as
Chairman of the Joint Chiefs of Staff Committee. I heard him in
silence. He then said that Lieutenant-General Mirza Aslam Beg
would succeed me, and both the changes would be effective on
22 March 1987. General Zia looked at me and paused as if to
assess my reaction. I wished luck and success to both the general
officers.

It was not for me to point out a glaring contradiction in the
statement of the experienced president. General Rahim was
supposedly being retired because he was over sixty. But at the
same time Lieutenant-General Akhtar, also over sixty years of
age, was being promoted. Zia's illogical argument was hard to
defend. He really didn't have to justify or explain his acts to me.

A relieved General Zia became affectionate, almost nostalgic,
about our three decades long association. He recounted my
'valuable' contribution during the difficult martial law period
(1977-85) and desired that our personal relationship endure
beyond my retirement. He inquired about my post-retirement
plans, to which I replied that I would think about them. Zia was
looking for an opening like this. 'Would you like to get an
ambassadorial appointment?' he shot back quickly. I thanked
him for the consideration and declined to accept the offer for
personal reasons. He had done his home work before meeting
me. 'I would strongly recommend to the Prime Minister,' said
General Zia, 'that you may be appointed as his adviser with the
status of a federal minister,' and added that, 'the Prime Minister
was keen to utilize your talents in some suitable manner.'

I thanked the President once again and stated that in my
humble judgment a nominated adviser had no place in an elected
government and declined the offer.

It was my turn to speak. I profoundly thanked General Zia for
his kind words and the consideration he had shown to me in our
long association. 'I leave it to posterity', I said, 'to judge my
performance.' Then looking at him, I stated that since I had never
hesitated in bringing unpalatable things to his notice, even at the

risk of earning his annoyance, I would like to maintain this on the eve of my retirement. There was a change in General Zia's mood. He held himself back and became somewhat serious.

I asked him to recall the details of a news item carried by a section of the government-controlled National Press Trust newspapers in March 1986. That news item had speculated about changes in the appointments of the Chairman of the Joint Chiefs of Staff Committee and the Vice Chief of the Army Staff. I reminded him that at the time of it's publication I had told him that the news item was inspired and the source of leakage was a federal intelligence agency.

Taken by surprise, General Zia stated that no evidence had come to light to prove the involvement of an intelligence agency in that 'unfortunate false report.' I told him that it was strange that the government had not contradicted the false report. General Zia could not and did not answer and I did not wish to embarrass him further on the issue. It was not my business to bring the obvious to the notice of the President.

I asked General Zia if I had lost his confidence. 'Oh, no' he promptly and vehemently denied the suggestion. This gave me an opening to complain. 'Then why were my movements kept under surveillance by junior officers?' I asked. An astonished General Zia vehemently denied having ordered any intelligence agency to keep me under surveillance.

I told him that while I would not speculate on who had issued the orders, I had enough evidence to conclude that the Vice Chief of the Army Staff was being shadowed. General Zia said that, 'knowing Akhtar, as I do, he could not have done such an act.' I provided him essential information in support of my claim. General Zia heard me patiently but remained unconvinced and argued that my apprehensions might have been based on some misunderstanding. I decided to disclose the facts in totality and gave him full details, chapter and verse, of a particular case, concerning my surveillance, by naming an agent, identifying the location, and disclosing to him the name of a serving corps commander, Lieutenant-General Raja Saroop Khan, who had investigated the case and personally brought the incident to my notice and to the notice of the Director General of Intelligence. During the investigation the concerned agent had disclosed that he had acted 'on orders from above.'

A bewildered Zia looked blank and promised to ascertain the details. I told him that the senior military commanders should either be fully trusted or instantly removed from their high risk assignments. I then gave him the names of some other senior military officers who had received similar treatment in the past. General Zia knew that the authenticity of my statement was based on knowledge and he wisely refrained from contradicting it.

I asked General Zia if I could complain about a service matter. He nodded his approval. I requested him not to misunderstand me as I had consistently tried to develop the institution. I then told him that I was constrained to point out that he, the Chief of the Army Staff, had downgraded the image of the army by retiring two four-star generals, Raheemuddin and Arif at just seven day's notice. The dignity of their high offices demanded that their retirement should have been announced much in advance. Such an act, I said, should have been done with grace and in accordance with recognized norms of military service and not in a state of confused hurry. A grim and tight-lipped Zia listened to me with commendable patience. I envied his capacity to take criticism from others.

The President then informed me that he had already informed Generals Akhtar and Beg about their respective promotions and appointments and the Ministry of Defence would issue a press notice later that day. He had prepared the ground with meticulous care. The retiring person was the last to be officially informed about his own retirement.

Soon after General Zia left my office, I flew to Nowshera on a pre-planned visit to the School of Armour. A couple of hours later, while at Nowshera, I received a telephone call from the President. He said that my criticism about the short notice of retirement was justified and, after discussing the issue with the Prime Minister who was outside Islamabad, it had been decided to retire General Rahim Uddin Khan and myself one week later. I suggested to the President that since the Government decision was already known to the Ministry of Defence, no change be made at that belated stage. The President almost pleaded that I accept the change and I bowed to his wish. Later that day, the Ministry of Defence issued a press note announcing my retirement on 29 March 1987.

After leaving General Headquarters, General Zia directed Ijlal Zaidi, the Defence Secretary, to convey my complaint about the short retirement notice to the Prime Minister and to get the date suitably extended. Ijlal contacted Junejo at his village Sindhri, Sindh. Fussy on minor issues, the Prime Minister initially expressed reluctance but he soon had second thoughts and told Ijlal to modify the date to April 1. Ijlal pointed out that this date might be inadvisable because a social taboo was sometimes associated with it. 'In that case,' said Junejo, 'let it be 29 March.' So, it was.

I spent the next two weeks on farewell visits to formation headquarters that extended warm hospitality in the best tradition of the Pakistan Army.

At 1330 pm Saturday, 28 March 1987, my last day in uniform, I inspected a smartly turned out guard of honour at the Army Stadium, Rawalpindi. It was given by the officers, junior commissioned officers and men of 11th Cavalry (FF), the regiment which I had joined in 1949. My professional life had thus completed a full circle. It was a historic day for me, and an honour that I shall remember. The ceremony was attended by a large number of military officers and their families. The President, General M. Ziaul Haq, and the Prime Minister, Mr Muhammad Khan Junejo, not only graced the occasion and stood with me on the dais as I took the salute, but also made warm and generous remarks about me and my contribution to the Pakistan Army. As I left the guard of honour ceremony, leaving the President and the Prime Minister standing on the dais, and a host of spectators waving at me, Arif, the soldier, faded away into history after serving the Pakistan Army and Pakistan for thirty-eight years.

My retirement earned me rest and, to my delight, distanced me from official engagements. This provided a long-awaited and much-cherished freedom of action which regretfully turned out to be short-lived. My newly acquired privacy was soon invaded from a different quarter. I received a number of lucrative work offers from the private sector. I had a hunch that most employers wanted to use my name and contacts with the government to promote their own business interests. I disqualified myself from playing such a role and declined the invitations with thanks. Some foreign firms of repute also contacted me with offers to promote their defence-related sales in the country. I rejected them with contempt because their motives were transparent.

A couple of months after my retirement there was a death in the family of Major-General Hamid Gul who had replaced General Akhtar Abdur Rahman as the Director General of Intelligence. My wife and I went to his house to offer condolences. He told me then that on my complaint the President had directed DGI to check the facts behind the incident of surveillance, Hamid Gul stated that since Akhtar had assumed his new responsibilities it fell on him to comply with the President's orders. He could not find evidence to substantiate my charges. Amused at the approach, I told Hamid Gul that since he was not on the scene of occurrence it was no use talking to him on the subject. I requested him to convey to Akhtar that he should speak to me personally if he could muster enough courage to do so. I did not hear anything again on this issue either from General Zia or from Akhtar.

My contacts with the President became rare and brief and were invariably restricted to an exchange of pleasantries. Under the circumstances, I was surprised when I received an invitation to attend the oath-taking ceremony of retired Mr Justice Aslam Riaz Hussain who was being sworn in as the acting *Wafaqi Mohtasib* (Ombudsman). I attended the function in which the oath of office was given by General Zia.

In early August 1988, I met General Zia at his house. Little did I know then that this was to be my last meeting with him. The discussion over, I sought permission to leave. General Zia was in no hurry to end our meeting. I sensed some load on his chest that he wanted to unburden. He questioned me on how I kept myself busy and said, 'I have kept an important slot ready for you for the last one year. Fill it in whenever you want' This unexpected disclosure surprised me. I was still speechless when he added, 'Remember that the Ombudsman was appointed on an acting basis and he still remains so. If you are interested, I shall give you this post tomorrow. Under the Constitution the President is the appointing authority of the Ombudsman and the appointment has a five year tenure.'

I learnt then why Aslam Riaz was made acting Ombudsman and the purpose of inviting me to his oath-taking ceremony. I pretended that I no longer remembered the detailed functioning of this organization. Zia was quick to mention that I had participated in drafting the charter of responsibilities and he would send me relevant documents to refresh my memory. I made no commitment but thanked the President for his consideration. Three days later, the President's staff sent me the documents promised by him. A week later Zia died in a plane crash.

The Pakistan Army that I joined in 1949 was very different from the one that I left behind on the eve of my retirement in 1987. During the interregnum it was transformed in many ways to meet the requirements of time and modernization. These changes transformed the army from an ill-equipped colonial force to a well-chiselled, hard-hitting and fairly modern war machine capable of defending the motherland. The experience gained included the wars imposed on the country and a variety of arduous, and often little-known low intensity operations in the fields of internal security, disaster relief, counter-insurgency and international peacekeeping operations.

The army also tasted political power—intoxicating and bitter—and in the process learnt a lesson or two, the most important being that politics and soldiering are full time professions each requiring undivided attention. The military interventions in Pakistan bore heavy price tags for the country and for the army itself. This cost is best avoided in the greater interests of both. The army faces a great responsibility and a bright future. The future of the country is inseparably linked with democracy.

EPILOGUE

It was originally planned to include events up to August 1997 in this book to coincide with the first fifty years of Pakistan's independence. However, the dramatic developments that took place in 1998, and 1999 have led to this epilogue. On 11 and 13 May 1998, India conducted five nuclear tests without justification or provocation. These tests were part of a premeditated plan. India then launched a well orchestrated campaign of anti-Pakistan propaganda, creating an atmosphere of war hysteria. The Indian Prime Minister Atal Behari Vajpayee advised Pakistan to 'forget about Kashmir'. In an even more strident tone, India's Home Minister, Mr L. K. Advani warned Pakistan to 'roll back her Kashmir policy' and arrogantly declared that henceforth India's Kashmir policy would be 'proactive and not reactive'. Mr K. L. Sharma, Vice President of the ruling BJP, threatened Pakistan to be 'prepared for India's wrath'. Minister Madanlal Khurana pointedly declared that Pakistan might 'choose between friendship and war with India'. This one-sided and sustained war of words was transformed into action when India activated the Line of Control in Kashmir with machine gun and artillery fire. Ominous war clouds were seen on the political horizon.

Global reaction to India's nuclear tests and the war hysteria created by the country was mild and niggardly. While the nuclear tests were condemned and the escalation of tension along the Line of Control deplored, sustained diplomatic pressure was exerted on Pakistan by the West to exercise restraint and avoid a tit-for-tat reaction to the nuclear tests. This partisan approach and India's aggressive initiative convinced Pakistan that her national security faced a grave threat and she only had two options: to either unilaterally surrender her nuclear test capability, or to make Pakistan a *de facto* nuclear power. This was a hard choice to make and the proven unreliability of external crutches that we had tried to hold onto in the past made it harder still. Pakistan adopted the latter course and carried out six nuclear tests on 28 and 30 May 1998. The era of nuclear ambiguity in South Asia ended. It was now known to the world that both India and Pakistan possessed nuclear weapons.

Other important developments also took place. A summit meeting was held between Muhammad Nawaz Sharif of Pakistan and Prime Minister Atal Behari Vajpayee of India in the historic city of Lahore. Symbolically, Vajpayee took a bus ride to Lahore under a blaze of media publicity where he was given red carpet treatment. Both the Prime Ministers signed what came to be known as the Lahore Declaration on 21 February 1999, pledging, among other things, a commitment from their respective governments, to 'intensify their efforts to resolve all issues, including the issue of Jammu and Kashmir'.[1] The Lahore Declaration created an air of euphoria, largely government sponsored, suggesting that Indo-Pakistan relations were on the mend. The world welcomed the development.

The hopes raised were short-lived. Both the adversaries soon reverted to their traditional one-step forward, two-steps back syndrome. Soon after the Lahore summit, the Kargil crisis erupted in the disputed State of Jammu and Kashmir. Once again, there were war clouds on the horizon. The Indian military forces were caught napping when the Kashmiri freedom fighters occupied the Kargil-Drass heights just across the Line of Control. The surprised military command in India woke up to the capture of territory in Kashmir several weeks later, and made repeated attempts to recover the area. Their attacks failed and their mounting casualties in combat raised a hue and cry among the Indian public. Faced with an adverse military situation in Kashmir and unrest within the country, India launched a vigorous diplomatic effort to get the disputed area vacated. The situation in Kashmir was eventually defused with the intervention of President Bill Clinton who prevailed on Prime Minister Nawaz Sharif to advise the Kashmiri freedom fighters to vacate the heights occupied by them. They agreed albeit with reluctance. An uneasy calm returned to the state but tension prevailed for a long while.

The Kargil crisis was perceived in Pakistan as a setback for the Nawaz Sharif government. It also created undercurrents of unease between the government and the army although both publicly declared that Pakistan's Kargil policy enjoyed total harmony between the top civil and military policy makers. On the contrary, in India, a sense of euphoria was purposely created by its electronic and print media, and as a part of government policy to divert public attention from the failure of the Indian army in Kargil and adjoining sectors in Kashmir. The West blamed Pakistan rather than India for the crisis that had developed in Kashmir. International pressure mounted on Islamabad. Perforce, an isolated Pakistan had conceded under extreme foreign pressure. The Kashmiri freedom fighters vacated captured territory as agreed with Pakistan. India, despite its vast numerical superiority in combat forces, had failed to regain the area even after repeated attempts.

In the immediate post-Kargil crisis period relations between India and Pakistan nose-dived. Bilateral negotiations on the Kashmir dispute and other issues were stalled and the hopes raised after the signing of the Lahore Declaration were negated.

A year after the Kargil affair, Pakistan was confronted with another crisis. On 12 October 1999, Prime Minister Nawaz Sharif suddenly ordered the immediate retirement of General Pervez Musharraf, Chief of Army Staff. The General's retirement was announced in the country on the state-controlled electronic media in a special bulletin.

The ISI chief Lieutenant-General Ziauddin was chosen to replace General Musharraf. General Ziauddin was summoned by the Prime Minister and promoted to the rank of a four-star general. His badges of rank were affixed by the Prime Minister under the focus of television cameras. The peremptory retirement of General Pervez Musharraf and the promotion and elevation of General Ziauddin to the position of army chief were repeatedly telecast and broadcast by the electronic media in special bulletins.

At the time when General Pervez Musharraf was insultingly retired as Chief of Army Staff, he was out of the country on an official visit to Sri Lanka. In fact, Prime Minister Nawaz Sharif had timed his announcements to coincide with General Musharraf's return flight from Sri Lanka to Pakistan. Therefore, as things moved in Pakistan, General Musharraf was on board an airliner and completely unaware of these developments.

The crisis deepened, however, with the Prime Minister's decision to refuse landing rights to the PIA airliner carrying General Musharraf and 198 other passengers and crew at Karachi. The pilot was ordered to divert the flight to any Gulf state. He requested permission to land at Nawabshah. He was told that this airport was also closed. The pilot expressed his inability to reach the Gulf because of low fuel endurance. He also reported the situation to General Pervez Musharraf. By this time, the runway at Karachi airport had been blocked and its lights switched off to prevent a forced landing. Finally, permission was given to land at Nawabshah Airport, and the airport management was directed to refuel the aircraft and permit it to take-off immediately for any airport outside Pakistan. At the other end of the spectrum, the military was alerted and an army contingent took control of Karachi Airport. Necessary steps were taken to clear the blocked runways and open landing lights till flight 805 finally landed with only seven minutes of fuel left in its tanks. A major catastrophe involving 198 people in an airliner had been averted. Prime Minister Nawaz Sharif and his colleagues were apprehended and detained by the military.

Even though the constitution authorized Mr Nawaz Sharif to retire General Pervez Musharraf, prudence demanded that the matter be dealt with in a dignified manner. Instead, General Pervez Musharraf was denied the required courtesies and was surreptitiously retired in a stage of confused hurry. Further, the retirement was publicised in a manner insulting to the Army Chief. Later, it transpired that the Prime Minister had neither consulted the ruling Muslim League nor had he taken the federal cabinet into confidence. The President of Pakistan Rafiq Ahmad Tarar was requested, at short notice, to approve the retirement order that was prepared in the Prime Minister's Secretariat instead of in the Ministry of Defence.

The hush-hush 'Get-Pervez Musharraf' drama was allegedly conceived and implemented by a small group of politicians and bureaucrats who constituted the Prime Minister's inner circle of policy makers. It was later learnt that the Prime Minister had personally spoken to the Director-General, Civil Aviation Authority, Mr Aminullah Chaudhry, and ordered that 'the aircraft of the army chief should not be allowed to land in Pakistan.'[2] This was a bizarre revelation. For Pakistan to prohibit its own national airliner from landing on its own soil, in peacetime, was an act that made no sense.

Prime Minister Nawaz Sharif had overplayed his hand and underestimated the reaction of the top military brass. Just over a year earlier, the circumstances under which the previous army chief, General Jahangir Karamat, was forced to seek premature retirement from the army were well known. This time the military intervened. Nawaz Sharif and his colleagues were picked up from the Prime Minister's house and detained.

Once again, for the fourth time in the history of Pakistan, the national democratic order was derailed. The government of Mr Nawaz Sharif was dismissed, the Constitution was held in abeyance, Parliament was suspended, and General Pervez Musharraf assumed control of the country as its Chief Executive. He promised to replace 'sham democracy' with a genuine one. Once again 'khaki shadows' loomed large over Pakistan.

The events of 12 October 1999, dipped Pakistan' image low. Mr Nawaz Sharif and his accomplices were tried in a court of law. Aminullah Chaudhry turned approver. Several months after the event, one commentator had this to say about the fate and functioning of democracy in Pakistan, 'The Prime Ministers of the day, and his or her relatives, always assume more power than is good for the country. The incumbent government runs roughshod over parliament, provincial governments, and even the financial system. All governments have robbed the financial system directly and indirectly. The exchequer remains perennially poor because of spendthrift governments and the manner in which the politically powerful refuse to pay any taxes.'[3]

Despite the faults and failures of democratic governments in the country, the military is not a panacea for Pakistan's political and administrative failures. It has no magic wand to put the wrongs right. Nor does the constitution authorise it to administer the country. Its organising ability and efficiency are best utilised for the defence of the motherland. It performs other tasks at the cost of its defence obligations.

The military establishment itself at the professional plane may critically evaluate the balance sheet of gains and losses sustained by the country and by the military itself during the military rules of Generals Ayub, Yahya and Zia. An in-depth and in-house discussion in GHQ and in the premier training institutions—National Defence College and Staff Colleges—may provide a well-researched analytical review of military rule. Such an effort by military researchers and academics would be beneficial both for the country and the military in the future.

NOTES

1. *Dawn*, Karachi, 22 February 2000.
2. *Dawn*, Karachi, 17 February 2000.
3. Dr Abdus Samad, *The News*, Islamabad, 15 February 2000.

INDEX

Musa, Gen Mohammad:
on Operation Gibralter, 47; on
Foreign Office, 48; loyalty, 53; on
Gen Akhtar Hussain Malik, 58; on
Gen Yahya Khan, 58; accepting
blame, 59; on army raisings, 65;
officers superseded, 374
Musharraf, Gen Pervez, 327, 357,
382, 441, 442, 443
Mutual Defence Assistance Agree-
ment, 392, 395
Muzaffar, Brig Mohammad, 17
Muzaffar, Nawab, 212

N

Naik, Niaz A., xvii
Narayan, Jayaprakash, 44
Nawaz, Gen Asif, 229, 365
Nawaz, Maj-Gen Mohammad, 101
Nawaz, Shah, 416
Nayyer, Vice Admiral K.K., 253
Nazimuddin, Khawaja, 10, 98, 278,
342, 360
Nehru, Pundit Jawaharlal, 37, 38, 40,
43, 53, 303, 328, 386, 387, 389,
399
Niaz, Lt-Gen Arbab, 164, 373
Niazi, Lt-Gen A.A.K., 69, 79, 80, 86,
127, 129, 130, 134, 136
Niazi, Maulana Kausar, 155, 196
Nishtar, Sardar Abdur Rab, 360
Nixon, Richard M., 184, 409
Noon, Prime Minister Firoze Khan,
27, 360
Noorani, Maulana Shah Ahmad, 118
Noorani, Zain, 273
Nusrat, Justice S.A., xvii, 301, 303
Nusserwanjee, Jamshed, 203

O

Omar, Maj-Gen Ghulam, 406
One Unit, 104

P

Palejo, Rasool Bux, 212
Patel, Sardar, 37
Peerzada, Lt-Gen S.G.M.M., 102,
113, 136, 279
Pirzada, Sharifuddin, 290, 291, 308,
313
Prasad, Maj-Gen Naranjan, 62

Q

Qadir, Lt-Gen Saeed, 159, 164, 171,
313
Qadri, Justice Shamim Hassan, 309
Qayum, Sahibzada Abdul, 118
Qayyum, Col Abdul, 103
Qazi, A.G.N., 367
Qazi, Capt Aftab Ahmad Jan, 87
Qureshi, Hafiz, 212
Qureshi, Shoaib, 389

R

Rahim, J.A., 279
Rahim, Khawaja Tariq, 319
Rahimtoola, Habib, 389
Rahman, Capt Fazal-ur-, 18
Rahman, Justice Hamoodur, 133, 279
Rahman, Lt-Gen M. Attiqur, 65, 105
Rahman, Shaikh Mujibur, 98, 106,
107, 109, 112, 126, 132, 137, 213,
343
Rahman, Tufail Ali Abdul, 285
Rana, Lt-Gen Bakhtiar, 63
Rasgotra, M., 256
Rashid, Lt-Col Abdul, 6
Raza, Maj Syed Nayar, 6
Reagan, Ronald, 184
Refaqat, Lt-Gen Syed, xvii, 200, 359
Rehman, Lt-Col Abdul, 78
Rehman, Maj Abdul, 87
Rehman, Maj Zia-ur, 119
Rhee, Syngman, 390

W

Waheed, Abdul, 417
Waheed, Maj-Gen Malik Abdul, xvii
Wilson, Harold, 42

Y

Yusuf, S.M., 406, 407

Z

Zafar, S.M., xi
Zafrullah, Sir Mohammad, 10
Zahid, Anwar, 367
Zahid, Justice Nasir Aslam, 311
Zaidi, Bushra, 226
Zaidi, Capt Syed Mohammad
    Muslim, 21
Zaidi, Ijlal Haider, 367, 436
Zaidi, Maj Syed M. Hatim, 86
Zedong, Mao, 29
Ziauddin, Lt-Gen, 366, 441
Zia-ul-Haq, Gen M.:
    Arif-Zia association, xv, 140-141;
    meets Zia-ur-Rahman, 119; the
    person, 141-144; the soldier,
    144-145; the Commander,
    145-147; the friend, 147-149; the

family man, 149-150; as Army
Chief, 151-152; Martial Law, 153,
287, 327, 345; the politician,
153-155; Z.A. Bhutto's visit to,
154; supports Bhutto government,
169; on Afghanistan policy,
179-181; praised on Afghanistan
issue, 181, 182, 185; cause of
success, 183; debate on Afghan
policy, 186; institutions weakened,
191; welfare measures by,
192-193; as President, 225; on
Exercise Brass Tacks, 270, 273;
on Pakistan National Alliance,
288; birth of democracy, 230;
dismissal of Mohammad Khan
Junejo, 330; Army dragged in,
333; 8th Amendment, 333; death,
347; on Bhutto, 352; on Junejo,
352; Soviet withdrawl from
Afghanistan, 377; presidental form
of government, 383; reluctant
ruler, 413; external developments,
413, 420; training FAG officers,
415, 416; relations with USA,
418; relations with India, 420
Zinni, Gen Anthony, xi
Zuberi, Maj-Gen Mohammad Aslam,
160